# PATHWAYS TO THE PRESIDENCY

# PATHWAYS
## TO THE
# PRESIDENCY

*A Guide to the Lives, Homes,*
*and Museums of the U.S. Presidents*

**GERALD AND PATRICIA GUTEK**

THE UNIVERSITY OF SOUTH CAROLINA PRESS

© 2011 University of South Carolina

Published by the University of South Carolina Press
Columbia, South Carolina 29208

www.sc.edu/uscpress

Manufactured in the United States of America

20  19  18  17  16  15  14  13  12  11    10  9  8  7  6  5  4  3  2  1

*Library of Congress Cataloging-in-Publication Data*
Gutek, Gerald Lee.
  Pathways to the presidency : a guide to the lives, homes, and museums
of the U.S. presidents / Gerald and Patricia Gutek.
      p. cm.
  Includes bibliographical references and index.
  ISBN 978-1-57003-997-3 (cloth : alk. paper) — ISBN 978-1-57003-998-0
(pbk : alk. paper)
  1. Presidents—United States—Biography. 2. Presidents—Homes
and haunts—United States. 3. Presidents—Museums—United States.
4. Presidential museums  I. Gutek, Patricia, 1941– II. Title.
  E176.1.G88 2011
  973.09'9—dc22
  [B]

                              2011000903

This book was printed on Glatfelter Natures, a recycled paper with
30 percent postconsumer waste content.

Dedicated to our grandchildren—
Claire Elizabeth, Abigail Lee, Luke Kenneth,
and Drew Christopher Swiatek
and
Charles Milford and Anna Hope Jordan

CONTENTS

viii
.....
CONTENTS

ILLUSTRATIONS

# George Washington

FIRST PRESIDENT OF THE UNITED STATES
*April 30, 1789, to March 3, 1797*

..............................................................

George Washington is an American icon, a symbol of the national struggle that won independence from England, a great European power. He served as the commanding general of the American Revolutionary Army and as the first president of the United States from 1789 to 1797. His success as a military leader led to the presidency.

George Washington was born to Augustine Washington and Mary Ball Washington on February 22, 1732, at Wakefield, a house on Popes Creek in Westmoreland County, Virginia. Although Washington's birthday is celebrated on February 22, his birth according to the old-style British calendar occurred on February 11, 1732. The British later reconciled their calendar with that used in Europe by adding eleven days, which changed his birth date to February 22. Augustine had two sons from a prior marriage and four children with Mary; of those four George was the eldest.

In 1735 Augustine moved his family to a farm later known as Mount Vernon. They then moved to Ferry Farm near Fredericksburg, Virginia. Augustine Washington died at the age of forty-nine on April 12, 1743, when George was eleven years old. George inherited Ferry Farm, more than two thousand additional acres, property in Fredericksburg, and ten slaves.

George's only formal education was in local schools. He studied surveying and in 1749 became the official surveyor of Culpeper County, Virginia. He also became a land speculator and by the age of twenty-one had purchased fourteen hundred acres.

Washington married Martha Custis, the widow of Daniel Parke Custis, on January 6, 1759. Through his marriage to Martha, Washington became one of the wealthiest men in Virginia. Martha had two children, John and Martha Parke Custis.

During the years leading up to the revolution of the English colonies, Washington was a member of the House of Burgesses from Frederick County, Virginia; a justice of the peace for Fairfax County; a delegate to the Williamsburg Convention; a member of the First Virginia Provincial Convention; and a delegate to the First Continental Congress and the Second Continental Congress. Relations between England and her colonies in North America were strained when the British Parliament enacted the Stamp Act in 1765 and the

Townshend Acts in 1767. The Virginia House of Burgesses argued that these acts were unconstitutional and violated the colonists' rights as Englishmen. Washington was instrumental in drafting a protest of the Townshend Acts and organizing a boycott against the British products on which duties had been imposed.

At the Second Continental Congress in Philadelphia in May 1775, a Continental army was formed. The colonists wanted independence from England. In June 1775 George Washington was unanimously approved as general and commander in chief of the Army of the United Colonies. On July 4, 1776, the Second Continental Congress endorsed the Declaration of Independence.

The Revolutionary War was a long, slow, hard-fought series of battles with victories and losses on both sides. In October 1781 at Yorktown, Virginia, Gen. Charles Cornwallis surrendered the British troops. A formal peace treaty was signed in September 1783.

After the war Washington headed the Virginia delegation to the Constitutional Convention in Philadelphia in May 1787 and was unanimously selected as president of the convention. By 1790 the Constitution had been endorsed by every state. The Bill of Rights was added in 1791.

The first United States Congress convened in New York City on March 4, 1789. When the electoral votes were counted by the newly seated Congress in New York in April 1789, Washington was the unanimous choice for first president of the United States. John Adams was elected as vice president.

On Inauguration Day, April 30, 1789, Robert R. Livingston administered the oath of office to George Washington at Federal Hall. Washington swore that he would faithfully execute the office of president of the United States and would to the best of his ability preserve, protect, and defend the Constitution of the United States. He then added, "So help me, God."

In December 1792 the Electoral College elected Washington for a second term with 132 positive votes and 3 abstentions. John Adams won the office of vice president by a 77–50 vote. Washington took the oath of office in the Senate chamber in Congress Hall in Philadelphia.

After completing two presidential terms, George Washington retired to Mount Vernon. At age sixty-seven he was diagnosed with quinsy, an inflammation of the throat. He died on December 14, 1799. After an elaborate funeral, the first president was buried at Mount Vernon. Martha Washington, who lived another three years, died in 1802 and was buried next to him.

. . . . . . . . . . . . . . . . . . . . . . . . . . . . . . . . . . . . . . . . . . . . . . . . . . . . . . . . . . . .

George Washington Birthplace National Monument
Washington's Birthplace, Virginia

ADDRESS: 1732 Popes Creek Road, Washington's Birthplace, VA 22443
TELEPHONE: 804-224-1732

WEB SITE: www.nps.gov/gewa

LOCATION: On Popes Creek, off the Potomac River, thirty-eight miles east of
Fredericksburg, Virginia, via State Route 3 and Route 204

OPEN: Daily, 9:00 A.M. to 5:00 P.M.; closed Thanksgiving, Christmas Day, and
New Year's Day

ADMISSION: Adults 16 and over, $4.00

FACILITIES: Visitor center; memorial home area; colonial farm; Washington
family burial ground; hiking trails, beach, and picnic area; special events;
ranger-led tours; administered by the National Park Service; wheelchair
accessible

*The birthplace of George Washington,* the Father of Our Country, the colonial
general who achieved victory in the Revolutionary War against Great Britain,
and the first president of the United States, is not a major American historical
site. The original house in which George Washington was born burned down
in 1779 and was never rebuilt. The house at the George Washington Birthplace
National Monument, called a memorial house, was meant to be a re-creation
of Washington's birth house. Built in 1930 six years before archaeologists discovered the original house site, its design was inferred from other eighteenth-
century southern plantation houses.

The first Washington ancestor in the colonies was Col. John Washington,
who immigrated to Virginia in 1656. When John married Anne Pope in 1658,
her father, Nathaniel Pope, gave them seven hundred acres for a tobacco farm.
John eventually owned ten thousand acres. Augustine Washington inherited
property on nearby Bridges Creek. When he subsequently purchased the
adjacent Popes Creek land, a house built prior to 1718 was on the property.
Augustine paid five thousand pounds of tobacco for an addition constructed
between 1722 and 1726. This was the house in which George Washington was

born. A second addition was built between 1743 and 1762, and a third addition was added between 1762 and 1775. In its final form the structure was a ten-room U-shaped house of unknown style with four chimneys and a cellar.

George Washington was born at Popes Creek Farm on February 22, 1732, to Augustine and Mary Ball Washington. The Washington family lived at Popes Creek until George was three and one-half years old. They then moved eighty miles up the Potomac River to Hunting Creek Plantation, later renamed Mount Vernon. When the future president was six years old, the family moved to Ferry Farm near Fredericksburg. Five years later, when Augustine died, eleven-year-old George inherited Ferry Farm.

George Washington's half brother Augustine Jr. inherited Popes Creek Plantation. The Commonwealth of Virginia acquired the home site and burial ground in 1858 and in 1882 donated the property to the federal government. The Wakefield National Memorial Association was formed in 1923 to restore George Washington's birthplace; the property was designated a National Monument in 1930. More land was acquired, increasing the property to 394 acres. The park officially opened in 1932, the two hundredth anniversary of Washington's birth.

The site was restored by the National Park Service and interpreted as a working eighteenth-century colonial Virginia tobacco farm, with costumed interpreters, animals, and gardens adding to the traditional atmosphere. Living history demonstrations include colonial cooking, blacksmithing, and spinning wool.

Displays in the visitor center include ceramic, glass, and metal artifacts found during archaeological excavations; Augustine Washington's wine bottle seal; and George Washington's christening gown. On the farm property are the memorial house, the kitchen house, a weaving room, a barn, a farm workshop, a kitchen garden, an ox yard, fowl yards, an herb garden, and an orchard.

The memorial house was constructed on the foundation of what was thought to be the farmhouse but was later learned to be a farm building. The two-story house made of local brick has a spacious central hallway with front and back doors facing each other and a view of Popes Creek. On the first floor are a withdrawing room, a dining room, and guest and main chambers. Second-floor bedrooms include the south chamber, the north chamber, the west chamber, and the children's room. The mid-eighteenth-century furniture decorating the memorial house does not include Washington family possessions.

The original kitchen was built in a separate structure away from the house to prevent fire. The reconstructed kitchen has been rebuilt on its original site. George Washington's father, grandfather, great-grandmother, great-grandfather, and half brother Augustine Washington, Jr. are buried in the farm's burial ground.

The 550-acre site along Popes Creek is a scenic natural area located in the Chesapeake Bay ecosystem. Its terrain includes upland forest, marshland, open fields, and Potomac River beaches. There is a one-mile nature trail.

. . . . . . . . . . . . . . . . . . . . . . . . . . . . . . . . . . . . . . . . . . . . . . . . . . . . . . . . . . . . . . . . . . . . . . . . . . . . . . .

Ferry Farm
George Washington's Boyhood Home
Fredericksburg, Virginia

ADDRESS: 268 Kings Highway, Fredericksburg, VA 22405
TELEPHONE: 540-370-0732
WEB SITE: www.kenmore.org
LOCATION: Fredericksburg is fifty miles south of Washington, D.C.
OPEN: Daily, 10:00 A.M. to 5:00 P.M.; closed Easter, Thanksgiving Day,
December 24, 25, and 31
ADMISSION: Adults, $5.00; seniors, $4.00; children 6–17 and students, $3.00
FACILITIES: Visitor center; hiking trails; picnic area

*George was six years old when, in 1738,* the Washington family moved to Ferry Farm, a six-hundred-acre farm on the Rappahannock River near Fredericksburg, Virginia. Augustine Washington, George's father, was a managing partner of the Principio Company, which operated Accokeek Iron Furnace, located only six miles from Ferry Farm. A ferry landing had been on the property since 1732 but was never operated by the Washingtons.

When Augustine Washington died in April 1743, he left Ferry Farm and ten slaves to his son George, who would not receive his inheritance until he was twenty-one years old. Mary Ball Washington managed the farm until her son came of age. Two hundred acres were under cultivation, and crops included tobacco and corn.

George Washington's residence when he was an adult was at Mount Vernon, a farm he inherited from his half brother Lawrence. Mary Ball Washington remained at Ferry Farm until 1772, when she moved to the town of Fredericksburg. In 1774 George Washington sold Ferry Farm.

The Fredericksburg area was the site of intense Civil War battles. Union soldiers camped there, and farm buildings served as the headquarters for Union commanders. President Abraham Lincoln visited the Union camp at Ferry Farm in May 1862. Union troops from Ferry Farm engaged in the bloody Battle of Fredericksburg in December 1862. Most of the farm buildings were torn down and the lumber used for shelters during this period.

Because Ferry Farm was threatened by development, Historic Kenmore purchased the property in 1996. Kenmore was the home of George's sister, Betty, and her husband, Col. Fielding Lewis. Their restored plantation and Ferry Farm are operated by the George Washington's Fredericksburg Foundation.

No original buildings from the Washington era remain at the eighty-four-acre Ferry Farm today. Archaeologists have recently located the Washington house site as well as its outside kitchen and slave quarters. Evidence indicates that the Washingtons lived in a large eight-room, one-and-one-half-story clapboard-covered wood structure. Located on a bluff overlooking the Rappahannock River, the house had a central hallway, a dormered roof, two chimneys, two stone-lined cellars, and two root cellars. Artifacts excavated from the cellars include pottery, glass, pipes, tea sets, wine bottles, knives, forks, and fragments from the ceilings and walls. There is also evidence of a fire in the house that occurred on Christmas 1740. There are plans to reconstruct Washington's home.

A self-guided tour of this picturesque farm includes the visitor center, which houses paintings of George Washington, exhibits on his life, and artifacts found during archaeological excavations. A 1770s-style, 24 x 48–foot oak pavilion was built as an interpretive and education facility. There are a nineteenth-century surveying office and an icehouse of an undetermined date. Steps lead to the site of the ferry landing that was on this property. A demonstration garden is filled with eighteenth-century plants and vegetables.

Other Washington-related sites to visit in the Fredericksburg area include Kenmore, the home of Fielding Lewis and his wife, Betty Washington, 1201 Washington Avenue, Fredericksburg, 540-373-3381; and the Mary Washington House, 1200 Charles Street, Fredericksburg. Mary lived the last seventeen years of her life at the Charles Street location. The site includes her charming house, an outside kitchen, and a restored garden.

. . . . . . . . . . . . . . . . . . . . . . . . . . . . . . . . . . . . . . . . . . . . . . . . . . . . . . . . . . . . . . . . . . . . . . . . . . . . . .

## Mount Vernon
### Mount Vernon, Virginia

ADDRESS: 3200 Mount Vernon Memorial Highway, Mount Vernon, VA 22121; mailing address: Mount Vernon Ladies' Association, P.O. Box 110, Mount Vernon, VA 22121

TELEPHONE: 703-780-2000

WEB SITE: www.mountvernon.org

LOCATION: Sixteen miles south of Washington, D.C., and eight miles south of Alexandria, at the southern terminus of the George Washington Memorial Parkway

OPEN: Mansion open daily, 8:00 A.M. to 5:00 P.M., April–August; 9:00 A.M. to 5:00 P.M., March, September, and October; 9:00 A.M. to 4:00 P.M., November–February. Gristmill and distillery open daily, 10:00 A.M. to 5:00 P.M., March 15–October 31

ADMISSION: Mount Vernon: adults, $15.00; seniors, $14.00; children 6–11, $7.00.

Annual pass: adults, $25.00, children 6–11, $1.00. Gristmill and distillery
site: adults, $4.00; children 6–11, $2.00
FACILITIES: Mansion, site and first floor are wheelchair accessible; Ford
Orientation Center; Donald W. Reynolds Museum and Education Cen-
ter; Mount Vernon Inn Restaurant; food court; shops; rental audio tour;
George and Martha Washington tombs; gristmill and distillery on a sepa-
rate site three miles from the mansion; sightseeing cruises. National
Register of Historic Places, National Historic Landmark

*Mount Vernon, the home of George Washington,* the first president of the
United States, is an American national shrine. Even before President Washington died in 1799, people curious about this legendary figure traveled to Mount
Vernon to see their leader in person. Thanks to a private preservation group,
the first such organization in America, Mount Vernon has been beautifully preserved and restored. The property belonged to the Washington family from 1674
until 1858, when it was purchased by the Mount Vernon Ladies' Association.

Mount Vernon includes five hundred acres containing Washington's mansion; twenty plantation outbuildings; an outdoor exhibit devoted to American agriculture as practiced by George Washington; fifty acres of restored
flower, kitchen, and botanical gardens; a greenhouse; the Ford Orientation
Center; the Donald W. Reynolds Museum and Education Center; a memorial
to eighteenth-century slaves; and George and Martha Washington's tomb. At a
separate site three miles from the main site are the gristmill and the re-created
distillery.

In 1674 the Mount Vernon homesite was granted to George Washington's
great-grandfather, who was a pioneer settler in the area between the Potomac
and the Rappahannock rivers referred to as the Northern Neck. It was part of

a five-thousand-acre site along the upper Potomac River granted to John Washington and Nicholas Spencer by Lord Culpeper, proprietor of the Northern Neck under King Charles II. In 1690 this tract of land was divided between Lawrence Washington's son, John, and the Spencers. The Washington property, known as Hunting Creek Plantation, was sold in 1726 to Augustine Washington, George Washington's father.

George Washington was born in 1732, and when he was three years old, Augustine moved his family to Hunting Creek Plantation. After four years they relocated to Ferry Farm, near Fredericksburg. In 1740 Augustine Washington deeded the Hunting Creek Plantation to his son Lawrence, who renamed the estate Mount Vernon in honor of Adm. Edward Vernon, under whom he had served in the Caribbean. George spent part of his youth at Mount Vernon with Lawrence. After Lawrence died in 1752, George leased Mount Vernon from his brother's widow until her death in 1761. Then George Washington inherited the 2,126-acre estate, which increased under his ownership to 8,000 acres.

Although George Washington would live at Mount Vernon until his death in 1799, his residency was interrupted by extended periods of service to his country during the turbulent revolutionary years. In 1775 Washington was appointed commander in chief of the Continental forces. After resigning his commission in 1783, General Washington retired to Mount Vernon until 1787, when he presided over the Constitutional Convention in Philadelphia. From 1789 to 1797 he served as the first president of the United States.

John Augustine Washington Jr., the last Washington family owner of Mount Vernon, sold the mansion, outbuildings, and two hundred acres to the Mount Vernon Ladies' Association in 1858. Restoration began immediately, and the estate was opened to the public. Three hundred additional acres have been added to the site.

The house at Mount Vernon was built by Augustine Washington between 1735 and 1739 and was expanded by both Lawrence and George Washington. The five hundred acres surrounding the mansion, called Mansion House Farm, were landscaped in the style of an English gentleman's country seat. There were rolling meadows; groves of trees; a vineyard; a bowling green; lawns; formal flower, botanical, and kitchen gardens; and a greenhouse.

On Washington's eight thousand acres there were five farms, each a complete unit with its own overseer, slaves, livestock, equipment, and buildings. General Washington was a progressive farmer who personally supervised farm activities when in residence. Farm managers reported to him on a weekly basis, even during the presidential years. African American slaves constituted the bulk of the workforce. Living in simple outbuildings at Mount Vernon, slaves worked as blacksmiths, carpenters, gardeners, shoemakers, painters, brick makers, herdsmen, house servants, coachmen, cooks, dairy maids, millers, coopers, and field hands. After the Revolution, General Washington's attitude toward slavery changed and he became an advocate of emancipation. He freed his slaves in his will.

Mount Vernon has been restored to its appearance in 1799, the year of George Washington's death. The mansion was originally one and one-half stories high and was raised to two and one-half stories in the late 1750s. George Washington further enlarged the house beginning in 1774. Additions were constructed on the south and north ends of the dwelling, and wing buildings and connecting colonnades were added. A high-columned piazza extending the full length of the side of the house facing the Potomac River was erected in 1777.

Fourteen rooms in the colonial-style mansion are open for viewing, with costumed interpreters in each room. Many of the furnishings are original. Room settings are based on a 1799 fifty-page inventory prepared after President Washington's death.

The large dining area in the north addition is a two-story room that extends the width of the house. When used for social functions that required dining tables, trestles and boards were moved into the room and covered with linen tablecloths. Nine of the twenty-four chairs are original; they were made by John Aitken of Philadelphia, as was one of the Hepplewhite mahogany sideboards. After George Washington's death and according to his wishes, he lay in state in this room for three days.

The passage or central hall, which runs the width of the house, is a paneled room that contains the stairway to the second floor. All of the wood in the passage has been grained to resemble mahogany, as it appeared in 1797. A key to the French Bastille, a gift to Washington from General Lafayette in 1790, hangs in the passage. Also on the first floor are a little parlor, a west parlor, a small dining room, and a downstairs bedroom.

There are five bedchambers on the second floor. Of greatest interest is General and Mrs. Washington's bedchamber in the south addition, from which General Washington's first-floor study was accessed by a narrow stairway. These rooms were designed and added by George Washington to provide privacy for him and Martha in a busy household that included Martha's two children and two grandchildren as well as guests and servants.

It is a moving experience to enter the private bedroom of the first president of the United States and see the bed, made in Philadelphia about 1794, in which George Washington died on December 14, 1799. From his study George Washington managed his estate at the tambour secretary desk made by John Aitken. Other original furnishings in the study are the presidential chair, a terrestrial globe, a gold-headed walking staff, a portrait of Lawrence Washington, and many books.

Ten outbuildings have been restored, including the white servants' hall; the kitchen, storehouse, and clerk's quarters; the smokehouse; the washhouse; the coach house; the stable; the overseer's quarters and spinning room; the garden house; and the salt house. Washington's 1785 greenhouse with adjoining slave quarters, which was destroyed by fire in 1835, has been reconstructed on its original site.

Sixty-five percent of the 66,700-square-foot Ford Orientation Center and Donald W. Reynolds Museum and Education Center is situated under the four-acre pasture just inside Mount Vernon's main gate so as to preserve the pastoral setting. Galleries feature hundreds of objects from Mount Vernon's collections, including furnishings, china, silver, clothing, jewelry, Revolutionary War artifacts, rare books and manuscripts, and personal effects of the Washington family. The Ford Orientation Center has life-sized bronze sculptures of the Washington family, a miniature of the mansion house, and theaters showing films on Washington.

The grounds and gardens at Mount Vernon, designed by George Washington, have been restored to their eighteenth-century appearance. The mansion opens onto an oval courtyard. Beyond it is a bowling green, a broad expanse of lawn bordered by shrubs and trees. On the sides of the bowling green are the upper garden, a flower garden with annuals and perennials of the period, and the lower garden full of fruits, vegetables, and herbs. A re-created sixteen-sided treading barn has been built. A four-acre working eighteenth-century farm nearby is known as the George Washington: Pioneer Farmer site.

George and Martha Washington are buried at Mount Vernon. In his will George requested that a new brick family vault be constructed. After it was completed in 1831, the bodies of George and Martha were moved there. Nearby is a burial ground for the African American slaves who died at Mount Vernon from 1760 to 1860.

Washington operated both a gristmill and a distillery. A site three miles from the mansion features the gristmill and the newly re-created distillery. Washington built a gristmill in 1771 of locally quarried sandstone. He built the distillery in 1797 at the urging of his Scottish overseer, who had experience producing whiskey. In 1799 George Washington's distillery produced more than eleven thousand gallons of rye whiskey. Both the mill and the distillery ceased operating in the mid-nineteenth century. In 1932 the Commonwealth of Virginia reconstructed the gristmill on its original site. In the 1990s the Mount Vernon Ladies' Association restored the gristmill to operating condition. The re-created distillery opened in 2007.

# John Adams

SECOND PRESIDENT OF THE UNITED STATES
*March 4, 1797–March 4, 1801*

. . . . . . . . . . . . . . . . . . . . . . . . . . . . . . . . . . . . . . . . . . . . . . . . . . . . . . . . . . . . . . . . . . . . . .

John Adams was a distinguished public servant during the revolutionary and early national periods. He signed the Declaration of Independence, served as a European diplomat, was the first vice president of the United States, and became the second president of the United States.

John Adams was born on October 30, 1735, in Braintree, Massachusetts, the oldest of the three sons of Susanna Boylston Adams and John Adams, a farmer, leather craftsman, and church deacon. President Adams was a great-great-grandson of the Pilgrims John and Priscilla Alden.

In a rough draft of his autobiography, John Adams described his ancestors, "My Father, Grandfather, Great Grandfather, and Great Great Grandfather all lived and died in this Town of Quincy, for so many Years the First Parish in the Ancient Town of Braintree, and are buried in the Congregational Church Yard. They were all in the middle rank of People in Society: all sober, industrious, frugal and religious: all possessed of landed Estates, always unencumbered with debts, and as independent as human nature is, or ought to be in the World."

At the age of sixteen John entered Harvard College, and he received a bachelor of arts degree in 1755. After studying law he was admitted to the Massachusetts Bar in November 1758 and established a law practice in Braintree. John inherited a saltbox cottage, a barn, and forty acres of land from his father, who died in 1761.

John met Abigail Smith, a daughter of Rev. William Smith of Weymouth, in 1759, and the couple married on October 25, 1764. Residing at his farm in Braintree, John practiced law and also was a surveyor of highways and a selectman for Braintree. The couple's first child, Abigail, was born in 1765 and was followed in 1767 by a son, John Quincy, who would become the sixth president of the United States. Charles and Thomas Boylston were born in 1770 and 1772 respectively, and Susanna was born in 1768 but died in infancy.

John Adams played an active role in the founding of a new nation and establishing its diplomatic relationship with the Old World. On July 4, 1776, the Continental Congress issued a Declaration of Independence from Britain. Adams served on the committee charged with drafting the declaration, which was largely written by Thomas Jefferson.

After four years as a Continental Congress delegate, John spent a decade (1778–88) as an American diplomat in France, the Netherlands, and Britain. The War for Independence ended with the signing of the Treaty of Paris on September 3, 1783. This treaty was negotiated by Benjamin Franklin, Adams, and John Jay. The British agreed to recognize the independence of the United States and withdraw their troops from the new nation.

Under the newly ratified Constitution of the new republic, in February 1789 sixty-nine electors voted for a president and a vice president. There was a general consensus that the Revolutionary War hero George Washington should be president, and he was elected unanimously. John Adams received thirty-four votes, the second-highest number, and thus was elected as the first vice president of the United States, serving from 1789 to 1797.

When Washington chose not to run for a third presidential term, the Democratic-Republicans supported Thomas Jefferson and former secretary of state Aaron Burr. On the Federalist ticket were John Adams and Thomas Pinckney. Seventy-one electors voted for Adams, and Jefferson received sixty-eight votes. Under the Constitution, the first-place Adams was elected as president and the second-place Jefferson was elected as vice president. Thus the president and the vice president were from opposing parties.

Sixty-one-year-old John Adams was inaugurated on March 4, 1797, in the House of Representatives chamber in Philadelphia's Federal Hall. During Adams's administration the Navy Department was founded, the U.S. Marine Corps was created, and the Public Health Service and the Library of Congress were established. Washington, D.C., became the nation's capital, and Adams was the first chief executive to live there.

Hostility developed between Adams and the leaders of the Federalist Party, which had split into two wings. The party leader Alexander Hamilton published a bitter attack on Adams, which assured Adams's defeat in the election of 1800. Thomas Jefferson received seventy-three electoral votes to Adams's sixty-five votes.

After serving one term as president, John Adams retired to his home in Quincy, formerly Braintree, Massachusetts. He occupied himself with writing, including his autobiography. Abigail Adams died in 1818. John lived to see his son John Quincy become the sixth president of the United States in 1825. John Adams lived twenty-five years after his presidency and died on July 4, 1826, at the age of ninety. He and Jefferson, his vice president and successor to the presidency, died on the fiftieth anniversary of the Declaration of Independence, which both men had signed.

Adams National Historical Park
Quincy, Massachusetts

ADDRESS: The visitor center is at 1250 Hancock Street, Quincy, MA 02169
TELEPHONE: Visitor center: 617-770-1175
WEB SITE: www.nps.gov/adam
LOCATION: Quincy is approximately ten miles south of Boston, accessible
   from I-93 south to Route 3 south and also accessible from the Red Line T
   to Quincy Center Station
OPEN: The three Adams houses are open daily, 9:00 A.M. to 5:00 P.M., mid-
   April through mid-November; the visitor center is open daily, 9:00 A.M.
   to 5:00 P.M., mid-April through mid-November; Wednesday–Friday,
   9:00 A.M. to 5:00 P.M., mid-November through mid-April
ADMISSION: Adults 17 and over, $5.00
FACILITIES: Guided tours; visitor center; special events; trolley transportation;
   limited handicapped accessibility

*Adams National Historical Park preserves the sites* where the nation's second
and sixth presidents were born and lived. The Adams Memorial Society gave
the Adams property to the federal government in 1946, and it is operated by the
National Park Service. The houses where John and John Quincy Adams were
born are the two oldest extant presidential birthplaces in the country.

The National Park Visitor Center, the two simple birth houses of the presidents, the Adams mansion or Old House, the United First Parish Church where
the two presidents and their wives are interred, and Hancock Cemetery are all
in Quincy, Massachusetts. Adams National Historical Park is not a contiguous
site. Guided tours of the park begin at the visitor center, 1250 Hancock Street,
Quincy, on the first floor of the Presidents Place Galleria. The visitor center
features video presentations and a time line of four generations of the Adams
family. Visitors take a trolley from the visitor center to the two Adams birthplaces, where docents give guided tours. Visitors then go by trolley to the Old
House for a guided tour, after which they return by trolley to the visitor center.

United First Parish Church is a short distance from the visitor center, and
church members give tours of the Adams family crypt in the lower level of the
church for a fee. Hancock Cemetery, located just across the street, can be visited on a self-guided tour.

The John Adams Birthplace was built in 1681 by Joseph Penniman. In 1720
the house and six acres of land were purchased by John Adams (1692–1761),
father of the president, who was a deacon in the Congregational Church. The
two-and-one-half-story frame house is the birthplace and early home of President John Adams, who was born on October 30, 1735.

Old House, Adams
National Historical Park,
Quincy, Massachusetts

The modest saltbox-style house had two rooms on the first floor and two on the second floor, with a large central chimney between the rooms. Eighteenth-century additions included two downstairs rooms and two upper rooms. The house is simply decorated with Windsor chairs and hooked rugs; none of the furnishings is original Adams furniture. Peter Boylston Adams, the president's brother, inherited this house on his father's death in 1761, and in 1774 Peter sold the house to his brother John.

The John Quincy Adams Birthplace was built in 1663 and purchased by Deacon John Adams in 1744. The future president John Adams inherited this house from his father, and after John's marriage to Abigail Smith in 1764, the couple moved into it. Their son John Quincy Adams, the future president, was born there on July 11, 1767.

The small, saltbox-style, frame, two-and-one-half-story house originally had two rooms on each of the two floors, with a large central chimney. John Adams used the kitchen as his law office and built a two-room kitchen addition on the back of the house. Restored by the Quincy Historical Society, the house has been open to the public since 1897.

Old House was built in 1731 as a summer home by Leonard Vassall, a sugar planter from the West Indies. The brick-end, two-and-one-half-story colonial-style structure originally had four rooms, a garret, and an unattached kitchen. A kitchen wing was added in the mid-eighteenth century.

John Adams bought Old House in 1787. John and Abigail were living in England at that time and wished to have a larger home when they returned. The colonial-style house was not as large as John and Abigail remembered, however, consisting of a paneled room, a dining room, and a kitchen on the first floor; two bedrooms on the second floor; and some attic rooms. Abigail supervised the addition of an east wing with a new entry, a hallway, and a large room for entertaining guests on the first floor; a hallway and a study on the

second floor; and attic bedrooms. The kitchen was substantially remodeled also, and a front porch was added.

Old House was occupied from 1788 to 1927 by four generations of the Adams family: John Adams, second U.S. president; John Quincy Adams, sixth U.S. president; Charles Francis Adams, minister to the Court of St. James during the Civil War; Henry Adams, a prominent historian; and Brooks Adams. Changes made by successive generations remain. John Quincy Adams added the second-story passageway that connected the kitchen wing and the east wing at the back of the house. Charles Francis Adams added a larger kitchen, servants' quarters, an English garden, a greenhouse, and a carriage house.

Old House served as the summer residence for John and John Quincy Adams while they served as president. It is filled with furniture and artwork from a collection of seventy-eight thousand Adams family artifacts. President John Adams died there on July 4, 1826. Visitors see the wing chair in which he died as well as the desk at which he worked.

In his will John Quincy Adams requested a fireproof building be built to house his books and papers. In 1870 Charles Francis Adams supervised the construction of a medieval-style stone library designed by Edward Cabot. Over fourteen thousand historic volumes and the book collection of John Quincy Adams were moved from the study in Old House to the stone library. Brooks Adams added the wooden front gates, electricity, and central heating. The grounds of Old House include a historic orchard and an eighteenth-century-style formal garden containing annual and perennial flowers.

United First Parish Church (Unitarian) of Quincy, 1306 Hancock Street, built in 1827–28, was designed by the architect Alexander Parris. This two-story granite structure, frequently referred to as the Church of the Presidents, is considered New England's finest extant Greek-revival church. John Adams donated the land for United First Parish Church, and John Quincy Adams and his wife worshipped there. John, John Quincy, and their wives are buried in the Adams crypt below the sanctuary. Visitors to the crypt see the four granite tombs, each with the name of the family member buried there carved into the stone. American flags from the eras when they were president adorn the presidents' tombs. There are fifteen stars on John Adams's flag and twenty-four stars on John Quincy Adams's flag.

Both President John Adams and President John Quincy Adams were initially buried in the Adams family vault in Quincy's Hancock Cemetery, which dates to 1640. Hancock Cemetery is named for Rev. John Hancock, father of John Hancock. Several generations of Adamses are buried there. At the request of John Quincy Adams, John and Abigail Adams were reinterred in United First Parish Church in 1828. In 1852 John Quincy and Louisa Adams were reinterred there.

# Thomas Jefferson

A many-sided Renaissance man, Thomas Jefferson was an amateur scientist, a philosopher, and an agriculturalist as well as a political leader. Although a U.S. president, he wanted to be remembered for introducing the Bill for Religious Freedom in the Virginia legislature and for creating the University of Virginia.

Thomas Jefferson, born on April 13, 1743, at Shadwell, Virginia, was the son of Peter Jefferson (1708–57) and Jane Randolph Jefferson (1720–76). The third of ten children, Thomas was born into a prestigious Virginia family. His father owned nearly ten thousand acres of land and more than sixty slaves, and he served in the Virginia House of Burgesses.

Thomas Jefferson entered the College of William and Mary in Williamsburg at the age of seventeen and graduated in 1762. After studying law for five years with George Wythe, in 1767 Jefferson was admitted to the Virginia Bar.

When Jefferson was fourteen, his father died, and at age twenty-one Thomas took charge of the family plantation, managing five thousand acres in Albemarle and adjacent counties. Interested in architecture, he studied the designs of James Gibbs and Robert Morris, which he implemented in building, redesigning, and adding to Monticello throughout his life.

On January 1, 1772, Jefferson married Martha Wayles Skelton (1748–82), who was the daughter of the prosperous lawyer and estate owner John Wayles and the widow of Bathurst Skelton, a fellow student of Jefferson's at William and Mary. Thomas and Martha Jefferson were the parents of six children—five daughters and one son—four of whom died in childhood. The two surviving daughters were Martha, born in 1772, and Mary, born in 1778. On September 6, 1782, after only ten years of marriage, Martha Wayles Skelton Jefferson died. Thomas Jefferson never remarried.

Jefferson was elected to the Virginia House of Burgesses in 1769. For the next decade he supported the colonial cause against Great Britain. In 1775 he was one of Virginia's representatives to the Continental Congress in Philadelphia, which on July 2, 1776, voted to separate from British rule. Jefferson was named to the committee to draft a statement of the colonialists' grievances against England and was the principal author of the Declaration of Independence, which asserted that individuals possess "inalienable rights of life, liberty, and happiness." The Declaration of Independence was officially proclaimed on July 4, 1776.

A strong believer in separation of church and state, Jefferson introduced the Bill for Establishing Religious Freedom in the Virginia Assembly in 1779. Jefferson's bill, which argued against religious tests as a basis for citizenship, was enacted in 1786.

In July 1784 Jefferson and his daughter Martha sailed to England, where he would serve as an American commissioner to Europe to negotiate treaties of commerce and friendship. Jefferson was accompanied by his servant James Hemings, a slave, and his personal secretary, William Short. When Benjamin Franklin, the American minister to France, resigned in 1785, Jefferson was named to replace him, and he served in that post for the next four years. Jefferson's eight-year-old daughter Mary arrived in Paris in July 1787 accompanied by a fourteen-year-old slave, Sally Hemings, James's sister.

Jefferson, a slave owner, had inherited 52 slaves from his father and 135 slaves from his father-in-law. Among the 135 slaves were Elizabeth Hemings (1735–1807) and her ten children. The daughter of an African slave and an English sea captain, Elizabeth is purported to have been the mistress of John Wayles, Martha Jefferson's father, and to have borne him several children, including Sally and James Hemings. If John Wayles was the father not only of Martha Wayles Skelton Jefferson but also of Sally Hemings, the women were half sisters.

Controversy continues over the nature of the relationship between Thomas Jefferson and Sally Hemings. During his lifetime allegations against Jefferson charged that Sally Hemings was Jefferson's mistress and that he was the father of her children. DNA tests indicate that Hemings's descendants have Jefferson ancestry. Sally's four children who survived to adulthood were freed by Jefferson—two in his lifetime and another two in his will. The Thomas Jefferson Foundation, which operates Monticello, has taken the position that there is a strong likelihood that Thomas Jefferson is the father of one or more of Sally Hemings's children.

In 1789 Jefferson and his daughters returned to the United States, and he served as President George Washington's secretary of state from 1789 to 1793. In the early nineteenth century American political parties were organized. Those who favored a strong central government with limited state power organized as the Federalist Party, while those who believed in limited federal power and championed states' rights were the Democratic-Republicans, led by Thomas Jefferson.

In 1796 John Adams, a Federalist, ran for president and was opposed by Thomas Jefferson. Adams received seventy-one electoral votes, while Jefferson received sixty-eight. This resulted in a Federalist president, John Adams, with a Democratic-Republican vice president, Jefferson. Adams and Jefferson opposed each other again in 1800. The election held on December 3, 1800, resulted in a tie (seventy-three votes each) in the Electoral College between Jefferson and Aaron Burr, the candidate for vice president, while Adams received only sixty-five votes. After thirty-six ballots, the House of Representatives elected Jefferson president on February 17, 1801.

In 1803 Jefferson's administration successfully negotiated the Louisiana Purchase from France for fifteen million dollars, which more than doubled the size of the United States. In 1804 Jefferson commissioned the transcontinental explorations of Meriwether Lewis and William Clark, which took the two explorers from St. Louis, Missouri, to the Pacific Ocean.

Jefferson was elected to a second term in 1804. His Federalist opponent, Charles Pinckney, received 14 electoral votes to Jefferson's 162. In March 1807 President Jefferson signed a bill that abolished the slave trade and banned the importation of slaves.

After leaving the presidency, Jefferson retired to Monticello. In the last years of his life he established the University of Virginia and was elected as its first rector. On March 7, 1825, the first class of thirty students entered the University of Virginia.

Jefferson died on July 4, 1826, and was buried at Monticello. Per his request, his tombstone reads: "HERE WAS BURIED THOMAS JEFFERSON, AUTHOR OF THE DECLARATION OF AMERICAN INDEPENDENCE, OF THE STATUTE OF VIRGINIA FOR RELIGIOUS FREEDOM, AND FATHER OF THE UNIVERSITY OF VIRGINIA."

. . . . . . . . . . . . . . . . . . . . . . . . . . . . . . . . . . . . . . . . . . . . . . . . . . . . . . . . . . . . . . . . . . . . . . . . .

## Monticello
### Charlottesville, Virginia

ADDRESS: Thomas Jefferson Memorial Foundation, P.O. Box 316, Charlottesville, VA 22902

TELEPHONE: 434-984-9800 or 434-984-9822

WEB SITE: www.monticello.org

LOCATION: In north central Virginia on Route 53, three miles southeast of Charlottesville near the intersection of Route 20 and I-64; Charlottesville is 125 miles southwest of Washington, D.C.

OPEN: Daily, 8:00 A.M. to 5:00 P.M., March–October; 9:00 A.M. to 4:30 P.M., November–February; closed Christmas Day

ADMISSION: Adults, $20.00, March–October and $15.00, November–February; children 6 to 11, $8.00; group rates and student rates available

FACILITIES: Restored home, gardens, and grave of Thomas Jefferson; house designed by Jefferson; Thomas Jefferson Visitor Center and Smith History Center with shops and café; guided tours of house; garden tours; foreign language tours; the house, visitor center, and much of the grounds are handicapped accessible; archaeological excavations; Thomas Jefferson

Monticello, Charlottesville, Virginia. West front view. Photograph by R. Lautman, Monticello

Center for Historic Plants; Monticello Research Center; garden shop and picnic area; shuttle service from parking lot. National Register of Historic Places, National Historic Landmark, Historic American Buildings Survey

*"Genius" is the word that springs to mind* when visiting Monticello, the thirty-three-room residence designed and continually remodeled by Thomas Jefferson from 1769 to 1809. Monticello was the home of the third president of the United States, Thomas Jefferson, along with his wife, children, and grandchildren. Jefferson's five-thousand-acre estate consisted of farms, gardens, orchards, slave dwellings, and shops. Monticello is a historical site because of its association with one of the nation's most illustrious presidents, but it is also an architectural showplace. It has been restored to its appearance in 1809, the year Jefferson retired to his estate after completing his second term as president.

When Thomas was fourteen years old, his father, Peter Jefferson, died, leaving five thousand acres of land along the Rivanna River to the boy. Eight years later Jefferson began constructing a home of his own design on the property. Over the next forty years Jefferson remodeled, enlarged, furnished, redesigned, and rebuilt this house. He was a self-taught architect who saw architecture as a process rather than the creation of a final product. In order to situate his home on a mountaintop to take advantage of the view, Jefferson had the mountaintop cleared and leveled in 1768. The eight-room house that Jefferson designed consisted of a center block with flanking wings in a modified neo-classical style. "Monticello" means "Little Mountain" in Italian.

Many of the building materials for Monticello, including bricks and nails, were made on the plantation, which had a blacksmith shop, a nailery, a joiner, a utility shed, a dairy, a smokehouse, slave quarters, workers' quarters, and an icehouse. Structural timber came from Jefferson's land, and the stone and limestone were quarried there. Construction workers came from the plantation's residential labor force, composed of free white workers and about sixty adult African American slaves. At Monticello tobacco, wheat, corn, potatoes, and small grains were grown on four farms. Cattle, hogs, and sheep were raised.

After returning from France in 1789, Jefferson decided to redesign and enlarge Monticello. He removed the upper story and enlarged the house from eight to twenty-one rooms. A dome was erected over the center portion of the building. Piazzas or arched loggias were placed on the north and south ends of the building. The house appeared to be one story, though steep, narrow stairs led to second and third floors.

Jefferson acquired a large collection of art and furnishings in Paris and purchased furniture from cabinetmakers in Williamsburg, London, New York, and Philadelphia. He also designed furniture, which he had made by his own cabinetmakers. Jefferson's landscape designs include ornamental flower gardens near the house, fruit orchards, and a one-thousand-foot-long garden where Jefferson experimented with hundreds of varieties of vegetables.

Monticello's furnishings were sold after Jefferson's death to pay off debts. Monticello was sold in 1831 to James Barclay, who sold it to Commodore Uriah P. Levy in 1834. It remained in the Levy family until 1923. Monticello is owned and operated by the Thomas Jefferson Memorial Foundation, Inc., a private, nonprofit organization formed in 1923. Two thousand of Jefferson's original five thousand acres remain.

Restored to its 1809 appearance, Monticello has eleven rooms on the first floor and six bedrooms on the second floor, which is reached by steep stairways. On the third floor are three bedrooms with skylights and a large octagonal room below the dome. Only the first floor is open to the public. Nearly all of the furniture and artifacts in the house were owned by Jefferson or his family. There are also rooms in the cellar and in the attached dependency wings.

On the first floor is the entrance hall, which served as a reception area and a natural history, Indian, and art museum with Native American artifacts from the Lewis and Clark expedition. The hall has twenty-eight reproduction Windsor chairs made according to Jefferson's specifications. An unusual calendar clock designed by Jefferson has faces both inside and outside the house and tells the days of the week.

Jefferson's private suite of rooms for sleeping, reading, writing, and conducting scientific experiments includes the bedroom, the book room, the cabinet, and the greenhouse. Jefferson's bedroom in the south portion of the house is a two-story room with a skylight and the alcove bed in which Jefferson died on July 4, 1826. His cabinet or study includes five presses used to store papers, a revolving chair, and a polygraph that was a two-pen, letter-duplicating device. An adjacent book room contains hundreds of his books. The greenhouse is a glassed-in piazza used by Jefferson for horticultural experiments.

In the south square room, which was used as a sitting room, is a portrait of Jefferson's daughter, Martha Randolph. The parlor, a large, elegant room with a semi-octagonal bay, is separated from the entrance hall by single-acting double glass doors. Jefferson was intrigued by gadgetry and incorporated some of it in the house, such as the parlor doors and the dining room's dumbwaiters. The two-story dining room has a skylight and is where breakfast and dinner were served. In the tearoom are busts of Adams, Washington, Franklin, and Lafayette. The north octagonal room, or Madison bedroom, and the north square room, or Abbe Correia bedroom, are guest bedrooms.

Monticello's complex roof system has been restored. The house has L-shaped wings connected to the cellars by an all-weather passageway that contained dependencies. Their roofs formed terraces that extended from the main floor of the house. Beneath the north terrace were stables, carriage bays, and an ice-house. Beneath the south terrace were the kitchen, the cook's room, house servants' rooms, a smokehouse, and the dairy.

In addition to the house tour, a tour of Mulberry Row and of house dependencies is available April through October. The tour focuses on the lives and activities of the plantation's African American slaves. Mulberry Row refers to the shops and dwellings along a plantation road lined with mulberry trees. The structures along Mulberry Row have disappeared with the exception of the foundations and chimney of the joinery, part of a stone stable, and a stone workman's house that is now attached to a modern gift shop and office. Artifacts from Mulberry Row can be seen at the visitor center. The kitchen and the cook's room in the dependency are also open to visitors.

In 1939 the Garden Club of Virginia restored the gardens, and tours are available from mid-April through October. Jefferson's flower gardens included twenty oval-shaped beds planted with a variety of flowers, including Columbian lilies, cardinal flowers, tulips, sweet Williams, Maltese crosses, and *Jeffersonia diphyllas*. The fruit and vegetable gardens were replanted in the 1980s. In 1977 a project was started to re-create the grove of deciduous trees planted by Jefferson.

Monticello's graveyard was laid out by Jefferson in 1773. He is buried there next to his wife. Jefferson's tombstone refers to the Declaration of Independence, the Virginia Statute for Religious Freedom, and the University of Virginia but does not mention that he was both a vice president and a president of the United States.

The forty-two-thousand-square-foot Thomas Jefferson Visitor Center and Smith Education Center opened in 2008. Five pavilions around a central courtyard house a reception area for ticket sales and visitor information, a two-story museum for historical exhibits, a two-story education center that shows an orientation film, a café, and museum and garden shops.

. . . . . . . . . . . . . . . . . . . . . . . . . . . . . . . . . . . . . . . . . . . . . . . . . . . . . . . . . . . . . . . . . . . . . . . . . . . . . . . . . . . . . . . . . .

## Poplar Forest
### Forest, Virginia

ADDRESS: Thomas Jefferson's Poplar Forest, P.O. Box 419, Forest, VA 24551-0419
TELEPHONE: 434-525-1806 or 434-534-8120
WEB SITE: www.poplarforest.org
LOCATION: On Route 661, southwest of Lynchburg
OPEN: Wednesday–Monday, 10:00 A.M. to 4:00 P.M., April–November; closed Tuesdays and Thanksgiving
ADMISSION: Adults, $10.00; seniors, $9.00; youths 12–18, $5.00; children 6–11, $2.00
FACILITIES: Retreat house designed by Thomas Jefferson; guided tours; museum shop; picnic tables; self-guided tours of grounds; house is not handicapped accessible; National Register of Historic Places, National Historic Landmark

*As much as Thomas Jefferson loved Monticello* and the family and friends who gathered there, he occasionally sought solitude. His other house, used as his personal retreat at his Bedford County plantation, was Poplar Forest, a National Historic Landmark near Lynchburg. Thanks to the efforts of the Corporation for Jefferson's Poplar Forest, formed in 1984, this relatively unknown two-hundred-year-old site opened to the public in 1986. Restoration began in 1993 and is ongoing. Poplar Forest is a showplace and is more precious because of its age, its association with Jefferson, and because it was almost lost to posterity due to neglect.

In 1773 Jefferson's wife, Martha Wayles Skelton Jefferson, inherited 11,000 acres, including the 4,812-acre tobacco plantation known as Poplar Forest, from her father, John Wayles. During the Revolutionary War the Jefferson family fled Monticello and stayed in the overseer's house at Poplar Forest. While there Jefferson was injured in a horse-riding accident, forcing him to remain longer than he had expected. There he worked on the manuscript of his only published book, *Notes on the State of Virginia* (1784).

Construction of the Poplar Forest house that was designed by Jefferson began in 1806, when he was sixty-three years old and president of the United States. Over the next seventeen years Jefferson personally supervised the building of the octagonal house, its wing of offices, and the landscaping around it, usually by correspondence. After eight years as president, Jefferson returned to Monticello. Approximately four times a year he spent from two weeks to two months at Poplar Forest, which was ninety miles and a three-day ride from Monticello. The existence of Poplar Forest was a well-kept secret during Jefferson's lifetime.

In 1823 the eighty-year-old Jefferson made his last visit to Poplar Grove and gave the property to his grandson Francis Eppes. Jefferson died in 1826, and in 1828 Eppes sold the property. In 1983 the house and its fifty-acre site were purchased by the Corporation for Jefferson's Poplar Forest, which has acquired five hundred additional acres of the original plantation. Changes were made to Jefferson's house by its many owners; other structures were torn down.

Poplar Forest was designed by Jefferson as a place of beauty and seclusion in the midst of a working plantation. Surrounded by wheat and tobacco fields was a sixty-one-acre enclosed area with an octagonal house at its center. Within the acreage were orchards, vegetable gardens, slave quarters, a plant nursery, and farm buildings. A one-hundred-foot service wing extending from the east side of the house was added in 1814. The house and wing were in a ten-acre fenced area with formal landscaping.

Jefferson's octagonal house had four bedrooms, a parlor, a dining room, and two porticoes. Jefferson, who had served as minister to France, had a deep appreciation for French architecture. Design features influenced by French architecture included a large central dining room with a twenty-foot ceiling and a skylight, floor-to-ceiling windows in the parlor, alcove beds in the bedrooms, and an indoor toilet. Window frames, trim, doors, and nails were made in Monticello's workshops. Many of the craftsmen, brick masons, carpenters, joiners, and plasterers were white workers or African American slaves from Monticello.

The fourteen fireplaces used four symmetrical chimneys. The fireplace in the central dining room would have required a fifth chimney. To avoid placing an awkward fifth chimney on the roof, Jefferson ran the dining room fireplace flue through an adjacent diagonal wall to the northwest chimney. This solution to a design problem most likely caused the major 1845 fire as well as an 1825 roof fire.

A 100 x 23–foot wing was added to the house in 1814 but was removed by a subsequent owner. In the service wing were a kitchen, a cook's room, a storage room, and a smokehouse. This east wing has been reconstructed based on archaeological findings.

Jefferson, a serious gardener, landscaped five acres surrounding the house in a combination of Palladian forms mixed with British and French formal garden designs. The geometric layout featured a sunken lawn flanked by terraces on the south, a carriage turnaround road on the north, and earth mounds and rows of trees on the east and west sides of the house encircled by a round road lined with paper mulberry trees. Other species of trees planted by Jefferson included balsam and Athenian poplars, common and Kentucky locusts, redbuds, dogwoods, aspens, willows, and tulip poplars. Oval flower beds were planted with dwarf and large roses and prickly locust shrubs. A bowling green was lined with Kentucky coffee trees. In an 1821 letter to William Short, Jefferson wrote: "I was just returned from Poplar Forest. . . . I have an excellent house there, inferior only to Monticello, and pass my time there in a tranquility and retirement much adapted to my age and indolence."[1]

Restoration is ongoing based on extensive research by archaeologists and restoration architects. The exterior of the house has been returned to its appearance in Jefferson's time, and post-Jefferson components have been removed. The skylight above the central room with its thirty-two panes of glass made in Germany and separated by antique heart pine muntins was restored. At least one room will be left with its original brick walls to enable visitors to see construction techniques. Other rooms have been plastered and covered in lime wash as in Jefferson's time. Jefferson's alcove bed has been rebuilt.

Archaeologists have excavated the foundations of four slave cabins, including single-family log cabins and a duplex for extended families. Slave houses were build of logs and had wooden chimneys lined with clay. Visitors can take a self-guided tour of the grounds, which are being restored to their original design.

# James Madison

FOURTH PRESIDENT OF THE UNITED STATES
*March 4, 1809–March 4, 1817*

..................................................................................

Destined to be a chief executive of a yet-to-be established new republic, Madison, along with George Washington, Thomas Jefferson, and James Monroe, would be one of the Virginia dynasty of presidents. Madison enjoyed a lifelong friendship with Thomas Jefferson, his mentor.

James Madison Jr. (1751–1836), the eldest of James and Nelly Madison's twelve children, was born on March 16, 1751, in King George County, Virginia. The future president was descended from original Virginia settlers who owned thousands of acres of land. James Sr. (1723–1801), the president's father, inherited Montpelier plantation and twenty-nine slaves from his father. He built Montpelier's main house around 1760 and constructed a profitable iron foundry on the property. After his father's death in 1801, James Madison Jr. inherited Montpelier along with 108 African American slaves. Madison expressed much ambivalence in regard to slavery. However, he never freed his own slaves.

James graduated from the College of New Jersey, later named Princeton; entered the law; and was drawn to Jefferson's political circle on the eve of the American Revolution. One of the new republic's most intelligent political theorists, Madison had a special genius in translating abstract political philosophy into practice.

A leading delegate from Virginia to the Constitutional Convention, which met in Philadelphia in 1787, Madison recognized the weaknesses of the confederation of states established after the Revolution and proposed a federal system of checks and balances based on interests and regions. His famous essay "The Federalist" argued that the popular will, expressed through representative government, could overcome narrowly prescribed special interests and sectional differences. Madison was a key mover in developing the Virginia Plan, which proposed a federal system with power divided between legislative, judicial, and executive branches. In 1789 he introduced the ten amendments to the Constitution known as the Bill of Rights, designed to protect from government interference the individual rights of speech, press, assembly, religion, speedy and impartial jury trial, and the right to bear arms. Madison served in the Virginia legislature from 1776 to 1777, was a Virginia delegate to the Continental Congress from 1780 to 1783, served as a member of the U.S. House of

Representatives from 1789 to 1797, was Jefferson's secretary of state from 1801 to 1809, and served as U.S. president from 1809 to 1817.

In 1794 Madison, a forty-three-year-old bachelor, fell in love with Dolley Dandridge Payne Todd (1768–1849), a twenty-six-year-old widow and mother. They were married on September 15, 1794. Dolley Madison was a charming and vivacious First Lady who hosted lively dinners, receptions, and entertainments at the President's House.

Madison served two presidential terms, from 1809 to 1817. His administration faced serious foreign policy tests from France, which was ambitiously aggressive under Napoleon, and from Great Britain, which sought revenge for losing its American colonies. The "War Hawks," led by Henry Clay, thundered against British humiliations of the United States, such as the impressment of American seamen into the British navy and the seizure of American ships. They charged the British with provoking the Indian tribes on the frontier to attack American settlements. They also dreamed of annexing Canada. A beleaguered President Madison asked Congress for a declaration of war against Britain on June 1, 1812.

The War of 1812 consisted of seesawing battles in Canada, in New York, on the Great Lakes, and on the Atlantic. As the war dragged on, it became increasingly unpopular in the New England states, where Madison's Federalist opponents derided it as "Mr. Madison's War."

On August 19, 1814, Sir George Cockburn, the British commander, landed four thousand troops between Baltimore and Washington, and they marched to the nation's capital. The much smaller American defensive force retreated, and President Madison and his cabinet fled the city. British troops set fire to the public buildings, burning the President's House, the Treasury, and the War Office. The British then besieged Baltimore. During the city's bombardment by British ships, on September 13 Francis Scott Key, watching the attack on Fort McHenry, wrote "The Star Spangled Banner," which was adopted as the national anthem in 1931. The Treaty of Ghent ended the war on December 24, 1814.

After completing his second presidential term in 1817, Madison retired to Montpelier. He died there in 1836 and was buried on the estate. Dolley Madison was forced to sell the house and its furnishings in 1844. She died in 1849.

. . . . . . . . . . . . . . . . . . . . . . . . . . . . . . . . . . . . . . . . . . . . . . . . . . . . . . . . . . . . . . . . . . . .

**Montpelier**
**Orange, Virginia**

ADDRESS: James Madison's Montpelier, P.O. Box 911, Orange, VA 22960
TELEPHONE: 540-672-2728
WEB SITE: www.montpelier.org

LOCATION: Montpelier is located four miles southwest of Orange, Virginia, on Route 20, approximately twenty-five miles north of Charlottesville and seventy miles south of Washington, D.C.

OPEN: Daily, 9:00 A.M. to 5:00 P.M., April–October; 9:00 A.M. to 4:00 P.M., November–March; closed Thanksgiving and Christmas Day.

ADMISSION: Adults, $14.00; children 6–14, $7.00

FACILITIES: Guided tours of James Madison's home; 2,650-acre site with gardens; visitor center with William duPont Gallery, Grills Gallery, a café, and a museum shop; shuttle bus and picnic areas; James Madison National Landmark Forest, Education Center, and Madison Family Cemetery; special events

*Montpelier was the plantation home* of James Madison, father of the U.S. Constitution, chief proponent of the Bill of Rights, and the fourth U.S. president. Madison was the third generation of his family to live on this extensive plantation in Virginia's piedmont.

The Madison family owned Montpelier for more than a century. In 1723 the future president's grandparents, Ambrose Madison and Frances Taylor Madison, moved to Virginia's piedmont, where they had acquired several large land tracts, including the Montpelier site. Although the origins of the name are uncertain, it may have been named for Montpellier, a French resort area. Ambrose built the first house on the property, called Mount Pleasant. Archaeologists are excavating the Mount Pleasant site, which is located near the Madison Family Cemetery.

Ambrose's son James inherited Montpelier. The future president, James Madison Jr., the eldest of James and Nelly Rose Conway Madison's twelve children, was born there on March 16, 1751. James Madison Sr., who built the central part of Montpelier's main house in the 1760s, probably designed it and supervised its construction by a workforce of enslaved African Americans.

Between 1797 and 1800 James Madison Jr. doubled the size of the main house, extending it thirty feet to the north. In September 1794 James Madison Jr. married Dolley Dandridge Payne Todd. James Jr.'s family occupied one wing of the house while his parents resided in the other wing. After his father's death in 1801, James Madison Jr. inherited Montpelier. Further additions were built between 1809 and 1812. The interior was renovated and one-story wings added to each end of the house. The kitchens, located in the basements of the wings, were brought into the main house for the first time.

After completing his second presidential term in 1817, Madison retired to Montpelier. At his death in 1836 Madison was buried in the family cemetery on the estate. Because of financial indebtedness, Dolley Madison was forced to sell the house and auction its furnishings in 1844. She lived in Washington,

D.C., until her death in 1849. Dolley was originally interred in the Congressional Cemetery on Capitol Hill and in 1858 was reinterred at Montpelier.

After leaving Madison family ownership, Montpelier changed hands six times until it was purchased in 1900 by Anna Rogers and William duPont who was a grandson of the industrialist E. I. duPont. The duPonts enlarged the house to fifty-five rooms, which were wrapped onto and around the Madison rooms. Marion duPont Scott, wife of the actor Randolph Scott, acquired possession of the property in 1928. The Scotts built barns, greenhouses, staff houses, a country store, a train station, a racetrack, a steeplechase course, and assorted horse stables. Mrs. Scott bequeathed Montpelier to the National Trust for Historic Preservation on her death, which occurred in 1983.

One of the last homes of the Founding Fathers to pass into public hands, Montpelier posed significant problems for historic preservation and interpretation. The radically altered main house was in poor structural condition and virtually empty of original furnishings. The trust decided to preserve the grounds and the exterior of the mansion as it was during the duPont era while identifying and restoring the interior areas that were part of the original Madison house. The trust opened the Montpelier mansion to the public in 1987 as part of the bicentennial celebration of the U.S. Constitution.

In 2000 the Montpelier Foundation assumed stewardship of Montpelier in cooperation with the National Trust, which retained ownership. After further study, the two entities changed their minds about Montpelier. In 2003 the foundation began restoring the mansion to the 1809–36 era. The duPont additions have been removed, and the house has been returned to the Madison period with twenty-two rooms. The exterior renovation of the mansion has been completed, although the interior is still being renovated.

In the Education Center the exhibit "Search for the Treasures" from the Madisons' collections is presented as a time line of James and Dolley Madison's lives through Madison-period pieces. "Public Places, Private Spaces" exhibits a re-creation of the Madisons' 1820 dining room. "James Madison: Architect of the Constitution and the Bill of Rights" focuses on Madison's role in the development, writing, and implementation of two of America 's most important documents.

A visitor center houses a theater with an orientation film about President Madison and the archaeological research and preservation at Montpelier. Its Grills Gallery is a museum with Madison furnishings and artifacts. Those of us who visited Montpelier when it was a fifty-five-room mansion appreciate the duPont Gallery, which displays the reinstalled red room and the grand salon.

A number of special tours, offered on weekends from April through October, include the Garden and Grounds tour and the Montpelier Enslaved

Community tour. The Montpelier gardens, designed by Bizet, a French gardener, were originally planted as a large four-acre terraced garden containing vegetables, fruit trees, flowers, and ornamental shrubs in the landscape style of the early nineteenth century. Anna Rogers duPont reconfigured the neglected garden into a formal garden. Restoration of the two-acre, early-1900-style formal garden began in 1990. Tours offered quarterly are the James Madison Landmark Forest Tour, also called the Big Woods Walk, and the Freedman's Farm and Confederate Winter Camp Site Walking Tour.

Designated by the U.S. Department of Interior as a National Natural Landmark, "Big Woods" is recognized as the best example of an old-growth forest. The two-hundred-acre deciduous forest contains five varieties of oaks, tulip trees, poplars, and hickories. Understory plants include dogwoods, redbuds, spicebush, honeysuckle, and grapevines. The mature tulip poplars of the forest date to President Madison's lifetime. A system of self-guided, interlocking trails, nearly two miles in length, has opened this natural treasure to visitors.

The Montpelier Enslaved Community tour focuses on the lives of the approximately one hundred African American slaves owned by President Madison and his father. Visitors see the sites of their homes and workshops and the slave cemetery. The Civil War Encampment and Gilmore Farm tour is a guided walking tour of the 1863–64 winter encampment of the Confederate South Carolina Brigade and the Gilmore Farm, the restored home built in 1872 by George Gilmore, a freedman who was born a slave at Montpelier around 1810.

Sites of archaeological work dot the landscape as evidence of an ongoing effort to interpret more of Montpelier's rich history. President James Madison and Dolley Madison are buried in the Madison Family Cemetery.

# James Monroe

FIFTH PRESIDENT OF THE UNITED STATES
*March 4, 1817–March 3, 1825*

. . . . . . . . . . . . . . . . . . . . . . . . . . . . . . . . . . . . . . . . . . . . . . . . . . . . . . . . . . . . . . .

James Monroe, U.S. president from 1817 to 1825, continued Virginia's legacy of leadership to the nation. President Monroe is remembered as the originator of the Monroe Doctrine, which stated that North and South America were no longer open to European colonization and that attempts to expand European interests in the Western Hemisphere would be interpreted as a threat to U.S. security.

James Monroe, born on April 28, 1758, in Westmoreland County, Virginia, was the second of the five children of Spence Monroe and Elizabeth Jones Monroe. When Spence Monroe died in 1774, sixteen-year-old James inherited the family property located only five miles from George Washington's plantation.

In June 1774 James entered the College of William and Mary in Williamsburg, Virginia. It was a turbulent time in the colonial capital as relations between the British and the colonists worsened. In 1776 the young patriot enlisted in the Third Virginia Regiment, and he served under General Washington when Washington's forces crossed the Delaware in December 1776. James was wounded in the Battle of Trenton.

Monroe reached the rank of lieutenant colonel before leaving the army in 1780. On the advice of Thomas Jefferson, Monroe reentered the College of William and Mary and began reading law with him. Monroe began his law practice in Fredericksburg, Virginia.

In February 1786 James married Elizabeth Kortright, the daughter of Laurence and Hannah Aspinwall Kortright of New York City. Eliza was born in December 1786, and a son was born in May 1799 but died in September 1801. Maria Hester was born in 1803.

Interested in politics, Monroe was a member of the House of Delegates, the lower house of the Virginia legislature, from King George County. He was a member of the Governor's Council in Richmond and represented Virginia in Congress, which was operating under the Articles of Confederation. Monroe was elected to the House of Delegates from Spotsylvania County in spring 1787 and was an anti-Federalist delegate to the Virginia ratifying convention in June 1788.

Though Monroe ran unsuccessfully against his friend James Madison for Congress in 1789, in fall 1790 he was elected to the U.S. Senate. Over time he emerged as a party spokesman for Jefferson and a leader of the Republican Party against Alexander Hamilton's opposition Federalist Party. In early 1791 Monroe proposed that the Senate open its sessions to the public, and in February 1794 that policy was adopted.

In May 1794 President Washington appointed Monroe as minister to France. France had declared war on Great Britain in 1793, and each country suspected the United States of favoring its enemy. Members of the Federalist administration accused Monroe of being pro-French and agitated for his removal from his diplomatic post. Eventually President Washington recalled Monroe, which made Monroe feel deeply wronged by the Washington administration. To defend himself, in late 1797 Monroe wrote a book, *A View of the Conduct of the Executive in the Foreign Affairs of the United States Connected with the Mission to the French Republic during the Years 1794, 5 & 6.*

Monroe served three terms as governor of Virginia. Then he was appointed by President Jefferson as minister to France to assist Minister Robert Livingston in acquiring the right of free navigation of the Mississippi River or to purchase land near New Orleans. In May 1801 Spain transferred control of the Louisiana Territory to France, ruled by Napoleon. Jefferson feared that Napoleon would close New Orleans to American trade. However, Napoleon offered to sell the entire territory. Monroe and Livingston negotiated the sale of Louisiana for sixty million francs.

Monroe was nominated for the presidency against Madison in early 1808 but received only three votes to Madison's eighty-three in the congressional caucus of Republicans. He was elected governor of Virginia again in early 1811, but shortly thereafter he was named by President Madison to be secretary of state, a position he held from April 1811 until he became president.

In December 1816 Monroe was elected as the fifth president of the United States. Daniel Tompkins won the vice presidency. The Monroe period, from 1816 to 1824, was known as the "era of good feelings." The United States and Spain disagreed about the boundaries of the Louisiana Territory. Secretary of State John Quincy Adams negotiated the Transcontinental Treaty, in which Spain ceded Florida to the United States and settled Louisiana's boundaries.

A serious challenge to the balance between free states and slave states arose in 1819 over Missouri's admission to the Union. At that time there were eleven slave and eleven free states. The Missouri Compromise of 1820, largely engineered by Speaker of the House Henry Clay, preserved the balance of free and slave states. An amendment to the Missouri Compromise prohibited slavery in the territory that was north of but allowed it south of latitude 36 degrees 30 minutes.

In 1820 Monroe was reelected as president without opposition, garnering all but one of the 232 electoral votes. Most of Spain's colonies in Central and South America had recently won their independence. President Monroe gave diplomatic recognition to Mexico and Colombia in 1822, to Chile and Argentina in 1823, to Brazil and the Federation of Central American States in 1824, and to Peru in 1826.

Monroe included a far-reaching foreign policy statement in his annual message to Congress on December 2, 1823. This statement, which came to be known as the Monroe Doctrine, declared that the United States would oppose any further European colonization in the Americas and any European efforts to extend political systems to the Americas. In return the United States would not involve itself in Europe's internal affairs.

President Monroe, who was succeeded by his secretary of state, John Quincy Adams, retired to Oak Hill in Loudoun County, Virginia in 1825. Elizabeth died on September 23, 1830, and James died on July 4, 1831. The former president's funeral was held in New York's St. Paul's Episcopal Church, and he was buried in the Gouverneur vault in Second Street Cemetery in New York. In 1858 Monroe's body was reburied in Hollywood Cemetery in Richmond, Virginia.

. . . . . . . . . . . . . . . . . . . . . . . . . . . . . . . . . . . . . . . . . . . . . . . . . . . . . . . . . . . . . . . . . . . . . . . . .

## Ash Lawn–Highland
## Charlottesville, Virginia

ADDRESS: 1000 James Monroe Parkway, Charlottesville, VA 22902-8722

TELEPHONE: 434-293-8000

WEB SITE: www.ashlawnhighland.org

LOCATION: Near I-64 and Route 250, two and one-half miles beyond Monticello on County Road 795, James Monroe Parkway

OPEN: Daily, 9:00 A.M. to 6:00 P.M., April–October; 11:00 A.M. to 5:00 P.M., November–March; closed Thanksgiving, Christmas, and New Year's Day

ADMISSION: Adults, $10.00; seniors, $9.00; children 6–11, $5.00; group rates and tour packages available

FACILITIES: Plantation home of President James Monroe; picnic area; gift shop; nature trail; special events; summer music festival; house is handicapped accessible; National Register of Historic Places

*James Monroe's Ash Lawn–Highland recalls* the history of America's fifth president and re-creates the atmosphere of an early nineteenth-century small Virginia plantation. Ash Lawn–Highland, situated on a 535-acre estate in a range of mountains near Charlottesville, Virginia, was the home of James Monroe from 1799 to 1823.

Motivated by his long friendship with Thomas Jefferson, Monroe purchased acreage adjacent to Monticello in 1793 to live near Jefferson in what Jefferson called "a society to our taste." Jefferson advised Monroe on the location of the house site and sent gardeners to prepare the gardens and orchards. Monroe built a one-story frame structure of about six rooms, which he intended to

Ash Lawn–Highland,
Charlottesville, Virginia

be a temporary dwelling until he could build a grander house, the plans for which never materialized.

In November 23, 1799, Monroe and his wife, Elizabeth, moved to their plantation, named Highland. Monroe may have selected that name because his ancestors had emigrated from the Scottish highlands or because of the plantation's location in Virginia's upland country. Monroe intended Highland to be a working plantation. Thirty slaves cultivated tobacco on thirty-five hundred acres. After growing tobacco for several years, Monroe realized that it was rapidly depleting the soil. He then turned to grain cultivation and raising cattle and sheep. He also planted French Bordeaux grapes for wine.

In 1816 Monroe put an addition on the north side of the house, which contained the study and the children's room. In 1818 he converted the three-room servants' quarters to guest accommodations.

The Highland farm suffered during Monroe's prolonged absences in Europe and in Washington and rarely made a profit. Although he had planned to retire to Highland, Monroe was indebted by his public service and so sold the property to repay a bank loan in 1826. Highland was renamed Ash Lawn in 1838. A wing of the house was damaged and partially removed in 1840. In the 1880s the owner, John Massey, added a two-story Victorian section over the foundation of the damaged wing.

In 1930 Jay Winston Johns, a wealthy industrialist, purchased Ash Lawn. Johns, who appreciated the house's historical significance, sought to maintain it and began furnishing it with Monroe furniture and artifacts. He opened it to the public in 1931. Johns, who died in 1974, bequeathed Ash Lawn, its furnishings, and 535 acres to the College of William and Mary, which Monroe had attended from 1774 to 1776 and again briefly in 1780.

The College of William and Mary began the process of historical restoration and preservation. Based on archaeological and historical research, the house was carefully restored. In April 1975 it was reopened to the public, and in 1985 it became known officially as Ash Lawn–Highland.

Monroe's "cabin-castle," as he referred to it, is accessed through an entrance hall featuring exhibits on the Monroe family and James Monroe's political career. Excerpts from the Monroe Doctrine are displayed. In the drawing room are items the Monroes purchased while in France, including 1800 neoclassical chairs. The Chaudet bust of Napoleon on display was given by him to Monroe. The portraits of Queen Hortense of Holland, her brother Eugene, and Madame Campan were given to the Monroes by Queen Hortense, who was a classmate of Eliza Monroe in France.

The study has a Louis XVI desk similar to the one President Monroe used when writing the Monroe Doctrine speech. An ongoing effort is being conducted to rebuild Monroe's three-thousand-book collection based on an inventory. The dining room furnishings owned by the Monroes include an elegant eighteenth-century Hepplewhite dining table and French Empire chairs that were used in the White House.

The Monroe bedchamber contains a four-poster bed and a Sheraton writing desk owned by President James Madison. The children's room has a hand-carved crib. There is a basement kitchen where food was cooked over an open fire.

On the grounds are the overseer's cottage, the smokehouse, and the re-constructed slave quarters. The Ash Lawn–Highland grounds have been carefully landscaped with flower, vegetable, and herb gardens. Peacocks walk about the lawns. The pastures with grazing cattle, horses, and sheep recapture an earlier time. James Monroe Historical Trail, a three-mile nature and ecology hiking path, begins at the museum gift shop and leads to the top of Carter's Mountain.

. . . . . . . . . . . . . . . . . . . . . . . . . . . . . . . . . . . . . . . . . . . . . . . . . . . . . . . . . . . . . . . . . . . .

### James Monroe Museum and Memorial Library
### Fredericksburg, Virginia

ADDRESS: 908 Charles Street, Fredericksburg, VA 22401

TELEPHONE: 540-654-1043

WEB SITE: www.umw.edu/jamesmonroemuseum

LOCATION: Fredericksburg is located south of Washington, D.C., about
    halfway between Washington and Richmond, off I-95 at Route 3 East

OPEN: Monday–Saturday, 10:00 A.M. to 5:00 P.M., and Sunday, 1:00 P.M to 5:00
    P.M, March–November; Monday–Saturday, 10:00 A.M. to 4:00 P.M., and
    Sunday, 1:00 P.M. to 4:00 P.M., December–February; closed Thanksgiving,
    Christmas Eve, Christmas Day, New Year's Eve, and New Year's Day

ADMISSION: Adults, $5.00; children, $1.00

FACILITIES: Guided tours; gift shop

*Located in the historic town of Fredericksburg,* the James Monroe Museum and Memorial Library is a small, low-key presidential museum compared to the huge complexes of the most recent presidents. It is located on the site of Monroe's law office where he practiced law from 1786 to 1790. The office was in a frame building on a half-acre site in downtown Fredericksburg, which Monroe purchased for £105 in 1786.

James Monroe studied law with Thomas Jefferson and was admitted to the bar of the Courts of Appeal and Chancery in October 1786. In 1790 he left the practice of law to serve in the U.S. Senate.

Monroe sold his Fredericksburg property in 1792, and over the next sixty years three brick buildings were erected on the site. Monroe's great-granddaughter Rose Gouverneur Hoes and her son Laurence Gouverneur Hoes purchased this property in 1927 with the intention of making it a museum. The James Monroe Law Office Shrine was officially dedicated on April 28, 1928, Monroe's 170th birthday.

The stewardship of the museum passed to Lawrence Hoes in 1933. The James Monroe Memorial Foundation was created in 1948 with Lawrence Hoes as its president. A library wing added in 1962 doubled the size of the museum. In 1964 the foundation gave the museum to the Commonwealth of Virginia, and it is administered by the University of Mary Washington. Knowledgeable docents conduct guided tours of the small museum.

The museum has a fine collection of President and Mrs. Monroe's artifacts and furnishings. Displayed in room settings, much of the furniture is from France, including the desk at which President Monroe wrote the Monroe Doctrine. Many years after Monroe's death, secret compartments in the desk were opened, and notes from Madison, Franklin, and other of the nation's founders were discovered.

A small harp that belonged to Eliza, Monroe's daughter, is displayed. While attending school in France, Eliza became friends with a stepdaughter of Napoleon named Hortense who later became the queen of Holland. In a vivid green room are portraits of Lawrence Gouverneur, Eliza Monroe, the queen of Holland, and James Monroe. The dining room furniture is from Oak Hill, the Monroes' retirement home, which is privately owned. The silver is adorned with a Scottish crest of the Clan Munro. Elizabeth Monroe's jewelry and her cloth shoes are displayed in a cabinet that was owned by Monroe descendants.

The 1824 New Year's Day White House reception is re-created in another room. On display are Elizabeth's black velvet dress and her jewelry. President Monroe collected clocks, including an eight-day clock that dates from 1810–20. There is an 1824 portrait of James Monroe by Rembrandt Peale.

Exhibits include the following: "James Monroe, an American Life"; "The Making of a Revolutionary"; "The Era of Good Feeling: The Monroe Family in Washington"; "Americans in Paris: Monroe as Diplomat"; and "The Jay Treaty and the Monroe Doctrine." There is a time line on Monroe's life from his birth in 1758 to his death in 1831.

# John Quincy Adams

SIXTH PRESIDENT OF THE UNITED STATES
*March 4, 1825–March 3, 1829*

John Quincy Adams was one of this country's most intellectual presidents. His life revolved around literary pursuits in almost equal proportion to his ambition that led to his life as an American statesman. In addition to being fluent in French, he spoke German and Spanish and frequently translated Greek and Latin classics. A poet, linguist, classical scholar, acclaimed orator, political analyst, able diplomat, Harvard professor, and well-published author, Adams lived many years of his life in Europe, where he interacted with royalty and powerful governmental figures. A son of the second president of the United States, he served as the sixth president of the United States as well as senator, congressman, and secretary of state in addition to diplomatic assignments in Russia and England.

John Quincy Adams was born on July 11, 1767, in Braintree, Massachusetts. He was the oldest son and second of the five children of President John Adams and Abigail Smith Adams. As a young boy, "Johnny" accompanied his father on diplomatic assignments to France and Holland and attended European schools. In July 1781 he and Francis Dana, John Adams's secretary, traveled two thousand miles to St. Petersburg, Russia, on a diplomatic assignment. In May 1784 Johnny returned to America to study at Harvard College, and he graduated in July 1787.

John Quincy studied law with Theophilus Parsons in Newburyport, Massachusetts; was sworn in to the office of attorney in July 1790; and launched his legal practice in Boston. In 1794 he was appointed as minister to Holland. In England he met Louisa Johnson, the daughter of Joshua Johnson, the American consul there. Louisa and John Quincy were married in London on July 26, 1797. Their children were George Washington, born on April 12, 1801; John, born on July 4, 1803; Charles Francis, born on August 18, 1807, who was destined to be a distinguished historian; and Louisa Catherine, who was born in Russia on August 11, 1811, and died on September 15, 1812.

President John Adams dispatched John Quincy to Prussia as America's minister in Berlin in late 1797. In July 1801 the Adams family returned to America. It was Louisa's first visit to the United States.

John Quincy was elected as a state senator on the Federalist ticket in April 1802, and in 1803 he was elected as a senator from Massachusetts, a role he served until June 1808. In June 1805 John Quincy was elected as Harvard's Boylston Professor of Rhetoric and Oratory. He did not resign his Senate seat but worked in both capacities.

In March 1809 President Madison appointed John Quincy as minister to Russia. He did not return home for another eight years. Adams was then appointed as minister to England. He was the secretary of state under President James Monroe and was instrumental in formulating the Monroe Doctrine.

John Quincy Adams was one of four candidates in the presidential campaign of 1824. The other candidates were William H. Crawford of Georgia, Henry Clay of Kentucky, and Gen. Andrew Jackson of Tennessee. Jackson was the front-runner in the popular vote, with 43 percent versus 31 percent for Adams. In the Electoral College, Jackson received ninety-nine electoral votes, followed by Adams with eighty-four, Crawford with forty-one, and Clay with thirty-seven. In such an electoral impasse, the Constitution provides that the House of Representatives will elect the president from the three candidates with the highest number of electoral votes. Clay, who came in fourth, threw his support to Adams. On February 9, 1825, Adams won the presidency on the first ballot in the House of Representatives with thirteen votes for Adams, seven for Jackson, and four for Crawford. The vice president was John Caldwell Calhoun of South Carolina.

When President Adams named Henry Clay as his secretary of state, many Jackson supporters saw Jackson, the biggest vote getter in the election, as the victim of a corrupt bargain. This widely held perception severely impacted Adams's effectiveness as president. When Sen. John Randolph denounced the corrupt bargain between Adams and Clay, Henry Clay challenged Randolph to a duel, which occurred without injury to either man.

Adams pursued reelection, but Andrew Jackson won the 1828 presidential election with an electoral vote of 178 and more than 647,000 popular votes. President Adams received 83 electoral votes and more than 508,000 popular votes. Like his father, John Quincy Adams was a one-term president.

President Adams's twenty-eight-year-old son George died on April 30, 1829, an apparent suicide. John Quincy ran for the House of Representatives in November 1830 and served in the House for seventeen years. He resumed writing, turning out poetry and political essays.

On February 21, 1848, the eighty-year-old Adams collapsed in the House chambers, and he died on February 23. A funeral service was held on February 25 in the chamber of the House. After a service in the United First Parish Church, Adams's coffin was placed in the family vault in the Quincy cemetery. Louisa died on May 14, 1852, at the age of seventy-seven. In December 1852 the bodies of Louisa and John Quincy Adams were reinterred in the crypt beneath the United First Parish Church in Quincy, where John and Abigail Adams also lie.

# Andrew Jackson

SEVENTH PRESIDENT OF THE UNITED STATES
*March 4, 1829–March 3, 1837*

. . . . . . . . . . . . . . . . . . . . . . . . . . . . . . . . . . . . . . . . . . . . . . . . . . . . . . . . . . . . . . . . . . . . . . . . .

Glorified in song and story as the victor of the Battle of New Orleans in the War of 1812, Andrew Jackson is an American hero. He is also remembered for his unrelenting policy to relocate the eastern American Indians across the Mississippi River.

Andrew Jackson, the youngest of the three sons of Andrew Jackson and Elizabeth Hutchinson Jackson, was born on March 15, 1767, in the Waxhaw settlement, South Carolina. He was the sole member of his nuclear family born in America. His parents, natives of Ulster, Northern Ireland, immigrated to America in 1765 with two-year-old Hugh and six-month-old Robert. In the Waxhaw region they settled on a two-hundred-acre farm near Twelve Mile Creek on the border between the Carolinas. Andrew Jackson Sr. died suddenly in March 1767 a few days before Elizabeth gave birth to the future president.

During the American Revolution the British army invaded the Waxhaw region, killing more than a hundred Continental soldiers at the Battle of Stono Ferry. Sixteen-year-old Hugh Jackson, a Continental volunteer, died of heat exhaustion on May 29, 1780, after the battle.

On August 1, 1780, thirteen-year-old Andrew Jackson, who had enlisted as a Continental soldier, was with the troops that attacked the British at Hanging Rock. Andrew and his brother Robert were taken prisoner, escaped, and then were recaptured and sent to the British base at Camden. A British officer struck Andrew with his sword when the young rebel refused to polish the officer's boots. Andrew's head and hand carried the scars throughout his life. Smallpox spread quickly among the 250 American prisoners at Camden, and both Andrew and Robert contracted the disease.

When she learned that her sons were imprisoned at Camden, Elizabeth Jackson successfully pleaded for their release in a prisoner exchange, which took place in early August. Fifteen-year-old Robert, who was very ill, died on August 6, 1780. Elizabeth then went to care for two of her nephews who were on a prison ship in Charleston Harbor. She contracted cholera and died in November 1781. At age fourteen Andrew was the only surviving member of his family.

Andrew Jackson studied law, was admitted to the North Carolina Bar in 1787, and became a public prosecutor for the Western District of North Carolina, now part of eastern Tennessee. In Nashville, Jackson lodged with Mrs. John

Donelson, whose daughter Rachel Donelson Robards would be his future wife. Although Andrew and Rachel were to be lifelong partners, their relationship was mired in mystery, scandal, and legalities that plagued Jackson's political career. When Andrew met Rachel in 1788, she was married to Lewis Robards of Kentucky. Because of a quarrel, Rachel had returned to her family's home in Nashville, but Robards followed her. After Robards accused Jackson of being too intimate with his wife, Jackson threatened to cut off Robards's ears. Robards swore out a peace warrant against Jackson but returned to Kentucky. Accusing Rachel of adultery and desertion, he filed for divorce and subsequently claimed to have obtained a decree of divorce issued in Virginia, of which Kentucky was then a part. In fact Robards, on December 20, 1790, had obtained an enabling act that permitted him to bring suit against his wife in the Supreme Court of the District of Kentucky.[1] This act declared that if the charges of adultery and desertion were upheld, a divorce would be granted, but a divorce was not actually granted at that time.

According to the official but undocumented story, Rachel and Andrew Jackson were married in Natchez in the summer of 1791.[2] On September 27, 1793, Lewis Robards was granted a divorce from the Court of Quarter Sessions of Mercer County in Harrodsburgh, Kentucky. When Rachel and Andrew Jackson learned about the now-legal divorce, they immediately obtained a marriage license. Rachel's brother-in-law, Robert Hays, a justice of the peace, married the couple on January 17, 1794.

Andrew Jackson was both a political and a military figure. During the War of 1812 against Britain, Creeks massacred 250 white men, women, and children at a stockade forty miles north of Mobile, Alabama, on August 30, 1813. Jackson, commissioned as a U.S. major general, led a coordinated attack against the Creeks near Horseshoe Bend, Alabama, in March 1814. Nine hundred Creek warriors were killed, and Jackson lost sixty men. The Creek chiefs were forced to accept the Treaty of Fort Jackson, by which twenty million acres of Creek land—three fifths of the present state of Alabama and one fifth of Georgia—were ceded to the United States.

As Jackson's troops approached Alabama, they destroyed the Indian village of Tallushatchee, savagely killing 186 men and capturing 84 women and children. Jackson, a man of contradictions, sent a ten-month-old captive Indian boy named Lyncoya, whose mother had been killed, to the Hermitage, his home in Nashville, where he and Rachel raised him as their son. The Jacksons, who had no children of their own, also adopted one of the twin sons of Rachel's brother Severn Donelson. Named Andrew Jackson Jr., he was born on December 4, 1809. Lyncoya died on June 1, 1828.

During the War of 1812 the British landed at New Orleans on January 8, 1815. Jackson's troops won a stunning victory with only 13 American soldiers killed while the British lost 2,037 men. News arrived after the battle that the Treaty of Ghent had already ended the war. The Battle of New Orleans made Andrew Jackson into a national hero.

Jackson was elected to the U.S. Senate on October 1, 1823. The leading candidates in the presidential election of 1824 were William Crawford of Georgia, Henry Clay of Kentucky, John Quincy Adams of Massachusetts, and John C. Calhoun of South Carolina. Andrew Jackson, Tennessee's favorite son, was nominated for president by the Pennsylvania state convention on March 4, 1824. Jackson came in first with 151,271 popular and 99 electoral votes, followed by Adams with 113,122 popular and 84 electoral votes. The third-place Crawford received 41 electoral and 47,531 popular votes, while Clay came in fourth with 37 electoral and 47,531 popular votes.

Although he won the popular vote and a plurality of electoral votes, Jackson lacked the needed majority of 131 electoral votes. The contested election was thrown into the House of Representatives, which was to choose from the three leading candidates. Clay, in fourth place, persuaded his electors to vote for Adams, who became president. When President Adams appointed Clay as his secretary of state, Jackson's supporters alleged that the two had made a corrupt deal to deprive Jackson of the presidency.

Jackson became the leader of a new political party, the Democratic Party. He and Adams vied for the presidency in 1828. Adams's party, the National Republicans, mounted a vicious attack on Jackson, dredging up the tangled legalities of his wife's divorce and his reckless duels. Jackson and his vice-presidential running mate, John C. Calhoun, won a landslide victory with 642,553 popular and 178 electoral votes. The incumbent, President John Quincy Adams, received 500,897 popular and 83 electoral votes.

Rachel Jackson suffered a heart attack on December 18, 1828, and died on December 22. She was sixty-one years old. Rachel was buried in the Hermitage garden. Ten thousand people attended her funeral.

Andrew Jackson was inaugurated on March 4, 1829. He called for the removal of all the eastern tribes beyond the Mississippi, and Congress passed the Indian Removal Act in 1830. All the southeastern tribes except the Cherokee had signed treaties to leave by 1833. The Cherokee held tribal land in Georgia, Alabama, North Carolina, and Tennessee. In 1838, during the Van Buren administration, federal troops rounded up the Cherokee for a forced march to the Indian Territory, now Oklahoma, and one quarter of them died on the "Trail of Tears." Forty-six thousand Indians were relocated west of the Mississippi River, and the United States gained one hundred million acres of Indian land.

In the election of 1832 the Democrats nominated Andrew Jackson and his running mate, Martin Van Buren, while the National Republicans nominated Henry Clay. Jackson won 701,780 popular and 219 electoral votes to Clay's 484,205 popular and 49 electoral votes.

In 1837, after Martin Van Buren was inaugurated as president, Andrew Jackson retired to his Nashville home, the Hermitage. He died on June 8, 1845, at age seventy-eight and was buried at the Hermitage next to his beloved wife Rachel.

......................................................................................

## The Hermitage
## Nashville, Tennessee

ADDRESS: 4580 Rachel's Lane, Nashville, TN 37076

TELEPHONE: 615-889-2941

WEB SITE: www.thehermitage.com

LOCATION: Twelve miles northeast of Nashville, on Old Hickory Boulevard, just off U.S. 70 north

OPEN: Daily, 8:30 A.M. to 5:00 P.M., April through mid-October; 9:00 A.M. to 4:30 P.M., mid-October through March; closed Thanksgiving, Christmas, and third week of January

ADMISSION: Adults, $17.00; seniors, $14.00; students 13–18, $11.00; children 6–12, $7.00

FACILITIES: Home of Andrew Jackson; guided tours of the mansion; gardens; President Jackson's grave; church; slave cabins

*Andrew Jackson was twenty-one years old* when he traveled to western North Carolina, now the state of Tennessee. It was Jackson's home for the rest of his life. There he met his wife, Rachel Donelson Robards Jackson.

In 1804 Andrew and Rachel purchased a 420-acre farm about ten miles from Nashville, which they named the Hermitage. Originally the Jacksons lived in a two-story block house that consisted of one room on the first floor and two rooms on the second floor. Later another small house was built nearby, and the two structures were connected by a covered passageway.

Rachel managed the farm during her husband's frequent absences, and slaves provided the farm labor. Jackson also operated a cotton gin, a distillery, a boatyard, a tavern, several mercantile stores, and a racetrack. In addition he raised racehorses.

In 1819 Jackson began building a house at the Hermitage plantation. The two-story brick federal-style house had a central hall with two rooms on each side of the hall on both the first and second floors. A large nineteenth-century garden designed by William Frost was laid out next to the mansion. In 1823 Jackson built a brick Presbyterian church for his wife. Rachel Jackson died on December 22, 1828.

In 1831, after a fire at the Hermitage, library and dining room wings were added on either side of the original house along with a one-story colonnade supported by ten columns on the facade. In front of the house was a large guitar-shaped lawn bordered by cedars.

The Hermitage,
Nashville, Tennessee

Another fire at the Hermitage in October 1834 destroyed much of the second floor and damaged the first floor. President Andrew Jackson rebuilt the house on its original site based on the 1831 house plan, although the exterior of the house was redesigned in the Greek-revival style with six two-story massive Corinthian columns. The ceilings of all the rooms were raised, and the windows were enlarged and rearranged. A new single-story west wing housed the dining room, a service pantry, and a storage pantry, while the east wing contained Jackson's study and library. It is this impressive 1836 mansion that visitors to the Hermitage see today.

In 1837, after the presidency, Andrew Jackson retired to the Hermitage. He died on June 8, 1845. Andrew Jackson Jr., Andrew and Rachel's adopted son, inherited the estate. Unable to manage financially, Andrew Jr. sold five hundred acres, including the mansion, to the state of Tennessee in 1856. In 1858 Governor Isham Green Harris asked the Jackson family to return as caretakers at the Hermitage. When Nashville was occupied by federal troops, Gen. George H. Thomas assigned soldiers to protect the Hermitage. Andrew Jackson Jr. died in 1865. After the war Andrew Jackson III returned to the Hermitage, where his mother, Sarah Jackson, lived. The Jackson family left the Hermitage in 1893.

The Ladies' Hermitage Association was founded in 1889 to preserve President Andrew Jackson's home. That year the state of Tennessee conveyed twenty-five acres, including Jackson's house and tomb, to the association. The association acquired additional acreage and now manages 1,120 acres, including the entire 1,050 acres owned by President Jackson. The house has been carefully restored to the era of President Jackson's retirement. Also at the historic site are Tulip Grove and the old Hermitage Church.

A video about the Hermitage and President Andrew Jackson is shown in the visitor center. Museum exhibits focus on the African Americans who lived on Jackson's plantation, archaeological research, the Ladies' Hermitage Association, and the restoration process. Jackson's dueling pistols and portraits of Jackson family members are displayed.

Few structural changes have occurred at the Hermitage since Jackson's death, and many of the furnishings are original to the family. A major refurbishing of the house occurred in 2000. The white Greek-revival-style mansion has a front portico and double doors leading to the central hall. The central hall's walls are covered with restored 1825 French wallpaper. Visitors can also see a magnificent curved staircase and an original chandelier that has been electrified.

Double parlors are connected by folding doors. The front parlor's reproduction gold and while wallpaper was copied from sample books in the Cooper Hewitt Museum. The invoice from Jackson's papers noted pattern numbers that match those in the sample books. A clock on the Italian marble mantel is stopped at the time that Jackson died. A formal table is set in the dining room in the west wing. The chairs, which were lost in a fire after 1889, have been reproduced.

To the right of the hall are the bedrooms of Andrew and Rachel and their son. Andrew Jackson died in his bedroom at the age of seventy-eight. Jackson's personal possessions include family portraits, a washstand, and a foot tub. Off a hall leading to the east wing are Jackson's library and the farm office. In the library are a walnut secretary desk and bookcases. Upstairs there are four guest bedrooms and a central hall. One bedroom was occupied by the artist Ralph E. W. Earl, who married a niece of Rachel Jackson.

Rachel Jackson's garden, designed by William Frost in 1819, is a nineteenth-century formal arrangement of hedges and flower beds edged with red bricks and boxwood and containing pebble paths. In the garden are roses, irises, black-eyed Susans, tree peonies, coreopsis, and old pink moss. Andrew and Rachel Jackson are buried in a corner of Rachel's garden under a stone cupola.

On the property is Tulip Grove, the 1836 brick home of Andrew Jackson Donelson, Rachel's nephew. It is used for special events.

# Martin Van Buren

.........................................................................

Martin Van Buren, a shrewd New York politician, maneuvered his way to the presidency through his friendship with Andrew Jackson. The popular expression "okay," used around the world to signify affirmation, is attributed to Van Buren, who signed his papers with O.K., the initials of his estate at Old Kinderhook.

A village tavern in New York's Hudson Valley was the birthplace of Martin Van Buren, the eighth president of the United States. He was born in Kinderhook on December 5, 1782, to Abraham Van Buren, a farmer and tavern keeper, and Marie Hoes Van Alen Van Buren. Martin was the third of the couple's five children.

The original settlers in New York's Hudson Valley were primarily from Holland. Van Buren's paternal great-great-great-grandfather, Cornelis Maessen, came to the New Netherlands in 1631. He returned in 1635 to Holland, where he married Catalyntje Martense and adopted the name Van Buren, which indicated his birthplace, the district of Buren.

Martin was baptized in Kinderhook's Dutch Reformed Church, and his first language was Dutch. He was apprenticed as a law clerk to a New York City lawyer, William P. Van Ness, who was active in Republican politics. Admitted to the New York Bar on November 25, Martin began his legal career in Kinderhook.

On February 21, 1807, Martin married Hannah Hoes, a cousin. They had four sons: Abraham, born on November 17, 1807; John, born on February 18, 1810; Martin, born on January 30, 1812; and Smith Thompson, born on January 16, 1817. After Smith's birth, Hannah remained in poor health. Two years later she died and was buried in Kinderhook.

Martin was an active member of the Republican Party, which at that time was an offshoot of the Democratic-Republicans founded by Thomas Jefferson.[1] In 1812 Van Buren was elected to the New York Senate, and he served until 1820.

Van Buren in 1820 bought a controlling interest in the newspaper the *Argus*. Under the editorship of Moses Cantine, his brother-in-law, the *Argus* disseminated Van Buren's political views. The New York legislature elected Van Buren to the U.S. Senate on February 6, 1821. When Gov. De Witt Clinton died suddenly in February 1828, Van Buren was the successful candidate for governor of New York.

Van Buren identified with Andrew Jackson's Democrats. As the 1828 election approached, the Jacksonians shortened the name of their party from Democratic-Republicans to simply the Democratic Party. The anti-Jacksonians, formerly the National Republicans, joined the emerging Whig Party. Van Buren supported Andrew Jackson in the 1828 presidential election. Fiercely attacking the incumbent, President John Quincy Adams, Van Buren's Albany *Argus* editorialized for General Jackson.

President Jackson appointed Van Buren as his secretary of state. The men were close friends as well as political allies. Van Buren was selected as the Democratic Party's vice-presidential nominee in 1832, and President Jackson was re-elected.

The Democratic convention in May 1835 nominated Van Buren, Jackson's handpicked successor, as its presidential candidate and Richard Mentor Johnson of Kentucky as the vice-presidential candidate. The Whigs held several state conventions that nominated three presidential candidates: William Henry Harrison, Daniel Webster, and Hugh L. White. The Whig strategy was to throw the election into the House of Representatives as had occurred in 1824. Willie P. Mangum was an independent Democratic nominee. Van Buren, with 764,176 popular and 170 electoral votes, triumphed. None of the vice-presidential candidates received a majority, so the election went to the Senate. Richard Johnson was victorious.

Van Buren faced a serious economic crisis—the panic of 1837. On May 10, 1837, New York banks suspended payments of specie, and shortly almost all of the nation's approximately eight hundred banks followed suit. The economy's downward spiral continued until late 1839. Van Buren did not believe that the Constitution provided for the federal relief of economic distress and unemployment, and he refused to recharter the national bank. He advocated depositing federal funds in an independent government treasury and issuing treasury notes based on them. In June 1840 Congress authorized the issuing of up to ten million dollars in treasury notes.

Van Buren continued President Jackson's Indian-removal policy. In 1838 Gen. Winfield Scott and his army troops forced Cherokee from North Carolina to march to Oklahoma. Thousands of Cherokee died en route on what came to be called the "Trail of Tears."

In the election of 1840 the Whigs nominated William Henry Harrison for president and John Tyler for vice president. President Van Buren was renominated by the Democratic Party. The Whigs contrasted the rugged Indian fighter Harrison, who was born in a crude log cabin and preferred to drink hard cider, with the "dandy" Van Buren, who enjoyed luxury and fine wines. The truth, however, was that Harrison had been born in a plantation mansion in Virginia.

Harrison was elected with 1,274,624 popular and 234 electoral votes, while Van Buren had 1,127,871 popular and only 60 electoral votes.

In the summer of 1839 Van Buren had purchased the Van Ness family estate in Kinderhook. In May 1841 he retired to his country home—named Lindenwald—with his son Martin, who had tuberculosis.

In 1848 Van Buren became a presidential candidate again, this time as the nominee of the Free Soil Party, a third party formed by disgruntled Democrats. The Free Soilers were joined by some northern Whigs, known as "Conscience Whigs," who defected from their party because it had nominated a slave owner, Zachary Taylor. Taylor won the election.

In 1853 Van Buren took his son Martin to Europe for his health. Martin Jr. died in Paris in March 1855. The former president died in July 1862 at the age of seventy-nine at Lindenwald. His funeral was held at the Reformed Dutch Church of Kinderhook, and he is buried next to his wife in Kinderhook Cemetery, Kinderhook, New York.

........................................................................

Martin Van Buren National Historic Site
Kinderhook, New York

ADDRESS: 1013 Old Post Road, Kinderhook, NY 12106
TELEPHONE: 518-758-9689
WEB SITE: www.nps.gov/mava
LOCATION: In New York's Hudson Valley, on N.Y. Route 9H, about two miles south of Kinderhook
OPEN: Daily, 9:00 A.M. to 4:30 P.M., mid-May through October; grounds are open 7:00 A.M. to dusk the rest of the year
ADMISSION: Individuals, $5.00; families, $12.00
FACILITIES: Retirement estate of President Martin Van Buren; guided tours of Lindenwald; visitor center

*Martin Van Buren, the eighth president* of the United States, was born in the village of Kinderhook in New York's Hudson Valley on December 5, 1782. Kinderhook was a Dutch settlement on the Albany or Old Post Road, the main thoroughfare between New York City and Albany. The Van Burens, who were from Holland, settled in Kinderhook in 1669. Martin's maternal ancestors, the Hoes, also came from Holland in the mid-1600s and by 1734 operated a gristmill on Kinderhook Creek.

Van Buren returned to the place of his youth for his retirement. In 1839 he purchased the Van Ness estate in Kinderhook, which included 130 acres of land and a 1797 house. Van Buren's estate, which eventually grew to 226 acres, was in a beautiful setting with a view of the Catskill Mountains.

Van Buren initially named his estate The Locusts and then Lindenwald for its abundant linden trees. In May 1841, after losing his bid for a second presidential term to William Henry Harrison, the former president retired to his country home. His son Martin, who suffered from tuberculosis, lived with him.

Van Buren farmed, raising rye, corn, oats, potatoes, and wheat. He had a large vegetable garden and a variety of fruit trees, and he raised cows, beef cattle, sheep, pigs, chickens, turkeys, geese, and ducks. He wrote his memoirs, corresponded, read books, and entertained visitors, including Washington Irving and Thomas Hart Benton.

Peter Van Ness's house was in a state of neglect when Van Buren purchased it in 1839. In 1849 Van Buren's son Smith, his wife, Ellen, and their three children moved to Lindenwald, and Smith renovated the house with the help of the prominent architect Richard Upjohn. He changed the exterior appearance from an eighteenth-century Georgian house to a mid-nineteenth-century Italianate-style villa with a four-story brick tower, a central gable, attic dormers, a new front porch, and a library wing. Additional rooms included a bedroom, a nursery, an entrance hall, and a bathroom. Renovations were completed by 1850, and the red brick house was plastered and painted yellow with brown trim.

Martin Van Buren died in July 1862 at Lindenwald and was buried next to his wife, Hannah, in the Kinderhook Cemetery. Lindenwald passed out of the Van Buren family and was privately owned until 1974, when it was acquired by the National Park Service. Martin Van Buren National Historic Site was established by Congress on October 26, 1974. Lindenwald was restored to its appearance in the 1850s and was opened to the public in 1982.

The thirty-eight-acre Martin Van Buren National Historic Site preserves Martin Van Buren's thirty-six-room home where he lived from 1841 until his death in 1862. Three quarters of the furnishings are associated with the Van

Buren family. Much of the property around the site is conservation land, which preserves the historic atmosphere. A video on Van Buren is presented at the visitor center.

Lindenwald's central hall is a high-ceilinged, spacious area papered with a spectacular historic mural. In 1841 Van Buren ordered from the Zuber Company of Rixheim, France, fifty-one panels of scenic wallpaper designed by Jean-Julien Deltil that depicts a hunting scene, *Paysage a Chasses* (Landscape of the Hunt). The wallpaper, which had deteriorated, was removed in the 1970s and carefully restored, cleaned, and rehung a decade later. Van Buren removed the staircase in the central hall so it could be used for formal dinners at a dining table that accommodated twenty people.

The formal parlor has a walnut table, couches, dark heavy draperies, a melodeon, and persimmon-colored mahogany armchairs. A piano, a harp, a sofa, and a table are in the sitting room. In the breakfast room are a sideboard and Van Buren's china. The library, added in the 1849 remodeling, was where Van Buren wrote his memoirs and correspondence. Anti–Van Buren political broadsides are displayed.

On the second floor Martin's son John and his wife Elizabeth's bedroom has sleigh beds and a clock with a picture of Martin Van Buren. Another bedroom was that of Abraham and his wife Angelica, Van Buren's White House hostess. President Van Buren died in his bedroom, which is furnished with a sleigh bed, a desk, and a shaving stand. Three adjoining servants' rooms are in the attic.

The basement kitchen has plastered stone walls, a sink with a hand pump, a coal-burning Moses Pond Union cookstove manufactured about 1850 in Boston, and a brick bake oven. A servants' dining room has flowered wallpaper, and there is a servants' bedroom.

The Lindenwald Wayside Trail is a one-half-mile loop on the grounds. Nearby is the Kinderhook Cemetery, where President Martin Van Buren is buried.

# William Henry Harrison

......................................................................

William Henry Harrison, the ninth president of the United States, has the undesirable distinction of serving the shortest presidential term. Because he died only thirty-one days after his inauguration, his vice president, John Tyler, served almost all of Harrison's four-year term.

Harrison rose to the rank of major general in the U.S. Army, served as governor of the Indiana Territory, fought in the Battle of Tippecanoe, and was secretary of the Northwest Territory, superintendent of Indian affairs, an Ohio state senator, a U.S. senator, minister to Colombia, and ninth president of the United States. In addition he was the grandfather of Benjamin Harrison, the twenty-third president of the United States—the only grandfather-grandson combination in presidential history.

William Henry Harrison was born on February 9, 1773, at Berkeley Plantation on the James River in Charles City County, Virginia. The youngest of the seven children of Benjamin Harrison V and Elizabeth Bassett Harrison, William was descended from politically active colonial and revolutionary-era Virginians, including a leading entrepreneur, Robert "King" Carter. Benjamin Harrison V was a friend of George Washington, a signer of the Declaration of Independence, a three-time governor of Virginia, Speaker of the House of Burgesses during the Revolution, and a Virginia delegate at the Continental Congress in Philadelphia.

William, at age eighteen, entered the Medical School of Pennsylvania University at Philadelphia but withdrew after his father's death in April 1791. Harrison enlisted in the army with a commission as ensign in the First U.S. Regiment of Infantry. In the early national period, the small and poorly trained U.S. Army was assigned to protect white settlements against hostile Indians and British agents in the region that would become Michigan, Indiana, and Ohio.

The Shawnee, Miami, Delaware, Ottawas, Wyandots, and Pottawatomie, alarmed by the westward-moving frontier of white settlement, organized a loose confederacy to repel the settlers who had crossed the Ohio River. In 1793 Congress enlarged the army, and Gen. Anthony Wayne was named its commander. Harrison was one of Wayne's aides-de-camp. Wayne's troops fought in the Battle of Fallen Timbers on August 20, 1794. Despite a force of over one thousand braves, the U.S. troops defeated the Native Americans, crushing

Indian resistance in the Northwest Territory. The Greenville Treaty, signed on August 3, 1795, ceded most of present-day Ohio and Indiana to the United States.

Lieutenant Harrison fell in love with Anna Tuthill Symmes, and they were married on November 25, 1795. They had ten children, including John Scott, born on October 4, 1804, in Vincennes, Indiana, who was the father of President Benjamin Harrison.

In 1798 Harrison was appointed as secretary of the Northwest Territory, and in 1799 he ran successfully for Congress as the delegate from the Northwest Territory. He introduced legislation to divide the Northwest Territory into two parts: the western Indiana Territory with its capital at Vincennes, Indiana; and the eastern Northwest Territory with Chillicothe, Ohio, as its capital. President Adams nominated Harrison as the governor of the Indiana Territory.

The Indiana Territory had been explored and settled primarily by the French and had a population of fewer than six thousand white people in 1800. William Harrison spent thirteen years as territorial governor of Indiana and superintendent of Indian affairs. He earned the respect of the local Native American tribes, held councils, and negotiated thirteen Indian treaties, adding millions of acres of land to the young republic. Aggressive but peaceful acquisition of Indian property was official government policy in the early nineteenth century.

Many Native Americans resented Governor Harrison's acquisition of their land, especially the Shawnee leader Tecumseh. He argued that Indian land was held in common by all the tribes and thus could not be sold by a single tribe. This logic challenged the validity of the treaties already signed. Tecumseh's brother, the Prophet, was a religious figure who preached a return to primitive ways and cultural separation. Throngs of Native Americans joined Tecumseh and the Prophet at Greenville in 1807 and at Prophetstown on Tippecanoe Creek, two hundred miles from Vincennes, the following year.

In September 1809 Governor Harrison called a council at Fort Wayne, which was attended by more than one thousand Miami, Wea, Delaware, and Pottawatomie. The Treaty of Fort Wayne resulted in the acquisition of three million acres in Indiana, which further enraged the tribes at Prophetstown. Tecumseh and Governor Harrison held a council at Vincennes in August 1810. The chief reiterated the invalidity of the Fort Wayne treaties, and war seemed inevitable.

On November 6, 1811, Governor Harrison and one thousand troops arrived at Prophetstown. Before dawn the next morning, Indian warriors mounted a fierce attack on the sleeping soldiers. The Prophet administered a potion to his braves to protect them from injury and assured them that many of the soldiers were already dead. Harrison's troops repulsed the warriors, resulting in a loss of credibility for the Prophet. The Battle of Tippecanoe was a victory for Harrison.

During the War of 1812 against Great Britain, Harrison was appointed commander of the northwestern army. On October 5 Harrison defeated British forces on Ontario's Thames River. Tecumseh was killed in that battle, and his plan to unite the southern and northwestern tribes died with him. Harrison negotiated the Treaty of Spring Well, signed on September 8, 1815, by nine tribes, which confirmed previous treaties and ended hostilities with those tribes.

In 1816 Harrison completed the term of U.S. Congressman John McLean. Harrison served in the Ohio Senate from late 1819 through 1821, after which he ran unsuccessfully for the U.S. Senate in 1821.

When Harrison's father-in-law, Judge John Cleves Symmes, died, the Harrisons inherited his three-thousand-acre farm at North Bend, Ohio. While they were waiting for their house to be constructed, John Scott Harrison and his second wife, Elizabeth Irwin, lived at his parents' North Bend farm. There, on August 20, 1833, Elizabeth gave birth to Benjamin Harrison, the twenty-third president of the United States.

In the presidential election of 1836, Harrison was one of three candidates of the newly organized Whig Party. He won 550,818 popular and 73 electoral votes, but the Democratic candidate, Martin Van Buren, proved victorious.

At the Whig convention in December 1839, Harrison was chosen as the presidential nominee and John Tyler as the vice-presidential nominee. Using the campaign slogan "Tippecanoe and Tyler Too," Whigs described their candidate as a military hero who, through his victory in the Battle of Tippecanoe, cleared the way for the settlement of the western frontier. The log cabin became a strong Harrison symbol, which erroneously implied that Harrison had been born in a frontier log cabin. Harrison, with 1,274,624 popular and 234 electoral votes, defeated Van Buren.

Harrison returned to his birthplace, Berkeley Plantation on Virginia's Charles River, where he wrote his inaugural speech in the room in which he had been born. The inauguration took place on March 4, 1841. It was a cold day, but Harrison wore neither hat nor overcoat while he delivered a one-hour-and-forty-minute speech to a crowd of fifty thousand.

On March 27 the president was diagnosed with bilious pleurisy. President Harrison died in the White House at 12:30 A.M. on April 4, 1841. An Episcopal funeral service was held in the East Room of the White House. The next day President Harrison's casket was moved to the Capitol to lie in state.

Because the Harrison family in Ohio did not immediately learn of the president's death, the decision was made to bury him temporarily in the Congressional Cemetery. In June his body was taken to Cincinnati, where thousands of citizens paid their respects. Harrison's body was buried in North Bend, Ohio. Anna Harrison died on February 25, 1864, at the age of eighty-eight and was buried next to her husband.

Grouseland
Vincennes, Indiana

ADDRESS: 3 West Scott Street, Vincennes, IN 47591
TELEPHONE: 812-882-2096
WEB SITE: www.grouselandfoundation.org
LOCATION: In southwestern Indiana, near the Illinois border, 132 miles south-
west of Indianapolis and about 55 miles north of Evansville
OPEN: Monday–Saturday, 9:00 A.M. to 4:00 P.M., and Sunday, 11:00 A.M. to
4:00 P.M., March–December; daily, 11:00 A.M. to 4:00 P.M., January–
February; closed Thanksgiving, Christmas, and New Year's Day
ADMISSION: Adults, $5.00; seniors, $4.00
FACILITIES: House built in 1803–4 by William Henry Harrison; gift shop

*Vincennes, the oldest town in Indiana* and the capital of the Indiana Territory,
is in a region explored by the French, who established a fort about 1732. After
losing a battle against the Chickasaw Indians in 1736, the commandant of the
fort, François Marie Bissot de Vincennes, was captured and burned at the stake.
The town was later named for Vincennes.

In 1800 Congress created the Indiana Territory, formerly a part of the
Northwest Territory, and Vincennes became the territorial capital. William
Henry Harrison was the first governor of the Indiana Territory. He, his wife
Anna Symmes Harrison, and three of their children arrived in Vincennes in
January 1801; five more children were born there. Governor Harrison pur-
chased a three-hundred-acre farm and in 1803–4 built a three-story brick house
named Grouseland. The grouse is a pheasant-like bird that Harrison enjoyed
hunting.

The Harrison family left Vincennes in 1812 due to the danger caused by the
War of 1812. In 1818 Harrison's son Symmes was appointed as receiver of public monies in the state of Indiana. William Harrison gave Grouseland to
Symmes and his wife Clarissa Pike, who lived there until 1829. Their six children were born there. Symmes and Clarissa's minor children inherited Grouseland after their parents' deaths in 1830 and 1837. Ownership of the estate was
complicated by the variety of the children's guardians, and the house was not
sold until 1851.

Grouseland was used as a hotel and then a barn. The Vincennes Water
Company owned most of Harrison's land, and in 1909 it purchased Grouseland intending to tear it down. When the Francis Vigo Chapter of the Daughters of the American Revolution learned of this plan, they sought to rescue the
historic home. In 1909 the Vincennes Water Company gave custody of Grouseland to the chapter members who had the property restored and then opened

54

WILLIAM HENRY HARRISON

it to the public in 1911. In 1936 the Francis Vigo Chapter became the owners of the property.

In 1949–50 a major restoration program on Grouseland began. Architectural additions were removed. Because the house had not been owned by the Harrison family since 1851, none of their furniture remained, but Harrison descendants donated family items.

Grouseland is constructed of four hundred thousand bricks kilned on the property. The three-story house is insulated and has walls twelve to twenty-two inches thick. Grouseland consists of two buildings connected by a covered passage. The great house has two large rooms with a center hall on the first floor, two large and two small bedrooms on the second floor, and a large attic above. The dependency has two rooms on the first floor and two low-ceilinged bedrooms on the second floor. There is a small winding stairway at the back of the dependency between the first and second floors. The basement, which extends under the entire building, has four rooms.

The spacious central hall has curved walls and a curved, self-supporting cherry staircase. On one side of the hall is a large parlor furnished with pre-1812 pieces. This room is also referred to as a council room as Harrison's treaty councils with Native Americans may have occurred here. Furnishings include a round cherry table that belonged to the Harrisons. The portrait of William Henry Harrison in military uniform was painted by Rembrandt Peale.

The dining room has a Hepplewhite sideboard that was made for Anna Harrison in Cincinnati. The morning room was used as both an office and a family room.

On the second floor is the large Harrison bedroom, which contains several family items including a bed, a blanket chest, a candle table, and a bamboo-style chair. Also on the second floor are a large guest bedroom, a nursery, and another bedroom, and a passage leads to two more bedrooms.

In the basement, which has its original brick floors and most of its original wood beams, are a museum room, a wine room, a crafts room, and a warming kitchen. On display in the museum room are Harrison books and memorabilia along with exhibits on the Harrison genealogy and Harrison's military career. There are engravings of Harrison's death, broadsides of Harrison's log cabin campaign, and prints of Tecumseh and the Prophet, the Battle of Tippecanoe in 1811, and the Battle of the Thames River in 1813. A large colored print of the death of Tecumseh and memorabilia from the "Tippecanoe and Tyler Too" campaign against Van Buren can be seen as well.

## Berkeley Plantation
## Charles City, Virginia

ADDRESS: 12602 Harrison Landing Road, Charles City, VA 23030
TELEPHONE: 804-829-6018 or 888-466-6018
WEB SITE: www.berkeleyplantation.com
LOCATION: Thirty-five miles east of Richmond, eighteen miles west of
   Williamsburg, on State Route 5
OPEN: Daily, 9:30 A.M. to 4:30 P.M.; closed Thanksgiving and Christmas
ADMISSION: Adults, $11.00; children 13–16, $7.50; children 6–12, $6.00
FACILITIES: Birthplace of President William Henry Harrison; guided tours;
   Coach House Tavern; picnic area; gardens. National Register of Historic
   Places, National Historic Landmark, Historic American Buildings Survey

*President William Henry Harrison,* the youngest of the seven children of Benjamin Harrison V and Elizabeth Bassett Harrison, was born on February 9, 1773, at Berkeley Plantation on the James River, Charles City, Virginia. A soldier and a politician, Harrison was elected as the ninth president of the United States in 1840. He returned to Berkeley to write his inaugural address in the room in which he was born.

The president's great-great-great-grandfather Benjamin Harryson I came to Virginia from England in 1632. He and his wife Mary settled in the James River area of Virginia, where they acquired considerable property on both sides of the river.

In 1691 Berkeley was acquired by Benjamin Harrison III, William Henry Harrison's great-grandfather, who established a prosperous tobacco export business. His shipyard built vessels to transport tobacco from his warehouse to the Caribbean and England. Three Revolutionary War warships were also built there. His busy ship landing was dubbed "Harrison's Landing." Berkeley is said to be the site of the first official Thanksgiving in America, held on December 4, 1619.

Benjamin Harrison IV built a house in 1726 for himself and his wife, Anne Carter Harrison, the daughter of a leading Virginia entrepreneur, Robert "King" Carter. Their son, Benjamin Harrison V, was a signer of the Declaration of Independence and three-time governor of Virginia. He was a friend of George Washington, who was entertained at Berkeley. The first ten presidents of the United States all visited the Harrison family at Berkeley Plantation.

During the Revolution, Col. Benjamin Harrison V moved his family from Berkeley to Richmond. Subsequently Berkeley was raided by a detachment of British Loyalists led by Benedict Arnold. Family portraits and furniture were burned, cattle killed, and slaves seized.

During the Civil War, Berkeley Plantation became the temporary headquarters of Union general George B. McClellan and his troops. After McClellan's seven-day Peninsula Campaign failed to capture the Confederate capital of Richmond in July 1862, the Union Army of the Potomac moved back to the James River, which was protected by federal gunboats at Harrison's Landing. While General McClellan and his army were at Berkeley, President Lincoln visited them twice.

While camped at Berkeley, Gen. Daniel Butterfield composed the melody called "Taps." It was first played by the bugler Oliver W. Norton. Adopted by both the Union and Confederate armies, Taps is now the official bugle call of the U.S. Army.

Berkeley changed hands several times after the Civil War. In 1907 the plantation was purchased by John Jamieson of Scotland, who had been a drummer boy in McClellan's army. Jamieson's son Malcolm and his wife, Grace, restored the early eighteenth-century mansion in the 1930s and furnished it with eighteenth-century antiques. Because the mansion did not remain in the Harrison family, there are few original Harrison artifacts.

The Harrison mansion occupies a hilltop site overlooking the nearly one-thousand-acre property complete with formal gardens, pastures, woodlands, and ponds. Berkeley is a classic, early Georgian three-story brick building with two tall chimneys and six dormers. A circular date stone on the west end of the house bears the inscription *H* for Harrison, *B* for Benjamin, *A* for Anne Carter, a heart, and the date 1726.

Brick used in construction of the house was fired on the plantation. The window frames, floors, and masonry of the stately mansion are original, as are the hand-hewn floor joists in the basement. The entrance hall is forty-five feet long. There are two drawing rooms separated by double arches. Hung over the mantel in the south drawing room is a portrait of Thomas Jefferson's niece, who was the great-great-grandmother of Mrs. Jamieson. Hand-carved cornices and chair moldings were added to the drawing rooms in 1790. Ten presidents were entertained in the formal dining room.

A noteworthy room is the bedroom in which William Henry Harrison was born and in which he wrote his inaugural address. Benjamin Harrison's office was used for managing the business of the plantation.

Also on the property are the bachelor's quarters and the old kitchen, both built after 1726. Between the house and the James River lie the five-level, ten-acre terraced boxwood gardens designed by Benjamin Harrison IV. Monuments to the first Thanksgiving and to Taps have been erected in the gardens.

. . . . . . . . . . . . . . . . . . . . . . . . . . . . . . . . . . . . . . . . . . . . . . . . . . . . . . . . . . . . . . . . . . .

## William Henry Harrison Tomb State Memorial
## North Bend, Ohio

ADDRESS: Cliff Road, North Bend, OH 45052

MAILING ADDRESS: Harrison Tomb, c/o Site Operations Department, The Ohio Historical Society, 1982 Velma Avenue, Columbus, OH 43211

TELEPHONE: Harrison Symmes Memorial Foundation: 513-941-3744

LOCATION: North Bend is on the Ohio River, fifteen miles west of Cincinnati; the Harrison Memorial is on Cliff Road, one mile east of the intersection of Route 50 and Route 128

OPEN: Daily during daylight hours, March through mid-December

ADMISSION: Free

FACILITIES: Burial site of President William Henry Harrison

*In 1841, when William Henry Harrison* became president, he and his family were living on their farm in North Bend, Ohio. William and Anna Symmes Harrison inherited the three-thousand-acre property from Anna's father, John Cleves Symmes, who died in February 1814. He was buried on a hill overlooking the Ohio River on his North Bend land.

After Judge Symmes's house burned down in 1811, the Harrisons enlarged the log cabin where they had lived when first married into a sixteen-room house. Anna Harrison was still there, packing for her move to the White House, when her husband died on April 4, 1841, just a month after his inauguration. She did not immediately learn of her husband's death.

President Harrison's sudden death plunged the nation into mourning. On April 7 a funeral was held in the East Room of the White House. Along a parade route lined with grieving citizens, the president's body was taken to the Capitol to lie in state. Since officials were not sure of the family's wishes with regard to burial, the president was buried temporarily in the Congressional Cemetery. To comply with the Harrison family's desire to inter the president in Ohio, in June the president's body was moved to Cincinnati and was taken by boat to North Bend, where he was buried not far from Judge Symmes.

The cabin at North Bend burned down in 1858, and the Symmes-Harrison property eventually was sold. John Scott, the son of President William Henry

Harrison and the father of President Benjamin Harrison, donated three acres of the property, including President Harrison's burial site, to the state of Ohio on the condition that the plot be preserved as a shrine. Anna Harrison died on February 25, 1864, at age eighty-eight and is buried next to her husband.

Although close to the Cincinnati metropolitan area, the Harrison Tomb Memorial is on Mt. Nebo, an isolated area overlooking the Ohio River. Steps and stone columns with eagles perched on top form the entrance to the memorial. The right column is inscribed: "William Henry Harrison 1772–1841; Ninth President of the United States: Hero of Tippecanoe; Major General in War of 1812; United States Senator from Ohio; Governor of the Territory of Indiana." The left column is inscribed: "That the Memory of Ohio's First President and Gallant Soldier William Henry Harrison May Be Fittingly Commemorated This Memorial Is Erected by a Grateful State."

Harrison's grave is marked by a sixty-four-foot Bedford limestone obelisk erected by the Ohio Historical Society. In the mausoleum are the headstones of William Henry and Anna Harrison and their son John Scott Harrison.

# John Tyler

TENTH PRESIDENT OF THE UNITED STATES
*April 6, 1841–March 3, 1845*

..........................................................................

John Tyler became president on April 6, 1841, after President William Henry Harrison's death on April 4. Harrison had served only one month in office as president. Tyler, the first vice president to gain the presidency as a result of the death of the incumbent, served almost a full term. President Tyler had more children than any other president—fifteen—and fourteen lived to adulthood.

John Tyler was born on March 29, 1790, in Charles City County, Virginia. He was the sixth of the eight children of John Tyler and Mary Marot Armistead. John Sr. was a lawyer, judge of the circuit court, governor of Virginia, and the owner of Greenway, a twelve-hundred-acre plantation on the James River.

John Tyler entered the preparatory school of the College of William and Mary in Williamsburg, Virginia, at age twelve and graduated from that institution in 1807. John passed the bar by the time he turned twenty and established a successful law practice in Charles City County.

John fell in love with Letitia Christian, daughter of Col. Robert Christian of nearby Cedar Grove Plantation. They were married on March 29, 1813. Shortly before the wedding, John Tyler Sr. died and left his son Mons-Sacer, a five-hundred-acre portion of the Greenway estate, and a number of slaves. Soon afterward Letitia's parents died, and she received a sizable inheritance. John and Letitia had eight children.

During the War of 1812 with England, Tyler joined a local militia company, the Charles City Rifles, which earned him the rank of captain. He spent his life in public service almost continually from 1811 to 1845. He served in the Virginia House of Delegates from 1811 to 1816 and again from 1823 to 1825 and in 1839. Tyler served in the U.S. House of Representatives from 1816 to 1821, was elected governor of Virginia in December 1825 and reelected in 1826, and became a U.S. senator in January 1827.

Tyler was a strong advocate of states' rights and strict interpretation of the Constitution. He opposed the establishment of the second Bank of the United States, the protective tariff, federally financed internal improvements, and the Missouri Compromise. A slaveholder himself, he supported slavery.

In November 1832 the South Carolina legislature passed an Ordinance of Nullification that declared the tariffs of 1828 and 1832 null and void in that state. The state threatened secession if force were used against its citizens. President

Jackson rejected the concepts of nullification and secession and asked Congress for authorization to deploy the military to put down armed rebellion. Called the Force Bill, it passed with Senator Tyler casting the only opposing vote because he defended the right of secession.

In early 1834 Tyler condemned President Jackson's withdrawal of funds from the Bank of the United States as unconstitutional. A censure resolution against Jackson passed the Senate on March 28, 1834, with Senator Tyler voting for it. At the end of Jackson's term, a resolution to expunge the censure of Andrew Jackson was introduced, and Senator Tyler was directed by the Virginia legislature to vote for expunction. Rather than obey this order, Tyler resigned from the Senate in February 1836.

Tyler became involved in the formation of the Whig Party, a coalition of Jackson foes and Clay supporters. In the election of 1840, the Whigs nominated John Tyler to run as vice president with William Henry Harrison. They were victorious over the incumbents President Martin Van Buren and Vice President Richard M. Johnson.

After President Harrison died on April 4, 1841, Tyler was sworn in on April 6 as president. Since he was the first vice president to assume office on the death of a president, there were no precedents. Questions were raised whether Tyler was the president of the United States or the acting president serving until a new election could be held. Tyler's position was that he was the president with all the office's powers, responsibilities, and authority.

Though he had been elected as a Whig, Tyler believed in limited federal powers, in contrast to the Whigs, who wanted a larger federal role. Led by Clay, the Whigs, who controlled Congress, passed legislation to reestablish the Bank of the United States. Tyler vetoed the bill. The entire cabinet with the exception of Secretary of State Daniel Webster resigned in protest. Later, after negotiating a treaty with Great Britain to settle a boundary dispute between Maine and New Brunswick, Webster too resigned. The Whigs, derisively dubbing Tyler "His Accidency," expelled him from the party.

Passed over by both the Whigs, who nominated Henry Clay, and the Democrats, who nominated James K. Polk, Tyler attempted to run for a second term as the nominee of the Democratic-Republican Party. He failed to gain support and withdrew his candidacy. After Polk's inauguration, Tyler left for Sherwood Forest Plantation in Charles County, Virginia, which he had purchased in 1842.

In 1839 Letitia Tyler suffered a paralytic stroke that left her an invalid. She died on September 10, 1842, at the age of fifty-one. She was the first wife of a U.S. president to die while her husband was in office. Twenty-two-year-old Julia Gardiner married fifty-four-year-old President Tyler on June 26, 1844. Tyler and Julia had seven children.

When Lincoln's election to the U.S. presidency was immediately followed by the secession of South Carolina, the Union faced civil war. Tyler was elected to the Confederate House of Representatives, which convened in Richmond. There he became ill and died on January 18, 1862, at the age of seventy-one. The former president's body lay in state at the Confederate Congress, and his casket was draped in the Confederate flag. He was buried in Richmond's Hollywood Cemetery. Because the North regarded Tyler as a traitor for joining the Confederacy, the federal government took no official notice of his death.

## Sherwood Forest Plantation
## Charles City, Virginia

ADDRESS: 14501 John Tyler Memorial Highway, Charles City, VA 23030
TELEPHONE: 804-829-5377
WEB SITE: www.sherwoodforest.org
LOCATION: Eighteen miles west of Williamsburg and thirty-five miles east of Richmond on Va. 5
OPEN: Grounds: daily, 9:00 A.M. to 5:00 P.M., closed Thanksgiving and Christmas Day; house is not open to the public except for private, prearranged tours
ADMISSION: Grounds: adults 16 and older, $10.00; house: adults, $35.00
FACILITIES: Restored eighteenth-century plantation house and grounds; home of President John Tyler. National Register of Historic Places, National Historic Landmark, Historic American Buildings Survey

*Sherwood Forest Plantation was the last home* of President John Tyler, the tenth president of the United States, from 1842 until his death in 1862. The plantation has remained in the Tyler family, and the house is owned by Harrison Tyler, a grandson, who is responsible for its restoration. The plantation had also been owned by the ninth president, William Henry Harrison, who inherited it from his sister in 1789. It is not known whether Harrison actually lived there.

John Tyler married Letitia Christian in 1813, and they had eight children. Letitia Tyler died in the White House in 1842. Tyler married Julia Gardiner in 1844, and they had seven children. John Tyler became president on April 6, 1841, when as vice president he attained the office after the death of President William Henry Harrison, who had served only thirty days.

In 1842 Tyler purchased Walnut Grove plantation in Charles County, Virginia, from his cousin Collier Minge. He and Julia retired there after his presidency. A political foe, Henry Clay, said that like Robin Hood, President Tyler was going off to his Sherwood Forest. Amused by the comment, Tyler changed the name of the plantation to Sherwood Forest.

The plantation, originally named Smith's Hundred, dates back to a 1616 land grant. A house was built around 1660 but was destroyed between 1700 and 1730.

A second house, built over the original basement, was constructed around 1730. Wings were added to the house in 1780 and 1800–1830. John and Julia Tyler added to the house in 1844 and 1845.

The house and fifty acres were purchased by a grandson, Harrison Tyler, and his wife Payne in 1975. The house had been damaged during the Civil War, and time and neglect had also taken their toll. Restoration was aided by Julia's letters and an 1835 architecture book by Minard LaFever, which had been used by Julia Tyler to style the doors and door frames.

At three hundred feet long, Sherwood Forest has been called the longest wood manor house in the country. The Virginia Tidewater–style white frame house has twenty-four rooms and sixteen fireplaces. The 1730 house was a three-story English Georgian townhouse with a detached dependency. Around 1780 a three-story wing connecting the main house and the dependency was added. In the early 1800s an addition was placed on the other side of the house for balance and symmetry. Around that time a *garconnier,* or separate living quarters for the planter's sons, was built. John Tyler added a 68 x 12–foot ballroom, which connected the house and the *garconnier* on one side, and a colonnade between the house and a seventeenth-century kitchen/laundry on the other side. The Tylers remodeled the long, narrow house in the then-popular Greek-revival style.

Most of the eighteenth-century furniture, paintings, and artifacts in Sherwood Forest belonged to either the Tyler family or the family of Payne Bouknight Tyler, Harrison Tyler's wife and the house's primary restorer. Previously the plantation house was open for touring, but now guided tours are available to groups of ten or more only by advance registration.

Portraits of Julia and John Tyler hang in the entry hall, which also contains a French pier table that had been in the White House. In the dining room is a set of china used in the White House. In the gray room are President Tyler's books, thought to have been hidden during the Civil War and found in a hay-covered box in the barn. The long and narrow ballroom, designed for the Virginia reel, has floor-to-ceiling windows and a unique vaulted ceiling, designed by Julia Tyler.

The twenty-five-acre site includes outbuildings: an 1820 two-room overseer's house; a 1745 smokehouse; a 1660 wine house; an 1845 garden house or privy; a 1745 milk house; and a 1790–1830 slave house. The terraced gardens and lawn are based on the designs of the mid-nineteenth-century landscape architect Andrew Jackson Downing of New York. More than eighty varieties of trees over one hundred years old are on the grounds.

# James Knox Polk

ELEVENTH PRESIDENT OF THE UNITED STATES
*March 4, 1845–March 3, 1849*

.................................................................

James Knox Polk, along with Andrew Jackson and Andrew Johnson, is one of three presidents from Tennessee. While most historians agree that he was a hardworking and competent president, his motives and methods in foreign policy provoke controversy. His defenders praise him as the president who significantly enlarged the United States; his detractors condemn him for engineering an unjust war against Mexico.

James Knox Polk was born on November 2, 1795, in a log cabin near Pineville, Mecklenburg County, North Carolina. He was the oldest of the ten children of Jane Knox Polk and Samuel Polk, a planter with a four-hundred-acre farm in the foothills of the Appalachian Mountains. In 1806 Samuel Polk relocated his family to Maury County, Tennessee.

In January 1816 twenty-year-old James entered the University of North Carolina at Chapel Hill's sophomore class. He began studying law in late 1818 and was admitted to the bar in 1820. He opened a law office in Columbia, Tennessee. In 1823 he was elected to Tennessee's state legislature.

James married Sarah Childress in Murfreesboro, Tennessee, on January 1, 1824. Sarah, born on September 4, 1803, was the daughter of Joel Childress, a wealthy planter. The couple did not have children.

Polk served in the U.S. House of Representatives from 1825 to 1839 and was elected as its Speaker in 1835. A Democrat, Polk backed the presidential ambitions of his fellow Tennessean Andrew Jackson. In 1839 Polk ran successfully for the governorship of Tennessee, but he was not reelected.

In the presidential election of 1844, the two front-runners for their party's nomination, Martin Van Buren, the leading Democrat, and Henry Clay, the leading Whig, made a gentleman's agreement to keep the annexation of Texas out of the campaign. When Van Buren voiced his opposition to annexation, Andrew Jackson, who strongly endorsed annexation, switched his support to James Polk. At the Democratic Party convention in May 1844, Polk was nominated on the ninth ballot, and the vice-presidential nomination went to George Mifflin Dallas. Polk, possibly the first "dark horse" candidate for president, agreed not to seek reelection. He won the election against Sen. Henry Clay of Kentucky.

Sarah Polk served as the president's private secretary and his political adviser, held receptions on Saturdays for congressmen and senators, and redecorated the White House. James Polk, a slaveholder, continued to own slaves while in the White House. Polk strongly believed that it was America's Manifest Destiny to occupy the continental expanse of land from the Atlantic to the Pacific Ocean. He promised to take control of the entire Oregon Territory, which since 1815 the United States and Great Britain had both claimed and ruled by joint occupation. Polk notified Britain that he planned to terminate the joint occupation agreement in April 1847. When the British offered to divide Oregon at the 49th parallel, Polk agreed to the compromise.

Polk hoped to acquire California, a province of Mexico. California, along with Oregon, would secure the American boundary on the Pacific Ocean and give the nation the ports of Los Angeles and San Diego.

In March 1845 Mexico broke diplomatic relations with the United States, protesting the annexation of Texas. A border dispute erupted between Mexico and the United States over the extent of Texas, with Polk claiming all the disputed land.

Preparing for war with Mexico, Polk in July 1845 ordered Gen. Zachary Taylor to take a position south of the Nueces River. Simultaneously Polk issued secret orders to the U.S. Navy to seize the California ports as soon as hostilities began with Mexico. He also encouraged Americans living in California to revolt against Mexico and set up an independent republic, which, like Texas, could then be annexed to the United States. Polk dispatched troops, led by Col. John C. Fremont, to California to aid American rebels. In November 1845 John Slidell was sent to negotiate with the Mexican government, but the terms were refused. Taylor's army, ordered further south, took a position on the Rio Grande River.

On May 9, 1846, Polk sent a declaration of war to Congress, which affirmed that a state of war existed with Mexico. The president sought to secure the Rio Grande as the country's southern boundary. New Mexico and California were seized within six months. Gen. Winfield Scott moved on Mexico City, which fell to the Americans on September 14.

An antiwar movement began against what was by then called "Polk's War." Whig politicians attacked the president for provoking the war and failing to win a decisive victory. A first-term congressman from Illinois, Abraham Lincoln, charged Polk with fomenting an unconstitutional war as an excuse for expansion. The transcendentalist philosopher Henry David Thoreau was jailed for refusing to pay taxes to support the war.

Nicholas P. Trist on February 2, 1848, negotiated the Treaty of Guadalupe Hidalgo, in which Mexico agreed to give the United States the Rio Grande border, New Mexico, and California in exchange for fifteen million dollars. The nation gained a half-million square miles including the present-day states of California, Utah, New Mexico, most of Arizona, and parts of Colorado and Wyoming. Approximately eighty thousand Mexicans living in the conquered territories became American citizens.

After the inauguration of Zachary Taylor, the Polks returned to their home in Nashville. In April a cholera epidemic reached the city. On June 3, 1849, James Polk evidenced cholera symptoms, and he died on June 15 at the age of fifty-three. He was buried in the Nashville City Cemetery, and a year later his body was moved to Polk Place. Sarah Polk died on August 14, 1891, and was buried next to her husband. In 1893 Sarah and James Polk were reinterred on the state capitol grounds in Nashville.

..........................................................................

## James K. Polk Ancestral Home
## Columbia, Tennessee

ADDRESS: 301 West Seventh Street, P.O. Box 741, Columbia, TN 38402
TELEPHONE: 931-388-2354
WEB SITE: www.jameskpolk.com
LOCATION: Columbia is in the middle of Tennessee, about fifty miles south-
   west of Nashville
OPEN: Monday–Saturday, 9:00 A.M. to 5:00 P.M., April–October; Monday–
   Saturday, 9:00 A.M. to 4:00 P.M., November–March; Sunday, 1:00 P.M. to
   5:00 P.M., year-round
ADMISSION: Adults, $7.00; seniors, $6.00; children 6–18, $4.00; families, $20.00
FACILITIES: Restored 1816 Polk house; visitor center with museum, orientation
   video, and gift shop. National Historic Landmark

*The James K. Polk Ancestral Home consists* of the restored 1816 residence owned by President James K. Polk's parents, a reconstructed kitchen behind the house, and the adjacent 1820 Sisters' House, built by James's sister and brother-in-law, which is used as a visitor center and museum. The site is a Tennessee State Historical Site, and the home and the museum are operated in cooperation with a local historical society.

The Polk house, the only extant residence of James K. Polk, was built and possibly designed in 1816 by Samuel Polk, James's father. When the house was built, James was a student at the University of North Carolina at Chapel Hill. After his graduation he returned to Columbia and lived intermittently in the new family residence until his marriage in 1824. During this period he served a legal apprenticeship in Nashville and was in the Tennessee legislature in Murfreesboro. Also living in the home were his parents, two of his sisters, and his five brothers. In 1924 the Polk house was purchased by the James K. Polk

Memorial, which had been founded by Saidee Fall Grant, who was the daughter of Sarah Jetton Fall, Sarah Polk's great-niece. Mrs. Polk adopted Sarah Jetton after her mother's death..

In 1937 the Polk Memorial acquired property adjacent to the Polk Ancestral Home. In 1946 a kitchen and an adjoining room were reconstructed on
their original foundations as determined by archaeological investigation. A
few years later the adjoining house that had been built by James Polk's sister
Jane Maria Polk and her husband James Walker in 1820 was added to the site.
The Walkers lived there for twenty-three years, after which the house was
occupied for ten years by another sister, Ophelia Polk, and her husband Dr.
John Brown Hays. The sisters' house remained in the family until 1870 and is
now the visitor center and museum. The exhibits in the Polk home visitor center feature the following: Polk as a lawyer and legislator; the road to the presidency; inauguration and inaugural balls; Polk's presidency from 1845 to 1849;
Polk's cabinet; life in the White House; and the enlargement of U.S. territory
as a result of the Mexican War and settlement of the Oregon territory dispute.

Built of handmade brick, the two-story federal-style house has a classic
design with a parlor and a dining room downstairs and bedrooms upstairs.
The floor plan, the arrangement of windows and doors, the fireplaces and
chimneys, the mantels, the floors, the woodwork, and the paint colors of the
house have been carefully restored to their 1816 appearance.

Most furnishings in the house are original to the Polk family. Over fifteen
hundred objects including furniture, paintings, china, and silver that belonged
to President and Mrs. Polk are in the collection. Many objects are from Polk
Place, the Polks' Nashville, Tennessee, retirement home, which was torn down
in 1901.

In the front hall hangs an etched lantern from Polk Place. The parlor furniture, from Polk Place, consists of rosewood sofas and mahogany armchairs

upholstered in red velvet and a round marble table with a colored mosaic top showing an American eagle and the thirty states that made up the United States at that time.

Dining room furnishings include a table set with the china used by President and Mrs. Polk in the White House and several portraits of the former president. The presidency weakened Polk's health, as is illustrated by portraits of him painted before and after his term.

For exhibit purposes one of the bedrooms on the second floor has been converted into Polk's law office and contains books, the daybed and Sleepy Hollow chair the president used in the White House, and Sarah's chair with a desk arm.

The south bedroom contains a four-poster bed that belonged to Saidee Fall Grant. The secretary belonged to Samuel and Jane Polk. In the northeast bedroom is a four-poster bed that belonged to Jane Maria Polk Walker and Sarah's writing desk.

The reconstructed kitchen has a large fireplace with ovens on both sides. A second room in the kitchen may have served as a laundry. The brick courtyard between the home and the kitchen is original. The grounds include a formal boxwood garden, a white azalea garden, and a wildflower garden.

# Zachary Taylor

TWELFTH PRESIDENT OF THE UNITED STATES
*March 4, 1849–July 9, 1850*

. . . . . . . . . . . . . . . . . . . . . . . . . . . . . . . . . . . . . . . . . . . . . . . . . . . . . . . . . . . . . . . . . . . . . . . . . . . . . . . .

Zachary Taylor served as U.S. president for less than one and one-half years. He was a career military officer from 1808 to 1848, rising from first lieutenant to major general, and served in the War of 1812, the Black Hawk War, the Second Seminole War, and the Mexican War. A southerner slave owner, he was Jefferson Davis's father-in-law.

Zachary, born on November 24, 1784, was the third of the nine children of Richard Taylor and Sarah Dabney Strother Taylor. The Taylors were a wealthy, prominent English family. James Taylor, Zachary's great-grandfather and one of the largest landowners in Virginia, was also the great-grandfather of President James Madison.

Zachary's father, Richard Taylor, was a Revolutionary War veteran who received a land grant of one thousand acres near Louisville, Kentucky. In 1784 he traveled to Kentucky, leaving his pregnant wife Sarah with relatives at Montebello, a Virginia plantation. It was there that Zachary Taylor was born. In Kentucky, Richard Taylor farmed, speculated in land, and acquired thirty-seven slaves.

Twenty-three-year-old Zachary Taylor was appointed as a first lieutenant in the Seventh Infantry on May 3, 1808. He joined a force in New Orleans, where he contracted yellow fever. He returned to Louisville to recuperate. There, Zachary met Margaret Mackall Smith, who was from Calvert County, Maryland, and they married on June 21, 1810. Richard Taylor gave his son a wedding present of 324 acres of land near Louisville.

Zachary and Margaret (Peggy) had six children: Ann Mackall was born on April 9, 1811; Sarah Knox was born on March 6, 1814; Octavia Pennill was born on August 16, 1816; and Margaret Smith was born on July 27, 1819. During the summer and fall of 1820 Peggy Taylor and her daughters contracted a fever, which killed Octavia and Margaret. Mary Elizabeth was born in 1824 and Richard in 1826.

The United States declared war on Great Britain on June 18, 1812, when Captain Taylor was stationed at Fort Harrison in Indiana Territory. In early September, Tecumseh led 450 Winnebago in an attack on Fort Harrison. Of the 50 men under Taylor's command, 34 were ill, but the fort held and the attackers retreated. It was the first U.S. victory in the War of 1812.

After the War of 1812 ended, the army was reduced in size. Taylor, who had been promoted to major in January 1815, was dropped to the rank of captain, resigned in June 1815. In mid-1816 Taylor returned to the military and was restored to the rank of major. Taylor's military assignments took him to Cincinnati, Ohio, to Washington, D.C., and to Baton Rouge and New Orleans. He was the commander of Fort Snelling in the Minnesota Territory and Prairie du Chien in the Michigan Territory.

In 1832 the United States was involved in the Black Hawk War. The Sauk and Fox Indians had signed treaties that ceded their property in northwestern Illinois to the United States, but in 1829 Chief Black Hawk challenged the legality of the treaties. When conflicts between the Indians and white settlers accelerated, additional troops were brought into Fort Armstrong at Rock Island. In spring 1832 the governor of Illinois called out the state militia. Thirteen hundred horsemen and three hundred soldiers reached Rock Island in May. Abraham Lincoln served as a militia captain. Taylor too arrived at Fort Armstrong in May. On August 2 the Battle of Bad Axe ended the war.

Typically, Taylor's wife and children joined him wherever he was stationed. Jefferson Davis, Zachary Taylor's adjutant and the future president of the Confederacy, began courting eighteen-year-old Sarah Knox Taylor in 1832. The couple married in Louisville, Kentucky, on June 17, 1835. A few months later, while visiting Davis's sister in West Feliciana Parish, Louisiana, the newlyweds contracted malaria. Sarah died on September 15, 1835.

Taylor successfully speculated in land in West Feliciana Parish, Louisiana. He then bought the nearly two-thousand-acre Cypress Grove Plantation on the Mississippi River north of Natchez. Eighty slaves were included in the Cypress Grove deal.

While negotiations with the Lone Star Republic about annexation to the United States went on in 1844, Zachary Taylor was the commander of the First Military District, which was prepared for action if Mexico should commence hostilities against Texas. When the Texas Congress accepted the terms of the resolution of annexation in July 1845, Taylor's orders were to move his troops near the Nueces River. In February 1846 Taylor and his troops were to relocate to the east bank of the Rio Grande, which marked the southern boundary claimed by Texas. It was more than one hundred miles south of the previous boundary of the former Mexican province of Texas. Mexico viewed Taylor's advance as an act of aggression and demanded that he retreat. Taylor not only did not retreat but also blockaded the river.

War with Mexico was officially declared on May 13, 1846. On September 21 General Taylor led six thousand soldiers in a fierce attack on Monterrey. After a few days the Mexican commander, Maj. Gen. Pedro de Ampudia, offered surrender terms, which Taylor accepted because he had been told that Mexico was about to accept a peace offer from the United States. When President Polk learned of the armistice, he was furious and replaced General Taylor. However, the American people celebrated the stunning victory at Monterrey, esteeming Taylor as a war hero.

In December 1847 a group of young Whig congressmen, including Abraham Lincoln, organized the Taylor-for-President Club. Taylor won the nomination for president at the Whig convention held in June, and the vice-presidential candidate was Millard Fillmore. Lewis Cass, a senator from Michigan, was nominated by the Democrats. Disgruntled Democrats formed a third party, the Free Soil Party, and ran Martin Van Buren, the former president. In the election of 1848 Taylor won 1,360,987 popular and 163 electoral votes to Lewis Cass's 1,222,342 popular and 127 electoral votes. Although he carried no electoral votes, Martin Van Buren won 291,263 popular votes.

General Taylor resigned from the army on January 31, 1849. While he was traveling to Washington for his inauguration, a trunk fell on the president-elect at Madison, Indiana, painfully injuring his side. In Cincinnati, Taylor's left hand was badly bruised. The steamboat on the Ohio River on which he was a passenger ran aground and then was delayed by ice jams.

On March 5, 1849, Taylor took the oath of office. On July 4, 1850, the president became ill and was diagnosed with cholera morbus. He died on July 9, 1850. Millard Fillmore was sworn in as president on July 10 in the House of Representatives.

President Taylor was buried in the Taylor family plot in Louisville, Kentucky. Peggy Taylor died on August 14, 1852, and was buried next to her husband.

. . . . . . . . . . . . . . . . . . . . . . . . . . . . . . . . . . . . . . . . . . . . . . . . . . . . . . . . . . . . . . . . . .

Zachary Taylor National Cemetery
Louisville, Kentucky

ADDRESS: 4701 Brownsboro Road, Louisville, KY 40207
TELEPHONE: 502-893-3853
LOCATION: Louisville is in northwestern Kentucky on the Indiana border.
The cemetery is in northeast Louisville on Brownsboro Road / U.S. 42, accessible from I-264
OPEN: Daily, sunrise to sunset
ADMISSION: Free
FACILITIES: Burial site of President Zachary Taylor

*At present there are no houses, museums, or libraries* associated with President Zachary Taylor that are open to the public. There is only his burial site in Louisville, Kentucky.

Taylor was born in Virginia, but his family moved to the Louisville area when he was only one year old. His father, Richard Taylor, owned a four-hundred-acre farm there and built a large brick house named Springfield circa 1790. After Richard Taylor's death in 1829, the house was owned by Hancock Taylor, Zachary's older brother. When President Zachary Taylor died, he was buried in Springfield's family plot. Springfield has not been owned by the Taylor family for many decades.

After serving as president for fifteen months, President Zachary Taylor died on July 9, 1850, at the age of sixty-five. Margaret Taylor, distraught by her husband's sudden death, refused to have the president's body embalmed, so it was packed in ice. On Friday, July 12, public viewing took place in the East Room of the White House. A funeral was held there at noon the next day. The president's casket was then borne in a two-mile-long procession viewed by one hundred thousand spectators to the Congressional Cemetery, where it was placed in a temporary vault. In October 1850 President Taylor's body was brought to Kentucky, and on November 1 it was placed in a limestone vault in the Taylor family cemetery. Peggy Taylor died on August 14, 1852, and is buried next to her husband.

In 1883 the state of Kentucky erected a granite shaft surmounted by a life-size figure of President Taylor at the burial site. In 1926 the federal government erected a limestone building with a marble interior. An inscription over its double glass-paneled bronze doors reads "1784 Zachary Taylor 1850."

At the request of the Taylor family, the Zachary Taylor National Cemetery was established in 1928 by an act of Congress. Over thirteen thousand military veterans are buried there. The Taylor vault and monument are now within the sixteen-acre national cemetery, although the half-acre Taylor burial site is not owned by the government.

Perhaps because of his short illness, there were persistent rumors that President Taylor had died of arsenic poisoning administered by political enemies. In 1991, over 140 years after President Taylor's death, his body was exhumed with the permission of Taylor descendants. Hair and fingernail tissue were analyzed using neutron activation in Tennessee's Oak Ridge National Laboratory. Scientists concluded that Taylor had not been poisoned.

# Millard Fillmore

THIRTEENTH PRESIDENT OF THE UNITED STATES
*July 10, 1850–March 3, 1853*

. . . . . . . . . . . . . . . . . . . . . . . . . . . . . . . . . . . . . . . . . . . . . . . . . . . . . . . . . . . . . . . .

Millard Fillmore today is considered an obscure and little-known American president. A largely self-educated man, he made his way to the White House by being an available compromise candidate.

Millard Fillmore was born on January 7, 1800, in a log cabin in Locke, Cayuga County, in the Finger Lakes region of western New York. He was the second of the nine children of Phoebe Millard Fillmore and Nathaniel Fillmore.

Nathaniel Fillmore and his brother Calvin purchased property in Cayuga County, New York, that was part of the Military Tract, the one and one-half million acres in central New York set aside to provide bonuses for veterans of the Revolutionary War. By 1799 this land was being sold to New England farmers. After the Fillmore brothers lost their farm because of a faulty land title, they leased a farm a few miles north of Sempronius, now Niles, near Lake Skaneateles. There, as a tenant farmer, Nathaniel scraped out a living.

Millard had little formal education. He was apprenticed to owners of a carding and cloth-dressing mill in New Hope, New York. There, Millard purchased a membership in a circulating library and attended classes in an academy.

While Millard Fillmore was in New Hope, his father farmed property owned by Judge Walter Wood. Nathaniel persuaded Wood to take Millard as a law clerk, and Millard began to study law. Because Millard needed to pay off his apprenticeship, Judge Wood arranged a teaching position in an elementary school in Sempronius. Millard then resumed his clerkship for Judge Wood until he was reprimanded for taking an outside legal job. In the summer of 1822 Millard began another clerkship, and in April 1823 the court of common pleas admitted Fillmore to the bar. He opened a law office in East Aurora, New York.

In New Hope, Millard fell in love with his teacher Abigail Powers, and they married on February 5, 1826. On April 25, 1828, Abigail gave birth to a son named Millard Powers Fillmore. A daughter, Mary Abigail, was born on March 27, 1832.

In 1826 Fillmore was admitted as an attorney and then a counselor by the New York State Supreme Court. He joined the newly formed Anti-Masonic Party, which attracted area politicians opposed to Andrew Jackson. Fillmore was elected in November 1828 to a one-year term in the New York State Assembly and was reelected in 1829 and 1830.

In November 1832 Fillmore was elected to the U.S. House of Representatives as a National Republican. In 1834 the Anti-Masonic Party officially ceased to exist and merged with other anti-Jackson groups into the Whig Party. In 1836 Fillmore, a Whig, was elected to the House of Representatives and served three successive terms. In Washington, D.C., Fillmore met Daniel Webster, who arranged for him to practice before the Supreme Court.

In 1837 a financial panic led to a severe economic depression. Buffalo, Fillmore's home district, was especially impacted. As banks failed and unemployment soared, Fillmore and other Whigs attacked President Van Buren's failure to alleviate the country's economic distress.

In the presidential election of 1840 the Whig candidate, Gen. William Henry Harrison, was lauded as a military hero who would lead the nation into an era of prosperity. The Whigs nominated John Tyler for vice president. Harrison was elected, and the Whigs won control of both the Senate and the House of Representatives. Fillmore's role as chairman of the powerful Ways and Means Committee of the House of Representatives elevated him to national prominence.

After serving in the House for eight years, Fillmore did not seek reelection in 1842 and lost his race for governor of New York. In 1847 Fillmore ran for comptroller of New York State and was elected. At the Whig National Convention held in June 1848, Zachary Taylor was nominated for president and Millard Fillmore was nominated for vice president. The pair defeated Martin Van Buren, the incumbent Democratic president.

When President Taylor unexpectedly died on July 9, 1850, Vice President Fillmore became president. He was inaugurated on July 10 before a joint session of Congress.

North-south sectional divisions over slavery sparked a contentious congressional debate over the Compromise of 1850, crafted by Henry Clay, the Whig leader in the Senate. Clay's bill would admit California as a free state, organize the territories of Utah and New Mexico without regard to slavery, assume the debts that Texas had incurred when it was a republic, end the slave trade in the District of Columbia, and enact a stringent new Fugitive Slave Law. The Compromise of 1850 was made into law.

The Fugitive Slave Law contained stringent provisions that runaway slaves could be pursued, even if in free states, and returned to their owners. It denied suspected fugitive slaves a jury trial and the right to testify on their own behalf. Anyone who aided escaped slaves was subject to fines and imprisonment. There were no effective safeguards against false identification and the kidnapping of legally free blacks. Many northerners condemned the law and Fillmore for signing it.

Abolitionists organized the Underground Railroad, a series of safe havens in which escaped slaves could hide in free states as they made their way to Canada. Harriet Beecher Stowe, angered by the Fugitive Slave Law, wrote *Uncle Tom's Cabin,* published in 1852, which became an instant best seller. Millions of readers sympathized with Uncle Tom and Eliza, escaped slaves, who were pursued by the villainous Simon Legree.

In the election of 1852 Fillmore's enforcement of the Fugitive Slave Law cost him the support of northern Whigs, who nominated Gen. Winfield Scott on the fifty-third ballot. Scott lost to Franklin Pierce, the Democratic nominee.

After Pierce's inauguration on March 4, 1853, the Fillmores moved to the Willard Hotel in Washington, D.C., because Mrs. Fillmore was too ill to travel. She died on March 30, 1853. Twenty-two-year-old Mary Abigail died of cholera the following year.

In 1856 the American Party nominated Fillmore as its presidential candidate, but James Buchanan, the Democratic candidate, was elected. In February 1858 fifty-eight-year-old Millard Fillmore married Caroline Carmichael McIntosh, a forty-four-year-old widow.

Millard Fillmore died on March 8, 1874, in Buffalo at age seventy-four. After a private funeral in his home, Fillmore's body was carried to St. Paul's Cathedral, where it lay in state. Millard Fillmore is buried in Forest Lawn Cemetery in Buffalo with both of his wives, his two children, and Abigail Fillmore's mother.

. . . . . . . . . . . . . . . . . . . . . . . . . . . . . . . . . . . . . . . . . . . . . . . . . . . . . . . . . . . . . . . . . . . . . . . .

## Millard Fillmore Museum
### East Aurora, New York

ADDRESS: 24 Shearer Avenue, East Aurora, NY 14052
TELEPHONE: 716-652-8875 or 716-652-4985
WEB SITE: www.nps.gov
LOCATION: East Aurora is southeast of Buffalo; from I-90 take Route 400 south to East Aurora
OPEN: Wednesday, Saturday, and Sunday, 1:00 P.M. to 4:00 P.M., June–October
ADMISSION: Adults, $5.00
FACILITIES: National Historic Landmark; guided tours; rose and herb gardens

*Several months before Millard Fillmore* and Abigail Powers married in February 1826, Fillmore, with the help of his friends, built a house on Main Street in Aurora (now East Aurora), New York. Millard began his law practice in a law office he built across the street from his home. The newlyweds lived in the house from 1826 until they moved to Buffalo in 1830. Their son, Millard Powers, was born there in 1828.

The Fillmore house changed hands many times and eventually fell into disrepair. In 1916 the house was moved to the back of its lot when a theater

building was built on Main Street. In 1930 the Fillmore house was purchased by Margaret Price, an artist, who moved the structure to its present location on Shearer Avenue and added a studio wing.

In 1975 the Aurora Historical Society purchased the Fillmore house with the intention of restoring it to its 1826 appearance. The house is a small frame, federal-period-style, two-story cottage painted light green. It has hand-hewn timbers fastened with wooden pegs. Although there were a kitchen wing and outbuildings on the property, when the Fillmore house was moved to Shearer Avenue in 1930, its kitchen wing, woodshed, and outbuildings were not moved, and they have since disappeared.

The Fillmore house has been restored to its 1826–30 appearance. Since the home had not been occupied by the Fillmore family for 150 years, no Fillmore family furnishings remained. Furnishings include period pieces and Fillmore pieces acquired by the museum.

The living room has a fireplace and stenciled walls. An empire-style settee and chairs belonged to the Fillmore family, while the federal-period lectern belonged to John Quincy Adams. There are portraits of Millard and his wife Abigail, who was a teacher and conducted school in this room. The living room windows, twelve panes over eight panes, contain original glass. The floor, of wide pine planks, is original. A reconstructed kitchen has a large brick fireplace with a beehive oven and a rustic table used by the Fillmores.

In the master bedroom upstairs is Fillmore's bed, covered with a silk and taffeta tumbling block quilt made by Abigail. The children's bedroom holds a toy collection.

Since Millard Fillmore's Main Street law office no longer exists, one room of the house is furnished as a law office. It contains a large secretary that belonged to President Fillmore.

The 1930 addition to the Fillmore house now serves as both a library and a museum. Abigail Fillmore was shocked to find that the White House had no library. Congress appropriated funds for her to found the first White House library. In the Fillmore house library are bookcases from the White House, as well as the piano and harp used there by Mary Abigail.

A reproduction carriage barn was built in the late twentieth century to house President Fillmore's sleigh, carriage, and a collection of nineteenth-century tools. Beams and other wood used to build the barn were salvaged from the recently razed barn owned by the president's father, Nathaniel Fillmore, in East Aurora.

The East Aurora Garden Club beautifully restored the grounds and gardens. The Presidential Rose Garden has varieties grown before 1840, and Abigail's Herb Garden features period herbs.

The Millard Fillmore Museum is owned and administered by the Aurora Historical Society, Inc. President Fillmore's parents and several other relatives are buried in East Aurora's old cemetery on Oakwood.

# Franklin Pierce

FOURTEENTH PRESIDENT OF THE UNITED STATES
*March 4, 1853–March 3, 1857*

.........................................................................

New Hampshire's only president, the often-overlooked Franklin Pierce served for one term. Pierce was a dark horse candidate nominated by Democrats at a divided convention. Serving at a time when tensions were rising between the North and the South over slavery, President Pierce tried to take a middle course and avoid conflict but pleased few.

Franklin Pierce was born on November 23, 1804, in a log house in Hillsborough, New Hampshire, to Gen. Benjamin Pierce and his second wife, Anna Kendrick Pierce. Franklin was the seventh of his father's nine children and the sixth of his mother's eight children.

Benjamin Pierce joined the colonial forces in the Revolutionary War and served under Gen. George Washington. Then Pierce purchased a fifty-acre farm and log house in Hillsborough. Soon after Franklin's birth, the Pierce family moved to a new home that Benjamin had built in Hillsborough's lower village. This structure also served as the Pierce tavern.

When he was sixteen years old, Franklin entered Bowdoin College in Brunswick, Maine. He graduated in 1824. Franklin then studied law and was admitted to the bar of Hillsborough County in 1827. In 1829, while his father was governor of New Hampshire, Franklin was elected to the General Court of New Hampshire, and in 1831 he became Speaker of the General Court. In 1833 Franklin was elected as a Democrat to the U.S. House of Representatives, where he served until 1837.

Franklin Pierce married Jane Means Appleton, the daughter of a former Bowdoin College president, on November 19, 1834. A son, Franklin Jr., was born on February 2, 1836, and died three days later. Frank Robert was born in September 1839, and Benjamin was born on April 13, 1841.

In March 1837 Pierce took the U.S. Senate seat to which he had been elected by the New Hampshire legislature. Jane, who was always uncomfortable with political life, pleaded with her husband to leave politics. He retired from the Senate early and returned to Concord in August 1838. The Pierces' four-year-old son Frank died of typhus on November 14, 1843.

Pierce served as chairman of the state temperance society. Although he sincerely believed in and worked for the temperance issue, Franklin struggled with alcoholism throughout his life. Public knowledge about his problem plagued him during the temperance debates.

After volunteering for the Mexican War, Pierce was appointed brigadier general in March 1847. He was with the eleven thousand troops who marched to Mexico City under the command of Generals Winfield Scott and Gideon Johnson Pillow. On August 18 American forces found that Mexican troops led by Gen. Gabriel Valencia were encamped at Contreras. During the battle General Pierce's horse went down; he was knocked unconscious and suffered leg and pelvic injuries. After receiving medical attention, he went back to the battle scene. Pierce returned to the United States in December 1847 and a few months later resigned his commission.

Although Pierce publicly stated that he did not want his name put forward at the Democratic convention held in June 1852, New Hampshire politicians gathered behind his cause. Pierce was initially named on the thirty-fifth ballot, and he received the presidential nomination on the forty-ninth ballot; William R. King of Alabama was nominated for vice president. Jane Pierce fainted when she learned of her husband's nomination.

Presidential campaigns were conducted by party leaders. Publicity consisted of authorized biographies and likenesses of the candidate. Nathaniel Hawthorne, Pierce's college friend, wrote a laudatory biography. Pierce sat for many daguerreotypes and portraits, from which engravings and woodcuts were made. He was a handsome, distinguished-looking man—the picture of a president. Pierce won with 1,601,474 popular votes and 254 electoral votes to Winfield Scott's 1,386,580 popular votes and 42 electoral votes.

Between the presidential election and the inauguration, on a train trip from Boston to Concord on January 6, 1853, the car that Franklin, Jane, and their son Bennie were riding in jumped the tracks and rolled down an embankment. Although his parents were unhurt, eleven-year-old Bennie was crushed in the wreckage. The parents' grief for their only remaining child was overwhelming, particularly for Jane, who dreaded becoming First Lady.

Chief Justice Roger B. Taney administered the oath of office, which the president-elect affirmed rather than swore on March 4, 1853. Vice President William R. King, in Cuba and very ill, was permitted to take the oath of office there by a special act of Congress. He died six weeks after taking office, and President Pierce served without a vice president. Jane Pierce lived a reclusive life and became known as the shadow of the White House.

Seeking to add territory to the United States, Pierce commissioned James Gadsen to negotiate the purchase of Mexico's Gila River region for construction of a proposed southern railroad route to the Pacific and to offer $50 million to Mexico for its northern provinces. The Mexican government agreed to sell only the Gila River region. In the Gadsen Purchase of 1854, the nation obtained over forty-five thousand square miles between Mexico's Rio Grande and Gila rivers, which became part of the Arizona Territory and enabled completion of a southern railroad route to the West.

During this period sectionalism and the debate over slavery divided the country. Pierce regarded slavery primarily as the right to property rather than as a moral issue. His major concern was for the preservation of the American system of government.[1]

The slavery issue gripped the nation when Stephen A. Douglas, Democratic senator from Illinois, introduced the Kansas-Nebraska Act in January 1854. Douglas's bill proposed repealing the Missouri Compromise line that excluded slavery north of the 36 degrees 30 minutes latitude and creating two territories, Kansas and Nebraska. Douglas's doctrine of "popular sovereignty" argued that it would be more democratic for the citizens of Kansas and Nebraska to make their own decision about slavery rather than having it imposed by Congress. The bill generated a firestorm of controversy, especially from northern antislavery groups.

President Pierce supported the Kansas-Nebraska Act, which passed despite fierce opposition. Kansas turned into a battleground between the pro- and anti-slavery forces. By late 1855 Kansas had two rival territorial governments, one slave and one free. A virtual civil war broke out. Early in 1857 federal troops restored order in Kansas.

In 1856 the Democrats bypassed President Pierce and nominated James Buchanan of Pennsylvania. The Republican Party, a new major party opposed to the extension of slavery in the territories, was formally organized at Ripon, Wisconsin, in 1854. Its nominee was John C. Fremont. Buchanan was the victor.

The Pierces retired to New Hampshire. Jane died in Andover, Massachusetts, in December 1863. Franklin Pierce died on October 8, 1869, in Concord, New Hampshire, at the age of sixty-four. He was buried in Concord's Old North Cemetery alongside his wife and three sons.

. . . . . . . . . . . . . . . . . . . . . . . . . . . . . . . . . . . . . . . . . . . . . . . . . . . . . . . . . . . . . . . . . . . . . . . . . . .

## Pierce Homestead
### Hillsborough, New Hampshire.

ADDRESS: Hillsborough Historical Society, Franklin Pierce Homestead, P.O. Box 846, Hillsborough, NH 03244

TELEPHONE: Hillsborough Historical Society: 603-478-3165

WEB SITE: www.franklinpierce.ws/homestead

LOCATION: Hillsborough is in southern New Hampshire, about twenty-five miles northwest of Manchester; the Pierce Homestead is near the junction of State Highway 9 and State Highway 31

OPEN: Monday–Saturday, 10:00 A.M. to 4:00 P.M., and Sunday, 1:00 P.M. to 4:00 P.M., July–August; Saturday, 10:00 A.M. to 4:00 P.M., and Sunday, 1:00 P.M. to 4:00 P.M., June and September

ADMISSION: Nominal charge for adults
FACILITIES: Childhood home of Franklin Pierce. National Historic Landmark

*The Pierce Homestead, the childhood home* of Franklin Pierce, is located in Hillsborough, New Hampshire, a small village in the southern part of the state. Benjamin Pierce, an officer in the Revolutionary War and father of President Franklin Pierce, built the Pierce Homestead in 1804.

Franklin Pierce was born in a log cabin on the family farm on November 23, 1804. That farm is now under a man-made lake. Benjamin Pierce built a larger home for his growing family on a two-hundred-acre site when Franklin was one month old. In the succeeding years Benjamin made a number of changes to the house. The structure was located on the Second New Hampshire Turnpike, and Benjamin operated a tavern there until 1810. He later added a two-story ell-shaped addition.

When Benjamin Pierce died in 1839, his house and property were sold to his oldest daughter, Elizabeth, and her husband, John McNeil. In 1855 their daughter Frances McNeil Potter inherited the property. The house continued to be owned by members of the Pierce family until 1890.

In 1917 the Franklin Pierce Birthplace Association and Frank Pierce Carpenter purchased the Pierce Homestead for restoration. Another relative, Hayward Kendall, purchased the buildings and almost thirteen acres in 1923, and in 1925 he gave the property to the state of New Hampshire. It was restored with the guidance of the New Hampshire Division of Historical Resources. The Pierce Homestead is maintained and operated by the Hillsborough Historical Society.

The two-story frame building is white, although the back of the house is painted red. White paint was expensive in the early 1800s; since red was cheaper, it was often used on the parts of the house that were not visible from the street.

Many Pierce family furnishings and artifacts are in the house, while other furnishings date from the period. The house has its original stenciling.

In the entry hall the portraits of Benjamin and Anna are copies that were done in 1815; the originals are in the collection at Greenfield Village and Henry Ford Museum. Franklin sat for his portrait when he was a candidate for president, and lithographs of it were put on campaign flyers.

During the period when Benjamin Pierce operated a tavern, the parlor would have been reserved for ladies traveling by stagecoach. Redecorated in 1824 as the family parlor, the room has its original wallpaper. Benjamin's gold-rimmed cup and saucer and Pierce china are displayed in the china cabinet. Between the two front windows is original stenciling in a rose border design.

From 1804 to 1810 the family sitting room was used as a tavern where travelers could stop for a meal and a drink. The bar was located in a closet left of the fireplace. Furnishings include a Pierce family dining table and a handmade sideboard constructed by a Mr. Pugh, who was a relative of the Pierce family, as a wedding present for Franklin and Jane. There is also a portrait of Franklin Pierce painted late in his presidency. Reproductions of that portrait were given to members of his cabinet, all of whom had the distinction of having remained in their positions throughout the president's full term.

There is a large four-poster bed with curtains in the master bedroom. The candlestick on the nightstand was owned by Benjamin Pierce. The small adjoining room may have been used as a nursery or a dressing room.

When Benjamin Pierce added a two-story ell to his house, the original kitchen, which had also served as the family's parlor and dining room, was turned into the dining room. It has a large fireplace with a bake oven. The chairs with cane seats are from a set of twelve owned by Benjamin and his wife.

Located in the two-story addition, the new or summer kitchen was equipped with a wood cooking stove. A justice of the peace certificate signed by Benjamin Pierce in 1835 is displayed on the mantel.

The ballroom was used for dancing, political meetings, and as a dormitory with portable partitions that divided it into sleeping rooms for the tavern's guests. It was also the site of the double wedding of sisters Elizabeth and Nancy Pierce to brothers John and Solomon McNeil. The restored stenciling in the Christmas holly, bent pine, and candles patterns was a reminder of Benjamin's Christmas birthday.

There are two bedrooms upstairs, each with a small adjoining room. The back left bedchamber was shared by Franklin and his four brothers, as was the four-poster rope bed. Franklin lived at home until age sixteen. He returned home after being admitted to the bar in 1827 and lived there until he married in 1834.

Items related to President Pierce, including a Japanese silk smoking jacket, are displayed in the Pierce Family Exhibition Room. Pierce was president when

Commodore Matthew Perry's fleet entered Tokyo Bay and trade opened with Japan. The sofa had been used in the White House reception area. The lithograph of the Washington Monument, which was still being constructed at the time of the Pierce presidency, bears the names of those who made a contribution, including Pierce, who gave fifty dollars to the fund. One of the letters displayed describes Franklin and Jane's 1834 wedding. Franklin Pierce's presidential seal and a letter authorizing its use are also in the room for viewing. The spoons engraved "Pierce" were used in the White House.

. . . . . . . . . . . . . . . . . . . . . . . . . . . . . . . . . . . . . . . . . . . . . . . . . . . . . . . . . . . . . . . . . . . . . . . . . . . . . . . . .

## Pierce Manse
## Concord, New Hampshire

ADDRESS: 14 Horseshoe Pond Lane, P.O. Box 425, Concord, NH 03301
TELEPHONE: 603-225-4555
WEB SITE: www.piercemanse.org
LOCATION: Concord is in south central New Hampshire on I-93; the Pierce
Manse is in the historic district at the end of North Main Street
OPEN: Tuesday–Saturday, 11:00 A.M. to 3:00 P.M., mid-June through Labor Day;
Friday–Saturday, noon to 3:00 P.M., mid-September through mid-October
ADMISSION: Adults, $5.00; seniors, $4.00; children and students, $2.00;
families, $12.00
FACILITIES: Home of President Franklin Pierce; guided tours. NHS

*Franklin Pierce was born, was raised,* and died in New Hampshire. However, Franklin lived in Washington, D.C., for thirteen years, from 1833 to 1842 and from 1853 to 1857. The Pierces owned only one house, which they purchased in Concord, New Hampshire, in 1842 and sold in 1848. During two of those six years, 1846–48, Franklin served in the Mexican War while Jane and their son, Bennie, lived with relatives. When the family reunited in Concord, they sold what is now called the Pierce Manse and boarded in the home of another family.

A historic restoration group rescued President Pierce's Concord residence from demolition in an urban renewal project. Called the Pierce Brigade, the preservation group was formed in 1966. They own and maintain the house that was originally located at 18 Montgomery Street in Concord. In 1971 the Pierce Brigade moved the house to its present location in the historic district. Close to expressways, the setting is less than idyllic.

The Pierce Manse is a white frame, Greek-revival, two-story house constructed in the late 1830s. It was purchased by Franklin Pierce in 1842 when he returned to his law practice in Concord. The Pierce family included Franklin's wife, Jane, and their sons, Franky and Benny. In 1843 four-year old Franky contracted typhus and died.

After the Pierces sold the house in 1848, it passed through many hands and was even divided into apartments. The residence has been restored to its appearance in the 1840s when the president's family occupied it. The upstairs floors are original, as are the stair treads and stair rails.

Members of the Pierce Brigade, who give guided tours, enthusiastically tell the story of New Hampshire's only president. The Pierce Manse has a fine collection of furnishings and artifacts that belonged either to the president or to members of his family. In the downstairs hall items that belonged to Franklin Pierce include a dressing table; a campaign chest that General Pierce took to the Mexican War; a letter from the president to Jefferson Davis, his secretary of war; and the Bowdoin College 1824 commencement program from Pierce's graduation.

Sliding doors divide a large room into a parlor and a dining room. Pierce possessions include the sofa from Jane's dowry, Franklin's writing table, and a center table referred to by the family as the White House Table. The secretary is from Pierce's Main Street law office. Franklin's ivory-headed cane engraved "Gen. Frank Pierce" was shortened by his grandniece Mary Pierce for her own use. Other Pierce items include Franklin's bookcase, presidential notepaper, Jane's writing case, a portrait of Pierce by the New Hampshire artist Adna

Tenney, and a print of Benjamin Pierce, the president's father. A place setting of White House china is displayed.

Flanking the kitchen's large open fireplace are two Shaker chairs; Pierce was the attorney for the New Hampshire Shakers at Concord. Silver spoons from Jane's dowry are displayed along with her silver folding fruit knife. The Bible belonged to Bennie; his mother always carried it with her after his death. The fire tongs and pearl card case belonged to Franklin. The mantel and two iron oven doors are original.

In the upstairs hall is a print of Pierce with his good friend and biographer Nathaniel Hawthorne when they were in Rome. In the master bedroom are Franklin Pierce's shaving kit with a folding mirror and a washstand that was used in the White House. The chest belonged to the Pierce family, as did the six-board chest with the Pierce crest inside its cover. The children's bedroom is furnished as it was when Franky and Bennie lived there.

The historic attached nineteenth-century carriage barn, which is much like the barn originally attached to the Pierce Manse, was moved from Belmont and reconstructed in 1993. It contains a Concord carriage and an exhibit on Franklin Pierce. President Pierce, his wife, and their sons are buried in Concord's Old North Cemetery, at State and Park streets.

# James Buchanan

..............................................................................

An astute politician and a capable diplomat, James Buchanan used negotiation rather than conflict to advance his career. Buchanan was elected to the presidency on the eve of the Civil War, and his skills failed to avert the nation's deepest and most dangerous crisis.

James Buchanan was born on April 23, 1791, in a log cabin in Cove Gap, Lancaster County, Pennsylvania. His father, James Buchanan, was born in County Donegal, Ireland, in 1761, and his mother, Elizabeth Speer Buchanan, was born in Greensburg, Pennsylvania, in 1767. James was the second of the eleven Buchanan children.

When James Jr. was sixteen, he enrolled in Dickinson College in Carlisle, Pennsylvania. In September 1808 he was threatened with expulsion because of disorderly conduct—drinking, smoking cigars, and disrespectful behavior toward the faculty. Given a second chance, James graduated from Dickinson in 1809. He then studied law in Lancaster, Pennsylvania, and was admitted to the bar in November 1812. In 1814 he and John Passmore purchased a small tavern on King Street in Lancaster, where they lived and had their law offices.

On August 24, 1814, during the War of 1812, Buchanan joined Shippen's Company, private volunteers from Lancaster who marched to Baltimore and offered their services. The British withdrew from Baltimore shortly afterward, and Shippen's Company was discharged. Buchanan, a Federalist, was elected as state assemblyman in August 1814 and was reelected in 1815.

In the summer of 1819 Buchanan became engaged to Ann Coleman. Because of what she perceived as James's inattentiveness to her, Ann ended the engagement in late 1819. A few days later she and her sister Sarah traveled to Philadelphia to visit their sister Margaret. On Wednesday, December 8, Ann was said to have had several fits of hysteria, and she died early the next day. In addition to his own grief, Buchanan faced accusations of responsibility for Ann's death. Although he lived to the age of seventy-seven, he never married.

In 1820 Buchanan, the Federalist candidate, was elected to the U.S. House of Representatives from the Lower Susquehanna. He served in Congress from 1821 to 1831. President Jackson appointed Buchanan as U.S. minister to Russia, where he successfully negotiated the commercial treaty that granted the United

States most-favored-nation status. In August 1834 Buchanan was elected to the U.S. Senate, where he served for the following decade.

President Polk named Buchanan as his secretary of state, although Buchanan often disagreed with Polk on foreign policy issues—especially the annexation of Texas, which involved border negotiations with Mexico. Polk wanted aggressive action against Mexico, while Buchanan tried to pursue peaceful negotiations. Polk and Buchanan also struggled with Britain over the Oregon Territory. An agreement was negotiated in June 1846 between the United States and Britain to divide Oregon at the 49th parallel.

Buchanan was an unsuccessful presidential candidate at the Democratic convention in 1844, which nominated James K. Polk, and the 1848 convention, which nominated Lewis Cass. After thirty years of political office, fifty-eight-year-old Buchanan retired to Lancaster, Pennsylvania, where in December 1848 he purchased a country estate named Wheatland. Buchanan was the favorite-son presidential candidate from Pennsylvania at the Democratic convention in June 1852, but Franklin Pierce won the nomination as well as the election. President Pierce appointed Buchanan to be the U.S. minister to England, in which capacity he served from 1853 to 1856.

At the 1856 Democratic National Convention, Franklin Pierce, the incumbent president, was bypassed and Buchanan was nominated for president on the seventeenth ballot. John C. Breckinridge of Kentucky was his vice-presidential running mate. The newly created Republican Party nominated John C. Fremont. Buchanan won the election with 1,832,955 popular and 174 electoral votes.

In 1857 the proslavery faction in Kansas held a convention at Lecompton, drafted a constitution recognizing slavery, and applied for statehood. Although a majority of the state's residents opposed slavery, Buchanan accepted the Lecompton constitution. After it was defeated in the House of Representatives, the Lecompton constitution was returned to Kansas for the voters' reconsideration, and in 1858 it was rejected. Kansas remained a territory until after the Civil War. Buchanan's support of the Lecompton constitution badly divided the Democrats.

President Buchanan looked to the Supreme Court to legally resolve the slavery issue through its decision in *Dred Scott v. Sanford.* He believed that the court, with a majority of southern justices, would render a decision favorable to slavery. Dred Scott, a Missouri slave, had lived several years with his master in Illinois, a free state, and in Minnesota, a free territory. Contending that they had been emancipated by virtue of their residency on free soil, Scott and his wife sued for their freedom. On March 6, 1857, the court rejected Scott's claim, ruling that as a slave Scott was not a citizen and had no legal right to sue in a federal court. Since he was owned by a citizen of Missouri, Scott's residence in Illinois, a free state, did not emancipate him. The Supreme Court ruled further that Scott's temporary residence in the Minnesota Territory did not make him free since the Missouri Compromise that had made this territory free was itself unconstitutional. The justices concluded that a slave was property and as such could be transported throughout the country.

Buchanan faced an issue with the Mormons in Utah, which became a U.S. territory in 1848. Mormons, led by Brigham Young, had traveled westward from Nauvoo, Illinois, after the assassination of Joseph Smith, their founder. They established the state of Deseret as a haven. Tension mounted between the government and the Mormons, who maintained their practice of polygamy. In 1857 President Buchanan sent a military force to establish control in Utah, but a peaceful agreement was reached in which the Mormons agreed to accept U.S. rule.

Buchanan announced that he would not seek reelection in 1860. The sharply divided Democratic Party split into northern and southern wings, which resulted in two Democratic tickets. Stephen A. Douglas headed the northern ticket, while John C. Breckinridge headed the southern one. The Republican Party nominated Abraham Lincoln, who got the highest vote and won in the Electoral College.

After Lincoln's election President Buchanan feared that South Carolina would seize the poorly garrisoned federal forts in Charleston Harbor. Maj. Robert Anderson, commander at Fort Sumter, asked Buchanan for reinforcements and on December 27 moved his troops from Fort Moultrie to Fort Sumter. On December 28 South Carolina seized Fort Moultrie, Castle Pinckney, and the U.S. Customs House at Charleston and demanded withdrawal of federal troops from the Charleston area.

Buchanan decided to supply Major Anderson with recruits and food. When the *Star of the West,* the U.S. Navy vessel bringing relief, sailed near South Carolina–held Fort Moultrie on January 9, it was fired on. Anderson protested to South Carolina's Gov. Francis Wilkinson Pickens, who demanded Fort Sumter's surrender. Anderson and Pickens agreed to a truce while negotiations took place. The stalemate over Fort Sumter lasted for the remainder of the Buchanan administration. On their way to the inaugural ceremony, Buchanan told Lincoln, "My dear sir, if you are as happy in entering the White House as I shall feel on returning to Wheatland, you are a happy man indeed."[1]

The former president was blamed for permitting the secession of the southern states and causing the Civil War. In December 1862 a Senate resolution censuring and condemning Buchanan accused him of "sympathy with the conspirators and their treasonable project" and with failure "to take necessary and proper measures" to prevent secession. The resolution was defeated after heated debate.[2] In response Buchanan wrote a book, *Mr. Buchanan's Administration on the Eve of the Rebellion,* that defended his administration.[3]

President Buchanan died at Wheatland on June 1, 1868. Although he had requested a simple burial, over twenty thousand people attended his funeral.

## Wheatland
### Lancaster, Pennsylvania

ADDRESS: 1120 Marietta Avenue, Lancaster, PA 17603
TELEPHONE: 717-392-8721 or 717-392-4633
WEB SITE: www.LancasterHistory.org
LOCATION: Lancaster is in southeastern Pennsylvania, about eighty miles west of Philadelphia; Wheatland is located approximately one and one-half miles west of Lancaster City on Route 23 (Marietta Avenue)
OPEN: Tuesday–Saturday, 10:00 A.M. to 4:00 P.M., April–October; Tuesday–Saturday, 10:00 A.M. to 3:00 P.M., and Sunday, noon to 3:00 P.M., November–December
ADMISSION: Adults, $10.00; children 6–11, $5.00; families, $25.00
FACILITIES: Home of James Buchanan; gift shops; guided tours. National Historic Landmark

*James Buchanan purchased Wheatland,* a twenty-two-acre estate, in 1848 while he was serving as secretary of state in President Polk's administration. He lived there, when not abroad or in Washington, until his death in 1868. After the president's death, Harriet Lane Johnston, Buchanan's niece, inherited Wheatland. Buchanan was a bachelor, and Harriet, a talented and accomplished young woman, served as his hostess both at the White House in Washington and at Wheatland. Harriet sold Wheatland in 1884 to George Wilson. The Wilson family bequeathed the property to the Lancaster County Historical Society.

Wheatland is now owned by the James Buchanan Foundation, which purchased the house in 1936. A National Historic Landmark, it has been restored to its appearance in the era that President Buchanan occupied the home, 1848–68. Wheatland, an excellent example of the then-popular federal style of architecture, was built in 1828 for William Jenkins, a wealthy lawyer and banker, who named his property "The Wheatlands" because of the fields of wheat and other grains that surrounded the mansion. Today the mansion is situated on four landscaped acres, and its outbuildings—the smokehouse and privy—still remain.

Visitors to Wheatland begin at the carriage house visitor center. The carriage house, probably built by George Wilson after 1884, was not there during the Buchanan years. A small museum contains artifacts and materials related to Buchanan's life, political career, and presidency.

Wheatland is an impressive two-and-one-half-story red-brick building with two recessed flanking wings surrounded by well-planted and landscaped grounds. The front of the house has a center entrance with fan and side lights and a portico with four white pillars, while the back entry porch is vine

covered. Upper-story windows are framed by green shutters, and lower-story windows have white shutters. There are round arched dormers in the upper story.

Approximately half of all the furnishings in the house belonged to Buchanan, and the other half are original period pieces. Much of the furniture is in the empire style. On a guided tour visitors use the rear doorway to enter the main hall, a corridor with an elliptical staircase and a stenciled floor cloth. After Buchanan's death, his body was placed in this hall for viewing.

Buchanan entertained Wheatland's guests in the spacious dining room. When a formal dinner was being served, the table would be covered by seven tablecloths, one for each course; a cloth would be removed after a course was finished. In the built-in wall cabinet are displayed several sets of French Limoges china that belonged to Harriet and a set of Buchanan's china.

Buchanan was a distinguished attorney as well as a skilled politician. During his campaign for the presidency in 1856, he met with supporters and wrote his inaugural address in his library. He also wrote his only book, *Mr. Buchanan's Administration on the Eve of the Rebellion,* there. The room is heated by a Benjamin Franklin stove. There are lithographs of President Buchanan and Vice President Breckinridge.

The formal Victorian parlor is furnished in the empire style found throughout the house. Here, Harriet, an accomplished pianist, entertained guests. Furnishings include her Chickery rosewood grand piano and her walnut lady's writing desk. The lithographs of Queen Victoria and Prince Albert were gifts of the royal couple to Buchanan, who served as ambassador to England. In June 1866 Harriet, age thirty-five, was married in the parlor to the Baltimore banker Henry Elliott Johnston.

On the second floor Harriet's bedroom is the biggest and brightest bedroom featuring several curtained windows and is furnished with Harriet's possessions. They include a pre dieu, a wooden prayer bench with the Book of Common Prayer, used by Harriet, who was an Episcopalian.

Buchanan's bedroom is elegant with heavily draped windows, carpeting, red flowered wallpaper, and a fireplace. Furnishings include a four-poster bed, a rocking chair used by Buchanan, and his gold watch and chain.

In the president's upstairs study, a portrait of Buchanan's fiancée, Ann Coleman, who died in 1819, hangs over Buchanan's desk. The Victorian-era bathroom was added by the Wilson family, and there is a servant's room for the head housekeeper.

An 1828 privy, which was used until the late 1800s, is on the grounds. The 1828 smokehouse and icehouse has three levels. Ice was stored in the basement area, fruits and vegetables were stored at ground level, and meats were stored on the top floor. The grounds also include a raised Victorian herb garden and many century-old trees.

President Buchanan died at Wheatland on June 1, 1868, at the age of seventy-seven. His body lay in state at Wheatland, where mourners paid their respects. Thousands of mourners lined the two-mile route to his burial site in Lancaster's Woodward Hill Cemetery, the address of which is 538 East Strawberry Street, Lancaster PA 17602–4434. His grave site, marked by an American flag, is left of the red brick church.

# Abraham Lincoln

Abraham Lincoln, of humble origins, led his nation during the most perilous test it faced, a civil war. Although Lincoln was self-educated, the clarity of his eloquence and wisdom of his policies saved the nation and liberated those who had been in the bondage of slavery.

Abraham Lincoln was born on February 12, 1809, on a farm on the south fork of Nolin Creek, near Hodgenville, Kentucky, to Thomas Lincoln and Nancy Hanks Lincoln. He was the couple's second child and the brother of Sarah. Thomas Lincoln soon moved his family to a farm on Knob Creek. In 1812 another child, Thomas, was born but died in infancy. In 1816 Thomas and his family moved to the sparsely settled territory on Pigeon Creek in Perry, later Spencer County, in southern Indiana. The Pigeon Creek community was devastated by an epidemic of what was called "milk sickness," probably brucellosis, which is caused by drinking milk from cows that fed on the poisonous white snakeroot plant. Lincoln's mother, Nancy, died of the disease on October 5, 1818.

The following year Thomas Lincoln married Sarah Bush Johnston, a widow with three children.[1] She was a kindly woman who cared for the two Lincoln children as her own. Abe attended what was called a "blab school." The pupils recited their lessons aloud, often in unison. The next year Lincoln began a six-month period at a school taught by Azel W. Dorsey. Lincoln had less than a year of formal education.

In 1830 the Lincoln family relocated to Macon County, Illinois. When Abraham Lincoln left home, he worked at the various occupations found on the frontier: carpenter, riverboat crewman, store clerk, soldier, merchant, postmaster, blacksmith, surveyor, lawyer, and politician. In 1831 he arrived in New Salem, Illinois, a small trading center of crude log buildings on the Sangamon River. Denton Offut, owner of the gristmill and sawmill, hired Lincoln as manager and clerk of his store.

Fearing that the projected central Illinois railroad and canal would bypass New Salem, several leading citizens urged Lincoln to run for the state legislature, where he could uphold the town's interests. In 1832 Lincoln finished eighth in a field of thirteen candidates. Also in 1832 the Sauk and Fox Indians, led by

Chief Black Hawk, crossed the Mississippi River in a futile effort to reoccupy their tribal lands in Illinois. Lincoln along with other volunteers from New Salem enlisted in the state militia on April 21. The Black Hawk War ended quickly in the Indians' defeat, and Lincoln did not experience combat.

In New Salem, James Herndon and J. Rowan Herndon sold their general store to Lincoln and William F. Berry. New Salem became increasingly isolated as the new railroad bypassed it, and dwindling business forced the closure of the Lincoln-Berry Store.

A great deal of speculation surrounds Lincoln's relationship with Ann Rutledge. It appears that Lincoln was romantically attracted to Ann, daughter of the owner of New Salem's tavern. Ann was engaged to John McNeil, a New Yorker, who lodged at the tavern. When McNeil returned to New York, Ann planned to seek a formal release from their engagement. There is a strong belief, unsubstantiated by documentary evidence, that Lincoln and Ann intended to become engaged. Unfortunately, Ann contracted typhoid fever and died on August 25, 1835. According to the Lincoln-Rutledge legend, Abraham, severely grieving Ann's death, fell into a deep depression.

Lincoln pursued an interest in the law, attending sessions of the Sangamon County Circuit Court in Springfield and studying law books. In September 1837 he was licensed to practice law, and his name was entered in the roll of attorneys in the office of the Illinois Supreme Court. On April 15, 1837, Lincoln relocated to Springfield, a frontier town with fifteen hundred residents, where he became a partner of John Stuart.

In Springfield, Lincoln met Mary Todd, the daughter of Robert S. Todd, a prosperous merchant and banker of Lexington, Kentucky. The Episcopal minister Charles Dresser married the couple on November 4, 1842. On August 1, 1843, Robert Todd was born. On March 10, 1846, Edward Baker, called "Eddie," was born; he died on February 1, 1850, from pulmonary tuberculosis. William Wallace, called "Willie," was born on December 21, 1849, and on April 4, 1853, Thomas, called "Tad," was born. In 1844 the Lincolns purchased a cottage on the corner of Eighth and Jackson streets from Reverend Dresser for twelve hundred dollars.

Lincoln entered into his second legal partnership with Stephen T. Logan. William "Billy" Herndon, who would become Lincoln's early biographer, was a law clerk studying with Lincoln and Logan. In the fall of 1844 Lincoln and Logan amicably dissolved their partnership, and Lincoln took Herndon as his partner.

Lincoln rode the legal circuit, following the district judge from county courthouse to county courthouse. The large Eighth Circuit stretched across two-thirds of the state. Lincoln, traveling on horseback or by horse and buggy, took ten weeks to complete the judicial circuit in the fall and spring of each year.

Running as a Whig, Lincoln was elected to the Illinois legislature in 1834, and he was reelected three times. In 1846 the Whigs nominated Lincoln for the U.S. House of Representatives, and he won. Lincoln, who had pledged to serve only one term in Congress, was not a candidate in 1848. He returned to his law practice. Lincoln handled a high volume of cases that earned him a handsome income of two thousand dollars a year. By 1860 he owned real estate valued at five thousand dollars and a personal estate of twelve thousand dollars.[2]

Lincoln, the Republican nominee, challenged the Democratic incumbent, Stephen A. Douglas, in the Illinois race for U.S. senator in 1858. In the nineteenth century senators were elected by the state legislatures rather than by direct popular vote. This meant that the contest between Lincoln and Douglas would be determined by the party that controlled the Illinois legislature. Lincoln and Douglas toured Illinois in a series of debates that they hoped would influence voters to elect candidates supporting their campaigns.

Lincoln and Douglas's seven debates focused on slavery, specifically the Fugitive Slave Law and slavery's extension into the territories. Douglas portrayed Lincoln as a dangerous, covert abolitionist determined to destroy slavery at all cost. Lincoln challenged Douglas's "popular sovereignty" doctrine as a subterfuge to extend slavery into the territories and revitalize it as a national institution rather than one limited to the South. Lincoln condemned slavery as "a moral, a social, and a political wrong."[3] Although the Republicans won a majority of the popular votes, they failed to win control of the Illinois legislature. Senator Douglas, who received fifty-four votes to forty-six for Lincoln, was reelected.

The Republican National Convention convened in May 1860. Lincoln was Illinois' favorite son. Lincoln was nominated for president with Hannibal Hamlin of Maine for vice president. The presidential election of 1860 was a four-way race. The Democrats' split into two rival factions virtually assured Lincoln's election. The national Democratic Party, but in reality its northern wing, nominated Steven A. Douglas, while the southern wing nominated John Breckinridge. A fourth party nominated John Bell of Tennessee.

Lincoln won a plurality of the popular vote: Lincoln 1,866,452; Douglas 1,376,957; Breckenridge 849,781; and Bell 588,879. In the Electoral College, Lincoln won 180 votes to Breckinridge's 72, Bell's 39, and Douglas's 12. Lincoln was the first Republican candidate to be elected president of the United States.

On December 20, 1860, South Carolina seceded from the Union. Mississippi, Florida, Alabama, Georgia, Louisiana, and Texas followed, seceding from January 9 to February 1, 1861. President Buchanan believed that while secession was unconstitutional, he could not prevent it. Jefferson Davis was inaugurated as provisional president of the Confederate States of America on February 18,

1861. Inaugurated as U.S. president on March 4, 1861, Lincoln astutely assembled his cabinet from his rivals for the Republican nomination—naming William Seward as secretary of state, Montgomery Blair as postmaster general, Salmon P. Chase as secretary of the treasury, Edward Bates as attorney general, and Gideon Welles as secretary of the navy.

Mary Lincoln delighted in her role as First Lady. Prior to the inauguration she made a shopping trip to New York to acquire a wardrobe suited to her position. She accumulated debts, which she concealed from her husband. In addition, while Congress appropriated twenty thousand dollars for repairs to the White House, Mrs. Lincoln overspent the congressional appropriation. Lincoln, though furious at the thought of requesting additional funds during a time of national emergency, asked Congress to pass two deficiency appropriations.

In February 1862 Willie Lincoln was diagnosed with "bilious fever," probably typhoid caused by pollution from the White House water system; he died on February 20. Tad also came down with the illness but survived.

Fort Sumter was the immediate crisis facing President Lincoln. In late December, Maj. Robert Anderson transferred his small garrison from Fort Moultrie, near Charleston, South Carolina, to the more defensible Fort Sumter. On January 9, 1861, the U.S. Navy ship *Star of the West,* carrying supplies and reinforcements, was fired upon and forced to retreat. On April 12 Confederate batteries bombarded Fort Sumter, and after thirty-four hours Major Anderson surrendered his garrison. The Civil War had begun. Lincoln asked for seventy-five thousand militiamen to suppress the rebellion.

Virginia, Arkansas, North Carolina, and Tennessee then joined the Confederacy. President Lincoln believed that the states of the South remained in the Union. For him, the Civil War was an insurrection, and he refused to recognize the Confederate States.

On January 1, 1863, Lincoln issued the Emancipation Proclamation, which declared "persons held as slaves" in states in rebellion to be "forever free." Lincoln authorized the enlistment of freed African Americans in the Union army.

The Republican Party, reconstituted as the National Union Party, nominated Lincoln for a second term. Andrew Johnson of Tennessee was the candidate for vice president. The Democratic nominee was Gen. George B. McClellan. Lincoln won 2,218,000, or 55 percent, of the popular vote to McClellan's 1,812,000, or 45 percent. Lincoln won 212 electoral votes to McClellan's 21 electoral votes.

As commander in chief of the Union army and navy, the president ran through a series of generals who were unable to defeat the skilled Confederate general Robert E. Lee. Lincoln at last found a determined general in Ulysses S. Grant. After Grant's successful siege and capture of Vicksburg opened the Mississippi River for the Union, Lincoln appointed him general in chief of the armies. Grant planned massive frontal attacks on the Confederate lines, sure that the much larger Union forces would defeat the South. Ably aided by Generals William T. Sherman and Philip H. Sheridan, Grant relentlessly pressed Lee's Confederate Army of Northern Virginia. As a result, Lee surrendered at Appomattox Court House.

As the Civil War approached its end, Lincoln tried to steer a moderate and reconciliatory course that would reestablish civil government, law, and order as quickly as possible. He announced a proclamation of amnesty and reconstruction that would give a "full pardon . . . with restoration of all rights of property, except as to slaves" to all rebels except high-ranking Confederate officials. Those pardoned would have to take an oath of loyalty to the Constitution. To encourage the political rehabilitation of the former Confederate states, he promised to recognize the state governments when they were supported by 10 percent of their 1860 voters who had taken the oath of allegiance.[4]

President and Mrs. Lincoln enjoyed going to the theater, attending plays, concerts, and operas. These outings gave John Wilkes Booth, a young actor, opportunities to carry out his plot to assassinate the president. Booth and his coconspirators, George A. Atzerodt, Lewis Powell (also known as Paine or Payne), John Surratt, Mary Surratt, and David E. Herold, planned a series of assassinations that would paralyze the federal government. In addition to Lincoln, they targeted Vice President Andrew Johnson and Secretary of State William Seward.

The Lincolns attended a performance of *Our American Cousin* at Ford's Theatre on April 14, 1865. Booth had gained access to the upstairs of the theater, where the presidential box was located. He quietly took a place behind Lincoln and shot the president in the back of the head at 10:13 P.M. Booth then jumped from the box, catching his heel in the flags decorating the box and breaking his ankle. Shouting "Sic semper tyrannis"—Thus always to tyrants— he escaped through the rear of the theater.

The first doctor to reach the presidential box was an army surgeon, Charles A. Leale, who gave artificial respiration to Lincoln, inducing shallow and irregular breathing. The president was carried to a house owned by William Petersen across Tenth Street. Lincoln never regained consciousness. On the morning of April 15 the president died. Secretary of War Edwin Stanton paid a final tribute to the fallen leader: "Now he belongs to the ages."[5]

Secretary of War Stanton closed all bridges and roads leading out of Washington and directed the military to hunt down the assassins. Atzerodt had decided not to kill Vice President Johnson, but Powell had attacked Seward, who was in serious condition. On April 26 Stanton's men tracked Booth to a farm in northern Virginia, where he was shot.

After a state funeral, a train carried Lincoln's body back to Springfield, Illinois. He was buried there in Oak Ridge Cemetery.

## Abraham Lincoln Birthplace National Historic Site
## Hodgenville, Kentucky

ADDRESS: 2995 Lincoln Farm Road, Hodgenville, KY 42748

TELEPHONE: 270-358-3137 or 270-358-3138

WEB SITE: www.nps.gov/abli

LOCATION: In north central Kentucky, fifty-five miles south of Louisville, eighty-seven miles from Lexington, about three miles south of Hodgenville, on U.S. 31E and Ky. 61

OPEN: Birthplace unit: daily, 8:00 A.M. to 6:45 P.M., Memorial Day through Labor Day; 8:00 A.M. to 4:45 P.M., Labor Day through Memorial Day. Boyhood home unit at Knob Creek: daily, 8:30 A.M. to 4:30 P.M., Memorial Day through Labor Day; Saturday and Sunday, 8:30 A.M. to 4:30 P.M., April 1 through Memorial Day. Grounds open daylight hours year-around

ADMISSION: Free

FACILITIES: Two units approximately ten miles apart: birthplace unit is 116 acres containing Sinking Spring Farm, where Abraham Lincoln was born in 1809, and a memorial building housing a Kentucky log cabin, visitor center, picnic area, hiking trails; boyhood home unit is at Knob Creek, with visitor center, hiking trails. National Register of Historic Places

*Abraham Lincoln Birthplace National Historic Site's* two units portray Lincoln's early years in Kentucky. The birthplace unit illustrates his humble origins with a symbolic birth cabin enshrined within a neoclassical memorial building. The boyhood home unit at Knob Creek Farm was Lincoln's home during his formative years.

The restoration of the birthplace began thirty years after President Lincoln' assassination when A. W. Dennett, a New York businessman, purchased Sinking Spring Farm. He believed that a log cabin on the property was Lincoln's birthplace. The cabin was dismantled and then reassembled at exhibitions in several cities.

About 1900 the Lincoln Farm Association was organized to preserve and commemorate Lincoln's birthplace. Members of the association included Mark Twain, William Jennings Bryan, Samuel Gompers, and Robert Collier. They purchased Sinking Spring Farm in 1905 and the cabin in 1906. A memorial to house the birthplace cabin was completed in 1911. Of the original 348-acre Sinking Spring Farm owned by Thomas Lincoln, 116 acres are preserved. Originally established as Abraham Lincoln National Park in 1916, the site was designated Abraham Lincoln Birthplace National Historic Site in 1959.

An early nineteenth-century Kentucky cabin, symbolizing the one in which Lincoln was born, is enshrined inside the memorial building at the site of Lincoln's birth. The memorial building is a Greek-temple-like, neoclassical marble

and granite structure approached by a flight of fifty-six stairs, one for each year of Lincoln's life. President Theodore Roosevelt laid the building's cornerstone in 1909, and President William H. Taft dedicated it in 1911. Research on the rustic 12 x 17–foot, one-room log cabin inside the memorial building indicates that it is probably not the log cabin in which Lincoln was born.

Abraham Lincoln, the son of Nancy Hanks Lincoln and Thomas Lincoln, was born on February 12, 1809, at Sinking Spring Farm in Hardin County, Kentucky. Sinking Spring, the deep limestone spring after which the farm was named, still runs on the property. In 1808 the Lincolns purchased the 348-acre Sinking Spring Farm for two hundred dollars. Their one-room log cabin had a dirt floor, a window, a door, and a fireplace. When Abraham was two years old, the family moved to the farm at Knob Creek. The Lincoln family rented 30 acres of the 228-acre Knob Creek Farm from the time Abraham was two until he was seven years old. It was the first home that Lincoln could remember.

The Lincoln boyhood home was established by the Howard family in the 1930s and was donated to the National Park System in 2001. The boyhood home unit at Knob Creek is currently administered by the Abraham Lincoln Birthplace National Historic Site, which has a visitor center and hiking trails.

### Lincoln's New Salem State Historic Site
### Petersburg, Illinois

ADDRESS: 15588 History Lane, Petersburg, IL 62675
TELEPHONE: 217-632-4000
WEB SITE: www.lincolnsnewsalem.com
LOCATION: In central Illinois, two hundred miles southwest of Chicago; on Ill. 97, three miles south of Petersburg and twenty miles northwest of Springfield

OPEN: Daily, 9:00 A.M. to 5:00 P.M., mid-April through mid-September;
Wednesday–Sunday, 9:00 A.M. to 5:00 P.M., March through mid-April
and mid-September through October; Wednesday–Sunday, 8:00 A.M. to
4:00 P.M., November through February

ADMISSION: Free; suggested donation: adults, $4.00; youths 17 and under,
$2.00; families, $10.00

FACILITIES: Reconstruction of the 1830s frontier village lived in by Abraham
Lincoln; State Historic Site; visitor center with orientation film and exhibits; campgrounds with two hundred campsites; hiking trails; restaurant; special events. National Register of Historic Places

*The frontier village of New Salem* is indelibly linked to the early Illinois years
of Abraham Lincoln. Lincoln arrived in 1831, entered into village life, opened
a small business, led a company in the Black Hawk War, and ran for political office for the first time. New Salem, located on the Sangamon River, was
founded in 1829 by James Rutledge and John Camron, who built a gristmill on
the river. Local farmers who brought their corn to be ground at the mill purchased provisions at nearby stores and gathered at the local tavern, where they
discussed politics, crops, and local gossip.

New Salem, with a population of one hundred residents, was the largest
community in which Lincoln had lived. He conversed with Dr. John Allen, a
graduate of Dartmouth College, and Mentor Graham, the local schoolteacher,

and was a member of New Salem's debating society. He became known for his sense of humor, storytelling ability, and jokes. Showing an interest in law, Lincoln frequently sat in on cases at the local court.

When in 1832 the Sauk and Fox Indians, led by Chief Black Hawk, crossed the Mississippi River seeking to return to their native lands in Illinois, Lincoln joined a company of militia volunteers from New Salem and was elected their commanding officer. The war ended quickly, and the New Salem volunteers did not see combat.

Lincoln became a partner in the Lincoln-Berry general store. Dwindling business and disagreements at the Lincoln-Berry store forced the partners to close. On May 7, 1833, Lincoln was appointed New Salem's postmaster, a part-time job he filled for three years. Lincoln also worked as an assistant to John Calhoun, the county surveyor.

In 1834 Lincoln made his second race for the Illinois legislature, running as a Whig. He was elected and then was reelected in 1836. Lincoln and Ann Rutledge, daughter of the owner of the town's tavern and inn, have been romantically linked. She died of typhoid fever on August 25, 1835. When the county seat was located in Petersburg, New Salem declined, and by 1840 it had been abandoned.

New Salem Village is a reconstruction of the town as it looked when Lincoln lived there. All tours are self-guided. The reproduction structures were constructed on their original foundations based on archaeological and historical research. The frontier town is arranged along a street with cabins on either side. On the site are twelve log houses, Rutledge Tavern, ten workshops, a sawmill, a gristmill, a blacksmith's shop, a cooper's shop, several stores, a tavern, and a school. Historically authenticated flower and vegetable gardens and trees re-create the original village setting.

The visitor center features an orientation film on Lincoln's life at New Salem, a diorama of New Salem, and a time walk on Lincoln and New Salem from 1809 to the present. Events in Lincoln's life at New Salem are told through stories, pictures, paintings, artifacts, documents, and models. Many of these artifacts were used in New Salem during the Lincoln era or date to that time.

The Henry Onstot Cooper Shop, built in 1830, is the only original building at New Salem. It was discovered in Petersburg in 1922, returned to its original foundation, and restored. Nearby is the Onstot cabin, built in 1830, where Henry and his family lived.

The Mentor Graham School (1830) is a simple log structure containing four half-log benches, a table, and a fireplace. Its teacher, Mentor Graham, conducted a subscription school where students paid tuition ranging from thirty to eighty-five cents a month per pupil, depending on the student's age. Church services were also held in the school building. Mentor Graham assisted Lincoln in studying grammar and surveying.

In 1831 James and Rowan Herndon arrived at New Salem and opened a store. William Herndon, their cousin, became a law partner of Lincoln in Springfield and authored an early Lincoln biography. The Herndon store was sold to William Berry and Abraham Lincoln in 1832. Lincoln signed a note for his share in the partnership. The Lincoln-Berry store faced competition from two other general stores—one owned by Samuel Hill and John McNeil and the other by Reuben Radford. The first Berry-Lincoln store did not stay in this location long but moved to Reuben Radford's store after the partners bought his stock in January 1833.

The second Lincoln-Berry store, built in 1831, is a frame structure. Its one large room was the store, and the rear lean-to was used as a storeroom and, on occasion, Lincoln's bedroom. Dr. John Allen's cabin (1831) is one of the better constructed buildings at New Salem. Sometimes Presbyterian services were held there.

The Rutledge Tavern and Inn was originally built as a home in 1829 by James Rutledge, a cofounder of New Salem and Ann Rutledge's father. Rutledge, who had a library of books, founded the debating society that Lincoln joined. In 1831 Rutledge converted his home into a tavern and built an addition for overnight guests. Lincoln lodged in the loft on several occasions.

The Rutledge-Camron saw- and gristmill, built in 1825, was the operation on which the village was founded. Lincoln worked for a time as manager of the Denton Offut store.

The New Salem Post Office was located in Hill's store, where Hill was postmaster. He was replaced by Lincoln on May 7, 1833. Lincoln held the post until May 30, 1836, when the post office was relocated to Petersburg.

. . . . . . . . . . . . . . . . . . . . . . . . . . . . . . . . . . . . . . . . . . . . . . . . . . . . . . . . . . . . . . . . . . . . . . . . . . .

### Lincoln Home National Historic Site
### Springfield, Illinois

ADDRESS: Lincoln Home Visitor's Center, 426 South Seventh Street, Springfield, IL 62701

TELEPHONE: 217-492-4150

WEB SITE: www.nps.gov/liho

LOCATION: In downtown Springfield, at the corner of Eighth and Jackson streets; accessible from I-55, Clear Lake Avenue exit

OPEN: Daily, 8:30 A.M. to 5:00 P.M.; closed Thanksgiving, Christmas, and New Year's Day

ADMISSION: Free; entry to the Lincoln home is by a National Park Service ranger-guided tour only; free tour tickets are available on a first-come, first-served basis at the visitor center

FACILITIES: Restored home owned by President Abraham Lincoln; visitor center with displays and introductory videos; bookstore; restored Great Western Railroad depot

Lincoln Home National Historic Site, Springfield, Illinois. Abraham, Tad, and Willie in yard. Photograph courtesy of Abraham Lincoln Presidential Library and Museum

103

ABRAHAM LINCOLN

*In 1844 Abraham Lincoln purchased* the only house he ever owned. He bought a cottage for twelve hundred dollars on the corner of Eighth and Jackson streets from the Reverend Charles Dresser, the Episcopal minister who had officiated at his marriage to Mary Todd. In May 1844 Abraham, Mary, and their son Robert moved into the one-and-one-half-story cottage. On the first floor were a parlor, a sitting room, and a kitchen, and in the half loft above were two bedrooms. Over the kitchen an attic was used for storage or as a maid's room. Fireplaces heated the downstairs rooms, and wood-burning stoves kept the upstairs bedrooms warm. Water came from a cistern and a well in the backyard.

In 1856 the Lincolns remodeled and expanded their home. When the contractors, Hannon & Ragsdale, had finished their work, the original house had been transformed into a spacious two-story Greek-revival house, painted brown with dark green shutters. The second story doubled the Lincolns' living space. When a census taker for the Eighth Census, Sixteenth District canvassed the Lincoln home on July 14, 1860, he listed the occupants as Abraham Lincoln, a fifty-one-year-old lawyer; his thirty-five-year-old wife, Mary (she was actually forty-two); their three sons, Robert Todd, William Wallace, and Thomas; a hired girl, M. Johnson; and a fourteen-year-old boy, Phillip Dinkell, a hired servant. The house today reflects the Lincoln home of 1860.

Since Springfield homes were not numbered until 1873, the Lincolns used a front door nameplate (still on the door) to identify their home to visitors. The entrance door opens into the front corridor or stair hall. To the right is a sitting room where the Lincolns hosted informal receptions or relaxed with their children.

The room to the left of the front hall was a formal parlor. It was here, on May 19, 1860, that a delegation from the Republican National Convention officially informed Lincoln that he was the party's candidate for president. The parlor was connected by double sliding doors with a back parlor that was Lincoln's library. For a large party the two rooms could be combined into one large room. Originally the back parlor had been Mary and Abraham's bedroom. Eddie, Willie, and Tad were born in the room, and Eddie died there.

The family ate their meals in the formal dining room. Visitors today will see a large table set with china, silver, and crystal as for a formal meal. As a lawyer and politician, Lincoln, along with Mary, hosted many large parties.

When the Lincolns moved their sleeping quarters to the second floor, they moved into separate bedrooms. For a time Mary shared her room with her two youngest children, Willie and Tad. When the children were old enough, they moved into their own room. The boys' room has several toys, including a wooden horse and hoops for hoop and stick. Family and friends of the Lincolns stayed in the guest room.

A recent refurbishing of the Lincoln home included historically correct decorating as ascertained from period documents and physical evidence uncovered in the house. The reproduction wallpaper and carpeting exemplify the Victorian love of mixing bold patterns and colors. The house was stylishly furnished with dark floral patterned carpeting. Rooms were wallpapered—the parlors with a light, patterned paper and the sitting room and bedrooms with a bold design. Windows were framed by heavy floor-to-ceiling cotton damask draperies. Much of the furniture in the home today was owned by the Lincoln family. In Abraham Lincoln's bedroom upstairs is the bed that was specially made to accommodate his tall frame.

For seventeen years the house at Eighth and Jackson in Springfield was the home of Abraham Lincoln's family. Because Lincoln planned to return to Springfield, he rented out the house and stored the furniture. In 1861 the Lincolns left their home forever. Willie died in the White House in February 1862 at the age of eleven. President Lincoln was assassinated in April 1865. Tad died in 1871 at the age of eighteen. Mary returned to Springfield but did not live in the house. She died in 1882 in her sister Elizabeth's house, where she had married Abraham Lincoln forty years earlier. In 1887 Robert, the only living member of the Lincoln family, donated his family's home to the state of Illinois on the condition that the public would always have free access to it. In 1972 the home was conveyed to the United States, which through the National Park Service continued the state's work in preservation and restoration of the home, along with acquisition and restoration of the surrounding four-block neighborhood.

The Victorian houses in the Lincoln neighborhood have been restored to their 1860 appearance. According to the 1860 census, there were twenty-five houses along these two blocks of Eighth Street; today there are twelve. Providing a link to the Lincoln era, some houses have been restored and others are in the process of restoration. The Dean house, owned and occupied by Harriet Dean, features a Lincoln exhibit that is entitled "What a Pleasant Home Abe Lincoln Has."

The special train that took President-elect Lincoln to Washington, D.C., left Springfield's Great Western depot on Monday, February 11, 1861. The depot, a red brick building located two blocks from Lincoln's home, has been restored to its appearance in the mid-1800s. The three-level train station has both gentlemen's and ladies' waiting rooms on the first floor. The balcony displays photographs of Lincoln's family, friends, neighbors, law partners, and political associates. On the third floor a film describes Lincoln's twelve-day journey to Washington, D.C., as well as the parallel trip of Confederate president Jefferson Davis to Montgomery, Alabama.

The Great Western Railroad constructed the depot in 1852, and it was heavily damaged in an 1857 fire. After it was closed as a railroad depot, it was used as a warehouse and storage space. In the 1960s a local group purchased the depot with the intention of restoring it. In 1987 the *State-Journal Register,* the corporate descendant of the newspaper Lincoln termed "always my friend," and the Lincoln Home National Historic Site entered into a cooperative agreement to operate the depot. Copley Press maintains the building, while National Park Service rangers provide interpretation from April through August, 10:00 A.M.–4:00 P.M. The depot is located at 10th and Monroe streets in Springfield, Illinois. Admission is free.

............................................................................

## Abraham Lincoln Presidential Library and Museum
## Springfield, Illinois

ADDRESS: 212 North Sixth Street, Springfield, IL 62701
TELEPHONE: 217-558-8844, 800-610-2094, or 217-782-5764; library: 217-558-8855
WEB SITE: www.alplm.org
LOCATION: In downtown Springfield, about 175 miles south of Chicago, accessible from I-55, West Clear Lake Avenue exit; the parking ramp is off Sixth Street between Madison and Mason streets
OPEN: Museum: daily, 9:00 A.M. to 5:00 P.M., closed Thanksgiving, Christmas, and New Year's Day; library: daily, 9:00 A.M. to 5:00 P.M.
ADMISSION: Adults, $10.00; seniors, college students, and military, $7.00; children 5–15, $4.00
FACILITIES: Abraham Lincoln's presidential museum, library, and archives; handicapped accessible

*The Abraham Lincoln Presidential Library and Museum,* operated by the Illinois Historic Preservation Agency, opened in April 2005. The library, the state's chief historical and genealogical research facility, is home to the world-renowned Lincoln collection as well as more than twelve million items of Illinois history.

As visitors enter the Lincoln Museum, they are met by lifelike manikins of Abraham and Mary Lincoln and their sons. There are two major exhibits,

"Journey One, the Pre-Presidential Years" and "Journey Two, the Presidential Years," in addition to the theaters and other exhibits. Tours are self-guided.

"Journey One: The Pre-Presidential Years" portrays Abraham Lincoln's early years from his birth in Kentucky, to his childhood in Indiana, to his young adulthood in Springfield, Illinois, to his election as president of the United States. Visitors begin at the small cabin where the Thomas Lincoln family settled at Pigeon Creek in southern Indiana after moving from Kentucky. The log cabin is a full-scale replica with lifelike manikins. Lincoln is portrayed as a teenager reading borrowed books by firelight in the dimly lighted room.

Another exhibit focuses on Lincoln's river experiences. Young Abe Lincoln from 1820 to 1828 often worked on flatboats hauling goods on the Sangamon and Mississippi rivers. In 1824 he encountered slavery in New Orleans. Exhibits on slavery show the division of the country into free and slave states, statistics on the number of slaves, and the various compromises regarding slavery. The evil of slavery is depicted by slave shackles, a slave auction, and photographs.

At New Salem the Berry-Lincoln store has been reproduced as it was in April 1833. Lincoln lived in the small village on the Sangamon River from 1830 to 1837. He was a partner in a store with Berry. The store is stocked with barrels, pots, blankets, and other goods. The display raises questions about Lincoln's early love affairs with Ann Rutledge and Mary Owens.

The Springfield exhibit focuses on Lincoln's life as a lawyer and politician, including his courtship of Mary Todd, his home life, his political career, his law practice, and the Lincoln-Douglas debates. Both Lincoln and his oftentimes adversary Stephen A. Douglas were Mary's suitors. Abraham is shown with his wife in their living room in October 1840. In the exhibit are the family tea set, a mantel clock, and Lincoln's home plate, key, and door knob. Lincoln's legal career is illustrated by his law book, eye glasses, and a picture of his law partner William Herndon.

Lincoln's political activities as a Whig and then a Republican are outlined in a time line from 1830 to 1840. Lincoln and Douglas are shown at their debate at Knox College in Galesburg on October 7, 1858, during their campaign for U.S. senator. Douglas defeated Lincoln in 1858, but Lincoln would defeat him in the presidential election of 1860. On exhibit is an outfit worn by women Wide Awakes, the name given to Lincoln supporters. The Lincoln-Herndon law office exhibit depicts Lincoln's cluttered office where Lincoln, a permissive parent, is lying on a couch engrossed in a newspaper while his young sons Willie and Tad are playing ball on the legal table.

The presidential campaign of 1860 is covered in contemporary style with multiple video monitors featuring a television news program analyzing the four-way race in which Lincoln won the presidency. Narrated by Tim Russert, the program puts the issues and strategies into the television sound bites of today. Campaign advertisements for Lincoln, Douglas, Breckinridge, and Bell flash across the screen followed by the election results. A manikin of President-elect Lincoln delivers his eloquent and emotional farewell speech at the Great Western Railroad depot on February 11, 1861, before leaving Springfield for Washington, D.C., to begin his first term as president.

"Journey Two" covers Lincoln from his first inauguration in 1861 through his assassination in 1865. Visitors enter a facsimile of the White House south portico, where they see the Union generals McClellan and Grant conferring. Manikins of the African American leaders Frederick Douglass and Sojourner Truth are there, and one of the actor John Wilkes Booth appears as a brooding presence.

Mary Lincoln's role in Washington high society is the subject of another exhibit. Mary is being fitted for a ball gown by her dressmaker in the Blue Room of the White House. The exhibit on Lincoln's early presidency and the beginning of the Civil War focuses on the secession of the southern states to form the Confederacy and the firing on Fort Sumter in Charleston Harbor. The Whispering Gallery is a winding, nightmarish hallway where unnamed voices attack President and Mrs. Lincoln both personally and politically. The walls of the passageway are lined with caricatures of Lincoln.

The deeply moving scene titled "Triumph and Tragedy" depicts the Lincolns standing in their son Willie's bedroom. A grand ball to celebrate Mrs. Lincoln's redecoration of the White House had been scheduled. Willie had fallen ill with typhoid fever, but doctors had assured the parents that he was recovering, so they proceeded with their plans. During the ball Willie had taken a serious turn for the worse. Abraham and Mary are seen in their formal party clothes at Willie's bedside. Two weeks after the scene depicted, Willie would die. The Hall of Sorrows is a small alcove with a figure of Mary Lincoln in black mourning dress weeping and grieving for her son Willie. Mary attempted to contact her dead son through mediums and séances.

In a reproduction of the White House kitchen, servants are gossiping in July 1862 about Mary Lincoln's mental health, the mounting war casualties, Lincoln's problems with his generals, and rumors that Lincoln is working on an Emancipation Proclamation to free the slaves. In a replica of Lincoln's White House office, Lincoln is telling his cabinet that he intends to issue the Emancipation Proclamation. Some cabinet members advise him to go further in freeing the slaves, and others warn him that he is going too far. There are texts of the Emancipation Proclamation issued in 1863.

"The Black Troops Go to War" exhibit concerns the enlistment of African Americans in the Union army. The African American leader Frederick Douglass pleaded with Lincoln to let freed blacks join in the struggle for emancipation. After the Emancipation Proclamation was issued, thousands of African Americans enlisted.

"The Civil War in Four Minutes" exhibit features an electronic map that plots the course of the Civil War. Each week of the war is reduced to one second. Battle lines move back and forth, showing the military campaigns and battles and the slowly shrinking Confederacy. A casualty counter tracks the growing number of soldiers killed, reaching a climax of 702,000 Union and 621,000 Confederate soldiers. The human side of the war is portrayed by the stories of eight soldiers: four from the North and four from the South. A photograph, a brief biography, and a letter written by each soldier to his loved ones are on display.

The forty-two-foot-long Gettysburg Mural portrays the battle, the cemetery, the dedication ceremony, and Lincoln's immortal Gettysburg address. "The Tide Turns and Washington Celebrates" includes a series of historical paintings and artifacts depicting Lincoln's last months, including Lincoln's reelection in 1864, ratification of the Thirteenth Amendment ending slavery, the fall of Richmond, Lincoln's tour of the Confederate capital, Lee's surrender to Grant at Appomattox, and Lincoln's speech to celebrating crowds in Washington.

The Ford's Theatre exhibit displays theater bills advertising *My American Cousin*. In the re-created presidential box, Lincoln holds Mary's hand. Behind him John Wilkes Booth, the actor turned assassin, is entering from behind the curtains.

The exhibit "The Funeral Train" displays the route of Lincoln's funeral train and his last journey from Washington, D.C., to Springfield, Illinois, April 21 to May 3, 1865. The long-lost and only remaining photograph of Lincoln lying in state was discovered in the library's collection by a fourteen-year-old student.

The body of Abraham Lincoln lay in state in Representatives Hall in Springfield's Old State Capitol on May 3 and 4, 1865. Here the re-creation of the scene, with the casket and flowers, portrays the mood and decor of a Victorian-era funeral. It is realistic, haunting, and quite moving. The concluding exhibit shows how individuals have commemorated and remembered Lincoln.

The Treasures Gallery exhibits Lincoln possessions, including the president's glasses, shaving mirror, pen, and his son Tad's toy cannon. Also on display are Mary Lincoln's music box, jewelry, wedding skirt, and shawl. The Everett Copy of the Gettysburg Address, the Lincolns' marriage license, and Lincoln's presidential portfolio, or briefcase, can also be seen.

In the "Ask Mr. Lincoln" interactive exhibit, visitors can ask the president questions. The Union Theater uses special effects to feature "Lincoln's Eyes," which focuses on the personal and political dramas and key issues of Lincoln's presidency.

"The Ghosts of the Library Theater" uses Holavision to describe the purpose and functions of a presidential library and museum. A combination of a live host and state-of-the-art special effects explains the activities, the detective work, and the discoveries waiting to be made in a great presidential archive. Holavision permits the magical "fade away" or disappearance of the on-stage actor, with astonishing impact to audiences of all ages.

"Mrs. Lincoln's Attic: is a play area where children can dress in period costumes, build a log cabin with Lincoln Logs, and play with a dollhouse modeled after Lincoln's Springfield home. In addition they can play with nineteenth-century toys.

. . . . . . . . . . . . . . . . . . . . . . . . . . . . . . . . . . . . . . . . . . . . . . . . . . . . . . . . . . . . . . . . .

## Lincoln-Herndon Law Office State Historic Site
### Springfield, Illinois

ADDRESS: Sixth and Adams Streets, Springfield, IL 62701

TELEPHONE: 217-785-7289

LOCATION: In downtown Springfield, across from the restored Old State Capitol

OPEN: Monday–Sunday, 9:00 A.M. to 5:00 P.M., May through Labor Day; Tuesday–Saturday, 9:00 A.M. to 5:00 P.M., September–April; closed major holidays

ADMISSION: Free; donation suggested

FACILITIES: Restored law office of President Abraham Lincoln and his law partner William Herndon; handicapped accessible; National Register of Historic Places

*As a Springfield lawyer Abraham Lincoln* worked in a variety of law offices. The Lincoln-Herndon Law Office is in the only remaining building in which Abraham Lincoln maintained a law office.

The red brick Greek-revival-style building had been recently constructed when Lincoln and his partner Stephen T. Logan moved into it in 1843. Their office on the third floor overlooked the state capitol and the county court-house. There was a post office on the first floor, and the U.S. District Court was on the second floor.

After Lincoln and Logan amicably dissolved their partnership in 1844, Lincoln took William Herndon (1818–91), who had been their law clerk, as his partner. Lincoln practiced law in that office from 1843 to about 1852. While Lincoln served in Congress, Herndon maintained the practice.

The site consists of the surviving portion of a three-story brick, Greek-revival commercial block constructed in 1840–41. In 1978 the building was listed on the National Register of Historic Places as part of the Central Springfield Historic District.

The law office building has a first-floor visitor center consisting of an exhibit gallery and an audiovisual theater, along with a room interpreted as a 1840s post office facility. On the second floor are rooms representing those used by the federal court, and on the third floor are a common room and three lawyers' offices. Two of the offices were used by Lincoln and his partners. Visitors receive a guided tour of the historic rooms.

The Lincoln-Herndon Law Office was sparsely furnished with a table, a small desk, a sofa, and a half-dozen plain wooden chairs. Over the desk some shelves had been installed to hold a small law library. The practice prospered, and the partners shared equally in the firm's profits. Lincoln focused primarily on bankruptcy cases, wills, and petitions. Lincoln and Herndon prepared cases for the federal courts, the Illinois Supreme Court, and the state's Eighth Judicial Circuit, which covered most of east central Illinois. Lincoln rode the circuit for a total of six months during the year, while Herndon usually stayed in Springfield. Before he left for the White House, Lincoln told Herndon that he planned to resume his law practice after leaving the presidency.

Herndon described his law partner's habits in the office: "When he reached the office, about nine o'clock in the morning, the first thing he did was to pick up a newspaper, spread himself out on an old sofa, one leg on a chair, and read aloud, much to my discomfort. Singularly enough Lincoln never read any other way but aloud." Another of Herndon's complaints was that Lincoln frequently brought his young, unruly sons to the office.

The office had a bare wood floor and a long table, which stood at the center of the office, crossed by a shorter one. Both were covered with green baize cloth. An old-fashioned secretary desk with pigeonholes and a drawer held legal documents. A bookcase contained law books. Also in the office were a couch and assorted chairs.

The Lincoln-Herndon Law Office is across from the beautifully restored Old State Capitol building, which was the center of Illinois' government from 1839 to 1876. Designed by the architect John Rague, it is a distinguished example of the Greek-revival style.

Lincoln served as a state representative from 1834 to 1841, and that body met on the second floor of the capitol. Here, as the Republican nominee for U.S. senator, he delivered his famous "House Divided" speech in 1858. It was also here that Lincoln's body lay in state on May 3, 1865, after his assassination.

The Old State Capitol was dismantled in 1966 and rebuilt. The interior was completely reconstructed. It is open Tuesday–Saturday, 9:00 A.M.–5:00 P.M., and closed on holidays.

......................................................................

## Lincoln Tomb State Historic Site
## Springfield, Illinois

ADDRESS: Oak Ridge Cemetery, 1500 Monument Avenue, Springfield, IL 62702
TELEPHONE: 217-782-2717
LOCATION: North of downtown Springfield
OPEN: Daily, 9:00 A.M. to 5:00 P.M., May through Labor Day; Tuesday–
    Saturday, 9:00 A.M. to 5:00 P.M., September–November and March–April;
    Tuesday–Saturday, 9:00 A.M. to 4:00 P.M., December–February
ADMISSION: Free
FACILITIES: Burial site of President Abraham Lincoln

*Springfield, Illinois, is the final resting place* for Abraham, Mary Todd, Tad, Eddie, and Willie Lincoln. Abraham Lincoln was buried in Springfield's Oak Ridge Cemetery at the request of Mrs. Lincoln after his assassination in 1865. Lincoln's body first arrived in the cemetery's public receiving vault on the hill below the present tomb. The coffin of his son William, who died in the White House, also rested there. Both had traveled nearly seventeen hundred miles in a special railroad car by a circuitous route from Washington, D.C.

The tomb is in the center of a twelve-and-one-half-acre plot. Designed by the Vermont sculptor Larkin Mead and constructed of Massachusetts granite, the tomb has a rectangular base surmounted by a 117-foot-high obelisk and a semicircular entranceway. A bronze reproduction of the sculptor Gutzon Borglum's head of Lincoln in the U.S. Capitol rests on a pedestal in front of the entrance. Four flights of stairs—two flanking the entrance at the front and two at the rear—lead to a level terrace. In the center of the terrace a large and ornate base supports the obelisk. In front of the obelisk and above the entrance stands a full-size statue of Lincoln.

As you enter the building, you will see bronze statues and excerpts from some Lincoln speeches. A circular hallway leads to the marble burial chamber, where Secretary Stanton's famous words command your attention: "Now he belongs to the ages."

The granite tomb contains the bodies of Lincoln, his wife, Mary, and three of his four sons— Edward, William, and Thomas. A red marble marker stands

Lincoln Tomb State
Historic Site, Springfield,
Illinois

112
.....

ABRAHAM LINCOLN

above the area where Lincoln's coffin lies. His body actually rests below the floor in a steel and concrete vault. This change was made in 1899 when the monument needed reconstruction, partly to deter grave robbers. An attempt to steal the body had been made in 1876.

Oak Ridge Cemetery was dedicated on May 24, 1860, five years before Lincoln's death, just outside the town where Lincoln lived most of his adult life. The committee that arranged his Springfield funeral formed an association to build this tomb, which was dedicated in 1874. In 1895 the association deeded the tomb and surrounding grounds to the state of Illinois.

Robert, the oldest Lincoln son, planned to be buried in this tomb with his parents and brothers. When his own son, Abraham Lincoln II ("Jack"), died in 1890, he brought the body to the Lincoln tomb. Robert's wife, Mary Harlan Lincoln, chose a plot in Arlington National Cemetery for Robert, a former secretary of war. He was buried in Arlington in 1928, and Jack was moved there in 1930.

# Andrew Johnson

SEVENTEENTH PRESIDENT OF THE UNITED STATES
*April 15, 1865–March 3, 1869*

........................................................................

Like Vice Presidents John Tyler and Millard Fillmore, who unexpectedly became president because of their predecessors' deaths, Andrew Johnson was an accidental chief executive, the first to succeed because of a president's assassination. On the death of Abraham Lincoln, who was only a month into his second term, Johnson became president, serving for almost one full term. An unlikely candidate for the nation's highest office, Johnson never attended school, grew up in poverty, and was apprenticed to a tailor who taught him to read and write. President Johnson faced the issue of Reconstruction, the restoration of the defeated Confederate states to the Union, and his policies put him on a collision course with a Republican-dominated Congress that led to his impeachment. Johnson is remembered as the only president to be impeached until President William Clinton also attained that dubious distinction.

Andrew Johnson was born on December 29, 1808, in a log cabin in Raleigh, North Carolina, to Jacob Johnson (1778–1812) and Mary McDonough Johnson (1783–1856). He was the youngest of their three children, one of whom had died in infancy. In early 1812 thirty-three-year-old Jacob died suddenly. Mary, whose sons were three and eight years old, took in laundry to support her children. She apprenticed her sons to James Selby, a tailor, who taught Andrew to read and write.

When Andrew was fifteen, he, his brother, and two companions pelted a neighbor's house with pieces of wood, possibly to attract the attention of the daughters of the family. The owner threatened to sue the boys, which frightened them so much that the Johnson brothers ran away to Laurens, South Carolina. They remained there for two years, during which time Andrew worked as a tailor. In 1826 Andrew and his mother and stepfather moved to Tennessee.

Andrew fell in love with Eliza McCardle, and they were married on May 17, 1827, by Mordecai Lincoln, a cousin of Abraham Lincoln's father. Andrew was eighteen, and Eliza was sixteen. They rented a house on Greeneville's Main Street, living in the back while Andrew and his partner operated a tailor shop in the front. Andrew and Eliza had five children: Martha, born in 1828; Charles, in 1830; Mary, in 1832; Robert, in 1834; and Andrew, in 1852.

In 1830–31 the Johnson family and the tailoring business moved to College and Depot streets. In September 1851 Johnson purchased a house on Greeneville's Main Street. Eventually Johnson left the tailoring business. He purchased a farm for his mother and stepfather and acquired several slaves.

Johnson organized a Mechanics or Workingman's Party in spring 1828. He successfully ran for alderman in 1829 and was reelected each year for the next four years. In 1834 the Greeneville Board of Aldermen chose Johnson to be mayor, and in 1835 Johnson was a successful candidate for the state legislature. He was defeated by Brookins Campbell in 1837, but in 1839 he ran against Campbell as a Democrat and won. From that time on Johnson was a loyal member of the Democratic Party. In 1841 he gained a seat in the Tennessee Senate.

In 1843 Johnson was elected to the U.S. House of Representatives, where he served five two-year terms. In March 1846 Johnson introduced his Homestead Bill, which provided for 160 acres of public land to be given free to the head of a household who would cultivate it for five years. Johnson's bill passed the House in December 1852. Johnson was elected governor of Tennessee in 1853 and was reelected in 1855.

Andrew Johnson was elected as a U.S. senator by the Tennessee legislature in October 1857. He was a strong Union supporter—a Southern Unionist. South Carolina seceded from the Union on December 20, 1860, followed by Mississippi, Florida, Alabama, Georgia, Louisiana, and Texas the next year. On May 7, 1861, Tennessee voted to join the Confederacy. With his home state now in the Confederacy, Johnson fled to Washington. The Johnson home was confiscated by Confederate troops.

President Lincoln appointed military governors to administer Confederate territory recaptured by Union troops. In March 1862 he appointed Andrew Johnson as military governor of Tennessee. Johnson regarded preservation of the Union rather than slavery as the central issue of the Civil War. Still, in 1863 Johnson endorsed emancipation of the slaves, a complete reversal of his lifelong position.

In the presidential election of 1864, the Democratic candidate was Gen. George McClellan. The Republicans, reorganized as the National Union Party, renominated Lincoln and named Johnson as his vice-presidential running mate. On April 14, 1865, the tragic shooting of President Abraham Lincoln by John Wilkes Booth occurred. Andrew Johnson took the oath of office about three hours after Lincoln's death on April 15, 1865.

For all intents and purposes, the Civil War had ended days before Lincoln's death when Gen. Robert E. Lee surrendered the Army of Northern Virginia on April 9 at Appomattox Court House, Virginia. President Johnson alleged that the Confederate states had never legally seceded, thus retaining their constitutional right to self-government. He directed the Confederate states to establish new constitutions that disavowed secession and to ratify the Thirteenth

Amendment abolishing slavery. By December 1865 the Thirteenth Amendment had been ratified and every former Confederate state except Texas had met Johnson's conditions for reentry to the Union.

When Congress convened in early December 1865, the Republican majority was aghast at Johnson's lenient reconstruction of the South and refused to seat the recently elected southern members of Congress. The Republican majority in Congress passed the Fourteenth Amendment, which extended citizenship to "all persons born or naturalized in the United States" and was designed to protect the freed slaves from restrictive state laws. The amendment was sent to the states for ratification, with an understanding that the former Confederate states' representatives to Congress would be seated only if their states ratified the amendment. Johnson opposed the Fourteenth Amendment.

Congress in 1867 enacted its own policy of Reconstruction, which reorganized the South into five military districts. The Congressional Reconstruction Act, passed over Johnson's veto on March 2, 1867, two years after the end of the Civil War, put the South under military rule but prohibited Johnson, the commander in chief, from giving orders to officers in command of the military districts. States seeking readmission needed to ratify a new state constitution that ensured black voting rights.

Because Johnson dismissed federal officeholders who supported congressional reconstruction, Congress passed the Tenure of Office Act, which required Senate approval to fire federal officials whose appointments needed the Senate's advice and consent. In January 1868 Johnson decided to replace Secretary of War Edwin Stanton. After several conspirators had been tried and hung for Lincoln's assassination, including the mother of a conspirator, Mary Surratt, Johnson learned that the judges in her case had advocated leniency. When Stanton brought the execution orders to the president, he removed the document regarding Mrs. Surratt. When President Johnson reread the file, he saw the missing document and realized Stanton's duplicity. Stanton refused to resign and was protected by the Tenure of Office Act.

Calls for Johnson's impeachment came from the Radical Republicans. The House Judiciary Committee recommended Johnson's impeachment on November 20 but with a vote of 57–108 failed to pass an impeachment resolution. According to the Constitution, the House of Representatives decides, through the impeachment process, if there is sufficient evidence to warrant a Senate trial. The House votes impeachment, while the Senate tries the case. Impeachment is an accusation of wrongdoing, and removal from office occurs only after a conviction by the Senate.

On February 24, 1868, the U.S. House of Representatives voted 126–47 to impeach the president on eleven Articles of Impeachment. President Johnson was charged with violating the Tenure of Office Act by attempting to fire Secretary of War Stanton. On May 16 the Senate vote was 35 guilty to 19 not guilty.

Since 36 votes were needed to convict, President Johnson was acquitted by 1 vote.

In July 1868 President Johnson granted a full pardon to all former Confederates except those under indictment for treason. On Christmas Day that same year, he issued an executive pardon to all former Confederates, including Jefferson Davis.

After his presidency Johnson and his family returned to Tennessee. In 1874 Andrew Johnson was elected to the U.S. Senate. Johnson died on July 31, 1875, at the age of sixty-six. In Greeneville his casket was placed in the parlor of the house. The funeral was held on August 3, and over five thousand people walked in the funeral procession to his grave site nearby. The following January 15 Eliza McCardle Johnson died.

. . . . . . . . . . . . . . . . . . . . . . . . . . . . . . . . . . . . . . . . . . . . . . . . . . . . . . . . . . . . . . . . . . . . . . . . . . . . . .

### Andrew Johnson National Historic Site
### Greeneville, Tennessee

ADDRESS: 121 Monument Avenue, Greeneville, TN 37743-5552

TELEPHONE: 423-638-3551

WEB SITE: www.nps.gov/anjo

LOCATION: Greeneville is located in northeast Tennessee, with access from I-81, approximately fifty miles northeast of Knoxville; the visitor center is on the corner of College and Depot streets.

OPEN: Daily, 9:00 A.M. to 5:00 P.M.; closed Thanksgiving, Christmas, and New Year's Day

ADMISSION: Free

FACILITIES: Guided tours; visitor center; special events. The visitor center and the early Johnson home are handicapped accessible.

*The Andrew Johnson National Historic Site,* operated by the National Park Service, consists of four properties in Greeneville, Tennessee: the visitor center and tailor shop; Andrew Johnson's early home; the President Johnson Homestead; and the president's burial site at the Andrew Johnson National Cemetery.

Although Andrew Johnson was born in Raleigh, North Carolina, he settled in Greeneville, Tennessee, in 1827 at the age of eighteen. In Greeneville, Johnson earned his living as a tailor and rose from an impoverished background to become a wealthy owner of a tailor shop, two houses, a 350-acre farm, flour mills, town lots, and the property where he was buried. On his death in 1875 his estate was estimated at two hundred thousand dollars.

After his death much of Johnson's property was retained by his daughters, Martha Patterson and Mary Stover, and their children. In 1906 Martha J. Patterson bequeathed fifteen acres of land in Greeneville, including the Johnson burial site, to the U.S. government. The tailor shop, owned by family members

until 1921, was purchased by the state of Tennessee. In 1941 the tailor shop was conveyed to the U.S. government, which in 1942 purchased the Johnson Homestead from the Patterson family. These sites, originally known as the Andrew Johnson National Monument, have since 1963 been known as the Andrew Johnson National Historic Site.

The bookstore, the museum, and the tailor shop are located in the visitor center. A video on Andrew Johnson focuses on Johnson's presidency, especially his impeachment by the House of Representative and trial by the Senate. Museum exhibits focus on Johnson's family, Johnson's life at the White House, the Johnson administration, foreign affairs, the Alaska purchase, statehood for Colorado and Nebraska, and Johnson's vetoes of the Civil Rights Bill.

Andrew Johnson's tailor shop is enclosed within the visitor center. President Andrew Johnson's occupation as a tailor is unique, and his tailor shop is the only such business at a U.S. presidential site. Johnson purchased the structure in 1831 and moved it to its present site. It became a gathering place for local political discussion. The small frame tailor shop measures approximately twenty-four feet by fourteen feet and has a fireplace. Its exterior is yellow poplar weather boarding, and its interior is wide pine boarding, with a pine tongue-and-groove floor. On display is a wedding coat made by Johnson. The exhibit includes a tailor's table, tools, scissors, shears, and an iron thimble.

The early Johnson house, located near the visitor center, is a small, two-story brick structure where the family lived from the 1830s to 1851. It is used as a museum and contains exhibits on the Johnson family tree, his apprenticeship as a tailor, his early years in Greeneville, and his marriage and family. There is a time line of major events in American history during Johnson's life. Other exhibits focus on Johnson as a representative of the working classes, his political career, and the restoration of the house as a museum.

The Andrew Johnson Homestead can be seen by guided tours, which originate on the porch. The house was built circa 1849 by James Brannon. Johnson paid Brannon $950 and deeded his former home and lot at Water and Main streets. This was Johnson's home from 1851 to 1875 and reflects his status as a man of wealth.

The original house was a two-story brick building with a one-story rear ell. There were eight rooms on three levels. For at least six years during the Civil War, the house was occupied by Confederate troops and later Union troops. In March 1869 the former president and his family returned to Greeneville to a heavily damaged home. Johnson proceeded to restore and remodel the house. He added a second story to the ell and a large porch at the rear, papered the walls, installed corner cupboards in several rooms, replaced broken windows, and repainted the trim. After Johnson's death the exterior of the house was remodeled into a Victorian structure and the interior was modernized. Additional houses were built on the property.

The Johnson Homestead has been restored to its 1869–75 appearance, reflecting the changes made by President Johnson. It is a ten-room block front brick structure situated close to the street. A center entry has a rectangular room on either side with fireplaces, and the second-story rooms follow the same pattern. In the ell, which is two steps lower than the rooms in the basic block, there are two rooms on each level, and there are two more rooms in the semibasement. A double-deck veranda flanks the back side of the basic block and the northeast side of the ell.

Many of the furnishings and artifacts in the Homestead are original to the Johnson family. The first floor has a parlor, a dining room, and two bedrooms, and there are four bedrooms on the second floor. The kitchen and storeroom are in the semibasement.

In the parlor are a piano, a portrait of Martha Johnson, Johnson's favorite chair, and an 1860 portrait by Samuel Shaver of Andrew Johnson with the Homestead Act. Andrew Johnson's bedroom contains portraits of Eliza McCardle and their son Robert Johnson and a secretary desk with thirteen panels of glass, one for each of the original colonies. The girls' bedroom was occupied by the Johnson daughters, Martha and Mary. The bedroom has a wooden ceiling and a straw mat on the floor. Another children's bedroom contains a large sleigh bed and toys. This bedroom belonged to Robert, Johnson's second son, who was a consumptive like his mother. He was treated with laudanum, an opiate, and became addicted to it. He died in this room.

The dining room is in a location that was originally used as a kitchen. It contains an original family dining table. The basement kitchen was once a laundry room and has a cast-iron stove, a fireplace, and kitchen utensils.

President Johnson is buried in Greeneville's Andrew Johnson National Cemetery, a National Historic Site operated by the National Park Service. From 1906 until 1942 the cemetery was administered by the Department of the Army.

Veterans from the Civil War, the Spanish-American War, World Wars I and II, the Korean War, and the Vietnam War are interred there.

Johnson died on July 31, 1875. He selected his burial site on property he had purchased in 1852. The cone-shaped summit of Signal Hill on the western edge of Greeneville was one of Johnson's favorite places because of the panoramic views of the countryside and the Appalachian Mountains. Eliza Johnson, who had been ill with tuberculosis for many years, died six months after her husband and is buried beside him.

In 1878 the Johnson family erected a twenty-seven-foot-tall Italian marble monument at President Johnson's grave. The shaft is decorated with the American flag, a scroll of the Constitution above an open Bible, and an eagle perched atop a globe at the top. The inscription reads: "His faith in the people never wavered."

# Ulysses Simpson Grant

EIGHTEENTH PRESIDENT OF THE UNITED STATES
*March 4, 1869–March 3, 1877*

...............................................................................

Ulysses Simpson Grant was the Union general who turned the tide of the Civil War into a victory. Grant's genius was on the battlefield, where he was able to grasp the complexities of military strategy and quickly implement workable plans. Cast into political prominence as a war hero, Grant possessed a personal honesty that was insufficient to keep his presidency from being tainted by scandals involving his associates.

Hiram Ulysses Grant was born on April 27, 1822, in a two-room frame house in Point Pleasant, Ohio. He was the oldest of the six children of Jesse Root Grant (1794–1873) and Hannah Simpson Grant (1798–1883). A year after Ulysses' birth, the family moved to Georgetown, Ohio, where they remained until 1840. Jesse Grant operated a tanning business and also farmed.

Jesse obtained an appointment to the U.S. Military Academy at West Point for his seventeen-year-old son. Jesse had always called his son Ulysses, which the young man preferred over Hiram. When Congressman Thomas Hamer signed the papers for Grant's appointment to West Point, he erroneously entered the appointee's name as Ulysses S. Grant; Hamer knew that the young man was called Ulysses and that his mother's maiden name was Simpson. Because West Point insisted that the new student use that name, Hiram Ulysses Grant became Ulysses Simpson Grant. After graduation Grant was commissioned as a brevet second lieutenant in the Fourth Infantry Regiment, which in March 1846 took up positions at the Rio Grande. Mexico declared war, and the Fourth Infantry fought in ten battles.

Ulysses met his future wife, Julia Dent, in February 1844, and they were married on August 22, 1848. The elder Grants, who were adamant abolitionists, did not attend their son's wedding, possibly because Julia was the daughter of a southern slave owner. Slavery was not a contentious issue between Julia, who accepted it, and Ulysses, who opposed it. On May 30, 1850, Julia gave birth to Frederick Dent Grant. Ulysses Simpson Grant Jr. was born on July 22, 1852; Ellen Wrenshall was born on July 4, 1855; and Jesse Root was born on February 6, 1858.

In winter 1852 Grant, who was lonely and depressed when he was at a military post away from his family, became concerned about his drinking. Joining the Sons of Temperance, Rising Sun Division, Lodge No. 210, he pledged to abstain from liquor, attended weekly meetings, and marched in temperance parades. Grant did not keep the pledge for a lifetime.

In July 1852 the Fourth Infantry was ordered to the Pacific Coast. From New York 650 members of the Fourth Infantry sailed to Panama, traveled the isthmus by mule, and then sailed to California on the steamer *Golden Gate*. One third of the troops contracted cholera in Panama, but Grant did not. He broke his Sons of Temperance pledge and drank only wine, not Panama's contaminated water.

On April 11, 1854, Captain Grant resigned his army commission. Practically penniless from a series of failed business ventures, he rejoined his family at his father-in-law's farm, White Haven, near St. Louis, Missouri. Julia had received an eighty-acre farm as a wedding gift, but the land was poor—rocky, uncleared, and unimproved. Jesse Grant, whose tanning business had made him rich, provided the start-up funds for stocking the farm and building the house. Ulysses farmed and built a two-story home. When the price of prairie wheat plummeted in the depression of October 1857, Grant gave up farming. In early 1860 Ulysses took a job in his father's leather store in Galena, Illinois.

Abraham Lincoln was elected president in 1860, and civil war loomed as eleven southern slave states seceded from the Union. Grant returned to the army in 1861 as a brigadier general with command that included twenty thousand troops in Missouri, Illinois, and Kentucky. In February 1862 Grant, commanding a joint army-navy operation, captured Fort Henry on the Tennessee River and Fort Donelson on the Cumberland River. Grant told Confederate general Simon B. Buckner that no terms except unconditional and immediate surrender could be accepted. After this Grant's initials, U. S., were dubbed "Unconditional Surrender."

In the Battle of Shiloh, Tennessee, on April 6–7, 1862, eighty thousand troops, almost evenly divided between General Albert Sidney Johnston's Confederates and General Grant's Union army, engaged in two days of fierce fighting. Grant's victory at Shiloh cost thirteen thousand Union and twelve thousand Confederates lives.

In 1863, as commander of the Army of the Tennessee, General Grant had eighty thousand troops in western Tennessee and northern Mississippi. The Confederates held only a narrow stretch of the Mississippi, at Vicksburg. Grant's objective was to take Vicksburg, located on a high bluff on the east side of the Mississippi River and protected by heavy Confederate artillery. Marching 180 miles in three weeks, Grant's forces fought five battles. In March 1863 Grant's army, surrounding Vicksburg, commenced the siege of the city. On July 3 Confederate general John C. Pemberton asked for an armistice. Grant demanded unconditional surrender. On July 4 thirty-one thousand Confederate troops surrendered at Vicksburg. With the Union in control of the Mississippi, the Confederacy was split in two.

In the fall of 1863 Grant became commander of the Division of the Mississippi, which included the Armies of the Ohio, the Tennessee and the Cumberland. Chattanooga, an important southern railroad hub, was Grant's next target. After a fierce battle that raged November 23–25, Grant was victorious.

In March 1864 Lieutenant General Grant was given supreme command of the country's armies. To win the war Grant designed a two-front offensive. Gen. William Tecumseh Sherman would invade Georgia and march from Atlanta to the sea, while Grant would pursue Lee's Army of Northern Virginia on its home territory.

In May and June, Grant and Lee fought a series of bloody battles in northern Virginia. Grant forced Lee to abandon Richmond and Petersburg on April 2, 1865. General Lee surrendered to Grant at Appomattox Court House on April 9, 1865. Over the next several weeks the remainder of the Confederate army surrendered.

On April 13 General Grant informed President Lincoln that the war was effectively over. The next day the Lincolns invited the Grants to accompany them to Ford's Theatre. The Grants declined, a decision that spared them from the bullets of John Wilkes Booth, the assassin of Abraham Lincoln.

The Republican National Convention in May 1868 nominated Grant as its presidential candidate on the first ballot, with Schuyler Colfax as the nominee for vice president. The Democratic candidate was Horatio Seymour. In a decisive victory Grant won 214 electoral and 3,013,421 popular votes to Seymour's 80 electoral and 2,706,829 popular votes.

Though President Grant was not personally involved, his administration was marred by repeated scandals involving his staff and extended family. Unscrupulous gold speculators, Jay Gould and Jim Fisk, in 1869 schemed to corner the gold supply and enticed Abel R. Corbin, the husband of Grant's sister Jenny, to join their plot. An angry Grant ordered Secretary of the Treasury George Boutwell to sell $4 million in gold. The price of gold plummeted, foiling Fisk and Gould's plan. Seeking revenge, Fisk and Gould implied that President Grant had profited by the plot, but he was exonerated by a congressional investigation.

The Republican Party nominated Grant for a second term in June 1872. Henry Wilson was nominated for vice president. In 1872 Republican reformers formed a third party, the Liberal Republicans, which nominated Horace Greeley, editor of the *New York Tribune,* for president; Greeley was also the Democratic Party's nominee. In a landslide victory Grant won 3,598,235 popular votes, or 55.6 percent, to Greeley's 2,834,761 popular votes, 43.8 percent. Grant won 286 electoral votes. Greeley, who died before the meeting of the Electoral College, did not receive any electoral votes.

For more than two years after Grant's presidency, Ulysses and Julia traveled through Europe, Egypt, Palestine, Syria, Turkey, India, China, and Japan.

Because Ulysses again had financial problems, his friends raised money that enabled him to buy a house in New York. He became president of the Mexican Southern Railroad. After he fell and injured his left leg, he used crutches for the rest of his life.

Ulysses invested with Grant and Ward, a partnership of his son Ulysses Jr. and Ferdinand Ward. Ward was running a pyramid scheme that Ulysses Jr. did not comprehend. The former president lost his total investment along with an additional $150,000 borrowed from William Vanderbilt in an effort to save the failing partnership. Wiped out financially, Grant sold the Galena house and the St. Louis farm he had purchased from his father-in-law. When Julia Grant refused to accept Vanderbilt's offer to cancel her husband's debt, Vanderbilt took some of Grant's military memorabilia as payment.

In the summer of 1884 Grant was diagnosed with throat cancer from a lifetime of cigar smoking. Mark Twain, a friend of Grant's, urged him to write his memoirs. Charles L. Webster & Co., a publishing firm set up by Twain, published the two-volume work. Congress restored Grant to his rank as general so that he, and later Julia, would receive a pension.

Ulysses S. Grant, age sixty-three, died on July 23, 1885, at Mount McGregor, New York. He was buried on August 8, 1885 in Riverside Park, New York City. In 1897 President McKinley dedicated Grant's Tomb overlooking the Hudson River. Julia died at the age of seventy-six.

........................................................................

## Grant Birthplace
## Point Pleasant, Ohio

ADDRESS: 1551 State Road 232, P.O. Box 2, New Richmond, OH 45157

TELEPHONE: 800-283-8932

WEB SITE: www.ohiohistory.org/places/grantbir/

LOCATION: In Point Pleasant, Ohio, in Clermont County, about five miles east of New Richmond, on the Ohio River, twenty-seven miles east of Cincinnati, at the corner of Routes 232 and 52

OPEN: Wednesday–Saturday, 9:30 A.M. to 5:00 P.M., and Sunday, noon to 5:00 P.M., April–October; closed holidays

ADMISSION: Adults, $2.50; seniors, $2.00; children 6–12, $1.50

FACILITIES: National Register of Historic Places, National Historic Landmark

*For a man who spent much of his life living* on military bases, there are certainly many sites preserved and dedicated to President Ulysses S. Grant, several of which he resided in for brief periods of time. The Union general lived in a house in Mount McGregor, New York, for only six weeks and did not own it, but he did die there. Grant occupied another house near St. Louis, Missouri, for only three months, but he did build it himself. Another site is the southern

plantation near St. Louis owned by his wife's family and occupied by Ulysses only as a guest in the early years of his marriage. Grant purchased this property in later life but did not return to it after his presidency. He was given a house in Galena, Illinois, which he resided in between the end of the Civil War and the beginning of his presidential term. The only house he actually occupied for any length of time—sixteen years—was his boyhood home in Georgetown, Ohio. His tomb, of course, is in a separate category.

The first house Grant lived in, his birth home, was located in Point Pleasant, Ohio, and he lived there for a year. The oldest child of Jesse and Hannah Simpson Grant, Grant was born on April 27, 1822, in a small house on the Ohio River and was named Hiram Ulysses Grant. The year after Grant's birth, the family moved to Georgetown, Ohio.

The house, which was built in 1817 of white Allegheny pine, is a small, three-room, single-story cottage painted white and with a wood shake roof. The main part of the house measures sixteen by nineteen and one half feet. There is a large chimney and fireplace. The interior has a kitchen, a living room, and a bedroom.

The building is property of the state of Ohio. Also on the site is a marker to Jean De Lannoy, 1570–1604, a Huguenot ancestor of President Ulysses S. Grant.

## Grant Boyhood House
### Georgetown, Ohio

ADDRESS: 219 East Grant Avenue, Georgetown, OH 45121

TELEPHONE: 937-378-4222 or 937-378-9470

WEB SITE: www.usgrantboyhoodhome.org

LOCATION: In southeastern Ohio, about seven miles north of the Ohio River and Kentucky border; near Routes 68 and 125; thirty-five miles east of Cincinnati

OPEN: Wednesday–Sunday, noon to 5:00 P.M., Memorial Day through Labor
  Day; Saturday–Sunday, noon to 5:00 P.M., September–October; closed
  holidays
ADMISSION: Adults, $3.00; children 12 and under, $1.00
FACILITIES: Childhood home of President Ulysses S. Grant, National Register
  of Historic Places, National Historic Landmark; Grant School at 508
  South Water Street

*President Ulysses S. Grant, who was born* on April 27, 1822, in the small village
of Point Pleasant, was one year old when his family moved to Georgetown,
twenty-five miles away. Grant spent his entire youth and received his early
education there, leaving when he was seventeen years old to study at the U.S.
Military Academy at West Point, New York.

In the early nineteenth century Georgetown was a farming community
surrounded by oak forests, seven miles from the Ohio River. Ulysses' father,
Jesse Grant, a tanner, built a tannery at the corner of Water and Main Cross
streets (renamed Grant Street). The bark of oak trees was the source of tannic
acid used to tan leather. Jesse also farmed fifty acres.

Though Georgetown had only about a dozen families when the Grants
arrived in 1823, the town quickly grew. Between 1823 and 1825 Jesse built a two-
story brick house on Water Street, and in 1828 he constructed an addition for
his growing family. Five more Grant children were born there. Jesse Grant retained ownership of the house until 1847, though the family moved to Bethel
in 1840.

In 1977, 130 years later, John and Judy Ruthven purchased the Grant home,
which was in danger of being demolished. They began restoring the house to
its 1835 appearance, using many furnishings that had belonged to the Grant
family. Visitors have toured the house since 1982. In 1996 the Ruthvens' property went into the U.S. Grant Homestead Foundation, and in 2002 the Grant

Boyhood Home was acquired by the state of Ohio to be operated by the Ohio Historical Society in cooperation with the local U.S. Grant Homestead Association.

The Ohio Historical Society is in the process of restoring the house to its appearance in the 1820s. In preparation they are cataloging furnishings and other items in the house to determine if they are appropriate to the time period, conducting an archaeological investigation of the property, and installing new exhibits. White paint on the exterior of the house has been removed revealing red brick, and the metal roof of the house has been replaced with wood.

The Grant Boyhood Home is a one-and-one-half-story federal-style brick house that was built by the president's father between 1823 and 1825. The structure is a modified L shape with a recessed front off-center paneled entrance with a transom. There is an interior end chimney. A one-story rear kitchen was added in 1826, and in 1828 Jesse Grant built a two-story addition that included a parlor, a bedroom, and a staircase on the first floor and two additional bedrooms upstairs.

The Grant Public School—which Grant attended from about the ages of six to thirteen—is located at 508 South Water Street. Built in 1829, the one-room building was acquired by the Ohio Historical Society in 1941 and restored. The school is open the same hours as the home.

..........................................................................

## Ulysses S. Grant National Historic Site
## St. Louis, Missouri

ADDRESS: 7400 Grant Road, St. Louis, MO 63123-1801
TELEPHONE: 314-842-3298
WEB SITE: www.nps.gov/ulsg
LOCATION: In south St. Louis County, on Grant Road, off Gravois Road (Route 30), adjacent to Grant's Farm
OPEN: Daily, 9:00 A.M. to 5:00 P.M.; closed Thanksgiving, Christmas, and New Year's Day
ADMISSION: Free
FACILITIES: A ten-acre site with five historic structures, visitor center; guided tours; visitor center and restroom are handicapped accessible

*Ironically the Ulysses S. Grant National Historic Site* is located on a southern plantation, White Haven, where as many as thirty slaves lived. Grant, the general who led Union troops to victory in the Civil War, which effectively ended slavery in the nation, came from a strongly abolitionist family and never condoned slavery. Julia Dent Grant, the general's wife, however, came from a slaveholding family, and during her marriage she owned slaves until they were

emancipated. Incredibly, Ulysses and Julia had a long and happy marriage in an era when differing views about slavery divided the country and resulted in a bloody war.

Frederick Dent, Julia Dent Grant's father, owned a one-thousand-acre farm in Missouri and, in 1830, thirty slaves. The Ulysses S. Grant National Historic Site is located on part of that property. When Ulysses was in the military, Julia and her children frequently lived at White Haven, which was eventually purchased by Ulysses S. Grant.

Julia and Ulysses were married on August 22, 1848. As a wedding gift, Colonel Dent gave Julia and Ulysses eighty acres of his estate. Ulysses S. Grant resigned from the military in 1854 and returned to Missouri to farm. Because there was no house on his land, the Grant family lived with the Dents at White Haven. Ulysses eventually built a two-story log house named Hardscrabble for his family, but three months after it was completed, Julia's mother died. Colonel Dent asked the Grants to move back into the main house so that Julia could help raise her younger sisters.

Though Ulysses Grant lived at White Haven from 1854 to 1859, his agricultural endeavors were unsuccessful, forcing him to sell his farm. In 1860 the Grant family moved to Galena, Illinois, where Ulysses worked with two of his brothers in their father's leather store. A year later when hostilities between the North and the South began, Grant returned to military service. When Julia and the children were not with Ulysses at his military camps, they lived at White Haven.

During the war years Ulysses became financially stable while Frederick Dent, like other plantation owners, suffered economic reverses. General Grant purchased White Haven's eleven hundred acres in the late 1860s and planned to retire to the farm. Yet after President Grant left office, he and Julia took an extended around-the-world trip and then settled in New York City.

Grant faced financial ruin again when he lost money in an investment scheme in which his son was involved. In April 1885 Grant formally conveyed his St. Louis property, including Hardscrabble, to William Vanderbilt to repay a loan of $150,000 he had obtained in a futile attempt to save his son's business. After Grant's death, a large part of White Haven farm was purchased by August A. Busch in the early 1900s. The house at White Haven was owned by the Wenzlick family from 1913 to 1986.

In 1985 interest in preserving the Grants' St. Louis–area property led to the formation of an association called Save Grant's White Haven, Inc. The Jefferson National Parks Association purchased the property and donated it to the National Park Service. On October 3, 1989, a 9.65-acre site was officially authorized by the National Park Service as the Ulysses S. Grant National Historic Site.

The house at White Haven was built by William Lindsay Long, a retired New England ship captain, in 1808 and purchased as a country home by Frederick Dent in 1820. Dent named the property White Haven after his family home in Maryland.

The Ulysses S. Grant National Historic Site has five original structures: the main house, a stone summer kitchen, a barn, a chicken house, and an icehouse. The property is heavily wooded with over fifty species of trees.

A visitor center, opened in 2005, houses a bookstore and a theater, where an orientation film is shown. Currently under restoration, the main house is the principal structure at the site. It is a work in progress as it is being restored to its 1875 appearance based on archaeological research and photographs taken by the Library of Congress in the 1940s for the Historic Building Survey. Guided tours are given of the first floor of the main structure, which is a two-story green frame house on a stone foundation with an attic, a cellar, and a two-story front porch. Recent additions have been removed, and the foundation and chimney have been repaired. A summer kitchen that had been removed at the back of the house has been rebuilt. The house is basically unfurnished because many Grant family possessions were lost in a fire.

The icehouse was used to store food in the warm summer months. The chicken house has a hayloft that provided insulation for the chickens in the winter. In an 1868 letter Grant directed his overseer to construct the barn. Exhibits focus on the life, military career, and presidency of Ulysses S. Grant as well as the life of his wife, Julia Dent Grant.

Hardscrabble, the log cabin built by Ulysses Grant, is located at Grant's Farm, which is adjacent to the National Historic Site. Grant's Farm, currently owned by Anheuser-Busch, Inc., a brewing company, is on former White Haven land. It is now a 281-acre family recreational site and wildlife preserve.

Although the Grant family occupied the cabin for only a few months, the house is unique because it was constructed by a president of the United States.

Construction began in the fall of 1855 on an elevated site. The two-story log cabin had four rooms: two rooms and a hall on each floor. Grant dug the cellar, built the stone foundation, shingled the roof, built the interior stairs, and laid the floors.

After Edward and Justin Joy purchased the cabin in 1891, it was disassembled and rebuilt in nearby Webster Groves. In 1903 C. F. Blanke purchased the Grant cabin and displayed it at the 1904 St. Louis World's Fair. In 1907 Adolphus A. Busch purchased the cabin and moved it back to White Haven about one mile from its original site. In 1977 Anheuser-Busch Inc. restored the cabin. Generally it can be seen only from the exterior. Grant's Farm is located at 10501 Gravois Road, St. Louis, MO; the phone number is 314–843–1700.

. . . . . . . . . . . . . . . . . . . . . . . . . . . . . . . . . . . . . . . . . . . . . . . . . . . . . . . . . . . . . . . . . . . . . . . . . . .

## Ulysses S. Grant Home State Historic Site
### Galena, Illinois

ADDRESS: 505 Bouthillier Street, P.O. Box 333, Galena IL 61036
TELEPHONE: 815-777-3310
WEB SITE: www.granthome.com
LOCATION: In northwest Illinois, near the Iowa border, 16 miles southeast of Dubuque, Iowa, 162 miles northwest of Chicago, on U.S. 20
OPEN: Wednesday–Sunday, 9:00 A.M. to 5:00 P.M., April–October; Wednesday–Sunday, 9:00 A.M. to 4:00 P.M., November–March; closed New Year's Day, Martin Luther King Jr. Day, Presidents' Day, Veterans Day, General Election Day, Thanksgiving, and Christmas Day
ADMISSION: Adults, $3.00; children, $1.00
FACILITIES: Restored home of President Ulysses S. Grant. National Register of Historic Places, National Historic Landmark

*Ulysses S. Grant came to Galena in 1860* to work in his family's business, a leather goods store founded by his father and operated by his brothers. After resigning from the army in 1854, Ulysses had struggled unsuccessfully to support his family by farming near St. Louis, Missouri. In dire financial straits, he turned to his father; Jesse Grant was a tanner who owned several leather stores. The Grant leather store in Galena was operated by Orvil and Simpson Grant, and Ulysses was their traveling salesman. His sales territory included southwest Wisconsin, southeast Minnesota, and northeast Iowa.

In his memoirs Grant said, "During the eleven months that I lived in Galena prior to the first call for volunteers, I had been strictly attentive to my business. . . . Upon the firing on Sumter President Lincoln issued his first call for troops. . . . As soon as the news of the call for volunteers reached Galena, posters were stuck up calling for a meeting of the citizens. . . . Although a comparative stranger I was called upon to preside. . . . The company was raised

Ulysses S. Grant Home State Historic Site, Galena, Illinois. Photograph courtesy of Galena / Jo Daviess County Convention and Visitors Bureau, Galena, Illinois

and the officers and non-commissioned officers elected before the meeting adjourned. . . . I never went into our leather store after that meeting."[1]

During the Civil War, Grant, who was a veteran of the Mexican War, became in 1864 general in chief of the Union armies. In 1865, after the Union triumph over the Confederates, Grant returned to Galena and was given a hero's welcome. Grateful citizens of Galena presented him with a furnished home purchased for twenty-five hundred dollars by Thomas B. Hughlett and other Republican supporters.

From 1865 to 1867 Grant divided his time between New York, Washington, and Galena. In 1867 he became secretary of war. After serving as president from 1869 to 1877 and then taking a world tour, Grant made occasional visits to his Galena home until 1881, when he moved to New York City. Grant died in Mount McGregor, New York, in 1885.

Galena, named after the Latin word for "lead sulfide," was a lead-mining town and river trading port that boomed in the 1820s, was the richest town in Illinois in the 1840s, and went bust in the 1860s. Steam transportation, which began on the Mississippi in 1816 and reached the upper Mississippi in 1823, facilitated shipping the ore, and Galena became a busy river port and trading center.

In 1845 Galena produced twenty-seven thousand tons of lead, 83 percent of the country's supply. After the surface veins were exhausted, the cost of mining lead made it unprofitable. Both the advent of the railroad in 1854 and the silting in of the Galena River contributed to the demise of river traffic. Farming replaced mining as the economic base.

Galena, a town built on hills along the Galena River, has steep streets lined with hundreds of architecturally diverse mansions constructed before 1900 in its historic district. Eighty-five percent of the town is listed in the National Register of Historic Places. The local architecture ranges from Greek revival, federal, Italianate, Queen Anne, and Second Empire mansions to Cape Cod cottages and New England–style churches. Because of periodic fires in the business district, by the 1850s commercial buildings were required to be built of brick. These have survived with little alteration.

Built in 1860, the Ulysses S. Grant Home is an Italianate bracketed style, red brick two-story building that was designed by William Dennison. It was Grant's official residence while he was president, and caretakers kept it prepared for visits by the chief executive. In 1904 Grant's children gave the Grant house to the city of Galena, which gave it to the state in 1931. Now owned by the Illinois Historic Preservation Agency, the Ulysses S. Grant Home is a State Historic Site.

Architectural features of the Grant Home include projecting eaves supported by brackets, a low-pitched roof, and balustraded balconies over covered porches. A small piazza at the left front corner of the house shelters the front entrance.

The house has been restored to its 1870s appearance. Most of the Victorian furnishings and artifacts in the home belonged to the Grant family. Many of the carpets and wallpapers are reproductions of the originals. There are front and rear interior staircases.

The parlor on the right of the entrance has a marble fireplace, a Brussels carpet, and several horsehair upholstered chairs. The dining room has a long table set with Grant family china, English white ironstone, and the silver that President and Mrs. Grant used in the White House. The furniture is oak, and the chairs have cane seats.

Mementos from Grant's military and presidential careers are found in Grant's library, along with comfortable chairs and a large collection of books in wood and glass bookcases. The kitchen is equipped with a wood-burning stove, a dry sink, a wooden work table, and a variety of kitchen utensils.

Upstairs there are five bedrooms—one for each of the four children and another for Ulysses and Julia. All of the bedrooms are wallpapered, carpeted, and simply furnished with oak beds, dressers, small tables, wardrobes, and rocking chairs.

. . . . . . . . . . . . . . . . . . . . . . . . . . . . . . . . . . . . . . . . . . . . . . . . . . . . . . . . . .

## General Grant National Memorial
## New York, New York

ADDRESS: Riverside Drive and 122nd Street, New York, NY 10027

TELEPHONE: 212-666-1640 or 212-666-1668

WEB SITE: www.nps.gov/gegr

LOCATION: Riverside Drive at West 122nd Street, on the upper West Side, Manhattan, in New York City

OPEN: Daily, 9:00 A.M. to 5:00 P.M.; closed New Year's Day, Thanksgiving, and Christmas Day

*Ulysses S. Grant, eighteenth president* of the United States and victorious Union general of the Civil War, died on July 23, 1885, at the age of sixty-three. A heavy cigar smoker, he succumbed to throat cancer. His death occurred at a summer home in Mount McGregor, New York, where he spent the last six weeks of his life finishing his memoirs.

As he contemplated his death, Grant's first wish was to be buried at his beloved West Point. He discarded this idea because Julia could not have been buried with him. His second choice was either Galena, Illinois, or New York City. His reason for choosing New York was "because the people of that city befriended me in my need."

After his death Grant's body lay in state for several days in both Albany and New York City. He was buried on Saturday, August 8, 1885, in Riverside Park, facing the Hudson River on the Upper West Side of Manhattan, New York City. This site was donated by a former mayor of New York City. Thousands of mourners turned out for the funeral procession.

The Grant Monument Association was founded to raise funds for a suitable tribute and burial place for the former president. Architects submitted designs, and the committee selected John Duncan's proposal for a granite and white marble tomb. Said to be the largest mausoleum in North America, it is situated on a 150-foot bluff overlooking the Hudson River.

Aspects of Grant's life are depicted in the allegorical reliefs on the vaulting and include Grant's birth, marriage, military life, political career, and death. Bronze busts of William T. Sherman, Philip H. Sheridan, George H. Thomas, James B. McPherson, and Edward O. C. Ord are displayed in the interior. Ceiling mosaics designed by Allyn Cox depict Lee and Grant at Appomattox Court House and the Battles of Vicksburg and Chattanooga.

On April 27, 1897, Grant's tomb was dedicated by President William McKinley. Julia Dent Grant, who died on December 14, 1902, is buried beside her husband. In 1958 the Grant Monument Association turned ownership of the tomb over to the National Park Service, which recently has refurbished the badly deteriorating monument.

# Rutherford Birchard Hayes

NINETEENTH PRESIDENT OF THE UNITED STATES
*March 4, 1877–March 3, 1881*

...............................................................................

Rutherford B. Hayes was among the Civil War generals from Ohio who were elected to the U.S. presidency. Although he was an advocate of African American voting rights, the compromise that made him president in 1876 had the effect of disenfranchising black voters in the South.

Rutherford B. Hayes, the youngest of the five children of Rutherford Hayes Jr. and Sophia Birchard Hayes, was born on October 4, 1822, in Delaware, Ohio. His was a posthumous birth, as his father had died on July 20, 1822, at age thirty-five. Only two Hayes children survived to adulthood—Fanny Arabella, born in 1820, and Rutherford. Both Sophia and her husband were born in Vermont: Rutherford Jr. in Brattleboro and Sophia in Wilmington. In 1817 Rutherford Jr. and Sophia, their children, and Sophia's sixteen-year-old orphaned brother, Sardis Birchard, moved to a 125-acre farm in Delaware, Ohio. After her husband's death, Sophia Hayes supported her family with income from her tenant farmer. In 1827 Sardis Birchard moved to Lower Sandusky, where he became a prominent merchant and banker. A lifelong bachelor, Sardis was the legal guardian and a surrogate father for Fanny and Rutherford.

In 1837 Sardis sent Rutherford to Isaac Webb's Maple Grove Academy, a college preparatory school in Middletown, Connecticut. Rutherford entered Kenyon Hall College in Gambier, Ohio, in the fall of 1838 and was the valedictorian of his graduation class in 1842. In 1843 Rutherford entered Harvard University's Law School, and he was awarded his LL.B. degree in 1845. He was admitted to the Ohio Bar that year and in Lower Sandusky formed a partnership with Ralph P. Buckland. Hayes opened a law office in Cincinnati in December 1849.

Rutherford Hayes met Lucy Ware Webb in 1847 in Delaware. She was the daughter of Dr. James Webb and Maria Cook Webb. In 1833, when Lucy was two years old, James Webb died. After her husband's death, Maria Cook Webb relied heavily on her father, an associate justice of the common pleas court and a member of the state legislature. When he converted to the Methodist religion, Isaac Cook became a strong proponent of abstinence, and his grandchildren, including Lucy, signed abstinence pledges. In 1847 sixteen-year-old Lucy entered Wesleyan Female College in Cincinnati. She graduated in June

1850 with a liberal arts degree. Lucy would become the first First Lady to have a college degree.

Rutherford Hayes and Lucy Webb were married on December 30, 1852. The first of their eight children, a son initially named Sardis Birchard but whose name was later changed to Birchard Austin, was born on November 4, 1853. A second son, named James Webb and later changed to Webb Cook, was born on March 20, 1856. Rutherford Platt was born on June 23, 1858; Joseph Thompson was born on December 21, 1861; George Crook was born on September 29, 1864; Fanny was born on September 2, 1867; Scott Russell was born on February 8, 1871; and Manning Force was born on August 1, 1873.

After the bombardment of Fort Sumter on April 12, 1861, Hayes volunteered for the Union army. He was commissioned as a major in the Twenty-third Ohio Volunteer Infantry in June 1861 and served the entire length of the Civil War, until May 1865. Wounded four times, Hayes earned a battlefield promotion to brigadier general and received the brevet rank of major general of the volunteers.

In March 1863 Hayes's regiment moved to Camp White in the Kanawha Valley of West Virginia. Lucy and the children joined Rutherford that June. Joseph, who was eighteen months old, became ill and died on June 24. In April 1866 Birch contracted scarlet fever, and the other children were soon infected with the disease. George, who was twenty months old, died on May 24, 1866.

In December 1858 Hayes was appointed to an unexpired term as Cincinnati's city solicitor, and he was elected to a two-year term in 1859. In October 1864 Hayes was elected as a Republican candidate to the U.S. House of Representatives, where he served for four years. A Radical Republican, he supported the congressional plan of Reconstruction, opposing President Andrew Johnson's policies.

In 1867 Hayes was the successful candidate of the Union Republican Party for governor of Ohio, and he won reelection in 1869. Instead of seeking a third term as governor, Hayes ran for Congress but was defeated. In 1875 the state Republican convention nominated Hayes for a third, though not consecutive, gubernatorial term, and he won. Upon his Uncle Sardis's death in January 1874, Hayes inherited Spiegel Grove, Sardis's home in Fremont.

When the Ohio Republican Convention met in late March 1876, it unanimously endorsed Rutherford Hayes as the state's presidential candidate. When the Republican National Convention convened in Cincinnati in June 1876, the field of presidential hopefuls included the front-runner James G. Blaine of Maine as well as Benjamin H. Bristow of Kentucky, Roscoe Conkling of New York, Oliver P. Morton of Indiana, John F. Hartranft of Pennsylvania, and Hayes of Ohio. On the seventh ballot Hayes became the Republican presidential nominee. William A. Wheeler of New York was nominated for vice president. Gov. Samuel J. Tilden of New York was the Democratic nominee for president with Thomas A. Hendricks of Indiana running for vice president. When the votes were counted on November 7, 1876, Tilden led in the popular vote with 4,288,456 to Hayes's 4,034,311. On election night Lucy and Rutherford believed that Tilden had won.

Tilden did not have the necessary majority of electoral votes because the electoral votes of three southern states still controlled by Republicans—South Carolina, Florida, and Louisiana—were contested. These three states cast two sets of electoral votes, and there was one disputed electoral vote in Oregon. Without these contested electoral votes, Tilden was ahead with 184 electors to Hayes's 165. To win a majority of the 349 electoral votes, Tilden needed only 1 while Hayes needed all of the disputed votes.

Congress passed the compromise Electoral Commission Bill, which established a bipartisan commission of five senators, five members of the House, and five Supreme Court justices to determine which candidate should receive the disputed electoral votes. Of the commission's fifteen members, seven were Republicans, seven were Democrats, and Justice David Davis was an Independent. During the process the Illinois legislature on January 25, 1877, elected Davis to the U.S. Senate. William T. Pelton, Tilden's nephew, had persuaded Illinois' Democrats to support Davis. In return, Davis was expected to vote for Tilden, but instead he resigned from the commission and was replaced by a Republican, Justice Joseph P. Bradley.

On March 2, 1877, the commission, voting along party lines, eight to seven, awarded all of the disputed electoral votes to Hayes. The House Democrats threatened a filibuster to delay the final counting of Electoral College votes. If the filibuster succeeded, the election would go to the House, where the Democrats controlled enough states to elect Tilden.

Republican leaders secretly negotiated with southern Democrats, who agreed to abandon the filibuster if federal troops were withdrawn, "home rule" was restored to the South, and Republicans would end Reconstruction. With the acceptance of the commission's report by the House, Hayes was declared president. Hayes immediately ordered the army not to interfere in a Democratic takeover of the state governments in South Carolina and Louisiana. The South would be firmly controlled by white conservative Democrats until the election of Eisenhower in 1952. White control of the South and indifference in the North led to the disenfranchisement of most black voters in the southern states until the civil rights movement and the enactment of the Voting Rights Act of 1965.

At President and Mrs. Hayes's first state dinner, held in honor of Grand Dukes Alexis and Constantine of Russia, wine was served. Shortly thereafter Hayes announced that alcohol would not be served again in the White House while he was president. While the temperance movement endorsed Hayes's stand, others ridiculed it.

The federal supply and backing of U.S. currency was a major issue that Hayes and his successors faced. The currency issue originated during the Civil War when the U.S. Treasury issued "greenbacks," paper money not directly backed by specie (gold or silver) to pay the costs of the war. The circulation of greenbacks caused inflation. Hayes favored a return to "hard money," currency backed by gold, and supported the 1875 Specie Resumption Act, which increased the U.S. Treasury's gold supply. Congress in 1878 passed the Bland-Allison Act over Hayes's veto, which required the U.S. Treasury to purchase $2 million to $4 million of silver each month and mint silver dollars. While the Treasury purchased the minimum $2 million of silver, it redeemed silver dollars in gold coin, and the country went on the gold standard as scheduled.[1]

Supporting civil service reform, in June1877 Hayes issued an executive order prohibiting political assessments and forbade the direct involvement of civil servants in managing political campaigns. Sen. Roscoe Conkling, the boss of New York, was incensed by Hayes's reforms and told his patronage appointees to ignore them. When Hayes tried to remove Conkling's ally Chester A. Arthur as collector of the Port of New York, Conkling blocked Hayes's efforts in the Senate. On July 11, 1878, with Congress not in session, Hayes replaced Arthur with Edwin A. Merritt, a reformer. The New York Custom House was removed from political patronage.[2]

Hayes, who did not seek a second term, on March 4, 1881, escorted James Garfield to his inauguration. The next day he and Mrs. Hayes departed for Spiegel Grove. Their train crashed into a train of empty cars near Baltimore. Two persons died in the accident, but Hayes and his wife were unhurt. On June 22, 1889, Lucy suffered a stroke. She died on June 25 at the age of fifty-seven.

Rutherford Hayes served on the Board of Trustees of Ohio State University and was president of the Ohio Archaeological and Historical Society. He died on January 17, 1893, at the age of seventy. After a funeral in his home on January 20, a large procession followed the hearse to Oakwood Cemetery, where Rutherford was laid beside Lucy. On April 3, 1915, the bodies of Rutherford and Lucy were reinterred at Spiegel Grove.

.............................................................................

**Rutherford B. Hayes Presidential Center**
**Spiegel Grove**
**Fremont, Ohio**

ADDRESS: Spiegel Grove, Fremont, OH 43420
TELEPHONE: 419-332-2081 or 800-998-7737
WEB SITE: www.rbhayes.org
LOCATION: In northern Ohio, southeast of Toledo, in Sandusky County, in Fremont; Spiegel Grove is at the intersection of Hayes Avenue and Buckland Avenue

OPEN: House and museum: Tuesday–Saturday, 9:00 A.M. to 5:00 P.M.; Sunday and holidays, noon to 5:00 P.M.; closed Thanksgiving, Christmas, and New Year's Day. Library: closed on Sunday and holidays

ADMISSION: Home or museum: adults, $7.50; seniors, $6.50; children 6–12, $3.00. Both home and museum: adults, $13.00; seniors, $12.00; children 6–12, $5.00

FACILITIES: Presidential home of Rutherford B. Hayes, research library, museum, and grave site on twenty-five acres; guided tours of home; gift shop; special events. The home is not handicapped accessible, but most of the museum is handicapped accessible.

*The Rutherford B. Hayes Presidential Center,* operated and managed by the Hayes Presidential Center, Inc., and funded by the state of Ohio and the Rutherford B. Hayes–Lucy Webb Hayes Foundation, is affiliated with the Ohio Historical Society. At the twenty-five-acre wooded site in the town of Fremont is the retirement home of the nineteenth president of the United States, the Hayes presidential library, a museum related to the life of President Hayes, and the burial site of President and Mrs. Hayes. The museum opened to the public in 1916. The house at Spiegel Grove opened in 1966; prior to that time it was still occupied by the Hayes family.

The property that President Hayes's uncle Sardis Birchard purchased in 1834 was virgin timberland. He named his property Spiegel Grove because of the reflecting pools of water after a rainfall; *spiegel* is the German word for "mirror." In August 1859 Birchard broke ground for a residence at Spiegel Grove, but due to the Civil War, the sixteen-room brick home was not completed until 1863.

Rutherford Hayes, Sardis's nephew and heir, and his family moved to Spiegel Grove in 1873. When Sardis died in 1874, Rutherford inherited the property. At that time Hayes no longer held a government office and was, seemingly, retired from politics. He poured his energy into real estate investments, settlement of his uncle's estate, and improvements to his new home. He cleared several acres to plant fruit and nut trees, evergreens, berries, and a vegetable garden.

In 1877 Hayes became the nineteenth president of the United States. While in Washington, the president continued to plan improvements for Spiegel Grove. His son Webb traveled back and forth between Ohio and Washington to supervise these changes. Water closets, heating, water and soil pipes, and an elevator were installed. Additions in 1880 and 1889 doubled the size of the original structure, which grew to a thirty-one-room house with eighteen bedrooms. The original gabled brick front was duplicated. A large parlor, a library, and upstairs bedrooms were still unfinished when President Hayes completed his presidential term and returned to Ohio in 1881.

President Hayes died at Spiegel Grove in 1893, and in 1910 Col. Webb C. Hayes, the president's son, deeded Spiegel Grove to the state of Ohio on the condition that the state would erect a building to be used as a museum and a library to hold the president's papers and personal library. Built in 1916, the Hayes Library was the first presidential library in the United States, though it is not a part of the National Archives and Records Administration's Presidential Libraries system.

At each of the six entrances to Spiegel Grove there are black iron gates that formerly stood at the entry to the White House grounds on West Executive Avenue. In 1928 Congress presented these gates to Ohio for the nineteenth president's home.

The Hayes family resided in the homestead until 1966, more than one hundred years after it was built. Everything in the house belonged to the Hayes family, which makes it a rare collection of original presidential family artifacts. Over time the house was modernized, and some rooms reflect a 1960s decor. The Hayes Center is currently restoring most first-floor rooms to the era of Lucy and Rutherford's occupation, 1880–93.

Knowledgeable docents lead guided tours of the stately mansion. The red brick house is four stories high with a central staircase ending in a lantern effect at the top to let hot air out and light in. Walls are three bricks thick for insulation, and there are fifteen fireplaces, ten chimneys, and wide porches. In 1996 a new slate roof was installed and the chimneys were rebuilt.

In the front hall are portraits of President Hayes's mother, Sophia Birchard Hayes, and her brother, Sardis Birchard. The red parlor, part of the original house, is decorated with furniture with red upholstery, and the windows have red draperies, reminiscent of the Red Room in the White House. Butternut paneling throughout the house as well as on the staircase gives a light, warm look.

The bed in the master bedroom, a gift from Lucy's parents, is where both Lucy and Rutherford died. The president's rosewood dressing table has secret drawers to hide valuables. The Hayeses lost three of their eight children in infancy, and a portrait of two of them, Joe and George, hangs in this room.

The large parlor, added by Hayes, was used as a family room. A life-sized portrait of President Hayes stands in one corner. The wallpaper, brass chandeliers, and draperies between the parlor and office are original. The president's library, another Hayes addition, is a high-ceiling room lined with bookshelves holding twelve hundred books. Hayes claimed to have read every book in his extensive personal library.

A 1779 clock that was a wedding gift from Hayes's mother, Sophie, is in the carriage entrance hallway. The large dining room was designed to Lucy's specifications, although it was unfinished when she died. Around the table are twenty-four chairs used by the Hayeses in the White House. Lucy ordered an original Haviland porcelain dinner service decorated with American flora and fauna designs by Theodore R. Davis.

In an upstairs hallway there is an 1858 Wheeler Wilson sewing machine, a gift to Lucy from her mother. This expensive item, which sewed only the chain stitch, cost $112. Lucy, who used it to make her children's clothing and her husband's shirts, took her sewing machine to military camps and to the White House.

Sardis's bedroom, one of the rooms in the original house, has a four-poster bed and an 1862 mail-order fireplace. Fanny's bedroom holds the black lacquer furniture that her father had specially made in Boston for her White House bedroom. A portrait of father and daughter hangs in the room. The Hayes family cradle is in another bedroom. Several bedrooms used by Hayes family members in the twentieth century are attractively decorated in a 1960s style. On the third floor are six additional bedrooms.

The museum houses a collection of more than ten thousand objects that belonged to the president, his administration, and his family. Exhibits tell Hayes's life story beginning with his ancestors in Vermont. There is a replica of the Hayes Tavern, operated by the president's grandfather, in Brattleboro, Vermont. Hayes's educational years in Ohio and at Harvard Law School and his legal career are the subjects of displays.

A diorama of the Civil War campaigns in which Hayes fought show that his regiment served primarily in Virginia and West Virginia. In the political exhibit are Hayes's desk from the House of Representatives, gubernatorial campaign items, and photographs of the presidential inauguration. In another room are dresses worn by the First Lady, some of which she had on when posing for portraits. The elegant black White House carriage is displayed. The architectural changes in the residence at Spiegel Grove are the subject of another exhibit.

The presidential library and archives contains materials related to President Hayes, local history, genealogy, and U.S. history from 1850 to 1917. There are more than one million manuscripts and nearly one hundred thousand books and pamphlets collected here. Special collections can be used by the public.

Rutherford and Lucy Hayes are buried at Spiegel Grove. Lucy died on June 25, 1889, and was buried in Fremont's Oakwood Cemetery. Rutherford died at Spiegel Grove on January 17, 1893, and was buried next to his wife at Oakwood Cemetery. The two were reinterred at Spiegel Grove in 1915. The burial site is south of the house.

# James Abram Garfield

TWENTIETH PRESIDENT OF THE UNITED STATES
*March 4–September 19, 1881*

. . . . . . . . . . . . . . . . . . . . . . . . . . . . . . . . . . . . . . . . . . . . . . . . . . . . . . . . . . . . . . . . . . . . . . . .

One of America's martyred presidents, James Abram Garfield held the office of president for only four months before he was shot by the assassin Charles Julius Guiteau on July 2, 1881, in Washington, D.C. The forty-nine-year-old president lingered between life and death for two and one-half months, finally succumbing on September 19. Garfield, an Ohio native, was the last in a line of seven presidents who were born in log cabins. He was a graduate of Williams College, a Civil War general, a lawyer, a member of the House of Representatives for seventeen years, and a leader of the Republican Party.

James Abram Garfield was born on November 19, 1831, in a log cabin in Orange Township, sixteen miles from Cleveland, in Ohio's Western Reserve. He was the youngest of Eliza Ballou Garfield and Abram Garfield's five children. In 1833 Eliza and Abram converted to a new evangelical denomination founded by Alexander Campbell. Campbellites, who called themselves disciples, wanted to reunite all Christians and believed in literal acceptance of the scriptures. In 1833 thirty-three-year-old Abram Garfield died of pneumonia. On March 4, 1850, James was baptized in the Chagrin River after joining the Disciples of Christ. James, known for his speaking ability and religious zeal, preached in area churches.

Eighteen-year-old James entered the Baptist-run Geauga Academy in Chester, Ohio, in spring 1849 and remained there for four terms. He taught at local schools during the winters to defray his college expenses. In fall 1851 James transferred to the Western Reserve Eclectic Institute in Hiram, established by the Disciples of Christ. He was admitted as a junior at Williams College in Williamstown, Massachusetts, in July 1854 and graduated in 1856. Garfield, who spoke German and French, could write Latin with one hand and Greek with the other simultaneously. Garfield taught ancient languages and literature at Western Reserve Eclectic Institute. In spring 1857 twenty-five-year-old Garfield was named chairman of the faculty and given responsibility for managing the school in addition to his teaching duties.

James Garfield fell in love with Lucretia Rudolph, who was the daughter of Zeb Rudolph, a Hiram disciple and a trustee of the Eclectic Institute. Garfield married Lucretia on November 11, 1858, and the couple had seven children. Their daughter Eliza, born on July 3, 1860, died when she was three years old. Harry was born on October 11, 1863; James Rudolph was born on October 17, 1865; Mary was born on January 16, 1867; Irvin McDowell was born on August 3, 1870; and Abram was born on November 21, 1872. Edward, born on December 25, 1874, lived less than two years.

In August 1859 James was nominated for the Ohio Senate by the Republicans, and he was elected for a two-year term. Retaining his position at the college, he traveled to Columbus for the legislative sessions. He was admitted to the Ohio Bar in 1860.

When the Civil War began, James accepted a commission as a lieutenant colonel in the Forty-second Ohio Infantry. He commanded the Eighteenth Brigade, which fought in the Battle of Middle Creek, Kentucky. Garfield, commissioned as a brigadier general, led the Twentieth Brigade of General Wood's division, which was ordered to Shiloh on the third day of the battle. In 1862 Garfield was elected as the Republican candidate for Congress from the Nineteenth District in northern Ohio. On January 14, 1863, Garfield was appointed as chief of staff to Gen. William S. Rosecrans, commander of the fifty-thousand-man Army of the Cumberland at Murfreesboro, Tennessee.

Garfield debated whether to continue in the military or take his seat in the Thirty-eighth Congress. President Lincoln convinced him that his recent military experience was valuable to Congress. Garfield served in the U.S. House of Representatives for seventeen years. He was consistently antislavery and publicly stated, "Let us not commit ourselves to the senseless and absurd dogma that the color of the skin shall be the basis of suffrage."[1]

In 1879 Garfield was nominated for the U.S. Senate by the Republican caucus. Since the presidential race was up for grabs, Garfield was urged to become a candidate. The Republican National Convention that met in June 1880 nominated Garfield on the thirty-sixth ballot. Chester A. Arthur was nominated for vice president. The Democratic candidates were Gen. Winfield Scott Hancock for president and William English for vice president. Garfield received 4,454,415 popular votes to Hancock's 4,444,952, a plurality of slightly more than 9,000 popular votes. In electoral votes Garfield won 214 to Hancock's 155.

On March 4, 1881, James Garfield rode to the Capitol, where Chief Justice Morrison Remick Waite administered the oath of office. Eliza Garfield was the first woman to witness her son's inauguration as president of the United States.

Lucretia Garfield became very ill with malaria in May 1881. As the fever raged for twelve days, her survival was in doubt. Lucretia recovered but remained weak. President Garfield took his family to the seashore at Elberon, New Jersey, in mid-June, hoping that the sea air would speed Lucretia's convalescence. The president returned to Washington on June 27.

To celebrate the Fourth of July, President Garfield planned to pick up Lucretia at Elberon and then proceed to Massachusetts for Williams College's commencement. He was also enrolling his sons Harry and James at Williams, his alma mater. The train was to leave the Baltimore and Potomac depot at 9:30 A.M. on July 2, 1881. For the previous three weeks Charles Julius Guiteau, a disappointed office seeker with delusions of grandeur, had been stalking Garfield. As the president walked to the train, Guiteau ran up behind him and fired two pistol shots, wounding Garfield.

A Washington, D.C., policeman, Patrick Kearny, arrested Guiteau, who had a .44 caliber British Bulldog pistol in his pocket. In the railroad station police discovered Guiteau's autobiography written for press distribution and a letter to the White House, dated June 2, which stated, "The President's death was a sad necessity but it will unite the Republican Party and save the Republic."

Garfield had been shot twice at point-blank range. One bullet had entered his lower right back, and the other bullet had grazed his right arm. Garfield was moved to the second floor of the station, where cabinet members, including Robert Todd Lincoln, son of the assassinated President Abraham Lincoln, gathered around him. President Garfield was then taken by wagon to the White House.

Although initially he was not expected to live, the president rallied three days later. No attempts were made to remove the bullet surgically. Alexander Graham Bell, inventor of the telephone, devised an induction balance electronic apparatus to locate the bullet, which he tried on the president on August 1; he was unsuccessful.

The president's weight dropped from 210 pounds to 135. He longed to be moved to the seashore. Charles G. Franklyn offered his house on the beach at Elberon, and a spur track to that house was built. On September 6 the president was taken to the Washington railroad station and was placed in a specially made bed in a railroad car for the eight-hour trip. The president died at 10:35 P.M. on September 19, 1881, eighty days after he was shot.

Vice President Chester A. Arthur took the oath of office as the twenty-first president of the United States at his New York home on September 20. On September 21 the president's body was returned to Washington, where it lay in state in the Capitol Rotunda for two days and was viewed by more than one hundred thousand people. A funeral service was held in the Rotunda on September 23, after which the body was transported by train to Cleveland, Ohio. A funeral was held in Cleveland, and President Garfield was buried in Lakeview Cemetery.

Many people believed that Guiteau was insane. Of French Huguenot ancestry, Guiteau was born on September 8, 1841, in Freeport, Illinois. His mother died when he was seven years old. His father, Luther Guiteau, a school superintendent and banker in Freeport, remarried when his son was twelve, and Charles was sent to live with his sister and brother-in-law, Frances and George Scoville. In June 1860 he joined the perfectionists' intentional commune at Oneida, New York.

John Humphrey Noyes, founder and leader of the perfectionists, had countercultural ideas regarding Christianity, sexuality, and marriage. His group of several hundred followers flourished from 1840 to the late 1880s. Within a context of Christianity, Noyes and his followers abandoned conventional marriage for complex marriage in which each man was a husband to all wives and each woman a wife to all husbands. The Oneidans' sexual practices and beliefs antagonized many of their neighbors. Guiteau left Oneida in April 1865 but returned demanding nine thousand dollars from the commune. When Noyes refused his request, Guiteau sued. After Noyes wrote to Luther Guiteau threatening to bring extortion charges against his son, Charles Guiteau withdrew the lawsuit.

In Chicago in 1869 twenty-eight-year-old Guiteau married sixteen-year-old Annie Bunn. He was admitted to the Chicago Bar after answering a few questions and was a collector of delinquent bills. His wife divorced him in 1873. Between 1878 and 1880 he spent time in jail because of unpaid debts.

Guiteau was a Republican Stalwart who supported Ulysses S. Grant for the presidential nomination in 1880. After Garfield was nominated, Guiteau adapted a speech, which he had written for Grant, for Garfield. Although the speech was never delivered, Guiteau credited Garfield's victory to his speech. On March 8 Guiteau asked Garfield to appoint him as ambassador to France. Daily he barraged Garfield, Blaine, and the White House staff with letters and copies of his speech. Eventually he was banished from the White House. On June 6 Guiteau purchased a British Bulldog revolver and a box of cartridges. He selected a fancy white bone-handled revolver, thinking it would be impressive in a future museum exhibit on the assassination.

Guiteau was represented at the murder trial by his brother-in-law, George Scoville, who entered a plea of insanity. Guiteau claimed that he was not guilty because the president had died of medical malpractice and that since Garfield did not die immediately, he was not fatally shot. Unfortunately that may be true as the president's doctors repeatedly probed his wound with their unwashed fingers and unsterilized instruments. The trial ended on January 5, 1882, and the jury returned with a guilty verdict. Guiteau was hanged on June 30, 1882.

Lucretia Garfield lived thirty-seven years after her husband's death, spending most of that time at the family farm in Mentor. She collected and arranged her husband's papers and then donated them to the Library of Congress. Lucretia was almost eighty-six years old when she died in Pasadena, California, on March 13, 1918.

## James A. Garfield National Historic Site
## Mentor, Ohio

ADDRESS: 8095 Mentor Avenue, Mentor, OH 44060

TELEPHONE: 440-255-8722

WEB SITE: www.nps.gov/jaga

LOCATION: Twenty-five miles east of Cleveland, near Lake Erie; accessible from I-90, SR 306 Mentor-Kirtland exit

OPEN: Monday–Saturday, 10:00 A.M. to 5:00 P.M., and Sunday, noon to 5:00 P.M., May–October; Saturday, 10:00 A.M. to 5:00 P.M., and Sunday, noon to 5:00 P.M., November–April; closed New Year's Day, Memorial Day, Labor Day, Thanksgiving, Christmas Eve, and Christmas Day

ADMISSION: Adults, $5.00

FACILITIES: Lawnfield, the home of President James A. Garfield; visitor center with film, exhibits, and museum shop; guided tours of house. The visitor center and the first floor and memorial library in the Garfield house are wheelchair accessible.

*The James A. Garfield National Historic Site* consists of approximately 8 acres of James A. Garfield's original 157-acre working farm. In addition to the main house, there is a visitor center in the 1893 carriage house, a small 1880 campaign office, a reconstructed pump house / windmill, and some farm buildings, including a granary, an 1877 horse barn, a tenant house, a gasholder, and a chicken coop. The site is owned by the National Park Service and operated by the Western Reserve Historical Society, which owns the contents of the house.

Garfield bought the 118-acre Dickey farm in 1876 and later purchased an adjoining 40 acres, which he referred to as his Mentor Farm. The original farmhouse, built in 1832, was a two-room structure. It was expanded to nine rooms in the 1850s. In 1880 Garfield added eleven rooms that enveloped the original structure. After Garfield's death, his wife, Lucretia, added a wing to the house.

When Garfield was running for president, a railroad spur was extended to Garfield's home. Over seventeen thousand people took the campaign trains to Mentor Farm. Because Garfield usually spoke to visitors from his large front porch, he was said to be conducting a front porch campaign. Reporters dubbed Garfield's home "Lawnfield" because of the spacious lawns surrounding it.

After President Garfield's death in September 1881, a national fund for the Garfield family collected $350,000 in donations, which Mrs. Garfield used to add a wing to the house in 1886. The stone-faced wing transposed the farmhouse into a mansion.

Lucretia Garfield sold half of the farm acreage in 1908. The Garfield family owned the property until 1936, when they donated eight acres to the Western

Garfield National Historic
Site, Mentor, Ohio

Reserve Historical Society. Congress authorized the property as a National Historic Site in late 1980.

Restoration of the Garfield house began in 1997 and was completed in mid-1998. On our earlier visits we saw a big, dilapidated white house with black trim. On subsequent visits we hardly recognized the pristine gray mansion with red and dark gray trim, which has been restored to the period 1880 to 1886. Garfield's youngest son, Abram, an architect, worked on the restoration. The beautiful interior of the Garfield house has wallpaper reproduced from remnants found there. Eighty percent of the artifacts in the house are Garfield family possessions. The original woodwork and brass light fixtures have been preserved. There are two staircases, and the large house is somewhat of a maze.

The spacious entry hall has an 1810–20 tall case clock that belonged to Zebulon Rudolph, Lucretia Garfield's father. The summer bedroom, used by President and Mrs. Garfield, has the secretary desk that Garfield used when he was president of the Western Reserve Eclectic Institute. The parlor, used for entertaining guests, is furnished in the Victorian manner with velvet upholstered chairs and sofa. The dining room has a fireplace surrounded with tiles hand-painted by Lucretia and the children. Haviland china used in the White House is displayed in built-in china cabinets. Stained-glass windows were added in 1886. Eliza Garfield, the president's mother, lived with the family. Her bedroom and an adjoining sitting room are filled with pictures of her son.

Near the 1886 wing, a kitchen was remodeled into a spacious reception hall with a fireplace, oak wainscoting, and a staircase leading to the stunning Garfield memorial library. Lucretia built the library to hold the president's collection of books and papers. Although located in a family residence, President Garfield's library served as the precedent for presidential libraries, though it was not open to the public. Garfield's papers are now in the Library of Congress.

Red walls, rugs, and upholstery decorate this large, irregularly shaped arts-and-crafts-style library. It is paneled in white oak with a high wooden beamed ceiling, a fireplace, brass light fixtures, oriental rugs, window seats, and built-in bookshelves. Furnishings include Garfield's congressional desk purchased by him when new desks were installed and another desk made for Garfield with one hundred drawers and cubbyholes. A large walk-in vault contains copies of many Garfield speeches and funeral mementos, including a funeral wreath from Queen Victoria. In 1888 two of the Garfield children, Mary (Mollie) and Harry, were joined to their spouses in a double wedding ceremony in the library.

Garfield enjoyed reading in his small study sitting in a chair that was designed so that he could drape his legs over one arm while he read. He also used his study for meetings. A new kitchen, pantry and servants' quarters built below the library are used for exhibits on agriculture and the restoration of Lawnfield.

On the upper floor are bedrooms, one of which was occupied by Zebulon Rudolph, Lucretia's father, who lived with the family and managed the farm for eighteen years. Irvin and Abram shared a bedroom, and their collection of shells, maps, and drawing instruments are displayed. Mollie's bedroom has a pink floor and ebonized furniture. Lucretia's blue bedroom, used after her husband's death, has paintings of the two Garfield children who died young—Eliza and Edward. Four bedrooms on the third floor are not open for touring. The Garfields had a cook, a governess, and a couple of maids.

The visitor center is in the carriage house, built in 1893 by Lucretia Garfield. An introductory video gives an overview of the life of Garfield. Exhibits focus on Garfield's life.

The small frame campaign office, formerly a tenant house, was used during the 1880 presidential campaign by reporters and campaign staff and had a telegraph that linked Garfield to the outside world.

The windmill, built by Lucretia Garfield in 1894 and taken down in the 1930s after extensive wind damage, was reconstructed in 1998. The stone foundation and original stone pump house have been restored, and the sixty-foot white wooden tower and windmill were replaced. The original windmill was constructed at a cost of over two thousand dollars. Until 1939 water flowed into faucets in the kitchen, bathroom, and laundry room from a three-hundred-gallon galvanized holding tank on the third floor of the house. The 1885 gasholder building held the natural gas that was piped into the house for lamps and fireplaces.

. . . . . . . . . . . . . . . . . . . . . . . . . . . . . . . . . . . . . . . . . . . . . . . . . . . . . . . . . . . . . . . . .

## James A. Garfield Monument
## Lake View Cemetery
## Cleveland, Ohio

ADDRESS: Lake View Cemetery, 12316 Euclid Avenue, Cleveland, OH 44106
TELEPHONE: 216-421-2665

LOCATION: Cleveland is in northeast Ohio on Lake Erie; Lake View Cemetery
is about six miles east of downtown Cleveland
OPEN: Daily, 7:30 A.M. to 5:30 P.M.
ADMISSION: Free
FACILITIES: Burial site of President James A. Garfield

148

*When President James A. Garfield died* on September 19, 1881, eighty days after being shot by the assassin Charles J. Guiteau, the nation went into deep mourning. For more than two months citizens had hung on the daily medical reports issued by the president's doctors and prayed for his recovery. Now all that was left was to pay their respects. The White House was draped in black bunting. In the Rotunda of the Capitol one hundred thousand people filed by Garfield's casket, which lay in state for two days. Countless people lined the railroad tracks as Garfield's body was taken by train from Washington to Cleveland. After a huge ceremony in downtown Cleveland, Garfield's body was taken to Lake View Cemetery and placed in a burial vault.

American citizens wanted a fitting memorial for their slain chief executive. The Garfield National Monument Association raised $135,000 during the next two years. George H. Keller of Connecticut was the architect commissioned to design the project. Garfield's Victorian-era monument is the most elaborate burial site of any American president, filled with marble sculpture, bas-relief panels, granite columns, gold and stone mosaics, stained-glass windows, a balcony, and a domed ceiling. It is a remarkable work of art as well as a memorial. Costing $225,000, it was formally dedicated on May 30, 1890, in a ceremony attended by President Benjamin Harrison, former president Rutherford B. Hayes, and future president William McKinley.

Located on a hill in Lake View Cemetery, the massive monument consists of a 180-foot high circular tower built of native Ohio sandstone, which stands on a broad stone terrace with a square stone porch at the base of the tower. Five bas-relief panels with life-size figures depicting Garfield as a teacher, soldier, statesman, and president decorate the exterior of the porch. The last one shows the president's body lying in state in the Capitol Rotunda.

The interior of the tower, which was designed by the Tiffany Company, is dominated by a Carrara marble statue by Alexander Doyle of Representative Garfield standing in front of his congressional chair as he addresses the House of Representatives. Red polished granite columns support the interior dome, which is decorated with Venetian gold and stone mosaic winged figures symbolizing North, South, East, and West encircled by wreaths from every state and territory. Below that is an allegorical mourning procession in stone mosaic panels. Stained-glass windows represent the thirteen original states and Ohio.

James and Lucretia Garfield's bronze caskets are in the crypt below Memorial Hall. President Garfield's casket is draped in the American flag.

# Chester Alan Arthur

TWENTY-FIRST PRESIDENT OF THE UNITED STATES
*September 20, 1881–March 3, 1885*

......................................................................

Chester Arthur succeeded to the presidency after President James Garfield's death at the hand of an assassin. A Stalwart Republican machine politician, Arthur served as collector of the New York Custom House, a rich source of patronage. He was removed from that office by President Hayes because of allegations of corruption. Arthur is often referred to as a "spoilsman," one who serves his party for a share of the spoils—financial benefits and political power. As president, Chester Arthur redeemed himself by handling his position responsibly and with dignity at a time of sorrow over a slain president.

Chester Arthur was born on October 5, 1829, in Fairfield, Vermont. He was the fifth child and first son of the nine children of William Arthur and Malvina Stone Arthur. William Arthur was born in Ballymena, County Antrim, Ulster, Ireland, in December 1796. He was ordained as a Baptist minister in 1827. Malvina Stone was born on the family's Berkshire, Vermont, farm not far from the Canadian border.

Pastor Arthur moved his family frequently, so that Chester's earliest years were spent in the Vermont towns of North Fairfield, Williston, and Hinesburg. When he was about six years old, the family moved to New York, where they lived in the communities of Perry, York, Union Village, Schenectady, Lansingburgh, and Hoosick.

Chester entered Union College, Schenectady, New York, at the age of sixteen as a sophomore in the classical curriculum, as he had been well prepared by his father, who was proficient in Greek, Latin, and Hebrew. He graduated in 1848 and then attended law school at Ballston Spa. He continued to study law while teaching at North Pownal, Vermont. In November 1852 Chester Arthur became principal of an academy in Cohoes, New York.

Arthur was admitted to the bar in May 1854 and became a partner in a New York City law firm. After that firm was dissolved in 1856, Arthur and Henry D. Gardiner formed a law partnership. Chester Arthur, an abolitionist, was the attorney in an African American rights case. Because a black woman, Elizabeth Jennings, refused to leave a Third Avenue Railroad Company car reserved for whites, she was assaulted by the conductor. Arthur won the case, which resulted in the subsequent racial integration of all New York City railroad cars.

In 1856 Chester met nineteen-year-old Ellen "Nell" Lewis Herndon. The two were married on October 25, 1859, in New York City's Calvary Episcopal Church. A son, William Lewis Herndon, born on December 10, 1860, died on July 7, 1863. Chester Alan Jr. was born on July 25, 1864, and a daughter, Ellen Herndon, was born on November 21, 1871.

Arthur joined the state militia as a judge advocate of the Second Brigade. He was part of an unpaid social corps that attended Gov. Edwin D. Morgan on state occasions and was a member of Governor Morgan's general staff. The day after the attack on Fort Sumter, General Morgan's staff was called to active duty. Arthur was assigned to the quartermaster general's office in New York City and on July 10, 1862, was commissioned as a quartermaster general. When a Democratic governor took office on January 1, 1863, Arthur lost his commission.

When Governor Morgan was elected to the U.S. Senate in early 1863, Arthur became more involved in New York Republican politics. He was a friend of Thomas Murphy, a conservative Republican leader, and a member of Sen. Roscoe Conkling's Republican circle. In 1869, thanks to Murphy, Arthur became counsel to the New York City tax commission, a post created especially for him. Thomas Murphy was appointed as collector of the Port of New York in 1870. A congressional investigation of the New York Custom House resulted in Murphy's removal, but incredibly he was given the right to name his successor; he selected Chester Arthur.

The New York Custom House in December 1871 was the nation's largest federal office with a staff of over one thousand and millions of dollars of custom receipts. At a salary of more than fifty thousand dollars a year, it was the highest paid job in the federal government. The president's salary was fifty thousand dollars, and the vice president, cabinet members, and Supreme Court justices earned ten thousand dollars annually.[1] Financial success enabled the Arthurs to buy a brownstone dwelling, hire servants, and lead the good life.

President Hayes promised civil service reform. The New York Custom House was targeted for investigation by the Jay Commission. The committee's report recommended a 20 percent reduction of staff and revealed overstaffing, inefficiency, corruption, partisan politics, and party assessments of as much as 4 percent of salaries.

In June 1877 President Hayes issued an order that forbade party assessments and prohibited federal officeholders from participating in political caucuses, conventions, or election campaigns.[2] He asked for the resignations of top New York Custom House officials, including Chester Arthur, who refused. When President Hayes submitted names of replacements for Arthur and his associates to Congress, Senator Conkling blocked congressional approval. In mid-1878 another Custom House investigation was conducted by the Meredith

Committee, and its report documented fraud and built a case against Arthur and Alonzo Cornell. On July 11 President Hayes suspended Arthur and Cornell and appointed Edwin A. Merritt and Silas W. Burt, who received congressional confirmation in early February 1879.

In the 1880 election, James A. Garfield became the Republican presidential candidate at the Chicago convention in June 1880 and Arthur won the vice-presidential slot. Vice president Arthur took his oath of office on March 4. Prior to the election, Arthur's forty-two-year-old wife, Nell, contracted pneumonia and died on January 12, 1880, after a two-day illness.

On July 2 President Garfield was shot by Charles Guiteau in Washington, D.C. First reports said that the president was dead, and that is probably what Vice President Arthur was told initially. He went to Washington in the morning of July 3 and offered his sympathy to Mrs. Garfield. By July 13 the doctors were far more optimistic, and Arthur returned to New York City. Arthur did not assume any presidential duties during the eighty days that Garfield lay dying.

On September 19, 1881, at 11:30 P.M., Arthur was notified that President Garfield was dead. The presidential oath was administered by Justice John R. Brady in Arthur's home at 123 Lexington Avenue, New York. Arthur's son, Alan, witnessed it. Arthur repeated his oath of office on September 22 in the vice president's room of the Capitol in front of a group of legislators, judges, and cabinet members. He was the third president to serve in 1881 after Hayes and Garfield. Arthur had no vice president.

Political enemies accused Chester Arthur of not being an American citizen, a necessary qualification for the presidency. His father was from Ireland and his mother from Vermont, and as newlyweds the couple lived in Quebec before moving to northern Vermont. Arthur P. Himan, author of a book titled *How a British Subject Became President of the United States,* alleged that Chester Arthur had been born in Canada to a British father and an American mother and was therefore a British subject.

President Arthur found the White House in need of redecoration. For several months he lived at the home of Senator John P. Jones while extensive repairs and redecorating took place at the Executive Mansion. Twenty-four wagonloads of historic furniture were sold at auction. Louis C. Tiffany, the decorator hired by Arthur, redid the White House in the Victorian style using the finest furniture, fabrics, and wallpaper available. After Arthur moved into the White House on December 7, 1881, he entertained on a grand scale, hosting state dinners and musical entertainments.

The most ironic consequence of President Arthur's administration was reform of civil services. The Pendleton Act, signed by Arthur on January 16, 1883, created a Civil Service Commission of three members, which was to appoint a corps of examiners and provide for competitive examinations for prospective federal employees.[3]

Arthur did not receive the Republican nomination for president in 1884 as he had alienated his traditional base of support—the Stalwarts—with his support of civil service reform. The nomination went to James G. Blaine, who lost to the Democrat, Grover Cleveland.

Arthur returned to his New York City home and resumed practicing law. He suffered from a kidney ailment called Bright's disease, which gradually worsened until he became bedridden. During his final months he burned many of his presidential and private papers. Arthur said, "I may be President of the United States, but my private life is nobody's damned business."

Arthur had a stroke on November 17 and died on November 18, 1886. He was fifty-seven years old. His funeral was held at the Church of the Heavenly Rest in New York, and he was buried next to his wife in the Arthur family plot in Rural Cemetery, Albany, New York. Arthur had only one grandchild, who died childless, so he has no direct descendants today.

........................................................................

### President Chester A. Arthur State Historic Site
### Fairfield, Vermont

ADDRESS: Route 36, Fairfield, VT 05455
TELEPHONE: 802-828-3051
WEB SITE: www.historicvermont.org
LOCATION: Fairfield is the northwest corner of Vermont, near the Canadian border, off Route 36 or 108
OPEN: Saturday–Sunday, 11:00 A.M. to 5:00 P.M., July 4 through mid-October
ADMISSION: Free; donations appreciated
FACILITIES: Reconstructed childhood home of President Chester Alan Arthur. National Register of Historic Places

*Chester Alan Arthur, the son of William Arthur* and Malvina Stone Arthur, was born on October 5, 1829, in Fairfield, Vermont. William Arthur, a Baptist minister, was the pastor of a Fairfield congregation, and at the time of Chester's birth, the family lived in a cabin while a parsonage was being built. A short time later they moved into the parsonage.

Fairfield, a small farming town of under two thousand people, was founded in 1763. Located near the Canadian border, Fairfield is in a beautiful setting with mountain views. In 1950 the state of Vermont purchased the land around a 1903 granite monument that was said to be the site of President Arthur's birth. In 1953 the state reconstructed the parsonage on its original site. It had been torn down, and an old photograph guided the restoration. The small yellow frame house is used for exhibits on the life and career of President Arthur.

152

CHESTER ALAN ARTHUR

Northwest of the Arthur house is the North Fairfield Baptist Church, which in 1840 replaced the earlier church where Rev. William Arthur was pastor. The church building, now referred to as the Old Brick Church, was donated to the state in 1970 and can be toured. It is no longer used for church services but is used for weddings and memorial services. It has never been electrified.

# Grover Cleveland

TWENTY-SECOND PRESIDENT OF THE UNITED STATES
*March 4, 1885–March 3, 1889*

TWENTY-FOURTH PRESIDENT OF THE UNITED STATES
*March 4, 1893–March 3, 1897*

Stephen Grover Cleveland has the distinction of being the only president to serve two noncontiguous terms. He ran for the presidency three times, won twice, and lost once. Cleveland was the first Democrat elected after the Civil War. While president of the United States he married for the first time at age forty-nine.

Stephen Grover Cleveland, born on March 18, 1837, in Caldwell, New Jersey, was the fifth of the nine children of Richard Falley Cleveland and Anne Neal Cleveland. Richard Cleveland was an ordained Congregational minister, a Yale graduate, and the pastor of the First Presbyterian Church in Caldwell.

When Stephen was four, his father accepted a position at the Presbyterian Church in Fayetteville, New York, where the family resided for the next ten years. In 1850 Richard joined the Central New York Agency of the American Home Missionary Society in Clinton, New York. In 1853 he moved his family to Holland Patent, New York, to serve as pastor of its Presbyterian church. On October 1, 1853, forty-nine-year-old Richard Cleveland died; Stephen was sixteen years old.

Stephen's brother William Cleveland had graduated from Hamilton College and worked in the literary department of the New York Institution for the Blind in New York City. Stephen became an assistant teacher at the same institution. When he was about nineteen, he began signing his name S. Grover Cleveland. He dropped the initial a few years later and was thereafter known by his middle name, Grover.

In 1855 Grover Cleveland went to the Buffalo, New York, home of his uncle Lewis F. Allen, a stock breeder. Grover helped his uncle edit the *American Shorthorn Handbook*. Allen arranged to have his nephew study law, and in May 1859 Grover was admitted to the New York Bar. Grover was a Democrat, and his first elected office was that of ward supervisor in November 1862. A short time later he was appointed as assistant district attorney.

Grover Cleveland did not fight in the Civil War, although his brothers Lewis and Richard enlisted in 1861. Grover was left to help his widowed mother and two youngest sisters financially. According to the Conscription Act of March 3, 1863, men who were drafted were permitted to furnish a substitute or pay a commutation of $300. When Grover was drafted in July 1863, he paid George Bennisky, a thirty-two-year-old Polish immigrant, $150 to be his substitute. Bennisky survived the war.

In 1869 Cleveland formed a legal partnership with Albert P. Laning and Oscar Folsom, and in 1870 he was elected sheriff of Erie County. When his term as sheriff ended in 1873, Cleveland practiced law in Buffalo with a variety of partners. Their law offices were in the Weed Block building at the corner of Main and Swan, and Cleveland had a small apartment in a rear addition to the building. As he grew older, Grover gained weight. His nieces and nephews called him "Uncle Jumbo."

Grover Cleveland enjoyed good times with his friends in local beer halls and was an avid fisherman and hunter. He was a bachelor and one of the founders of the City Club, where he dined regularly, and the Beaver Island Club, a sports club on the Niagara River. Among his closest friends were his law partners Oscar Folsom and Wilson Bissell. When Oscar Folsom died in a buggy accident, Cleveland was appointed administrator of his estate and took on responsibility for Folsom's widow and young daughter, Frances, who would later marry Grover Cleveland.

Cleveland was elected mayor of Buffalo in 1881 and then governor of New York. At the Democratic National Convention in July 1884, he was nominated for president on the second ballot. Thomas Andrews Hendricks of Indiana was the vice-presidential candidate. The Republicans nominated Sen. James G. Blaine of Maine.

The 1884 presidential campaign was notable for its vicious attacks on the characters of the nominees. The Mulligan letters, which tied Blaine, when Speaker of the House, to a land-grant railroad scandal that had earlier curtailed his political career, were resurrected. In retaliation irate Republicans revealed a sexual relationship that Cleveland had had with a woman who had given birth to a son who subsequently was placed in an orphanage. When asked by party leaders what they should say after the scandal became public, Cleveland told them to tell the truth.

He fully disclosed his story. Cleveland and several other men in his circle had become sexually involved with Maria Halpin, an attractive young widow from Jersey City. Maria gave birth to a son on September 14, 1874, named him Oscar Folsom Cleveland, and indicated that Grover Cleveland was her child's father. Paternity was never established. Cleveland decided to admit paternity and provide for the boy. Unfortunately Maria drank heavily and neglected her child. Cleveland's friend Roswell L. Burrows, a former county judge, temporarily placed Maria in a mental institution while Cleveland took legal steps to place the boy in the Protestant Orphan Asylum in March 1876. He paid the asylum five dollars a week for the child's board. Maria hired a lawyer in an unsuccessful effort to regain custody of her son. She kidnapped him in late April, but he was found and returned to the orphanage. He was adopted by a family from western New York and became a doctor in adulthood.[1]

During the campaign a nasty story began circulating about Blaine's marriage. Documentation on the subject was offered for sale to Cleveland, who after determining that the packet of papers was complete, bought them. He then burned them. "The other side," he remarked, "can have a monopoly of all the dirt in this campaign."[2]

Cleveland defeated Blaine and was inaugurated on March 4, 1885. The president, who weighed three hundred pounds, proved to be an honest, hardworking chief executive. Committed to Jeffersonian principles of limited government, he sought to reduce the activities of the federal government, which had expanded since the Civil War. He was a reformer who applied efficient business practices to government.

Grover Cleveland was the only president to have a White House wedding. On June 2, 1886, he married Frances Folsom, his ward for over a decade. The bride was twenty-one, and the groom was forty-nine.

At their convention held in June 1888 the Democrats renominated the incumbent president. The Republicans nominated Benjamin Harrison, a senator from Indiana and the grandson of President William Henry Harrison. In a close election Cleveland won more than 90,000 popular votes than Harrison; he received 5,537,857 popular votes to Harrison's 5,447,129. In the Electoral College, Cleveland, with 168 electoral votes, lost to Harrison with 233.[3]

President Cleveland and his wife moved to New York City. A daughter, Ruth, was born on October 3, 1891. A candy bar, Baby Ruth, was named for her. After a four-year respite, Cleveland was nominated on the first ballot at the Democratic convention in June 1892. Adlai Ewing Stevenson III was the vice-presidential nominee. The Republicans renominated President Harrison. Grover Cleveland won 5,555,426 popular votes and 277 electoral votes to Benjamin Harrison's 5,182,690 popular and 145 electoral votes. Frances Cleveland, who had told the White House servants to take good care of the house as they would be returning in four years, had been right.

President Cleveland developed cancer of the mouth. Surgery to remove his upper left jaw from the first bicuspid tooth to just beyond the last molar and a part of the palate was secretly performed on July 1, 1893, aboard the yacht *Oneida* on Long Island Sound. In a second operation on July 17, the president was fitted with an artificial jaw of vulcanized rubber.

On September 9, 1893, the First Lady gave birth to a second daughter, Esther, who was the first child of a president to be born in the White House. A third daughter, Marion, was born on July 7, 1895.

President Cleveland expanded the civil service so that over 40 percent of federal employees were classified. The economic panic of 1893 resulted in the failure of fifteen thousand business firms and the closing of six hundred banks. In 1894 unemployment reached three million. That summer a severe drought hit the farm belt and caused farm foreclosures.

When the leading industrial firms sought to reduce wages as prices fell, the labor unions resisted, and in 1894 there were fourteen hundred strikes. Thousands of unemployed men roamed the country. In 1894 the Pullman strike, the largest in the nation's history up to that time, began.

Pullman was a Chicago-area company town in which employees were expected to rent company apartments and shop at the company's stores. As the economy declined, George Pullman announced wage reductions, but rents and prices at the stores remained the same. The Pullman workers went on strike. On June 26, 1894, the American Railway Union under Eugene V. Debs joined the strike, refusing to handle trains carrying Pullman cars. President Cleveland sent in federal troops on July 4. Mob violence resulted in the deaths of twelve people. On July 10 Debs and seventy other union officials and strikers were arrested for obstructing the mails. The strike was broken.

After Cleveland retired from the presidency, the family moved to Princeton, New Jersey. In 1899 Cleveland was appointed Henry Stafford Little Lecturer in Public Affairs at Princeton. On October 28, 1897, Richard Folsom was born, and on July 18, 1903, a second son, Francis Grover, was born. The Clevelands' oldest daughter, twelve-year-old Ruth, died of diphtheria on January 7, 1904.

President Grover Cleveland died of heart failure on June 24, 1908, at the age of seventy-one. Funeral services were conducted in his home, and he was buried in Princeton, New Jersey, next to his daughter Ruth. About five years after the president's death, Frances Folsom Cleveland married Thomas Preston Jr., a professor of archaeology at Princeton University. She died on October 29, 1947, at the age of eighty-three and was buried next to the president.

· · · · · · · · · · · · · · · · · · · · · · · · · · · · · · · · · · · · · · · · · · · · · · · · · · · · · · · · · · · · · · · · · · ·

## Grover Cleveland Birthplace State Historic Site
## Caldwell, New Jersey

ADDRESS: 207 Bloomfield Avenue, Caldwell, NJ 07006

TELEPHONE: 973-226-0001 ˙

WEB SITE: www.state.nj.us/dep/parksandforests/historic/grover_cleveland/ gc_home.htm

LOCATION: In northeastern New Jersey, twenty-two miles northeast of New York City, thirteen miles northeast of Newark, New Jersey

OPEN: Wednesday–Sunday, 10:00 A.M. to noon and 1:00 P.M. to 4:00 P.M.; closed state holidays, Thanksgiving, Christmas, and New Year's Day

ADMISSION: Free

FACILITIES: Birthplace of President Grover Cleveland, guided tours; picnic area; research library by appointment. National Register of Historic Places

*On March 18, 1837, Stephen Grover Cleveland* was born in the parsonage of the First Presbyterian Church of Caldwell, where his father, Richard Falley Cleveland, was the minister. The future president lived in the Presbyterian manse for the first four years of his life. In 1840 the family moved to Fayetteville, New York.

The birthplace, built in 1832, was used as a parsonage until 1913, when the Grover Cleveland Birthplace Memorial Association purchased the manse from the church and operated it as a house museum. It was acquired by the state of New Jersey in 1934. The New Jersey Department of Parks and Forestry maintains President Grover Cleveland's birthplace as a historic site. It has been restored to its appearance in the late 1830s when the Cleveland family resided here.

The two-and-one-half-story clapboard house has a stone foundation, inside brick chimneys, plaster interior walls, and a wood shingle roof. Most of the artifacts in the house belonged to the Cleveland family. Rooms on the first floor are open for viewing.

In the rear parlor on display are Frances Folsom Cleveland's Shaker-made cape that she wore to her husband's inauguration and a pastel portrait of Grover Cleveland. In the birth room are Grover's cradle, a quilt made by his mother, and the Cleveland family Bible.

The front parlor and the foyer contain exhibits on Cleveland's law and political careers and on his family. On display are President Cleveland's top hat, his pipe collection, and flags that flew in the inaugural parade. President Cleveland was the only president to marry in the White House. The first couple's marriage license, the bridal wreath, and a wedding cake box are displayed. Other items are Cleveland's cane rocking chair from his White House years and his desk when he was the mayor of Buffalo.

The manse's two-and-one-half-acre grounds feature three gardens planted with 1830s varieties of flowers and plants. Visitors are invited to dress up in 1890s costumes or play 1830s lawn games, including hoop rolling, marbles, tops, and hoop toss.

President Cleveland died on June 24, 1908, in his Princeton home. After a simple funeral in his home, he was buried in Princeton Cemetery next to his daughter Ruth, who died when she was twelve. Frances Cleveland remarried five years after Cleveland's death. She died in 1947 and is buried next to the president in Princeton Cemetery, which is located at 29 Greenview Avenue, Princeton, NJ 08542; the phone number is 609-924-1369.

# Benjamin Harrison

*March 4, 1889–March 3, 1893*

..................................................................

Benjamin Harrison has the distinction of being the only president whose grandfather was a president of the United States. William Henry Harrison, the ninth president, served an extremely brief term as he died on April 4, 1841, only thirty-two days after his inauguration.

Benjamin Harrison, born in North Bend, Ohio, on August 20, 1833, was the second of ten children of John Scott Harrison and Elizabeth Ramsey Irwin Harrison. Benjamin Harrison, the twenty-third president, was born in the home of his grandfather William Harrison. While John Scott Harrison was building a house on his eight-hundred-acre farm called The Point in 1833, he and his family lived temporarily with his parents.

When Benjamin was seven years old, his grandfather became president of the United States. At fourteen Benjamin and his older brother, Irwin, were sent to Farmers' College, a secondary school in a Cincinnati suburb, to prepare for college. In September 1850 Benjamin entered Miami University at Oxford, Ohio, a state university with strong Presbyterian roots. Oxford was the home of Caroline "Carrie" Scott, the daughter of a Farmers' College teacher, Rev. Dr. John W. Scott, who later founded the Oxford Female Institute. While at Miami University, Benjamin Harrison and Carrie Scott became secretly engaged.

Benjamin Harrison graduated from Miami University with an A.B. degree with honors on June 24, 1852. He began reading law in a Cincinnati law firm and in March 1854 was admitted to the Ohio Bar. After a religious revival conducted by university president Joseph Claybaugh, Benjamin joined the Presbyterian Church.

Benjamin and Carrie were married on October 20, 1853. Carrie Harrison gave birth to a son, Russell, on August 12, 1854, and a daughter, Mary, on April 3, 1858. A third child, born in 1861, died at birth.

Harrison began his law practice in Indianapolis, a city of sixteen thousand people. His partner, William Wallace, belonged to the newly formed Republican Party. Although Harrison's father and grandfather were Whigs, that party had virtually collapsed. Harrison ran for city attorney on the Republican ticket in May 1857 and was secretary to the Indiana Republican Central Committee. In February 1860 Harrison was elected as supreme court reporter for Indiana at the Republican state convention. In the national election held in November 1860, the Republican candidate, Abraham Lincoln, was elected president. Harrison heard President-elect Lincoln speak in Indianapolis on February 11, 1861.

After the surrender of Fort Sumter, President Lincoln called for seventy-five thousand three-month volunteers. Indiana exceeded its quota of six thousand men. When Lincoln called for three hundred thousand additional men in July 1862, Harrison enlisted. He was commissioned as a second lieutenant in the Seventieth Regiment, Indiana Volunteers, and proceeded to raise a regiment. Without any military experience, Harrison hired a drillmaster to train his company. The Seventieth Regiment became part of the First Brigade of the Twentieth U.S. Army Corps under Gen. William T. Ward on January 1, 1864, and later the Twentieth U.S. Army Corps was attached to the Army of the Cumberland.

On May 6, 1864, Sherman's Grand Army of the West moved south from Chattanooga, Tennessee, to execute his carefully prepared plan to take Atlanta, Georgia. Confederate troops commanded by Joseph E. Johnston were faced with stopping the march. At Resaca, Harrison's regiment was ordered to silence the rebel guns mounted on the crest of a hill and firing incessantly on Union troops. Under heavy fire they stormed the redoubt and engaged in hand-to-hand combat, and that night General Johnston and his troops retreated. Harrison's regiment fought in battles at New Hope Church, Golgotha Church, and Peach Tree Creek.

In late 1864 Harrison was asked by Governor Oliver Morton in Indianapolis to campaign for Republican candidates and to raise army recruits. When Harrison rejoined his regiment, he became ill with scarlet fever. By the time he recovered and returned to his regiment, General Lee had surrendered at Appomattox and President Lincoln had been assassinated.

Harrison received his military discharge on June 8, 1865. He returned to his law practice and Republican Party politics. In 1874 Carrie and Benjamin built a large brick house in Indianapolis on North Delaware Street.

In 1876 Harrison was the unsuccessful Republican candidate for governor of Indiana. When an Indiana seat in the U.S. Senate was vacated by the November 1877 death of Oliver P. Morton, Harrison was elected by the state legislature. He was defeated for reelection.

In 1888 the Republican presidential race was wide open. On the eighth ballot the convention nominated Benjamin Harrison. Levi P. Morton of New York was named Harrison's vice-presidential running mate. When they heard of Harrison's nomination, crowds of Indianapolis citizens gathered on the lawn of the family home on North Delaware Street. Harrison spoke then as he would more than eighty times during the campaign to crowds ranging from fifty to fifty thousand.

In a close election, Cleveland won more than 90,000 popular votes than Harrison; he received 5,537,857 popular votes to Harrison's 5,447,129. However, in the Electoral College, Cleveland, with 168 electoral votes, lost to Harrison, with 233. Harrison was inaugurated on March 4, 1899.

Harrison, author of a small book, *My Duty: This Country of Ours,* espoused a kind of civil religion, a deep Christian faith founded on Presbyterianism and Republicanism. Believing that the United States had been founded on ethical principles, he held individual freedom to be a God-given inalienable right. As the civil rights gains of the Reconstruction period were being undone, Harrison remained steadfast in his commitment to African American civil, political, and educational rights. He protested the Supreme Court decision of 1883 that overturned the Civil Rights Act, and he was especially concerned with the growing disenfranchisement of black voters in the South. He supported the Blair Federal Aid to Education Bill, which would have provided aid to public schools in the South and might have enabled more blacks to pass the literacy tests for voting. The bill failed.

The tariff was an issue dividing the two major parties. Harrison in 1888 enthusiastically supported the tariff, which he argued meant general prosperity and protection for American workers. The Republicans enacted the McKinley Tariff Act, which raised tariff duties from 38 to 50 percent, the highest rates in history.

The Republicans passed a pension act that provided pensions to one million Civil War veterans, their widows, and their children. They passed the Sherman Anti-Trust Act, the first federal attempt to regulate trusts and monopolies as illegal combinations in restraint of interstate commerce. In 1891 Congress passed the Forest Reserve Act, which gave the president authority to protect forested federal lands. Harrison withdrew thirteen million acres of timberland from cutting.

Harrison presided over the closing of the American frontier when the sole remaining Indian Territory in the county, Oklahoma, was opened to white settlement. In March 1889 Congress passed legislation by which the Creeks and Seminoles, two tribes that had been forcibly removed from the Southeast and resettled in the Indian Territory in the 1820s, ceded their land to the federal government. In what became known in history as the last great land rush, the Oklahoma District was proclaimed open to settlement at noon on April 22, 1889, by President Harrison. One hundred thousand persons on horseback, in carriages, or on foot lined the Oklahoma border ready to make a mad dash to stake their claims to homesteads. That day twelve thousand homesteads were claimed and 1,920,000 acres were officially settled.

Six states were added to the Union during President Harrison's term. In 1889 North Dakota, South Dakota, Montana, and Washington were admitted to the Union. Idaho and Wyoming became states in 1890.

With Harrison's encouragement, Secretary of State James G. Blaine designed a foreign policy to improve diplomatic relationships with and expand

U.S. business involvement in the Latin American countries. With representatives from nineteen American republics in attendance, Blaine opened the first Inter-American Conference on October 2, 1889. This conference created the International Bureau of the American Republics, which grew into the Pan American Union.

Carrie Harrison, an artistic woman who moved her kiln and other art equipment to the White House, designed the Harrisons' formal china and started the White House china collection after discovering in the attic and cupboards china used by former presidents in the White House. She developed tuberculosis and died in the White House on October 25, 1892, at the age of sixty. Funeral services were held in Washington, and she was buried in Indianapolis.

The election of 1892 again pitted Harrison, the incumbent Republican president, against Cleveland, the former Democratic president. Grover Cleveland won 5,555,426 popular votes and 277 electoral votes to Benjamin Harrison's 5,182,690 popular and 145 electoral votes.

Harrison returned to Indianapolis. On April 6, 1896, the sixty-two-year-old former president married his wife's thirty-seven-year-old niece, Mary Lord Dimmick, who had lived with the Harrisons in the White House. Mary Harrison gave birth to a daughter, Elizabeth, on February 21, 1897.

Harrison died of pneumonia in Indianapolis on March 13, 1901, at age sixty-seven. After his body lay in state at the Indiana State Capitol, a funeral service was held at the First Presbyterian Church in Indianapolis. Harrison is buried next to his wife Caroline in Crown Hill Cemetery in Indianapolis.

. . . . . . . . . . . . . . . . . . . . . . . . . . . . . . . . . . . . . . . . . . . . . . . . . . . . . . . . . . . . . . . . . . .

## President Benjamin Harrison Home
### Indianapolis, Indiana

ADDRESS: 1230 North Delaware Street, Indianapolis, IN 46202
TELEPHONE: 317-631-1888
WEB SITE: www.presidentbenjaminharrison.org
LOCATION: Indianapolis is in the center of Indiana; the house is just north of I-65, exit #113
OPEN: Monday–Saturday, 10:00 A.M. to 3:30 P.M., mid-February to December; Sunday, 12:30 P.M. to 3:30 P.M., June and July; closed major holidays
ADMISSION: Adults, $8.00; seniors, $6.00; children 5–17, $3.00
FACILITIES: Home of President Benjamin Harrison, research library; guided tours; gift shop; special events. National Historic Landmark, National Register of Historic Places

*Benjamin Harrison, the twenty-third president* of the United States, served from 1889 until 1893. In 1854, twenty-one-year-old Harrison moved to Indianapolis to begin a law practice. He had been admitted to the bar in 1854, soon

after he married Caroline Lavinia Scott. By the 1870s Harrison was wealthy enough to erect an impressive home for his wife and their children Mary and Russell.

Harrison had purchased a double lot on the west side of North Delaware at auction in 1867. The Harrison house, built by Benjamin Harrison in 1874–75 at a cost of twenty-five thousand dollars, is in the Italianate Victorian style. The three-story brick house, designed by the architect H. T. Brandt, had sixteen rooms, an attic, and a basement with a dirt floor. Originally the house was heated by a coal furnace and illuminated by gas lamps. In the 1890s Harrison remodeled the house adding plumbing, electricity, and a front porch.

The house figured prominently in Harrison's presidential campaign in 1888. Harrison gave eighty "front porch" speeches to an estimated three hundred thousand people. After being defeated for a second presidential term in the election of 1892, Harrison, now a widower as Caroline had died in the White House in 1892, returned to his home in Indianapolis. He resumed his law practice and extensively redecorated his Delaware Street home.

President Harrison married Mary Lord Dimmick, his first wife's niece, in 1896. A daughter, Elizabeth, was born in 1897. Benjamin Harrison died at his home at age sixty-seven on March 13, 1901. Mary Harrison and her daughter, Elizabeth, resided there until 1913, when they moved to New York. The house was rented until 1937, when it was sold to the Arthur Jordan Foundation for use as a dormitory for students at the Jordan Conservatory of Music. According to Mary Harrison's wishes, some rooms remained as they were when President Harrison was living in the house as a memorial to him. Mrs. Harrison contributed the furniture and artifacts for these historical rooms.

In 1966 the not-for-profit President Benjamin Harrison Foundation assumed the maintenance and operation of the house. In 1973–74 the Harrison house was renovated and decorated with Harrison family furniture, paintings, and other artifacts. A replica of the original carriage house, torn down in the 1930s, was built in 2000–2001.

The Harrison house has front and back staircases, thirteen-foot ceilings, butternut woodwork, oak floors, and Victorian-era carpets and wallpaper. Three quarters of the furnishings and artifacts in the home belonged to the Harrison family.

Restored rooms on the first floor of the Harrison house include the parlor, the sitting room, the dining room, the library, and the kitchen. Front parlor furniture is rococo revival. Windows are hung with lace sheers under long, heavy draperies. Floral patterns are seen in the wallpaper, carpet, and upholstery. Connected to the front parlor by sliding butternut pocket doors is the sitting room. Both rooms have cut-glass prism chandeliers and engraved walnut fireplace mantels. The couch and chairs are upholstered in red wine velvet.

The spacious dining room holds the family's original walnut Eastlake table and chairs and mahogany empire sideboard. The table is formally set with the Harrisons' Haviland White House china designed by Caroline Harrison, an artist who specialized in painting on china. The walnut china cabinet holds china painted or designed by Caroline Harrison.

A massive walnut bookcase designed and built for the library contains many of President Harrison's books. In addition to the president's White House desk and chair is a chair made of longhorn cattle horns and bobcat fur, which was a gift from a Texas rancher. Portraits of Abraham Lincoln, William Henry Harrison, and Benjamin Harrison hang in the library. The kitchen has its original wainscoting, a wooden icebox, and a Reliant stove.

On the second floor the spacious master bedroom holds the rosewood and satinwood bedroom set of Harrison and his second wife, Mary. A watercolor of the Harrison house at Cape May is by Caroline Harrison. The sunny upstairs sitting room, which is connected to the master bedroom, may have been used by Caroline Harrison as her studio.

Another bedroom has been decorated like Harrison's Indianapolis law office and contains Harrison's Moore desk, an unusual folding desk that could be closed and locked. There are photographs of Benjamin Harrison as brigadier general and his son, Russell, who served with Teddy Roosevelt's Rough Riders during the Spanish-American War. Also in this room are a portrait of Anna Harrison, President William H. Harrison's wife and President Benjamin Harrison's grandmother, and a charcoal drawing of the William H. Harrison house in North Bend, Ohio.

A large guest bedroom has a fireplace and a mahogany half-tester canopy bed. The nursery displays the crib used by the Harrison children and grandchildren.

The President Benjamin Harrison Research Library, located on the third floor of the house, contains President Harrison's personal book collection as well as many of his presidential papers. Other collections relate to the Harrison family genealogy, political pamphlets, family correspondence and papers, and photographs. Archives of the Daughters of the American Revolution, Seventieth Regiment, and the President Benjamin Harrison Home Foundation are located in the library. A third-floor ballroom is used for changing museum exhibits.

Benjamin Harrison died of pneumonia in Indianapolis on March 13, 1901. After his body lay in state at the Indiana State Capitol, a funeral service was held at the First Presbyterian Church in Indianapolis. Harrison is buried next to his wife Caroline in Crown Hill Cemetery in Indianapolis, 700 West Thirty-eighth Street, Indianapolis, IN 46208; the phone number is 317-925-8231.

# William McKinley

TWENTY-FIFTH PRESIDENT OF THE UNITED STATES
*March 4, 1897–September 14, 1901*

..................................................................

William McKinley, one of the three Civil War officers from Ohio who was elected president, was the third president to be assassinated. He led the country through the Spanish-American War, which made the United States a world power.

William McKinley, born on January 29, 1843, in Niles, Ohio, was the seventh of the nine children of William McKinley and Nancy Campbell Allison McKinley. William Sr. was an iron manufacturer in Pennsylvania and Ohio. The president's mother was a devout Methodist. William made a public profession of faith at a revival meeting when he was ten. His mother "often said that she was sorry he had only become president when he could have had such a useful and brilliant career in the church."[1]

When William was nine years old, the McKinley family moved to Poland, Ohio. William graduated from the Poland Academy at age seventeen. He attended Allegheny College in Meadville, Pennsylvania, for one term in 1860 but was unable to finish college because his father suffered financial reverses.

The McKinleys were staunch abolitionists. When the Civil War began, eighteen-year-old William enlisted as a private in the Twenty-third Ohio Volunteer Infantry in June 1861. He became a favorite of Rutherford B. Hayes, then an officer in the regiment, who in later years promoted McKinley's political career.

A commissary sergeant at Antietam, McKinley drove a mule team to the front lines to deliver cooked rations, meat, hardtack, and coffee to the hungry soldiers. Cited for bravery, McKinley was promoted to first lieutenant and then captain.[2] On March 13, 1865, President Lincoln promoted McKinley to brevet major of volunteers. The Twenty-third Ohio Volunteers were mustered out in July 1865.

McKinley read law and then attended the Albany Law School at Albany, New York. In March 1867 he passed the Ohio Bar and in Canton, Ohio, became a partner of Judge George Belden.

William fell in love with Ida Saxton of Canton. They were married on January 24 or 25, 1871, in Canton. A daughter named Katherine was born on December 25, 1871. A second daughter, Ida, was born on April 1, 1873, and died when she was four months old. That birth had been difficult, and subsequently Ida Saxton McKinley suffered from phlebitis, migraine headaches, and epileptic seizures that left her a semi-invalid. Katherine died on June 25, 1875, at the age of three.

In 1869 McKinley was elected as prosecuting attorney of Stark County, but he was defeated the following year. In spring 1876 coal miners in the Tuscarawas Valley went on strike. When violence broke out, Gov. Rutherford Hayes sent the militia and soldiers to quell the disorder. McKinley defended several miners arrested for disorderly conduct, and only one was convicted. From 1888 onward McKinley and one of the mine owners, Marcus Alonzo Hanna, formed a powerful political team. Hanna's organizational skills and fund-raising abilities were a great asset to McKinley's political career.

McKinley served in the U.S. House of Representative from 1876 until 1890 with one interruption. He won a narrow victory for a third congressional term in 1882, winning only eight votes more than Jonathan Wallace, his Democratic opponent. When Wallace contested the results, a congressional committee dominated by Democrats declared Wallace the victor. McKinley served as Ohio's governor from 1892 to 1896.

At the 1896 Republican National Convention in St. Louis, McKinley received 661.5 votes for president on the first ballot. Garret Augustus Hobart of New Jersey was his vice-presidential running mate. McKinley's Democratic opponent was Nebraska congressman William Jennings Bryan. McKinley won 7,102,246 popular and 271 electoral votes to Bryan's 6,492,599 popular and 176 electoral votes.

President McKinley treated Congress as an equal partner and consulted members of both parties. The telephone and the telegraph provided him with more rapid access to current information than his predecessors had. The Thomas Edison Company filmed the president during public appearances. Newspaper reporters were given space on the second floor of the White House, and twice a day the president's secretary spoke with them.

The Spanish-American War occurred during McKinley's administration. In 1895 a revolt broke out against Spanish rule in Cuba. Spain sent two hundred thousand troops to Cuba, and the Spanish army controlled the cities while the insurgents hit and ran in the countryside. Gen. Valeriano Weyler y Nicolau set up camps to concentrate the Cuban population and keep them from supporting the guerrillas. Because of overcrowding and unsanitary conditions, thousands of Cubans died of disease in these "re-concentration camps."

President McKinley continued President Cleveland's official neutrality policy but insisted to the Spanish minister that warfare in Cuba be conducted according to the military codes of civilization, within humane limits. McKinley offered to mediate the conflict. He ordered the U.S. battleship *Maine* to

Havana Harbor to show the flag as a sign of America's resolution. On February 15, 1898, an explosion tore through the hull of the *Maine,* which sank with 266 American lives lost. McKinley commissioned an investigation into the cause of the explosion. Although the cause is still debated, the explosion was attributed to Spain at the time.

On March 27 McKinley cabled Spain demanding an armistice between the Spanish army and the insurgents and the closing of the re-concentration camps. When Spain rejected those demands, McKinley sent a war message to Congress. Congress recognized Cuba's independence on April 19 and on April 25 passed a declaration of war against Spain.

On May 1, 1898, Commodore George Dewey, commander of the U.S. Asiatic Squadron, achieved a tremendous naval victory over the Spanish fleet in Manila Bay. His victory paved the way for the Spanish surrender of the Philippines twelve days later. On June 25 an American invasion force of seventeen thousand troops landed on Cuba's southeastern coast. Heavy fighting, marked by the charge of Theodore Roosevelt's Rough Riders, occurred at San Juan Hill. In addition U.S. Army forces occupied Puerto Rico.

The Spanish surrendered on July 17. Meanwhile, American troops were being decimated by yellow fever and malaria. The terms on which the United States and Spain would negotiate peace and end the fighting was signed on August 12. Lasting 113 days, the Spanish-American War claimed 5,500 Americans—379 in combat and the remainder from tropical diseases.

On December 10, 1898, the Treaty of Paris was signed. By its terms Spain granted independence to Cuba and ceded Puerto Rico, Guam, and the Philippines to the United States. Meanwhile, Filipinos who had rebelled against Spain now fought American occupation. The Filipino insurgency cost the lives of 4,300 Americans and over 50,000 Filipinos by the time it ended in 1902. The islands did not become independent until July 4, 1946, after they were liberated by U.S. forces from the occupying Japanese in World War II.

The issue of annexation of Hawaii had remained unsettled throughout the 1890s. McKinley proposed that Congress enact a joint resolution that needed approval by only a majority of the members of both houses of Congress. After Congress passed the joint resolution, McKinley signed it on July 7, 1898.

At the Republican convention in June 1900, McKinley was unanimously renominated for president and Theodore Roosevelt was nominated for vice president. William Jennings Bryan was again the Democratic presidential candidate, with Adlai E. Stevenson of Illinois in the vice-presidential slot. McKinley was reelected.

The Pan American Exposition in Buffalo, New York, featuring the newest scientific and technological innovations, opened in spring 1901. Vice President Roosevelt presided over the opening ceremony. On September 5 President and Mrs. McKinley arrived at the exposition. On September 6 the president stood in a receiving line in the Temple of Music. Leon F. Czolgosz, whose right hand was wrapped in a bandage to conceal a .32 caliber revolver, stood in that line. As the president extended his hand to him, Czolgosz fired two shots at point-blank range. One bullet ricocheted off a button, and the other struck President McKinley in the abdomen.

The president was rushed into surgery, but doctors were unable to extract the bullet lodged in McKinley's pancreas. Four days later a second surgery was performed, and McKinley was taken to the home of John Milburn, the exposition's president, to recover. McKinley died on September 14 at 2:15 A.M. He was fifty-eight years old. An autopsy revealed gangrene around the bullet. Theodore Roosevelt, who was vacationing in the Adirondacks, traveled to Buffalo and was sworn in as president.

President McKinley's casket was taken to Buffalo City Hall, where it lay in state. Then the president's body was transported by train to Washington, D.C. It was taken to the White House initially and then to the Capitol Rotunda, where it again lay in state. A funeral train transported McKinley's casket to Ohio, where a public service was held in Canton. The president's remains were temporarily interred at Westlawn Cemetery and reinterred in the William McKinley National Memorial in Westlawn Cemetery in 1907.

McKinley's assailant, Leon F. Czolgosz, a Detroit native of Polish heritage, was immediately apprehended and proudly admitted his crime. He was quickly tried, convicted, and sentenced to death by electrocution. The sentence was carried out on October 29, 1901. The Edison Company filmed the execution as well as McKinley's funeral. Ida Saxton McKinley died on May 26, 1907, and is interred next to her husband.

..............................................................................

## McKinley National Memorial and William McKinley Presidential Library and Museum
## Canton, Ohio

ADDRESS: 800 McKinley Monument Drive NW, Canton, OH 44708
TELEPHONE: 330-455-7043
WEB SITE: www.mckinleymuseum.org
LOCATION: Canton is in northeast Ohio, sixty miles south of Cleveland
OPEN: McKinley Monument and William McKinley Presidential Library and Museum: Monday–Saturday, 9:00 A.M. to 4:00 P.M.; Sunday, noon to 4:00 P.M.; closed major holidays
ADMISSION: Monument: free; museum: adults, $7.00; seniors, $6.00; children 3–18, $5.00
FACILITIES: Burial site of President William McKinley; McKinley National Memorial is handicapped accessible—mausoleum may be reached by elevator; McKinley Museum of Science, History and Industry; museum shop

McKinley National Memorial,
Canton, Ohio

*The McKinley National Memorial, owned* and operated by the Stark County Historical Society, is the burial site of the assassinated twenty-fifth president, William McKinley; his wife, Ida Saxton McKinley; and their daughters, Katherine and Ida. Paid for by voluntary contributions, the memorial was intended to be a tribute to an assassinated president by a grateful nation.

President William McKinley died in Buffalo, New York, on September 14, 1901, eight days after being shot by the anarchist Leon Czolgosz. The nation went into mourning. Funeral services for the slain chief executive were held in Buffalo, New York; Washington, D.C.; and Canton, Ohio's First Methodist Church. McKinley's body was interred in the Werts Memorial Vault in Westlawn Cemetery in Canton on September 19.

The McKinley National Memorial Association was formed in September 1901 to plan an appropriate monument for the slain president. Large numbers of schoolchildren donated their pennies to the fund. Over one million donors contributed $578,000 during the next two years.

In 1903 a twenty-six-acre site was purchased from Westlawn Cemetery in Canton. Sixty architectural designs for the McKinley Memorial were submitted to the Memorial Association, and the classic Greek plan by Harold Van Buren Magonigle of New York was selected. Magonigle's design was in the shape of a cross or sword, as can be seen in an aerial view. The mausoleum stands at the junction of the cross, and 108 main steps form the upright portion of the cross and the side steps form the arms.

Construction of the monument began in June 1905. Ida McKinley attended the cornerstone-laying ceremony the following November. The steps leading to the mausoleum are arranged in four tiers with terraces at each level. Midway up the steps to the dome is a statue of President McKinley by Charles Henry Niehaus based on a photograph of the president taken a few hours before he was shot. The president is seated in a bronze chair with a flag draped over it.

The mausoleum is double domed, and both the interior and exterior are of pink Milford granite from Massachusetts. Over the large bronze entrance doors is a lunette with figures depicting peace also designed by Charles Henry Niehaus. On the inside walls plaques contain information on President McKinley's life.

The sarcophagi in which the president and his wife are interred are on the top of the center pedestal made of black Berlin granite. The sarcophagi were carved from dark green granite from Vermont. The McKinley daughters were placed in the north wall in back of the sarcophagi. Katherine was born on December 25, 1871, and died on June 25, 1875; Ida was born on April 1, 1873, and died the following August 22. President Theodore Roosevelt presided at the dedication ceremony held on September 30, 1907.

Also on the site is the William McKinley Presidential Library and Museum, a private nonprofit organization of the Stark County Historical Society. Although it contains the McKinley Gallery, a large collection of McKinley artifacts as well as exhibits on McKinley, and the Ramsayer Research Library, which houses McKinley's papers and books, this is not a presidential museum but rather a museum of history, science, and industry. Discover World, the Children's Science Center, has interactive exhibits on Natural History Island, Ecology Island, and Space Station Earth.

The McKinley Gallery displays artifacts from the president's early life, military career, marriage, years as an attorney, political life, and life in the White House. On display are campaign ribbons and buttons, an 1897 inaugural badge, a bookcase from McKinley's Canton law office, and family portraits. The gallery also features photographs of the battleship *Maine;* the signing of the peace treaty with Spain on December 10, 1898; the Battle of Santiago; the destruction of the Spanish fleet; the charge up San Juan Hill; and Dewey's victory at Manila.

The Ramsayer Research Library houses photographs, correspondence, books, magazines, presidential papers, and copies of presidential papers from the Library of Congress, which are available for researchers. Historical Hall houses four nineteenth-century period room settings, while the exhibits in

Industrial Hall relate to Stark County companies and agriculture. The Street of Shops represents commerce in the late 1800s.

....................................................................

### National First Ladies' Library
### First Ladies National Historic Site
### Canton, Ohio

ADDRESS: William McKinley Historic Home: 331 S. Market Avenue, First Ladies National Historic Site Education and Research Center, 205 S. Market Avenue, Canton, OH 44702

TELEPHONE: 330-452-0876

WEB SITE: www.firstladies.org; www.nps.gov/fila

LOCATION: Canton is in northeast Ohio, sixty miles south of Cleveland, accessible from I-77; the McKinley home is on the corner of Market Avenue and Fourth Street

OPEN: Tuesday–Saturday, tours at 9:30 A.M., 10:30 A.M., 12:30 P.M., 1:30 P.M., and 2:30 P.M., and Sunday, tours at 12:30 P.M., 1:30 P.M., and 2:30 P.M., June–August; closed New Year's Eve, New Year's Day, Presidents' Day, Memorial Day, July 4, Labor Day, Thanksgiving and the day after, Christmas Eve, and Christmas Day

ADMISSION: Adults, $7.00; seniors, $6.00; children, $5.00

FACILITIES: William McKinley Historic Home, home of Ida Saxton McKinley, wife of President William McKinley; National First Ladies' Library Education and Research Center; guided tours; video; gift shop. National Register of Historic Places, NHS

*The First Ladies National Historic Site* is comprised of both the William McKinley Historic Home—known until September 2009 as the Saxton-McKinley House, the childhood home of First Lady Ida Saxton McKinley—at 331 S. Market Avenue and the Education and Research Center in the 1895 National Bank Building at 205 S. Market Avenue. Managed by the National Park Service and operated by the National First Ladies' Library, the site became a part of the National Park Service in October 2000.

The William McKinley Historic Home is distinctive because it is the restored home of a president's wife as well as of a president. Neither William McKinley's birthplace in Niles, Ohio, nor the Canton, Ohio, house that the McKinleys received as a wedding present from Ida's parents is extant. A 2009 study has documented the fact that the house was the longest-term residence of President William McKinley, serving as his home for nearly thirty years through his career as U.S. congressman, governor of Ohio, and U.S. president. The William McKinley Historic Home was in essence the "Canton White House."

Ida Saxton was raised in the house from the age of three, and she and William McKinley were married there in 1871. Originally owned by her grandfather John Saxton and then by her father, James Saxton, it became the home of her sister, Mary Saxton Barber, and Mary's family. While McKinley served in the U.S. House of Representatives their primary residence was in Washington, D.C. When they were in Ohio, Ida and William McKinley resided with the Saxton and Barber families. The house was the McKinleys' Ohio home from 1877 until 1891, and for twenty years William McKinley maintained a law office on the third floor.

The house remained in the Saxton and Barber families until the 1920s. Over the next fifty years it suffered much damage, and it was condemned in 1972. Not wanting to see this historic structure torn down, Marsh Belden, a local preservationist, purchased the Saxton house and spent over one million dollars stabilizing and restoring it. In 1979 it was listed on the National Register of Historic Places.

Although the restored William McKinley Historic Home recounts Ida and William McKinley's story, since June 1998 it has also served as the National First Ladies' Library. Mary Regula, wife of U.S. Representative Ralph Regula, spearheaded the drive to create a repository for the books, manuscripts, letters, and audiovisual materials related to the nation's first ladies. In June 1998 Rosalind Carter attended the opening ceremonies of the First Ladies' Library, and First Lady Hillary Rodham Clinton toured the facility in July 1999.

The seven-story 1895 City National Bank building at 205 S. Market Avenue serves as the Education and Research Center of the National First Ladies' Library. The building was donated to the library by the Marsh Belden Sr. family, and Laura Bush inaugurated the Education and Research Center in September 2003.

The William McKinley Historic Home, a three-story red brick federal-style structure, was built by John Saxton, Ida's grandfather, around 1840. Additions to the house were built in 1865 and 1920. John Saxton was the founder of the *Ohio Repository* newspaper (*Canton Repository*). Restoration has returned the appearance of the house to the McKinley era.

Guided tours of the elegant William McKinley Historic Home begin with a video by the former Smithsonian Institution curator Edith Mayo, who produced the first ladies' exhibits at the Smithsonian during the 1990s. Exhibits on the lower level include a heavy bronze plaque presented to Mrs. McKinley in 1907 as a memorial to her husband; the plaque depicts McKinley with children and a figure of liberty. Also on the lower level are photographs and watercolors illustrating the history of the house and photographs of the first ladies.

Docents, some dressed in the garb of various first ladies, start the tour in the front hallway. Reproductions of historic William Morris carpets and wallpaper are used throughout the house. Many furnishings are period reproductions. The parlor, now used as a reading room, houses Ida's desk and piano. The fireplace is original, and the bookcases belonged to Ida's maternal grandfather.

On the second floor, the sitting room and the bedroom are replicas of rooms in the McKinley house at 725 N. Market, which has been demolished. It includes a shrine that Ida made to her husband. After his death she visited his grave every day. The reclusive Ida knitted thousands of slippers in her lifetime and would present the slippers as gifts. A pair of those slippers is displayed in the bedroom. In the hallway is a set of Ulysses and Julia Grant's china.

An extensive photograph exhibit on the first ladies is displayed in the third-floor ballroom. Also on the third floor is the law office used by William McKinley for twenty years. Since McKinley lived at the beginning of the age of photography, photographs of his law office facilitated the accuracy of its restoration.

The Education and Research Center is a repository for over six thousand books, photos, audiovisual materials, and artifacts related to the wives of the U.S. presidents. The library has special exhibits and specially created educational curricula that are available to teachers.

# Theodore Roosevelt

TWENTY-SIXTH PRESIDENT OF THE UNITED STATES
*September 14, 1901–March 3, 1909*

Theodore Roosevelt began life as the frail child of a prestigious family. As president of the United States, the energetic, vigorous, and ambitious Roosevelt was known as a trust buster, a conservationist, and a builder of the Panama Canal. His presidency was a strenuous exercise in American politics.

Theodore Roosevelt Jr., born on October 27, 1858, in New York City, was the second child of Theodore Roosevelt and Martha Bulloch Roosevelt. The Roosevelts, descended from Dutch settlers, were a wealthy family who made their fortune in real estate and merchandising. Philanthropy was Theodore Roosevelt Sr.'s true interest. Martha Bulloch, raised at Roswell, a Georgia plantation, was considered a true southern lady.

The Roosevelts had servants, spent their summers in the country, took their children to Europe, and provided them with tutors. Theodore suffered from severe bronchial asthma as a child. Determined to overcome his frail physique, he at age fourteen began taking boxing lessons.

Theodore entered Harvard College in 1876 and graduated on June 30, 1880. He boxed and wrestled at Harvard. An outdoorsman and naturalist, he enjoyed hiking, climbing, and canoeing. He published a scientific catalog of ninety-seven species of birds, *The Summer Birds of the Adirondacks,* followed by *Notes on Some of the Birds of Oyster Bay.*

In 1878 Roosevelt met seventeen-year-old Alice Hathaway Lee, and on his twenty-second birthday, October 27, 1880, he married Alice in Brookline, Massachusetts. When Alice became pregnant, Roosevelt began building a large house, Leeholm, on 155 acres in Oyster Bay, New York.

Theodore briefly studied law at Columbia Law School but was more interested in writing a scholarly book, *The Naval War of 1812.* Published by Putnam in May 1882, the book was hailed as the definitive work on the subject. In 1881 Roosevelt was elected to the New York legislature, and he was reelected the following two years.

In September 1883 Theodore traveled to the small settlement of Little Missouri in the Dakota territories to hunt buffalo with a Canadian guide, Joe Ferris. He subsequently went into cattle ranching with Sylvane Ferris, his guide's brother, and a friend, Bill Merrifield.

Theodore was in Albany when he received a telegram notifying him that Alice had given birth to a daughter on February 12, 1884. A second telegram informed him that Alice was not doing well. By the time Theodore arrived at his mother's Manhattan house, where Alice had given birth, it was almost midnight of the thirteenth. Alice suffered from Bright's disease. In addition Theodore's mother was ill with typhoid. Forty-nine-year-old Martha Roosevelt died at 3:00 A.M. on February 14, while twenty-two-year-old Alice Roosevelt died that afternoon. A double funeral was held at the Fifth Avenue Presbyterian Church on February 16, and the women were buried in Greenwood Cemetery. The following day the baby was christened Alice Lee and Theodore's sister Anna became the baby's caretaker.

Roosevelt returned to his Elkhorn Ranch in the Dakota Territory. In the West, Theodore was a hunter and rancher while remaining an author who wrote by the light of a kerosene lamp in a room above Joe Ferris's store.[1] He wrote *Hunting Trips of a Ranchman* (1885), *Ranch Life and the Hunting Trail* (1888), *The Wilderness Hunter* (1893), and a biography, *Thomas Hart Benton.*

Roosevelt and Edith Kermit Carow were married at St. George's Church, Hanover Square, London, on December 2, 1886. They and two-year-old Alice settled at the house on Oyster Bay, Long Island, which was renamed Sagamore Hill. Theodore Roosevelt Jr. was born on September 12, 1887; Kermit was born on October 10, 1889; Ethel Carow was born on August 13, 1891; Archibald Bulloch was born on April 9, 1894; and Quentin Roosevelt was born on November 19, 1897.

Roosevelt's cattle business declined due to drought, overgrazing, and overproduction. Blizzards in the Badlands during the winter of 1886 were especially harsh. When Roosevelt went to assess the damage, he was met by indescribable scenes of rotting steer carcasses. He liquidated his western assets, enduring a large financial loss.

Theodore earned his living by writing. His literary work was well received and highly praised. His books reflected his strongest interests: history, literature, politics, and natural history. Between 1889 and 1895 he launched a four-volume series on the settlement of the United States called *The Winning of the West.* The western artist Frederic Remington did the illustrations for *Ranch Life and the Hunting Trail* (1888).

In 1889 President Benjamin Harrison appointed Roosevelt as a U.S. civil service commissioner, a position he held for six years. During his tenure twenty-six thousand jobs that had been political appointments were put under the merit system.

Theodore and his sisters were faced with the irresponsible behavior of their brother, Elliott, due to alcoholism. Elliott's lifestyle included excessive drinking, extramarital affairs, and the neglect of his wife, Anna Hall, and their three children: Eleanor, Elliott Jr., and Gracie Hall. Though treated in institutions at home and in Europe, Elliott suffered frequent relapses. Theodore quietly attempted to have Elliott declared legally insane so his brother's money could be placed in a trust for his wife and children, and Theodore was terribly embarrassed when this news appeared in newspaper headlines. In late 1892 Anna Hall Roosevelt died of diphtheria. Elliott Jr. died in 1893, and Elliott Sr. died in 1894. Now orphans, Eleanor, the future First Lady, and Gracie Hall were cared for by Grandmother Hall.

President McKinley on April 19, 1897, appointed Roosevelt as assistant to John D. Long, the secretary of the navy. Since the late 1890s growing independence movements in Cuba and the Philippine Islands sought to overthrow Spain. In Havana Harbor the *Maine* blew up on February 15, 1898, killing more than 260 men.

The United States severed diplomatic relations with Spain, and President McKinley asked Congress to declare war. Secretaries Long and Roosevelt purchased ships for conversion to military use. The U.S. Navy blockaded Cuba. On May 1, 1898, Commodore George Dewey won a decisive naval victory over the Spanish at Manila Bay.

Roosevelt resigned his navy post and organized the First Regiment of U.S. Volunteer Cavalry. The thousand-man regiment, known as the "Rough Riders," joined twenty-five thousand regular army troops at Tampa, Florida, in May 1898. They landed in Santiago de Cuba in late June with Colonel Roosevelt as commander of the Rough Riders.

On July 1, 1898, Roosevelt's regiment charged up San Juan Hill toward the Spanish who were shooting down on them. Press coverage made Roosevelt a war hero. On August 12, 1898, Spain and the United States signed a protocol ending the fighting. After seven weeks the Rough Riders departed Cuba, and the regiment disbanded with Roosevelt leaving military service on September 15.

Roosevelt was elected governor of New York and served from 1899 to 1901. In 1900 he was the Republican vice-presidential candidate, running with the incumbent president William McKinley. Six months into McKinley's second term, on September 6, 1901, Leon F. Czolgosz shot the president at the Pan American Exposition in Buffalo, New York. McKinley died on September 14. That day U.S. District Judge John R. Hazel administered the presidential oath of office to Theodore Roosevelt at the home of Ansley Wilcox of Buffalo, New York.

At age forty-two Roosevelt became the youngest man to serve as president of the United States. Roosevelt personified the national mood for progressive reforms such as regulation of trusts and monopolies, conservation of natural resources, safe working conditions, restriction of child labor, regulation of railroads, and pure foods and drugs.

In early 1902 Roosevelt instructed the U.S. Department of Justice to bring suit against the Northern Securities Company for violating the Sherman

Antitrust Act. Northern Securities, a gigantic interlocking company, exercised a railroad monopoly that included the Northern Pacific, Great Northern, and Chicago Burlington and Quincy railroads. In 1904 the Supreme Court ordered the company dissolved. The Department of Justice launched suits in 1906 and 1907 against the American Tobacco Company, the New Haven Railroad, the DuPont Corporation, and the Standard Oil Company.

In the early twentieth century the growth of labor union organization led to frequent strikes. Roosevelt intervened in the coal miners' strike in Pennsylvania in which the United Mine Workers, led by John Mitchell, demanded wage increases, an eight-hour workday, and company recognition of the union. When the coal companies rejected their demands, 140,000 mine workers went on strike in May 1902. As winter approached, schools, hospitals, railroads, and factories were running desperately short of coal. The mine owners refused Roosevelt's offer to mediate the situation until he threatened to use the army to seize the mines and return them to operation. In late October the miners returned to work. In March 1903 an independent arbitration commission awarded the miners a 10 percent wage increase and a reduction in workday hours. However, it did not recommend union recognition.[2]

Theodore Roosevelt was nominated for president at the Republican Party convention in June 1904, with Charles W. Fairbanks of Indiana as his vice-presidential running mate. Roosevelt's Democratic opponent was Alton B. Parker of New York. In a landslide victory Roosevelt received 7,623,486 popular votes and 336 electoral votes to Parker's 5,077,911 popular and 140 electoral votes. The Socialist candidate, Eugene V. Debs, received 402,489 popular votes. Roosevelt said that he would not accept another nomination for president, words he would regret when he ran for president in 1912.

Roosevelt organized the National Commission on the Conservation of Natural Resources to protect the nation's rivers, lakes, forests, and wilderness areas. The progressive conservationist Gifford Pinchot, chief of the Forest Service, increased federal preserves from 45 million acres in 1901 to 195 million in 1908.

Roosevelt saw the Caribbean and Central America as the United States' special region. When the Dominican Republic defaulted on its debts, Roosevelt issued the Roosevelt Corollary to the Monroe Doctrine, which warned Latin American countries to keep their affairs in order or face American intervention. Acting on that doctrine, the United States in 1905 took charge of the Dominican Republic's revenue system and paid off its European debts.

Roosevelt sought to link the Atlantic and Pacific oceans by digging a massive canal across the isthmus that joined North and South America. Selecting a route through the Panamanian region of Colombia for the canal, Roosevelt instructed John Hay, his secretary of state, to negotiate a ninety-nine-year lease for a six-mile-wide canal zone. When the Colombian senate balked at the proposal, Roosevelt made it known that he would support a Panamanian revolt and secession from Colombia. When the Panamanians rebelled in 1903, Roosevelt quickly gave diplomatic recognition to the Republic of Panama. The Hay-Bunau-Varilla Treaty granted the United States control of a ten-mile canal zone across the Isthmus of Panama. Begun in 1904, the canal was completed in 1914 at a cost of $275 million.

After Japan and Russia went to war in 1904 over their conflicting interests in Manchuria and Korea, Roosevelt in August 1905 convened a peace conference in Portsmouth, New Hampshire. On September 5, 1905, the Russo-Japanese Peace Treaty was signed. Secretary of War William Howard Taft negotiated the Taft-Katsura Agreement in 1905, which recognized Japan's dominance in Korea in return for a promise to respect U.S. possession of the Philippines. In 1906 Roosevelt was the first American president awarded the Nobel Peace Prize.

Roosevelt did not seek reelection in 1908. He had virtually handpicked his successor, William Howard Taft. Roosevelt and his son Kermit went on an African hunting and scientific expedition outfitted by the Smithsonian Institution.

Roosevelt was more progressive than the moderately conservative Taft, and the Republican Party split into progressive and conservative wings. Roosevelt challenged President Taft for the Republican nomination in 1912, but Taft was the Republicans' choice. Roosevelt then organized a third party, the Progressives, which enthusiastically nominated him. While campaigning in Milwaukee, Wisconsin, on October 14, 1912, Theodore Roosevelt was shot in a failed assassination attempt by John Schrank.

In the election of 1912 Woodrow Wilson, the Democratic Party nominee, scored a victory, winning 6,296,547 popular and 435 electoral votes. Roosevelt came in second with 4,118,571 popular and 88 electoral votes, while Taft, a distant third, won 3,486,720 popular and only 8 electoral votes.

In January 1914 Theodore Roosevelt and his son Kermit joined a South American expedition of the unexplored Rio Da Divuda, the River of Doubt. After six weeks of hacking their way through the jungle to the river's head, they began a difficult two-month journey by canoe of the fifteen-hundred-mile river. Roosevelt severely injured his leg, contracted malaria, and lost fifty-seven pounds. Scribner's published Roosevelt's account of the expedition, *Through the Brazilian Wilderness.*

When World War I broke out in Europe, Roosevelt publicly campaigned for the country to support the Allies' fight against Germany and advocated military preparedness. Wilson asked Congress for a declaration of war against Germany on April 2, 1917. The Roosevelt sons, Theodore, Kermit, Archibald, and Quentin, joined the military. Quentin was killed in France on July 14, 1918.

Theodore Roosevelt, sixty years old, died at Sagamore Hill on January 6, 1919. A private family funeral service held at Sagamore Hill was followed by a funeral service at Christ Episcopal Church in Oyster Bay. The former president was buried in Oyster Bay's Young's Memorial Cemetery. Edith Roosevelt survived her husband by almost thirty years, dying at the age of eighty-seven on September 30, 1948.

## Theodore Roosevelt Birthplace National Historic Site
## New York, New York

ADDRESS: 28 East Twentieth Street, New York, NY 10003

TELEPHONE: 216-260-1616

WEB SITE: www.nps.gov/thrb

LOCATION: In Manhattan, a block west of Gramercy Park, between Park Avenue South and Broadway

OPEN: Tuesday–Saturday, 9:00 A.M. to 5:00 P.M.

ADMISSION: Free

FACILITIES: Reconstructed birthplace of President Theodore Roosevelt; guided tours; special events

*The New York City brownstone* in which President Theodore Roosevelt was born on October 27, 1858, was demolished in 1916. After his death in 1919, organizations were formed to honor the memory of the twenty-sixth president. Their plans included the reconstruction of the president's birthplace in Manhattan.

Cornelius Van Schaak Roosevelt, the president's grandfather, purchased two adjoining Gothic revival brownstones on East Twentieth Street, Nos. 26 and 28, as wedding presents for his sons, Theodore Sr. and Robert. The row houses were built in 1848. Theodore Roosevelt Sr. and his wife, Martha, moved into their house in 1854 shortly after their marriage and lived there until 1872. All of their children were born there. In 1865 they redecorated the interior and built an additional story on the fashionable row house. The Roosevelt house remained in the family until 1896. As the neighborhood became increasingly commercial, numbers 26 and 28 were no longer used as residences. In 1916 No. 28 was demolished and a two-story commercial building was constructed on the site.

After Theodore Roosevelt's death in January 1919, two organizations were formed to perpetuate his memory: the Men's and Women's Roosevelt Memorial Associations. The Women's Roosevelt Memorial Association purchased Nos. 26 and 28 and razed both of them. Theodate Pope Riddle designed the reconstruction, an exact replica of the original four-story building at 28 East Twentieth Street. Erected on its original site in 1923, the rectangular row house is three and one-half stories over a high basement, with a mansard roof, dormers, a balustraded staircase that leads to the first floor, and an off-center double-door entrance with a transom. Memories of Theodore Roosevelt's sisters and widow assisted Riddle with interior details.

When Theodore Roosevelt's birth house and Robert Barnwell Roosevelt's adjoining structure were reconstructed, they were combined into a single unit, but the brownstone facade of Robert's house is slightly recessed and plainer. The Roosevelt birthplace opens at each level into the adjacent new wing, which is used as a museum and offices.

The reconstructed birthplace, which depicts the lifestyle of the wealthy Roosevelt family in a fashionable Manhattan neighborhood in the mid-1800s, was opened to the public in 1923. In 1963 the Theodore Roosevelt Association, the new name of the merged Roosevelt Memorial Associations, donated the site to the National Park Service. It is administered by the National Park Service and the Theodore Roosevelt Association.

The decoration of the house represents the period 1865–72, when Theodore Sr., Martha, and their four children lived there. Forty percent of the furniture and artifacts, donated by Roosevelt's widow and sisters, are original to the house. Other pieces came from Roosevelt relatives, and the rest are of the period.

The restored rooms include the parlor, the library, and the dining room on the first floor and the master bedroom, the children's nursery, and the gymnasium on the second floor of No. 28. The wing has museum galleries, and there is a bookstore on the lower level.

Leon Marcotte, a New York interior decorator, redecorated the Roosevelt house in 1865, the era to which the house has been restored. This upper-class, urban home's elegant rooms have high ceilings, fireplaces, painted woodwork, patterned wallpaper, chandeliers, carpeting, heavy draperies, and horsehair upholstery.

The formal parlor at the front of the house has rococo revival style chairs and sofas upholstered in blue, crystal chandeliers, and large mirrors. The library, which was used as a family room, has bookcases and horsehair upholstered chairs. A pair of obelisks from Egypt attest to the family's love of travel. A large table and horsehair upholstered chairs can be seen in the dining room.

On the second floor the master bedroom has the original rosewood and satinwood veneered furniture made for Theodore and Martha Roosevelt. This would be the room in which the future president was born. Because of Theodore's frail physique due to asthma, his father installed gymnasium equipment on the porch of the second floor, which was used by father and son regularly. The gymnasium was accessible by going up a few steps and then climbing through a nursery window. In the nursery are a child's chair that belonged to Theodore, a crib, and a sleigh bed.

Theodore Roosevelt's full and varied career is chronicled in exhibits that include newspapers, books, manuscripts, photographs, artifacts, and clothing such as his Rough Rider uniform. Trophies from his hunting days are displayed on the second floor. Special events are held in the auditorium on the fourth floor.

· · · · · · · · · · · · · · · · · · · · · · · · · · · · · · · · · · · · · · · · · · · · · · · · · · · · · · · · · · · · · · · · · · · · · · · ·

## Sagamore Hill National Historic Site
## Oyster Bay, Long Island, New York

ADDRESS: 20 Sagamore Hill Road, Oyster Bay, NY 11771

TELEPHONE: 516-922-4788

WEB SITE: www.nps.gov/sahi

LOCATION: On Cove Neck at the terminus of Cove Neck Road, about two miles northeast of the town of Oyster Bay, Long Island, accessible from the Long Island Expressway

OPEN: Daily, 9:00 A.M. to 5:00 P.M., Memorial Day through Labor Day; Wednesday–Sunday, 9:00 A.M. to 5:00 P.M., September–May; closed Thanksgiving, Christmas, and New Year's Day

ADMISSION: Adults and children 15 years or older, $5.00; first-floor viewing, adults and children 15 years or older, $3.00

FACILITIES: Home of President Theodore Roosevelt and his family, guided tours; visitor center and bookstore, Roosevelt Museum at Old Orchard; ranger-led grounds walks and bird walks, nature trail; Theodore Roosevelt's burial site in Youngs Memorial Cemetery is one and one half miles from Sagamore Hill, as is the Theodore Roosevelt Sanctuary

*When Theodore Roosevelt was a child,* he and his family spent many summers at Oyster Bay, Long Island. In 1883 twenty-five-year-old Roosevelt, now married and expecting a child, purchased 155 acres at Oyster Bay. He kept 95 acres and sold the remainder to relatives. A barn was the only structure on the property. Roosevelt hired the architects Lamb and Rich to design a house for his family on Cove Neck, a three-mile-long peninsula jutting into Long Island Sound.

In February 1884 Alice Hathaway Lee Roosevelt, Theodore's wife, died days after giving birth to a daughter named Alice. Despite his grief, Theodore proceeded building the house, called Leeholm, a twenty-two-room Queen Anne–style house. Completed in early 1885, this was the future president's home until his death there in 1919. Roosevelt, his daughter Alice, and his sister Anna moved into the house on Cove Neck shortly before he left for the Dakota Badlands, where he operated ranches.

In 1886 Roosevelt returned to New York, and on December 2, 1886, he married Edith Kermit Carow in London. After a European honeymoon, they settled in their Oyster Bay home, renamed Sagamore Hill for Sagamore Mohannis, chief of an Indian tribe that had inhabited this land in the seventeenth century. Writing was Theodore's main occupation then; he wrote over thirty-five books, several of them at Sagamore Hill.

Three of Theodore and Edith's children were born at Sagamore Hill: Theodore Jr. in 1887; Kermit in 1889; and Ethel in 1891. Two more children, Archibald

in 1894 and Quentin in 1897, were born in Washington, D.C., when Theodore served on the U.S. Civil Service Commission and as assistant secretary of the navy. Edith and the children spent their summers at Sagamore Hill. When Theodore Roosevelt became president of the United States on September 14, 1901, Sagamore Hill served as the summer White House.

After President Roosevelt's death in January 1919, Edith Roosevelt lived in Sagamore Hill until her death in 1948. In 1950 the Theodore Roosevelt Association purchased the house, its contents, and eighty-three acres. The association spent the next three years restoring Sagamore Hill to its appearance between 1901 and 1919. In June 1953, at a ceremony presided over by President Dwight D. Eisenhower and attended by President Herbert Hoover, Sagamore Hill was opened to the public.

After the 1960 death of Eleanor Alexander Roosevelt, widow of Theodore Jr., the Theodore Roosevelt Association purchased their adjacent home, Old Orchard, built in 1937–38. In 1963 the association donated both Sagamore Hill and Old Orchard to the National Park Service, which operates the property today. Old Orchard opened as a museum in 1966.

Sagamore Hill is a popular destination, with over seventy thousand annual visitors. The eighty-six-acre site, set among forests, meadows, salt marsh, and beach, includes not only the Roosevelt house but also Old Orchard Museum, a carriage barn, a tool exhibit barn, a visitor center, two garden areas, and nature trails. On weekends and during the summer months tour tickets sell out early each day.

The large Queen Anne house is painted blue-gray and gray and has a wide piazza. While Roosevelt was president the piazza was redesigned to create a speaker's platform. Sagamore Hill is furnished with original Roosevelt possessions as the house was occupied only by the president and his family. Restored to the period between 1901, when Theodore Roosevelt became president, and 1919, the year he died, the rambling house is filled with fireplaces, hunting trophies, personal mementoes, and thousands of books.

In the oak-paneled hall, an African Cape buffalo head hangs over the fireplace, a trophy from Roosevelt's post-presidential African safari. Many of Roosevelt's African safari specimens went to the Smithsonian Institution.

Roosevelt's library was his private office and study. It has a fireplace, walls lined with full bookshelves, comfortable chairs, a desk, and a bronze statue of a Paleolithic man by Frederic Remington. There is also a portrait of Oliver Cromwell, the subject of a Roosevelt biography. In 1902 a telephone was installed.

As president, Roosevelt needed a large area for meetings and receptions while at his summer White House. The north room, added in 1905, was designed by C. Grant LaFarge. The room, which is thirty feet wide and forty feet deep, has a vaulted ceiling, pairs of black walnut columns on each wall, a massive fireplace, and a mantelpiece and desk of Philippine camagon wood. Hunting trophies include a lion and a lioness from Africa, bison from North Dakota, and elk from Wyoming. There are sculptures by Augustus Saint-Gaudens, Frederic Remington, Gutzon Borglum, and James L. Clark. There are also lots of books, some in bookcases from the White House.

In the drawing room there is a 1908 portrait of Edith painted in the White House by Philip A. deLaszlo. The polar bear rug is from Adm. Robert E. Peary. A leather-covered table and rosewood étagère are Carow family pieces. Also on the first floor is the dining room with Italian dining room furniture purchased by Theodore and Edith in Florence on their honeymoon and a silver coffee and tea service owned by Martha Bullock, Theodore's mother.

On the second floor are the bedrooms for family and guests. Babies started out in the nursery and then progressed to the gate room. Children were bathed in the red bathroom, while adults took baths in tin tubs in their rooms. Alice had the southeast bedroom, the boys had the northeast bedroom, and the parents were in the northwest bedroom. The "modern gothic" bedroom furniture, bird's-eye maple veneer over walnut, was purchased in 1870. Adjoining the master bedroom is the president's dressing room. There are also a south bedroom, a single guestroom, and a double guestroom.

The third floor had the cook's room, the sewing room, the trunk room, the schoolroom, two maid's rooms, the linen closet, Theodore Jr.'s bedroom, and the gun room, which Theodore Sr. used as a study. He said that this room had the best views—so good, in fact, that he had to turn his chair to face the wall to avoid being distracted.

Old Orchard, the Georgian home built by the president's son Theodore and his wife in 1937–38, is a museum. Exhibits focus on the history and operation of the estate, the six Roosevelt children, Theodore Roosevelt's political life, the Dakota years, Rough Rider experiences, the presidential years, and the post-presidential era.

President Theodore Roosevelt is buried in Youngs Memorial Cemetery in Oyster Bay one and one half miles from Sagamore Hill at the intersection of Cove Neck Road and Cove Road. A private family service held at Sagamore Hill was followed by a funeral at Christ Episcopal Church in Oyster Bay. Roosevelt was buried on January 8, 1919. Also buried in the Roosevelt plot is the president's wife Edith as well as Roosevelt children, grandchildren, and great-grandchildren.

In 1932 Theodore's cousin Emlen Roosevelt purchased twelve acres surrounding the cemetery. Some of this land was added to the Roosevelt plot, while the remainder was given to the Audubon Society, which established the Theodore Roosevelt Sanctuary, a bird and nature preserve.

..........................................................................

## Theodore Roosevelt Inaugural National Historic Site
## Buffalo, New York

ADDRESS: 641 Delaware Avenue, Buffalo, NY 14202

TELEPHONE: 716-884-0095

WEB SITE: www.nps.gov/thri

LOCATION: Buffalo is in northwestern New York, on Lake Erie. The Theodore Roosevelt Inaugural National Historic Site is north of downtown Buffalo. The entrance is on Delaware Avenue, near North Street.

OPEN: Monday–Friday, 9:00 A.M. to 5:00 P.M.; Saturday–Sunday, noon to 5:00 P.M.; closed New Year's Eve and Day, Easter, Memorial Day, July 4, Labor Day, Thanksgiving, Christmas Eve and Day

ADMISSION: Adults, $10.00; senior citizens and students, $7.00; children 6–14, $5.00

FACILITIES: Guided tours; visitor center; audiovisual program; handicapped accessible

*On September 6, 1901, President William McKinley* was shot by Leon Czolgosz, an anarchist, while attending the Pan American Exposition in Buffalo, New York. Not a presidential residence, the Theodore Roosevelt Inaugural National Historic Site is the house in which Vice President Theodore Roosevelt took the oath of office as the twenty-sixth president of the United States. It is one of only a few inaugural sites outside of Washington, D.C.

Roosevelt stayed with his friend Ansley Wilcox when he arrived in Buffalo after learning about the assassination attempt on President McKinley. Wilcox, a lawyer, had served with Roosevelt on commissions on civil service reform. After being assured by McKinley's doctors that the president would recover, on September 10 Roosevelt joined his family vacationing in the Adirondack Mountains.

Theodore Roosevelt
Inaugural National
Historic Site, Buffalo,
New York

On September 13 Vice President Roosevelt received a telegram informing him that the president appeared to be dying and that he should return to Buffalo. President McKinley died on the afternoon of September 14. Judge John R. Hazel administered the oath of office to Roosevelt in the library of Wilcox's house at 3:30 P.M. on September 14, 1901. Most cabinet members witnessed the inauguration. The new president wore a long frock coat, gray trousers, a waistcoat, and a black tie, clothes he had borrowed from the men who attended the ceremony.

The Wilcox house was originally built in 1840 as officers' headquarters at Poinsett or Buffalo Barracks, a U.S. Army post. In response to the Upper Canada Rebellion of 1836–38, three companies of U.S. Artillery were ordered to Buffalo to establish a garrison for federal troops. They were to protect the American border from the British, who had seized and destroyed an American steamer, the *Caroline*. Rebellious Canadians were using Buffalo as a base to raise troops to fight the British. The United States wanted to remain neutral in the Canadian-British dispute.

The army post was built on land leased from Ebenezer Walden, who had owned the property since 1809. The Wilcox house, in a row of officers' quarters on Delaware Avenue, was a two-story, two-family brick edifice with a huge portico facing the parade ground. Buffalo Barracks was abandoned in the mid-1840s, and the inaugural site is the only remaining barracks structure. Albert P. Laning, the owner from 1863 to 1881, added a one-and-one-half-story frame service wing and basement, dug a full basement under the main house, moved the portico to the Delaware Avenue facade, and built a central doorway.

In 1883 Dexter P. Rumsey purchased the house for his daughter Mary Grace and her husband Ansley Wilcox. George Cary, an architect hired by Wilcox, replaced the frame service wing with a two-and-one-half-story brick addition, thus tripling the size of the house, which grew from a military duplex to a mansion with Greek-revival aspects. The Wilcoxes lived in the house until their deaths in the 1930s.

By the 1960s the Wilcox house had deteriorated and was threatened by demolition. Local citizens led a successful drive to preserve the historic building. In 1966 it was designated a National Historic Site, and in 1970 it was restored through the joint efforts of the Theodore Roosevelt Inaugural Site Foundation, Inc., the Buffalo and Erie County Historical Society, the Junior League, Erie County, the state of New York, and the National Park Service. It was opened to the public on the seventieth anniversary of President Roosevelt's inauguration, September 14, 1971. In 2008 the Wilcox mansion was renovated and a new visitor center was constructed. The visitor center, located on the site of the original 1901Wilcox carriage house, re-creates its exterior appearance.

Originally a duplex, the building was converted into a single-family residence with 1890s additions. The two-and-one-half-story, painted brick, restored, Greek-revival mansion has a full-width two-story pedimented portico with six columns and a center entrance with a fanlight Palladian window. Interior remodeling resulted in two parlors being combined into a large library.

The library, the dining room, the morning room/study, and a bedroom have been restored to their appearance in the 1901 era. Wilcox furnishings were auctioned after the couple's deaths, but some pieces are original and the rest are of the turn-of-the-century period.

The most impressive room in the house is the library, the site of Theodore Roosevelt's inauguration in September 1901. Vice President Roosevelt stood in front of the bay window as Judge Hazel administered the presidential oath of office. The president's first meeting with his cabinet was held here after the ceremony. Walls are lined with book-filled oak bookcases, some of which are original, as are the light fixtures.

The dining room features a large dining table set with Wilcox china. The Wilcox morning room/study was used by Mary Grace Wilcox and her daughters in the mornings and by Ansley Wilcox as a study in the evenings. Roosevelt prepared his first official document, a proclamation announcing McKinley's death and designating September 19 as a day of national mourning, at Wilcox's desk. His original draft has survived.

An upstairs bedroom has been restored as a Victorian lady's room with turn-of-the-century furniture and gas lamps. The Theodore Roosevelt room displays material related to President Roosevelt's opening of the Pan American Exposition in Buffalo on May 20, 1901; President McKinley's visit to the Pan American Exposition; his shooting by the assassin Leon Czolgosz; McKinley's death; Roosevelt's inauguration; and Czolgosz's trial.

A Victorian touching museum is located in the basement. There is a small herb garden behind the house.

Theodore Roosevelt's Maltese Cross Cabin
Theodore Roosevelt National Park
Medora, North Dakota

ADDRESS: Superintendent, P.O. Box 7, Medora, ND 58645

TELEPHONE: Park Headquarters: 701-623-4466

WEB SITE: www.nps.gov/thro

LOCATION: In Theodore Roosevelt National Park, in the Badlands of western North Dakota, near the Montana border. The south unit is 130 miles west of Bismarck, North Dakota, and 24 miles east of the Montana state line. The entrance is in Medora, exits 24 and 27 off I-94; adjacent to the south unit visitor center

OPEN: Theodore Roosevelt National Park is open daily, year-round; the Maltese Cross Cabin is open daily, 8:00 A.M. to 6:00 P.M., mid-June through Labor Day, for guided tours; 8:00 A.M. to 4:15 P.M., September through mid-June, for self-guided viewing; closed Thanksgiving, Christmas, and New Year's Day

ADMISSION: Park: $10.00 per vehicle or $5.00 per person

FACILITIES: President Theodore Roosevelt's ranch; guided tours; visitor center museum; south unit has 46,159 acres; campgrounds, hiking trails, ranger-led activities

*Theodore Roosevelt, who was born* in an elegant Manhattan townhouse, lived in a log cabin when he was a cattle rancher in the Badlands area of the Dakota Territories. His restored Maltese Cross Cabin is a little dwelling in a huge 70,447-acre North Dakota national park that in the nineteenth century was ranch land. Although a large ranch house and several outbuildings stood on Roosevelt's Elkhorn Ranch, miles from the Maltese Cross Cabin, nothing is left but the foundation of the ranch house.

In addition to being a naturalist and a conservationist who established fifty-one wildlife sanctuaries and doubled the acreage of the national parks, Theodore Roosevelt was a rancher, a hunter, and a working cowboy. He became so enchanted with the Dakota Badlands on a buffalo hunting trip in September 1883 that he invested fourteen thousand dollars in a cattle-raising business with Sylvane Ferris and Bill Merrifield of the Maltese Cross or Chimney Butte Ranch. His wife Alice was expecting a baby, and Theodore hoped that the cattle business would provide for his expanding family.

Alice died shortly after giving birth to a daughter in February 1884. Several months after this tragedy, Theodore settled in the Dakota territories. In addition to the Maltese Cross Ranch, he purchased the Elkhorn Ranch on the Little Missouri River. In the West, Theodore, a writer, wrote *Hunting Trips of a Ranchman* (1885), *Ranch Life and the Hunting Trail* (1888), *The Wilderness Hunter* (1893), and a biography, *Thomas Hart Benton.*

Roosevelt returned to New York in 1886. A terribly cold winter in 1886–87 killed about 60 percent of his cattle, a huge financial loss. By fall 1890 Roosevelt had abandoned ranching; he sold the ranches in 1898.

In 1934 federal and state governments agreed to start a Roosevelt Regional Park, and the following year the North and South Roosevelt Regional Parks were designated the Roosevelt Recreation Demonstration Area. The Works Projects Administration and the Civilian Conservation Corps built roads, trails, picnic areas, campgrounds, and buildings. In 1941, when the United States entered World War II, work on the park ceased. In mid-1947 President Truman signed the bill that created Theodore Roosevelt National Memorial Park. More land was added in 1948.

On November 10, 1978, President Carter signed a bill that gave the area national park status, and it was renamed Theodore Roosevelt National Park. It includes 70,448 acres, of which 29,920 acres are wilderness.

The Maltese Cross Cabin, built by Ferris and Merrifield in the winter of 1883–84, was Roosevelt's first home in the Dakota territories. It was located seven miles south of Medora in the bottomlands of the Little Missouri River. During Roosevelt's presidency the cabin was exhibited in Portland, Oregon, and St. Louis, Missouri, and then was moved to the grounds of the state capitol in Bismarck. In 1959 the restored cabin was returned to Theodore Roosevelt National Park. Seven miles from its original location, it is adjacent to the visitor center region of the south unit.

Roosevelt's cabin is a one-and-one-half-story ponderosa pine log structure with a steep shingle roof, a kitchen, a living room, a bedroom, a sleeping loft, and a cellar. The simply furnished interior has some of Roosevelt's furniture and other belongings. In the living room are Roosevelt's rocking chair, books, and the desk where he wrote *Hunting Trips of a Ranchman.* Ironstone china sits on the dining table. Roosevelt's wicker-lined canvas clothing trunk and a wooden bed are in the bedroom. Ranch hands slept in bunks in the loft. A coal-burning range and a Dutch oven are in the kitchen. The south unit visitor center museum displays personal items of Theodore Roosevelt, ranching artifacts including a scale model of Elkhorn Ranch, and natural history displays.

# William Howard Taft

TWENTY-SEVENTH PRESIDENT OF THE UNITED STATES
*March 4, 1909–March 3, 1913*

...........................................................................

William Howard Taft, the twenty-seventh president of the United States, who served from 1909 to 1913, was also the tenth chief justice of the Supreme Court from 1921 to 1930. He is the only person to have headed two of the three branches of the federal government: the executive and the judicial.

William Howard Taft was born on September 15, 1857, in Cincinnati, Ohio, to Alphonso Taft and his second wife, Louisa Torrey Taft. William, called "Will," was the seventh of Alphonso's ten children and the second of Louisa's five children. The Tafts lived in a large house in a prosperous suburb of Cincinnati called Mount Auburn. Alphonso Taft, a successful lawyer who was educated at Yale, was appointed as secretary of war and then attorney general by President Grant and also served as ambassador to Austria-Hungary.

Will, who attended Woodward High School, was big and was nicknamed "Lub" or "Lubber" by his classmates. He entered Yale in 1874 and graduated in 1878 as the class salutatorian. He studied law at the Cincinnati Law School and worked at his father's law firm, Taft and Lloyd. Will became an assistant prosecuting attorney and was the collector of internal revenue for the First District.

William Taft fell in love with Helen "Nellie" Herron, whose father had been a U.S. attorney in the Benjamin Harrison administration and a law partner of Rutherford B. Hayes. Will and Nellie were married on June 19, 1886. On September 8, 1889, Nellie gave birth to Robert Alphonso Taft. Helen was born on August 1, 1891, and Charles Phelps was born on September 30, 1897.

William Taft was appointed as a judge of the Superior Court of Ohio and then served as U.S. solicitor general from 1890 to 1892. In 1892 Taft became a judge of the U.S. Federal Circuit Court.

In 1900 President McKinley appointed William Taft to head a commission to establish a civil government in the Philippine Islands after the Spanish-American War. Maj. Gen. Arthur MacArthur, the father of Gen. Douglas MacArthur, had been the military governor of the islands. Taft became civil governor in July 1901. Two weeks after President McKinley was assassinated in September 1901, fifty American soldiers were massacred by Filipino rebel troops. At the time Taft was on a three-month medical leave of absence.

One problem facing the governor of the Philippines was the half million acres of land owned by Catholic orders of priests who had been driven out during the war. When the Spanish military took over the Philippines, they were followed by priests, who converted many native people. Four orders of priests were given civil authority and were authorized to collect taxes and draft men into the military. Members of the clergy owned huge tracts of land, which they leased to tenant farmers. When the rebellion against the Spanish occurred, the priests were seen as an arm of the government, and many were killed. Clergymen who survived intended to reclaim their land.

Knowing the resistance of the native people to the clergymen's return, U.S. officials preferred to purchase this land. President Theodore Roosevelt sent Taft to Rome to negotiate the sale with the pope, but Taft was unsuccessful. However, in late 1903 Congress passed the Philippine bill that stipulated the sale to the United States of 380,000 acres of land held by the Catholic orders for $7,543,000. This land was then sold to Filipino farmers.

Twice President Theodore Roosevelt offered Taft a seat on the Supreme Court, but he declined. He did accept a cabinet post as secretary of war. Roosevelt indicated that he would not run for a third term and that Taft was his choice as successor. In June 1908 the Republican National Convention nominated William Howard Taft on the first ballot. William Jennings Bryan was the Democratic candidate, and Eugene V. Debs was the Socialist candidate. Taft was victorious with 7,678,908 votes to Bryan's 6,409,104. Taft received 321 electoral votes, and Bryan received 162.

President Taft was a big man, and his weight fluctuated from 260 to 330 in his adult years. Battling obesity would be a lifelong struggle. Taft was also known for his hearty laugh and his good sense of humor.

Two months after Taft became president, Nellie had a serious stroke. Helen, who made her formal debut in December 1910 at a White House tea, left college so that she could act as hostess in the White House.

President Taft found himself in the middle of warring factions in his own party. The progressive and conservative wings of the Republican Party were locked in bitter policy and personality conflicts.

Theodore Roosevelt deliberately left the country—going on an African safari—after his presidency to allow Taft to establish himself independently. When Roosevelt returned to the United States in the summer of 1910, he was unhappy about Taft's deviations from his policies, especially in regard to conservation. President Roosevelt had set aside sixteen million acres of federal land bordering rivers and streams in the Rocky Mountains and in the Pacific Coast states because of their water-power potential. He relied heavily on Gifford Pinchot, his knowledgeable chief forester, for policies on the development of water power in the national forests. Taft's secretary of the interior, Richard Achilles Ballinger, sold some of this acreage.

Alaska coal mining was another controversial conservation issue. A series of articles in *Collier's Weekly* alleged that a coal shortage would result from fraudulent acquisition of Alaska land by mining and coal companies. Accusations of fraud came from a zealous chief of the Field Division of the Interior Department named Louis R. Glavis, who notified Pinchot that he had evidence of official misconduct by Secretary Ballinger. When he heard of Ballinger's proposed land sale, Pinchot strongly protested, and Taft fired Pinchot for insubordination. A major rift between Taft and Roosevelt occurred as a result of the Ballinger-Pinchot controversy, which obscured the fact that Taft actually conserved more land than Roosevelt had.

A congressional investigation into Alaska's coal mining situation lasted from January until May 20, 1910. A report by Attorney General Wickersham had been predated with the president's knowledge, opening him up to charges of dishonesty. Although the congressional investigation sustained the positions of Ballinger and Taft, the president emerged in the public mind with a stained character and as an enemy of conservation.

One of Taft's legislative victories was the passage of the Postage Savings Bill in June 1910. Citizens could deposit up to five hundred dollars at their local post offices and receive 2 percent interest. Legislation for the protection of railroad workers as well as railroad regulation were enacted by the Interstate Commerce Commission. Taft supported Democrat-sponsored measures to regulate safety in mines and on railroads, to create a federal Children's Bureau, and to institute an eight-hour workday for federal employees. He also supported the Sixteenth Amendment authorizing an income tax, which was ratified in 1913. Although Roosevelt earned the title "the trust buster," Taft initiated forty-three antitrust indictments during his four-year term as compared to the twenty-five brought by Roosevelt in seven years.

In 1910 progressive Republicans wanted Roosevelt back in the White House. In February 1912 Roosevelt announced that he was running for the Republican nomination. When the Republican convention met in June 1912, Taft was renominated. Roosevelt and his progressive followers claimed that Taft had stolen the nomination. In July progressive Republicans, calling themselves the Progressive Party, nominated Theodore Roosevelt for president. The Democrats nominated Woodrow Wilson. When the votes were tabulated, Woodrow Wilson won 6,296,547 popular and 435 electoral votes, Roosevelt won 4,128,571 popular and 88 electoral votes, and Taft won 3,486,720 popular and 8 electoral votes; Eugene V. Debs, the Socialist candidate, won 900,000 popular votes.

Taft became the Kent Professor of Law at Yale. He started a diet and went from 340 pounds to 270 pounds in eight months. Overtures of peace occurred between Taft and Roosevelt. Taft expressed sympathy to Theodore and Edith in July 1918 on the death of their son Quentin. They resumed their friendship prior to Roosevelt's death in 1919.

President Harding in June 1921 appointed Taft as chief justice of the Supreme Court. Taft showed signs of heart problems in 1924, suffering mild attacks in

February and April. Despite that, Taft was adamant about an appropriate building for the Supreme Court. Congress appropriated $1.5 million for the lot, and Cass Gilbert was selected as the architect.

Taft resigned as chief justice on February 3, 1930. He died on March 8, 1930, at the age of seventy-two. His body lay in state at the Capitol, and his funeral was held at All Souls Unitarian Church in Washington, D.C. William Howard Taft was buried at Arlington National Cemetery, the first U.S. president to be buried there. Nellie Taft died on May 22, 1943.

. . . . . . . . . . . . . . . . . . . . . . . . . . . . . . . . . . . . . . . . . . . . . . . . . . . . . . . . . . . . . . . . . . . . . .

## William Howard Taft National Historic Site
## Cincinnati, Ohio

ADDRESS: 2038 Auburn Avenue, Cincinnati, OH 45219

TELEPHONE: 513-684-3262

WEB SITE: www.nps.gov/wiho

LOCATION: Cincinnati is in southwestern Ohio, near the Kentucky border; the William Howard Taft National Historic Site is in the Mount Auburn area, north of downtown, accessible from I-71

OPEN: Daily, 8:00 A.M. to 4:00 P.M.; closed Thanksgiving, Christmas, and New Year's Day

ADMISSION: Free

FACILITIES: President William Howard Taft's birthplace and childhood home; education center with orientation film, exhibits, and gift shop; wheelchair accessible; special events

*William Howard Taft's restored birthplace* and childhood home on one-half acre of the original property is owned and operated by the National Park Service. Built in 1841, the exterior of the house has been restored to its appearance circa 1852–77, the years of Taft's childhood and youth.

The stately 1841 house in Mount Auburn was purchased in 1851 by the president's father, Alphonso Taft. He paid the estate of G. Bowen ten thousand dollars for the two-story square brick house, improvements, and 1.8 acres of land. Alphonso, his wife Fanny Phelps, their two sons, and his parents, Peter and Sylvia Taft, moved to this hilly community on the outskirts of the city.

Within a few months Alphonso Taft more than doubled the size of his home by building a three-story brick 41 x 23–foot ell-shaped addition to the rear of the 41 x 32–foot house. On June 2, 1852, a year after the move to Mount Auburn, Fanny Taft died. She had given birth to five children, only two of whom survived.

On December 20, 1853, Alphonso married Louisa Maria Torrey of Millbury, Massachusetts. William Howard Taft, the second of Louisa's five children, was born on September 15, 1857, in the Auburn Street home and lived there until

he left for college in 1874. More than a dozen people resided at the Taft home, including Louisa, Alphonso, Fanny Taft's sons Charles and Rossy, the surviving four of Louisa's five children, the senior Tafts, and a handyman, a cook, and two maids.

After a fire in 1877, the Tafts made a number of changes to their home. Alphonso and Louisa moved to California in 1890, and the house was sold in 1899. The residence had been remodeled into an apartment building before it was acquired by the William Howard Taft Memorial Association in 1961. In 1964 the birthplace achieved National Landmark status, and in 1969 it was designated as the William Howard Taft National Historic Site under the supervision of the National Park Service.

Restoration of the birthplace, which began in 1964, presented a prodigious challenge because almost every room was impacted by its conversion to apartments, and each unit had a kitchen and a bathroom. The roof, which had been raised after the 1877 fire, had to be lowered; the widow's walk rebuilt; the front porch, modern kitchens, and bathrooms removed; and the front stoop replaced.

The imposing three-story brick house is painted mustard yellow with green shutters. Although there are three full floors, from the front grading makes it look like a two-story house. There are two large chimneys and a widow's walk.

Rangers lead tours through the restored rooms of the house, while visitors take a self-guided tour through the rest of the house. Furniture is of the era and from Cincinnati. Portraits, books, and other items are Taft possessions. The four rooms that have been restored to William Howard Taft's childhood era are the library, the parlor, the nursery, and the master bedroom.

The parlor is decorated in the Victorian fashion with patterned wallpaper, lace curtains and heavy draperies on the windows, and a Chickering piano. Louisa loved music and had her rosewood piano shipped from Massachusetts.

The library was used every day by the family, especially the children, who did school work there. Alphonso Taft was a member of the local literary society and had one of Cincinnati's largest book collections. His love of books is evident in the library. Gas lighting was installed in 1863.

The nursery, for the youngest children in the family, is furnished with a trundle bed, a crib, a chest, and a small coal-burning stove. A nurse often slept with the children.

The rest of the house contains museum exhibits about the Taft family and their careers. One exhibit focuses on Alphonso Taft (1810–91) a diplomat in 1882 to Austria-Hungary and in 1884 minister to the tsar of Russia. Another exhibit is on Louisa Torrey Taft (1827–1907), William. H. Taft's mother. Charles P. Taft (1843–1929), President Taft's brother, served one term in the Ohio legislature and one term in the U.S. Congress and was the publisher of the *Cincinnati Times Start*. All of the Taft sons attended Yale and studied law.

There are photos of Taft when he attended Woodward High School, Yale, and Cincinnati Law School. Upstairs an exhibit covers William Taft's early public service career, his romance and marriage to Helen Herron, and their three children.

An exhibit on Taft's career covers the presidency, 1909–13. The "Presidential Firsts and Lasts" exhibit includes Taft as the first president to throw out the first baseball pitch, to be a golfer, to have a motor car at the White House, to preside over a nation of forty-eight states with the entry into the union of Arizona and New Mexico, and to have Pauline—the last family cow—at the White House. A new large bathtub was installed at the White House for Taft, who weighed 335 pounds while president.

An exhibit on the First Family and the First Lady has photographs of the Taft family while in the White House and pictures of the planting of Japanese cheery trees. There are exhibits on the presidential campaign of 1912 and on Taft as the tenth chief justice of the Supreme Court, serving from 1921 to 1930. The Taft Education Center features an animatronics figure of the president's son Charlie, who tells stories about his family.

# Woodrow Wilson

..................................................................................

Woodrow Wilson, the son of a Presbyterian minister, had a distinguished career as a scholar and politician. He brought to the presidency the belief that his policies were based on principles of religious morality. He was unwilling to compromise his principles, and his dream of world peace, guaranteed by the League of Nations, failed.

Thomas Woodrow Wilson was born in the Staunton Presbyterian Church manse in Staunton, Virginia, on December 29, 1856. He was the third of the four children of Joseph Ruggles Wilson, a Presbyterian minister born in Steubenville, Ohio, and Janet Woodrow Wilson, known as Jessie, who was born in Carlisle, England.

In 1858 the Wilson family moved to Augusta, Georgia, where Reverend Wilson was pastor of the First Presbyterian Church. During the Civil War he served as a chaplain for the Confederate army. In 1870 Joseph Wilson was appointed as professor of theology and rhetoric at Columbia Theological Seminary in Columbia, South Carolina.

The future president, who grew up in Virginia, Georgia, South Carolina, and North Carolina, witnessed the Civil War through the eyes of a southern child. Confederate soldiers marched through Augusta. Wounded soldiers were cared for in his father's church, and Union prisoners were held in the churchyard. In Augusta, Thomas saw Jefferson Davis and Gen. Robert E. Lee.

Tommy, as he was known as a child, received most of his education at home from his father. Because the boy did not read well until he was eleven years old, it is believed that he suffered from dyslexia. In 1873 he entered Davidson College in North Carolina, where he remained less than a year.

From 1875 to 1879 Woodrow Wilson attended Princeton University, a Presbyterian institution. He then entered the University of Virginia Law School, where he discontinued using the name Thomas, preferring to be called Woodrow. He passed the Georgia Bar in 1882. In 1883 Wilson was accepted to Johns Hopkins University in Baltimore, a new graduate-level institution created on the German research model.

Woodrow met Ellen Louise Axson in April 1883. Born on May 15, 1860, Ellen was the oldest child of Janie Hoyt and Samuel Edward Axson, the pastor of the First Presbyterian Church in Rome, Georgia. Woodrow and Ellen became engaged in September 1883. Ellen studied at the Art Students League in New York. Woodrow completed his course work at Johns Hopkins and secured a teaching position at Bryn Mawr, a new women's college in Pennsylvania.

On June 24, 1885, Woodrow and Ellen were married in her grandparents' home in Savannah, Georgia, in a service jointly conducted by Ellen's grandfather and Woodrow's father. Margaret was born on April 16, 1886; Jessie was born on August 28, 1887; and Eleanor was born on October 16, 1889.

Woodrow received his doctorate from Johns Hopkins in 1885, and his dissertation, *Congressional Government,* was published by Houghton Mifflin. He taught at Bryn Mawr, but in 1888 he became a professor of political science and history at Wesleyan University, a men's college in Middletown, Connecticut. In 1890 Wilson was appointed chair of jurisprudence and political economy at Princeton University. In addition to his duties at Princeton, he lectured annually at Johns Hopkins, published scholarly articles and books, and lectured throughout the country.

In October 1902 the Princeton Board of Trustees chose Professor Wilson as the school's president. Wilson introduced a tutorial system known as the preceptorial plan, restructured the curriculum, raised admission standards, expanded the physical plant, and severed the university's official ties with the Presbyterian Church.

Wilson sought to reconstruct the university's social eating clubs, which he regarded as elitist. The trustees, under pressure from the alumni not to tamper with the clubs, did not fund Wilson's plan. At the request of the trustees, Wilson resigned as president in October 1910.

Running as a Democrat, Wilson was elected governor of New Jersey in 1910. At the Democratic National Convention in June 1912, Wilson was nominated for president on the forty-sixth ballot. In the election Wilson defeated William Howard Taft, the Republican incumbent, and Theodore Roosevelt, who had mounted a third-party challenge as a Progressive. Wilson won 6,296,284 popular and 435 electoral votes. Roosevelt received 4,122,721 popular and 88 electoral votes. Taft came in a poor third with 3,486,242 popular and only 8 electoral votes. Eugene V. Debs, the Socialist candidate, received 901,873 popular votes. Wilson was the first southern-born president since the Civil War. He succeeded in having progressive legislation enacted, such as the Federal Reserve Act, which established a central financial system for the country; the Underwood-Simmons Tariff, which lowered tariffs substantially; the Federal Trade Commission Act; and the Clayton Antitrust Act.

Proclaiming a neutrality policy, Wilson sought to avoid U.S. involvement in World War I. Since 1914 the Allies—England, France, and Russia—had been at war with the Central Powers—Germany, Austria-Hungary, and Turkey.

Under international law, neutral countries were permitted to trade in non-military goods with countries at war. Great Britain, however, with the world's largest navy, imposed general economic sanctions, forbidding the shipment of all cargoes, including food, to Germany. As a result, British naval ships intercepted American ships and confiscated their cargoes.

To break the British blockade, the Germans resorted to submarine warfare in February 1915. When President Wilson protested, the Germans agreed not to sink American ships. However, many Americans traveled on British passenger ships. When German submarines in May and August 1915 sank the British ships *Lusitania* and *Arabic,* which had American passengers on board, Wilson demanded that the Germans protect passenger vessels and pay compensation for American losses. In February 1916 Germany declared unrestricted submarine warfare against all armed ships. In April, Wilson warned Germany that the United States would break diplomatic relations unless that country stopped attacking cargo and passenger ships.

At home Wilson's neutrality policy grew increasingly controversial. Although Wilson had begun to prepare for a possible war, he faced critics on two sides—those who charged him with not defending the national interest and those who felt he was leading the country into a European conflict.

First Lady Ellen Wilson died of Bright's disease on August 6, 1914. After a private funeral in the White House, she was buried in Rome, Georgia. The president's daughter Margaret served as the official hostess at White House social functions until Wilson remarried. President Wilson married Edith Bolling Galt on December 18, 1915. Edith, a widow, had been born on October 15, 1872, in Wytheville, Virginia.

In the presidential election of 1916, the Democrats renominated Wilson, while the Republican Party nominated Charles Evans Hughes, a Supreme Court justice. Wilson won a narrow victory with 9,127,695 popular and 277 electoral votes to Hughes's 8,533,507 popular and 254 electoral votes.

In January 1917 Wilson tried to negotiate a "peace without victory" settlement between the European belligerents. A desperate Germany, however, announced that on February 1 it would resume unrestricted submarine warfare in the seas around England and France. Wilson severed diplomatic relations with Germany, ordered the arming of American merchant ships, and authorized the navy to attack submarines.

On April 2, 1917, Congress, at Wilson's request, declared war against Germany and the Central Powers. Instituting a draft, Congress passed the Selective Service Act, which provided for the registration of all men between ages twenty-one and thirty. Of the twenty-four million men who were ultimately registered, two million were inducted into the armed forces, with the majority seeing combat in Europe.

Wilson faced the daunting challenge of mobilizing the American people and the nation's industry and agriculture for the war effort. To protect national security, Congress, at Wilson's request, passed the Espionage and Sedition Acts, which curtailed opposition to the war and limited civil liberties. He created the War Industries Board, headed by Bernard Baruch, to oversee industrial production, and the Food Administration, headed by Herbert Hoover, who organized a campaign to send food to starving Belgians.

By the end of October 1918 Turkey, Bulgaria, and Austria-Hungary had surrendered. On November 11 Germany accepted the armistice that ended the fighting. The American Expeditionary Force had suffered 48,909 killed and 230,000 wounded soldiers.

On January 8, 1919, Wilson announced his "Fourteen Points," which he regarded as a blueprint for world peace. They included open covenants, freedom of the seas, reduction of trade barriers, limitation on armaments, self-determination of peoples, restoration of Poland, and the creation of an international peace-keeping body, the League of Nations.

Wilson personally led the American delegation at the peace conference at Versailles, France, which began in January 1919. It was attended by Georges Clemenceau of France, David Lloyd George of England, and Vittorio Orlando of Italy. Germany was required to pay $33 billion in reparations. Wilson accepted the Allies' demands in return for their support of the League of Nations. On June 28, 1919, the treaty was signed in Versailles.

When Wilson returned home, he faced serious opposition from Republicans, who controlled both houses of Congress. Sen. Henry Cabot Lodge, head of the Senate Foreign Relations Committee, was determined to block ratification of the Versailles Treaty if it were not amended.

Taking his case to the American people, Wilson set out on a national speaking tour. At Pueblo, Colorado, Wilson on October 2 suffered a debilitating stroke. The extent of the president's illness was kept secret. Only family members, his secretary, and his physician were allowed to see him. Critics charged that his wife Edith Bolling Wilson was acting in the president's name.

The Senate took several votes on the Versailles Treaty without reservations as Wilson insisted and with amendments as Lodge demanded. None of them received the needed two-thirds vote. The war with Germany did not officially end until July 1921, when Congress passed a joint resolution terminating the conflict.

Wilson was awarded the Nobel Peace Prize on December 10, 1920. After he left office in 1921, the former president and Edith resided in Washington until his death on February 3, 1924. He is buried in the National Cathedral in Washington, D.C.

## Woodrow Wilson Presidential Library at His Birthplace
### Staunton, Virginia

ADDRESS: 18–24 North Coalter Street, P.O. Box 24, Staunton, VA 24401

TELEPHONE: 540-885-0897 or 1-888-4WOODRO (496-6376)

WEB SITE: www.woodrowwilson.org

LOCATION: Staunton is in west central Virginia, west of Charlottesville, near the intersection of I-64 and I-81

OPEN: Monday–Saturday, 9:00 A.M. to 5:00 P.M., and Sunday, noon to 5:00 P.M., March–October; Monday–Saturday, 10:00 A.M. to 4:00 P.M., and Sunday, noon to 4:00 P.M., November–February; closed Easter, Thanksgiving, Christmas Eve, Christmas Day, and New Year's Day

ADMISSION: Adults, $12.00; seniors/military, $10.00; students, $5.00; children 6–12, $3.00

FACILITIES: Birthplace of President Woodrow Wilson, museum with exhibits on Wilson's life; presidential library; learning center; gift shop; first and lower floors of the birthplace manse and the first floor of the museum are handicapped accessible. National Register of Historic Places, National Historic Landmark

*Woodrow Wilson, the twenty-eighth U.S. president* and the son of a Presbyterian minister, was born on December 29, 1856, in the Presbyterian manse in Staunton, Virginia. After a distinguished academic career as president of Princeton University, he served as governor of New Jersey and as U.S. president from 1913 to 1921. The Woodrow Wilson Presidential Library includes the restored birth home, the Woodrow Wilson Museum, and the Woodrow Wilson Research Library under the auspices of the Woodrow Wilson Birthplace Foundation.

A visit to the Woodrow Wilson birthplace provides fascinating insight into the president's family origins, education, career, and presidency. The Presbyterian manse, the home provided for the minister of the Staunton Presbyterian Church and his family, is a Greek-revival townhouse built in 1846. Located at the crest of a hill in downtown Staunton, Virginia, it has been beautifully restored to its appearance in the mid-1850s when the Wilsons were in residence. The two-story, twelve-room, painted brick house was built by John Fifer and is thought to have been designed by Rev. Rufus W. Bailey, the founder of Augusta Female Seminary. Bailey designed the seminary's classical main building in 1844, which is similar in style to the manse.

President-elect Wilson returned to his birthplace in 1912 to celebrate his fifty-sixth birthday. In 1938 the Woodrow Wilson Birthplace Foundation, with the active participation of Edith Bolling Galt Wilson, the president's widow, was incorporated to "purchase, preserve, and maintain" the old manse. Restoration work in 1940 returned the house to its appearance at the time of Woodrow

Wilson's birth in 1856. In May 1941 President Franklin Roosevelt dedicated the restored Woodrow Wilson Birthplace as a "shrine to freedom." The house was designated a registered National Historic Landmark in 1965. Recently additional exterior and interior restoration has occurred.

Since the spacious house has been restored to the time of Wilson's birth, additions and alterations that occurred since then have been removed. The rooms are painted in their original colors, revealed through paint analysis. A remarkable number of Wilson family artifacts, donated by Edith Wilson, are displayed throughout the house.

Four first-floor rooms, each with a fireplace, open off a central hall that runs from the front door to the back door. A formal parlor has lace curtains and heavy draperies at the windows and wallpaper on the walls. The original Wilson family Bible, Jessie Wilson's guitar, and Reverend Wilson's rocking chair are displayed. The Wilson's silver service is in the dining room. In the pastor's study there are maps of the United States as it was in 1846, the year the manse was constructed. The parents' bedroom, also on the first floor, is the room in which Woodrow Wilson was born. The four-poster bed belonged to the family.

Among the Wilson pieces displayed in the second-floor nursery are a baby crib used by President Wilson and his sisters and a rocking chair used by Jessie Wilson to rock her babies. In the guest chamber is a four-poster bed used by Woodrow and Ellen Axson Wilson at their home in Princeton.

Since the first floor of the manse served as a public area, the Wilsons used the lower level for dining, sewing, and other family activities. There is a family sitting room with a mahogany sideboard. Also on the lower level are a kitchen, a storage room, and simply furnished servants' rooms.

Wilson's fully restored 1919 Pierce-Arrow limousine was part of the White House fleet during Wilson's presidency. Upon his retirement it was purchased as a gift to Wilson by several Princeton friends and used until his death in 1924.

The automobile was a gift to the Wilson Birthplace Foundation from Wilson's widow, Edith Bolling Galt Wilson.

At the back of the Wilson house is a well-designed garden that is a restoration project of the Garden Club of Virginia. The Victorian gardens were designed by Charles F. Gillette in 1933. They included two terraces, one of which featured boxwood-lined bowknot beds. A brick terrace was added in 1968. In 1990 a forecourt and lawn and garden walkways connecting the museum with the rest of the grounds were added.

The Woodrow Wilson Museum, which was opened to the public in November 1990, is located in an adaptively renovated chateau-style mansion adjacent to Woodrow Wilson's birthplace and called the Dolores Lescure Center. The museum highlights Wilson's career as author, scholar, professor, university president, governor of New Jersey, and president of the United States.

The first floor contains seven exhibit galleries illustrating Wilson's life and career through artifacts, photographs, documents, and portraits. Among the exhibits are those dealing with Wilson's family origins and genealogy, his education and early career as a university professor and president of Princeton University, the governorship of New Jersey, the presidential years, World War I, the Treaty of Versailles, and the League of Nations. As guests tour the museum, they see exhibits on Wilson's books, his office at Princeton, Ellen Axson Wilson's art equipment, the campaigns of 1912 and 1916, and the events of Wilson's presidency and World War I.

The second floor contains the Woodrow Wilson Research Library, meeting rooms, and educational program space. The Wilson library has recently purchased a historic two-story mansion, Kenwood, adjacent to the Woodrow Wilson Museum. This building will be renovated into a separate Wilson library and research center, thus freeing up exhibit space in the museum. The carriage house has been renovated and is used as the First Families Research Center.

. . . . . . . . . . . . . . . . . . . . . . . . . . . . . . . . . . . . . . . . . . . . . . . . . . . . . . . . . . . . . . . . . . . . . . .

## Boyhood Home of President Woodrow Wilson
## Augusta, Georgia

ADDRESS: 419 Seventh Street, Augusta, GA 30901
TELEPHONE: 706-722-9828
WEB SITE: www.wilsonboyhoodhome.org
LOCATION: In downtown Augusta, Georgia
OPEN: Tuesday–Saturday, 10:00 A.M. to 5:00 P.M.
ADMISSION: Adults, $5.00; seniors, $4.00; children K–12, $3.00
FACILITIES: Boyhood home of President Woodrow Wilson, guided tours; visitor center; gift shop. National Register of Historic Places, National Historic Landmark, Historic American Buildings Survey

*The Wilson site in Augusta includes the home* of President Woodrow Wilson and the home of his boyhood friend Joseph Rucker Lamar (1857–1916), who became an associate justice of the U.S. Supreme Court. Lamar's house, on the adjoining property, serves as the Wilson house's visitor center. Historic Augusta, Inc., which owns and operates the site, acquired the Wilson home in 1991 and the Lamar home in 1995.

A visit to the Presbyterian manse reveals the early life of Tommy Wilson, a lad eager to experience life in Augusta during the Civil War and Reconstruction periods. Rev. Joseph Ruggles Wilson, Woodrow Wilson's father, accepted the position of pastor of the First Presbyterian Church in Augusta in 1857. He and his wife, Janet, and their three children, Marion (seven years old), Annie (four), and Thomas (one), moved to Augusta from Staunton, Virginia, in January 1858 and resided in the old parsonage on Greene Street.[1]

The trustees of the church purchased a new parsonage for the Wilson family in 1860. Built by A. H. Jones in 1859, the manse is located on a corner across from the First Presbyterian Church.[2] Considered a modern home, it was attached to the town's system of running water and illuminated by gas jets. Thomas "Tommy" Wilson lived in the new manse from age three to age fourteen, when his family relocated to South Carolina. The structure is now known as the Boyhood Home of President Woodrow Wilson and is a National Historic Landmark. Although his later public service was in the North as president of Princeton and governor of New Jersey, Wilson considered himself a son of the South.

During the Civil War, Tommy could look across the street to the church where the southern wing of the Presbyterian Church voted to create the Confederate Presbyterian Church in 1861. During the War for Southern Independence, as it was called in Georgia, this church was used as a hospital for wounded Confederate soldiers. Presbyterian services were held at the Baptist church. The churchyard was used as a prison camp for captured Union soldiers who were awaiting shipment to other prison camps.

From his front yard Tommy Wilson remembered seeing the wounded Confederates and the Yankee prisoners. He caught a glimpse of the Confederate president, Jefferson Davis, under arrest and stopping at the church on the way to prison. When Tommy was thirteen, he saw Gen. Robert E. Lee, who visited the church. During Reconstruction he saw federal troops patrolling Augusta's streets.

As governor of New Jersey, Woodrow Wilson returned to Augusta on November 18, 1911. He said he wanted to walk the streets of his boyhood and recapture the memories of his youth. At lunch in the manse, Governor Wilson sat in the same place at the dining room table he had occupied as a boy.

The Presbyterian Church owned the house until 1930, after which it was used variously as a private house museum, a florist shop, and the Woodrow Wilson Beauty Salon. On February 28, 1979, the house was listed on the National Register of Historic Places. Historic Augusta, Inc., purchased the house in 1991 for two hundred thousand dollars.[3] After extensive historical, architectural, and archaeological research, the house was restored to its 1860s appearance. It was opened to the public on September 29, 2001.

The two-story red brick house with white trim and green shutters was originally furnished with Renaissance-revival-style furniture, some of which was owned by the church and some by the Wilsons. Now it contains some original Wilson pieces and others of the period. In the entry hall is the Wilsons' marble-top table on which visitors placed their calling cards.

The front formal parlor was an often-used family room. The settee and chairs are original to the Wilsons. Ornate plaster medallions decorate the ceiling area where the gasoliers (gas lighting fixtures) were located. Reproductions are used in place of the original chandelier gasoliers, which were removed when the house was electrified.

In the dining room the table, original to the Wilsons, is set with china, glassware, and silver for a formal dinner. When Wilson visited the manse in 1911, he checked the table and verified it as the one the family had used when he was a boy. The marble-top sideboard is a Wilson piece, and there is an engraved silver butter dish inscribed to the Reverend Joseph Wilson and dated December 25, 1858.

The pastor's study/office contains a secretary desk original to the Wilsons. With a green felt writing leaf and four shelves of books, the desk was used by Reverend Wilson to prepare his sermons. Wilson's father taught him to read in this room. The Wilsons were a highly literate family as well as committed Presbyterians, so that the Bible, John Calvin's works, and religious tracts held a central place. They also enjoyed reading the novels of Charles Dickens, James Fenimore Cooper, and Sir Walter Scott. The guest room was used as the receiving room by Mrs. Wilson.

Tommy's bedroom, at the top of the stairs, overlooked the backyard. The room was his alone until the late 1860s, when his brother, Joseph Wilson Jr., was born. On a table are copies of sketches drawn by Tommy Wilson of a train, a dog, and a baseball diamond.

Wilson's two sisters' bedroom has cottage furniture, a cheaper kind of furniture painted to look more expensive. Two original gas sconces used to illuminate the house remain in this room.

An ornate Victorian-style sewing table, an original piece used by Mrs. Wilson, is in the master bedroom. There are two large unfurnished attic rooms on the third floor.

In the backyard are a garden plot and two additional buildings, a kitchen/laundry and a carriage house. The kitchen and laundry are in a two-story brick building; servants lived in the upper rooms. The brick carriage house was used for the family's horse and carriage, and the loft was used by Tommy and his baseball team for meetings.

. . . . . . . . . . . . . . . . . . . . . . . . . . . . . . . . . . . . . . . . . . . . . . . . . . . . . . . . . . . . . . . . . . . . .

### Woodrow Wilson Boyhood Home
### Columbia, South Carolina

ADDRESS: 1705 Hampton Street, Columbia, SC 29201
TELEPHONE: 803-252-1770; Historic Columbia Foundation: 803-252-7742
WEB SITE: www.historiccolumbia.org
LOCATION: Centrally located in South Carolina, Columbia is approximately 120 miles from Charleston and 150 miles from Myrtle Beach
OPEN: Closed for renovation in 2005; scheduled to reopen in 2010
FACILITIES: Boyhood home of President Woodrow Wilson

*Woodrow Wilson lived in Columbia, South Carolina,* from 1870 to 1874, when he was between the ages of fourteen and eighteen. He lived in the Woodrow Wilson Boyhood Home from the time it was built in 1872 until 1874.

The Wilson family moved from Augusta, Georgia, to South Carolina in 1870 when the future president's father, Rev. Joseph Ruggles Wilson, was appointed professor of theology and rhetoric at Columbia Theological Seminary. Reverend Wilson also served at Columbia's First Presbyterian Church.

Jessie Wilson, Woodrow Wilson's mother, in 1872 used her inheritance to build a large house, which she designed based on the architect Andrew Jackson Downing's plan of a Tuscan villa-style cottage. She oversaw the construction of the house and the design of its gardens. For the first time the Wilson family owned their own home instead of living in a church manse.

In 1873 Woodrow Wilson entered Davidson College in North Carolina, where he remained less than a year. In 1874 the Wilson family moved from Columbia to a pastorate in Wilmington, North Carolina, and Tommy, as he was known in his youth, moved with them. Wilson's sister Annie Josephine married Dr. George Howe and remained in Columbia. Joseph and Jessie Wilson, the president's parents, are buried at Columbia's First Presbyterian Church.

The Woodrow Wilson Boyhood Home, operated by Historic Columbia Foundation, was saved from demolition in 1928 and opened as a museum in 1932. It was closed for renovations in 2005, and a structural investigation of the house occurred in 2009. Renovation includes exterior repairs to the masonry foundation; wood sills, studs, and siding; restoration and replacement of windows; and the installation of a new wood-shingle roof. Other projects will involve landscaping and construction of a new outbuilding to house mechanical systems as well as visitor amenities.

........................................................................

### Woodrow Wilson House
### Washington, D.C.

ADDRESS: 2340 S Street NW, Washington, D.C. 20008
TELEPHONE: 202-387-4062
WEB SITE: www.woodrowwilsonhouse.org
LOCATION: In Washington, D.C., northwest of the White House, Du Pont Circle metro stop
OPEN: Tuesday–Sunday, 10:00 A.M. to 4:00 P.M.; closed Thanksgiving, Christmas, and New Year's Day
ADMISSION: Adults, $7.50; seniors, $6.50; students and children over 7, $3.00
FACILITIES: Retirement home of President Woodrow Wilson; audiovisual presentation; guided tours; gift shop; available for meetings and receptions; special events: May Garden Party and the September Kalorama House and Embassy Tour

*Woodrow Wilson, the twenty-eighth president* of the United States, lived only three years after leaving the presidency. During those years, 1921–24, he and his wife Edith resided in a Washington, D.C., Georgian revival town house designed in 1915 by Waddy B. Wood for Henry Fairbanks. Located in the heart of Embassy Row, it is the only presidential house museum in the nation's capital.

The twenty-two-room house on S Street is a symmetrical steel and concrete structure encased in brick with a central portico, Palladian windows, and limestone lintels. At a cost of $150,000, it was paid for with Wilson's $50,000 Nobel Peace Prize award along with $10,000 gifts from ten friends, including Bernard Baruch. Because Wilson was paralyzed after suffering a stroke in 1919, the house was adapted to accommodate his needs. An electric elevator was

installed, and a brick garage was erected for the Pierce-Arrow automobile in which Wilson enjoyed almost daily motoring trips.

After a video on Woodrow Wilson is shown, knowledgeable guides lead visitors through the impressive, yet comfortable house. Many items in the drawing room were gifts from foreign leaders. State gifts presented to contemporary presidents belong to the country, not the individual holding office, but that was not the case when Wilson was in the White House. On display are a mosaic of Saint Peter from Pope Benedict and a tapestry from the French government. After President Wilson's death on February 3, 1924, a private service was held in the drawing room before his body was taken to Washington's National Cathedral for a public funeral.

Wilson spent most of his time in his library, which is furnished with his large desk with a Tiffany desk set and a leather White House chair presented by his cabinet. He received guests here, including Justice Louis Brandeis, Franklin Roosevelt, David Lloyd George, and Georges Clemenceau. Edith's brother John Randolph Bolling, who helped Wilson with his correspondence, kept a daily log of Wilson's activities. On a radio microphone, which is displayed in the library, on Armistice Day 1923 Wilson broadcast a speech to three million people.

The dining room features a 1921 portrait of Edith Bolling Galt Wilson by Seymour Stone. Underneath the dining room is the street-level kitchen. Food was sent from the kitchen to the dining room on a dumbwaiter. The kitchen pantry holds china that was a gift from Belgium and English flo blue dishes. A modern house for the early 1920s, it has a GE refrigerator as well as a traditional large stone icebox.

In the third-floor hallway is a Robert Vonnoh portrait of Ellen Wilson and her three daughters on the veranda of a New Hampshire vacation house. Outside Wilson's bedroom is the satin rainbow flag that was America's design for the League of Nations flag.

In Woodrow's bedroom is a bed that is a duplicate of one in the Lincoln Bedroom in the White House. The desk is the one that Wilson used while he was president of Princeton. Edith's bedroom overlooked the garden and was connected to her husband's bedroom by a loggia. Pictures of Pocahontas, from whom Edith was descended, are in the room.

On the first floor is a museum displaying items in the Wilson House Collection. They include books written by and about Wilson, a presidential seal from the king of Belgium, a 1913 gold inaugural medal, a freedom casket from the city of London, Wilson's Ph.D. diploma from Johns Hopkins, an academic gown, a top hat, and Nobel Peace Prize documents. Three paintings by Ellen Axson Wilson that have been acquired by the Wilson House are *Madonna and Child*, *Landscape*, and *Landscape with Lake*.

After Woodrow Wilson's death in 1924, Edith Bolling Wilson continued to live in the house. In 1954 she gave the dwelling to the National Trust, though she continued to live there until her death in 1961. Edith wished the house to serve as a memorial to her husband.

# Warren Gamaliel Harding

TWENTY-NINTH PRESIDENT OF THE UNITED STATES
*March 4, 1921–August 2, 1923*

Consistently at the bottom of presidential rankings by historians, President Warren Harding was elected to the presidency by the largest percentage of the popular vote prior to 1920. He was a well-liked president who was deeply mourned by the nation when he suddenly died in office. Harding's historical reputation was tarnished by financial scandals perpetrated by his appointees and discovered posthumously. Personally, Harding has been linked to extramarital affairs, information not generally known during his lifetime.

Warren Gamaliel Harding, born on November 2, 1865, in Blooming Grove, Ohio, was the eldest of the eight children of Phoebe Elizabeth Dickerson Harding and George Tryon Harding. A Civil War veteran, George Harding farmed and became a homeopathic physician. In 1882 Dr. Harding relocated his family to Marion, Ohio.

Warren attended Ohio Central College in Iberia, Ohio, where he started a school newspaper—the *Iberia Spectator*. After graduation Warren became a reporter for the *Marion Democratic Mirror*. When he was nineteen, he and two associates purchased the *Marion Daily Pebble*, whose name was changed to the *Marion Star*. Warren soon bought out his partners.

Warren Harding married Florence Kling DeWolfe, daughter of Amos Kling, the richest man in Marion. Florence was a divorcee whose first husband was Henry DeWolfe, although the author Carl Anthony asserts that no record exists of a marriage between Florence and DeWolfe. Florence, who was pregnant, and DeWolfe allegedly wed in March 1880. "Their child was technically born out of wedlock. The elopement sometime in March 1880 was legend, not fact."[1] Eugene DeWolfe was born on September 22, 1880, and was called Marshall.

In December 1880 DeWolfe abandoned his wife and infant son. Because of the scandal, Florence's father cut off relations with her. Returning to Marion, Florence supported herself and her son by giving piano lessons. When Amos Kling offered to raise his four-year-old grandson, Florence accepted the offer and essentially gave up her maternal role. In May 1886 she filed for divorce. Although no marriage certificate was produced, a divorce was granted in June.

On July 8, 1891, Warren Harding married Florence in the home they had recently built on Mount Vernon Avenue in Marion. Warren suffered frequent bouts of indigestion accompanied by signs of depression and required frequent treatments by his father. During the first six months of his marriage, his symptoms reoccurred. On five separate occasions he sought treatment at the Seventh-day Adventists' Battle Creek Sanitarium in Michigan, operated by Dr. J. H. Kellogg. On January 7, 1894, Warren checked himself into the sanitarium, where he remained off and on for almost a year.

Florence, business manager of the *Star*, hired boys to deliver papers door-to-door and streamlined the bookkeeping system. Warren supervised editorial policy and solicited advertisements. Their efforts resulted in increased profitability for the *Star* and prominence for its editor.

In 1899 Warren Harding was nominated by the Republicans as a state senator. He was elected for two successive terms and became the Republican floor leader. He was nominated for lieutenant governor of Ohio in 1903 on a ticket headed by Myron T. Herrick, which proved victorious. In 1910 he ran for governor but was defeated.

Warren Harding won a U.S. Senate seat in 1914 and served until 1921. He was among the first group of senators to be directly elected by the people. Until the Seventeenth Amendment to the Constitution was passed in 1913, state representatives elected senators.

In 1920 the Republican presidential race was wide open. In addition to Harding, Leonard Wood, Hiram Johnson, Frank Lowden, and Herbert Hoover were candidates. At the Republican convention Harding came in fourth behind Wood, Lowden, and Johnson on the first ballot. After four deadlocked ballots, the party leaders retired to the legendary "smoke-filled room," where they settled on Warren Harding, who received the nomination on the tenth ballot. Calvin Coolidge was the vice-presidential choice. Harding's Democratic opponent was Gov. James M. Cox, with Franklin D. Roosevelt for vice president.

In the postwar period Harding as a candidate promised a return to normalcy, a term he invented. He delivered statements from the front porch of his Marion home to six hundred thousand curious citizens. Warren Harding looked presidential. Tall and erect, he was a handsome, distinguished, authoritative-looking statesman.

Three weeks before the election, brochures produced by Prof. William E. Chancellor of Wooster College in Ohio circulated asserting that Harding had African ancestry. Chancellor was a racial bigot who advocated segregation. Although Republican Party leaders were devastated, Democrats refused to capitalize on the story. Most newspaper editors declined printing the allegations. Warren Harding did not dignify the charge with a response. A Harding family tree produced by a reputable Pennsylvania historical society was distributed.

Warren Harding won a stunning victory with 16 million votes versus James Cox's 9 million votes. He garnered 404 electoral votes to Cox's 127 electoral votes. Women could vote in a presidential election for the first time throughout the United States in 1920.

Domestically, President Harding supported greater civil rights for Negroes, released World War I political prisoners including Eugene V. Debs, and appointed former president William Howard Taft to the Supreme Court. In foreign policy, the Washington naval conferences of 1921–22 ended the naval arms race between Japan, England, France, Italy, and the United States and adopted the Four-Power and the Nine-Power pacts. The Four-Power Pact pledged the United States, England, Japan, and France to maintain the peace of the Far East by respecting each other's territorial holdings and maintaining the region's military status quo. In the Nine-Power Pact, which added the countries of China, Italy, Belgium, the Netherlands, and Portugal, the signatories agreed to respect the territorial integrity, sovereignty, and independence of China.

Harding and his administration were probusiness. Secretary of Commerce Herbert Hoover pursued a policy to make American business more competitive on the world market and sought to reduce labor disputes through arbitration. Tariff rates were increased and federal government expenditures substantially cut.

President Harding and his wife left on a tour of the western states and Alaska on June 20, 1923, and returned through the Panama Canal. Harding made numerous stops to deliver speeches and attend special events. Suffering from an undiagnosed cardiovascular disease, President Harding died at the Palace Hotel in San Francisco on August 2, 1923.

The country was stunned by Harding's death. In Vermont, Calvin Coolidge was sworn in by his father as the next president of the United States. President Harding's body was transported by train, and millions of people reverently watched while his coffin passed through their area. His body lay in state in the East Room of the White House and then in the Capitol. After being moved to Marion, Ohio, President Harding was placed in a temporary vault until the Harding Memorial was completed in 1927.

Harding was a popular president who was sincerely mourned by the country. Not until after his death did his personal sexual improprieties and his administration's financial scandals become widely known. A young woman named Nan Britton claimed to have had a long affair with Harding and to have given birth to his daughter. She expected the Harding family to provide for her and her daughter after his death, as she claimed he had during his life. When the family refused, she wrote a book called *The President's Daughter.* Warren, who had been a friend of Nan's father, and Nan were thirty years apart in age. No documentary evidence to support her claims was produced.

In 1963 documentary evidence of an affair between Warren Harding and Carrie Phillips was uncovered by the biographer Francis Russell. Carrie was a grade-school teacher who was married to James E. Phillips. The affair began in 1905. In 1956, after Mrs. Phillips entered a nursing home, an attorney named

Donald Williamson found a locked closet in her home containing ninety-eight Harding love letters written between 1910 and 1920. When Russell learned of the letters, he informed Kenneth W. Duckett, manuscript curator of the Ohio Historical Society, of them. Russell and Duckett persuaded Williamson to give the letters to the Ohio Historical Society. Some historians were given access to the letters, and Duckett made photographic copies of them. Harding's heirs wanted the correspondence suppressed, if not destroyed, and sued the Ohio Historical Society over ownership of the letters. The court decided that Mrs. Phillips's daughter owned the letters. She sold them to Dr. George T. Harding III, the president's nephew, who donated them to the Library of Congress with the provision that they would be sealed until July 2014. The letters indicate that in 1920 Carrie was trying to blackmail Warren Harding.

The best-known scandal during the Harding administration concerned the Teapot Dome, a naval oil reserve near Salt Creek, Wyoming. Secretary of the Interior Albert B. Fall arranged for the naval oil reserve to be transferred to the Navy Department before he resigned from the Department of the Interior in 1923. Fall had financial problems, and Edward L. Doheny lent $100,000 and Harry F. Sinclair lent $304,000 in bonds and cash in return for leases on the oil land. Harding agreed to the transfer of the oil reserves to the Navy Department by executive act because he thought it would be a better administrative arrangement.

Because she told a Library of Congress official that she had burned all of President Harding's papers, it was believed that Florence Harding did just that soon after his death. She shipped between five and eight large wooden crates of papers from Harding's second-floor White House office to Marion, where she and an assistant went through them. It is estimated that the pair discarded more than half of the papers while the remainder went to the Harding Memorial Association.

The papers from Harding's White House executive office were discovered in 1929 in the basement of that building. They were given to the Harding Memorial Association along with papers from the *Marion Star* and from Harding's legislative career. Documents found in the basement of Harding's house in Marion in 1963–64 were transferred to the Ohio Historical Society. Florence Harding died on November 21, 1924, and is buried with her husband in Marion, Ohio.

................................................................................

Harding Home
Harding Tomb
Marion, Ohio

ADDRESS: 380 Mt. Vernon Avenue, Marion, OH 43302; Harding's tomb is at the corner of State Route 423 and Vernon Heights Boulevard in Marion,

about one and one-half miles west of U.S. Route 23 off State Route 95 in Marion County

TELEPHONE: 740-387-9630 or 1-800-600-6894

WEB SITE: www.ohsweb.ohiohistory.org/places/harding/

LOCATION: Marion is in northwest Ohio, fifty miles north of Columbus, ninety-five miles southeast of Toledo; on State Route 95, about two miles west of U.S. Route 23 in Marion County

OPEN: Thursday–Sunday, noon to 5:00 P.M., Memorial Day through Labor Day; Saturday–Sunday, noon to 5:00 P.M., September and October

ADMISSION: Adults, $6.00; children 6–12, $3.00

FACILITIES: Home built by President Warren Harding; burial site of President Harding

*For thirty years President Warren Harding* and his wife, Florence, lived in a home that they designed and built in Marion, Ohio. Harding, who was born, raised, educated, married, and buried in Ohio, moved with his family to Marion in 1883. There he purchased and edited a local newspaper, the *Marion Daily Star.* Warren met Florence Kling DeWolfe in Marion. Prior to their marriage the couple designed a house and had it constructed. They were married in its front hallway in July 1891. They lived there their entire married life, with the exception of Harding's years in the U.S. Senate, until 1920.

After Harding was elected the twenty-ninth president of the United States in 1920, he and his wife leased their house in Marion while they vacationed in Florida. Harding was inaugurated on March 4, 1921, and the Hardings moved into the White House. President Harding died in office on August 2, 1923. Florence returned to Marion but not to her home, which was still occupied by tenants. She died in November 1924.

Florence Harding bequeathed her house and its furnishings to the Harding Memorial Association, organized in 1923 to preserve the president's house and build his tomb. Two hundred thousand schoolchildren contributed pennies, and a total of $977,821 was raised. The structure was used as a house museum, and several rooms were opened to the public.

In 1978 the property and structures were donated to the state of Ohio. The site is operated by the Ohio Historical Society, which also owns its furnishings. In 1964–65 the house was restored, and the library was renovated in 2005.

The Harding house is a frame two-and-one-half-story Queen Anne–style structure with a gabled roof and green clapboard siding with cream colored trim. A distinctive feature of the home is its large colonial-revival porch with a rounded end. During what was called a "front porch campaign," Warren Harding gave forty formal speeches and one hundred informal speeches to the public and press from this porch while he was a presidential candidate. Six hundred thousand people traveled by train to Marion to see and hear Warren Harding. They walked along Mt. Vernon Avenue, dubbed "Victory Way," from the Marion train depot to Harding's home.

The original porch collapsed in 1903 when crowds came to congratulate Harding on his election as lieutenant governor. The wicker furniture on the current porch, which dates to 1904, belonged to the Hardings. The front lawn, which had been covered with gravel to accommodate the crowds, is now edged with roses.

Because the Harding house was occupied almost exclusively by the Hardings, it has an extensive collection of original furniture and artifacts. Patterned rugs and wallpaper, heavy velvet draperies, and oak woodwork lend a Victorian air. Many decorative objects were purchased by the Hardings while traveling. Stained glass windows from Germany decorate the parlor, the dining room, and the entrance hall.

On the first floor of the house are a reception hall, a dining room, a parlor, a library, and a kitchen. Warren and Florence were married in the spacious reception hall by Reverend Wallace of the Epworth Methodist Church; one hundred guests attended the ceremony. Appointments include a gas fireplace with Rookwood tile and original rugs, drapes, and gas light fixtures. On his fifty-fifth birthday Warren Harding sat at the Egyptian wooden table inlaid with mother-of-pearl waiting for election results.

The piano in the parlor belonged to Dr. Charles W. Sawyer, the Hardings' physician. Florence Harding studied piano at the Cincinnati Conservatory of Music and also gave lessons. The library, used by Harding the publisher and politician, has cherry bookcases and a desk used by Harding in the Ohio Senate.

The dining room has a gas fireplace, a built-in china cabinet, a buffet, and a table that could be expanded to seat twelve people. White House china is displayed here. In the kitchen there is a six-burner gas stove with two ovens made in Battle Creek, Michigan, and an icebox that could hold one hundred pounds of ice.

On the second floor are the master bedroom, Marshall DeWolfe's room, a guest bedroom, a maid's room, and a bathroom. The master bedroom, which has bird's-eye maple furniture, has twin beds. Warren Harding wore the top hat on the dresser at his presidential inauguration. Florence's dresses, shoes, and fur coat are displayed on mannequins.

It is said that Calvin Coolidge, William Howard Taft, and Herbert Hoover slept in the brass bed from Germany in the guest room. There is a chiffonnier purchased by the Hardings in Vienna.

In the maid's room is a Jenny Lind bed with a log cabin quilt made in the 1870s by Melissa Harding, Warren Harding's cousin. The bathroom sink has three faucets, one of which was for rainwater.

Adjacent to the Harding Home is a white, one-story clapboard structure known as the Press House. Believed to be a Sears and Roebuck precut house ordered from a catalog, it was built in the summer of 1920 for journalists covering the presidential campaign. It is now a museum in which are displayed the Harding family cradle, Harding's inaugural stand, and stamps issued in Harding's honor. Near the museum there is a horse-drawn Ohio voting-booth car used between 1880 and 1940.

Two miles from the Harding Home is the tomb of Warren G. and Florence Harding, located at the corner of State Route 423 and Vernon Heights Boulevard in Marion. After Harding's death, his body was placed in a temporary tomb at the Marion cemetery. Under the auspices of the Harding Memorial Association, a design competition was held in 1925 for the Harding tomb. The commission was awarded to Henry Hornbostel and Eric Fisher Wood of Pittsburgh. The original cost of the tomb was $783,108.

Set in ten acres of landscaped grounds, the circular monument of white Georgia marble is reminiscent of a Greek temple. Columns of white marble on both sides of a circular wall define a raised courtyard and a hanging garden. Japanese maples shade the black granite tombstones of Harding and his wife.

The tomb was dedicated in June 16, 1931, by President Hoover. Restored in 1990, the tomb is owned by the Ohio Historical Society. The Harding tomb is open daily during daylight hours, and admission is free.

# Calvin Coolidge

THIRTIETH PRESIDENT OF THE UNITED STATES
*August 3, 1923–March 3, 1929*

.........................................................................

Known as "Silent Cal" because of his reticence, Calvin Coolidge, a quiet and frugal New Englander, presided over the economic prosperity and dramatic social change of America in the 1920s. A private man in a public office, he became president on the death of President Warren Harding.

Only one president was born on Independence Day. John Calvin Coolidge was born on July 4, 1872, in Plymouth Notch, Vermont, in the eastern foothills of the Green Mountains. He was the oldest child of John Calvin Coolidge and Victoria Josephine Moor Coolidge. A daughter, Abigail (Abbie), was born three years later.

Plymouth Notch, a tiny community, consisted of a few farmsteads, a church, a school, and a general store. John Coolidge operated a general store and was a farmer and a state legislator. Victoria Coolidge, Calvin's mother, died on her thirty-ninth birthday, leaving a twelve-year-old son and a nine-year-old daughter. Grandmother Coolidge, Sarah Almeda Brewer Coolidge, stepped in to mother Calvin and Abigail. Grandpa Coolidge had died when Calvin was six, but he had already taught his grandson how to ride a horse standing up.

Calvin began attending the Black River Academy in Ludlow in February 1886 and lived in a family-run rooming house. Two years later Calvin's sister entered the academy. In March 1890 fourteen-year-old Abbie became ill and died a week later.

In 1891 John Coolidge married Carrie Brown, who had been Calvin's elementary teacher. Calvin was admitted to Amherst College in September 1891 and graduated cum laude with a bachelor of arts in June 1895. Coolidge read law, was admitted to the bar in July 1897, and opened an office in Northampton, Massachusetts.

In December 1898 Calvin was elected as a councilman for his ward in Northampton. In 1900 and again in 1901 he was appointed as city solicitor, and in 1903 he was appointed to the post of temporary clerk of courts for Hampshire County.

Coolidge was a political anomaly—a shy public man. The appellation "Silent Cal" was well earned, according to hundreds of witnesses. He did not engage in small talk, answered questions in monosyllables, and showed little facial expression. Yet Coolidge's writing is crisp, to the point, insightful, and heartfelt. His *Autobiography* is emotional and revealing.

In Northampton, Coolidge lived in a rooming house operated by Robert Weir, steward of the Clarke Institute for the Deaf. In 1903 Calvin fell in love with Grace Goodhue, a teacher at the Clarke school. A graduate of the University of Vermont, Grace was extroverted and vivacious and loved music, theater, and baseball. On October 4, 1905, Grace and Calvin were married in Burlington, Vermont. John was born on September 7, 1906, and was followed by Calvin Jr. on April 13, 1908.

Coolidge was elected to the Massachusetts House of Representatives in 1906, was reelected in 1907, and then served as mayor of Northampton from 1910 to 1911. He was elected to the Massachusetts Senate in 1911 and was reelected twice. During his third term he became president of the senate.

In 1915 Coolidge was the Republican nomination for lieutenant governor with the gubernatorial candidate Samuel McCall. The McCall-Coolidge ticket prevailed, and they were reelected in 1916 and 1917. Coolidge was elected governor of Massachusetts in 1918.

Coolidge's term as governor coincided with the end of World War I. There were tensions in the workforce and workers' strikes. In 1918 the Boston police force formed the Boston Social Club, which was granted a charter by the American Federation of Labor. When Police Commissioner Curtis threatened union leaders with firing, they threatened to strike. Governor Coolidge supported Commissioner Curtis. On September 8, 1919, Curtis suspended nineteen union leaders, and 1,117 policemen walked off the job on September 9. Mayor Peters replaced Curtis. Governor Coolidge reinstated Commissioner Curtis and called out the Massachusetts National Guard. He said, "There is no right to strike against the public safety by anybody, anywhere, any time."[1] The strikers were replaced by Boston's unemployed, many of them veterans.

Since no Republican candidate had the presidential nomination locked up in 1920, states pushed their favorite sons. Sen. Henry Cabot Lodge put Coolidge's name in nomination for president. When the 1920 Republican National Convention convened, Warren G. Harding was nominated for president and Coolidge was nominated for vice president. The Democrats nominated James Cox, governor of Ohio, for president and Franklin D. Roosevelt of New York for vice president. Harding and Coolidge won with a popular vote of over sixteen million votes to nine million for Cox and Roosevelt and nearly one million for Eugene V. Debs, the Socialist candidate.

On June 20, 1923, President Harding left Washington on a cross-country trip, and in San Francisco he became seriously ill. He died at the Palace Hotel in San Francisco on August 2. Vice President Coolidge, who was in Plymouth Notch, was aware that President Harding was ill but anticipated his full recovery.

When the agent at the Bridgewater telegraph office received the news of Harding's death, he telephoned the store at Plymouth Notch, which had the only telephone in town, but no one answered. Coolidge's chauffeur, Joseph McInerney, drove William Crawford, a newspaper man, and Coolidge's stenographer, Erwin Geisser, to Plymouth Notch and informed Vice President Coolidge of the president's death.

Attorney General Daugherty advised Coolidge to take the oath of office as president, and Secretary of State Hughes informed Coolidge that a notary could administer the oath. John Coolidge was a notary. In his sitting room illuminated by a kerosene lamp, John administered the presidential oath of office to his son at 2:47 A.M. on August 3, 1923. Witnesses included Grace and the Coolidge's sons.

Coolidge presided over the economic prosperity and booming stock market of the Roaring Twenties. Although most of the nation enjoyed prosperity, the country's farmers were beset by a deep depression. There were precipitous drops in the prices for agricultural commodities in the 1920s due to American overproduction and the decline of European importation of American wheat and cotton. Coolidge, who believed that such special aid was not a federal responsibility, vetoed farm-aid legislation.

Calvin Coolidge Jr. stubbed his toe while playing tennis on the White House courts. He developed blood poisoning and died on July 7, 1924. A funeral service was conducted in the East Room of the White House. Young Calvin was buried in the cemetery at Plymouth Notch.

Coolidge received the Republican Party's presidential nomination in the election of 1924. Charles G. Dawes, director of the budget under Harding, was nominated for vice president. The Democrats nominated John W. Davis from West Virginia for president and Charles Wayland Bryan, the governor of Nebraska, for vice president. The Progressives nominated Robert La Follette, senator from Wisconsin. Coolidge won with 15,717,533 popular and 382 electoral votes to Davis's 8,386,169 popular and 136 electoral votes. La Follette won 4,814,000 popular and Wisconsin's 13 electoral votes.

The president's grief for his son was overwhelming. He delegated more work as he had less energy. Yet his term was noted for having a stable economy, tax cuts, and reduction of the national debt. Coolidge announced that he would not seek reelection. Herbert Hoover was inaugurated as president in 1929.

The Coolidges returned to Northampton, Massachusetts, where Calvin began an ambitious writing program that included his *Autobiography* and, from mid-1930 to mid-1931, a syndicated daily column for the McClure Newspaper Syndicate. On January 5, 1933, Coolidge collapsed and died. He was sixty years old. His funeral was held in Northampton's Congregational Church and was attended by President and Mrs. Hoover. Calvin Coolidge was buried in the small cemetery in Plymouth Notch, Vermont, alongside his son, mother, father, and generations of relatives.

Grace died on July 8, 1957, at age seventy-eight. In her will Grace specified that her husband's birthplace be given to the state of Vermont.

....................................................................

## President Calvin Coolidge State Historic Site
## Plymouth Notch, Vermont

ADDRESS: 3780 Route 100A, P.O. Box 257, Plymouth Notch, VT 05056
TELEPHONE: (802) 672-3773
WEB SITE: www.historicvermont.org/coolidge
LOCATION: In mid-eastern Vermont, six miles south of US 4 on Vt. Route 100A
OPEN: Daily, 9:30 A.M. to 5:00 P.M., Memorial Day to mid-October
ADMISSION: Adults, $7.50; children 6–14, $2.00; family passes, $20.00
FACILITIES: Home, inaugural site, and burial site of President Calvin Coolidge; visitor center with exhibits, museum stores; Wilder House restaurant; nature trails; self-guided tour

*The President Calvin Coolidge State Historic Site* / Plymouth Notch Historic District ranks among the top presidential sites for ambiance, natural beauty, idyllic setting, and historic restoration. Because of its remote location in the Green Mountains, Plymouth Notch retained its rural character with tranquil mountain vistas. It is easy to step back into the Coolidge time frame here.

President Calvin Coolidge was born, spent his entire youth, attended school and church, was inaugurated as the thirtieth president of the United States, and is buried in Plymouth Notch, Vermont. His inauguration site is most unusual as after the first two presidents presidential inaugurations were held in Washington, D.C. The exceptions were inaugurations of vice presidents, such as Coolidge, who attained the office on the death of presidents.

Five generations of Coolidges lived in the small agricultural community of Plymouth Notch. President Coolidge's paternal great-great-grandfather, Capt. John Coolidge, was a Revolutionary War soldier. In the 1780s he purchased land in Plymouth Notch with his mustering-out pay. A house he built around 1815 eventually became the home of the president's paternal grandfather, Calvin Galusha Coolidge. The future president spent time in his youth at his grandparents' farm and often wore his grandfather's blue wool frock and boots.

The President Calvin Coolidge State Historic Site / Plymouth Notch Historic District is owned and operated by the Vermont Division for Historic Preservation, which has acquired twenty-five buildings, most of the village, and nearly one thousand adjacent acres of fields and forestland. Buildings open

to the public, most of which have been carefully preserved and contain their original contents, include the birthplace home, the Coolidge Homestead, and John Coolidge's general store and cheese factory.

The visitor center, a stone structure built in 1972, contains a museum and a gift shop. Museum displays focus on Coolidge's life, career, and presidency. Quotations from Coolidge's 1929 autobiography accompanied by photographs take the visitor from Coolidge's family and birth through his presidential years.

The Calvin Coolidge birthplace is a four-room house connected to a general store that had been operated by John Coolidge, the president's father. Calvin Coolidge was born on July 4, 1872. The family lived in this house until they moved to the Coolidge Homestead—a larger, separate house—in 1876. The birthplace has been restored to its 1872 appearance. Furnishings belonged to the Coolidge family.

In the sitting room are a corner cupboard and a sofa with horsehair upholstery. The first-floor bedroom, in which Calvin and his sister, Abigail, were born, has a rope bed. The kitchen has a cast-iron stove and a sink; there is crockery in the pantry.

The attached general store is stocked with food, kitchen utensils, dishes, tools, and fabric found in late nineteenth-century Vermont general stores and is also a gift and book shop. The upstairs of the general store is Coolidge Hall, originally used as a storage area. It was remodeled around 1890 for community meetings and dances, with music provided by the Plymouth Old Time Dance Orchestra. A bandstand, a piano, and musical instruments are displayed. At the entrance to the hall a silent video is shown of newsreels featuring President Coolidge.

Calvin and Grace Coolidge returned to Plymouth Notch in 1924, accompanied by eighteen Secret Service agents, the president's secretary, and his stenographer. The hall served as the official summer White House office. Telephones

and a telegraph were installed. President Coolidge and his staff worked at several large tables made for the president, which remain in the hall. In 1991 the hall was restored to the summer White House period.

The Coolidge Homestead, the boyhood home of President Calvin Coolidge, was purchased by John Coolidge in 1876, along with a blacksmith shop and several acres of land. The one-and-one-half-story white frame and clapboard farmhouse is connected to a barn by a shed—a common arrangement in New England so that farmers could tend their animals without going out in inclement weather. John Coolidge added the front piazza and the bay windows in the sitting room. Calvin lived here from the age of four until his graduation from Amherst College in 1895.

After President Coolidge's father died in 1926, his housekeeper Aurora Pierce remained in the Coolidge Homestead for thirty years, acting as its caretaker. She preserved and maintained it as it was in the early 1920s. In 1931 President Coolidge, now retired, put an addition on the Homestead. In 1956 John Coolidge, the president's son, gave the Homestead and all its contents to the state of Vermont. Restoration of the house was funded by the state legislature. The 1931 addition was removed.

Calvin and his family were visiting Plymouth Notch when he was notified of President Harding's death. The sitting room, the oath of office room, is the location of Calvin Coolidge's inauguration as president on August 3, 1923. The oath of office was administered at 2:47 A.M. by his father, John Coolidge, who was a notary public. Witnesses included Grace Coolidge and her sons John and Calvin, U.S. Representative Porter H. Dale, L. L. Lane of the Railway Mail Association, William Crawford, a newspaper man, Coolidge's chauffeur, Joseph McInerney, and his stenographer, Erwin Geisser.

The house has been restored to its appearance on Coolidge's inauguration day, and the room looks as it did on that fateful night in 1923, with the same table and kerosene lamp. Furnishings include John Coolidge's desk with his seal of notary public of Vermont.

The parlor, which was reserved for special occasions, has its original black walnut horsehair furniture and cast-iron stove. John Coolidge was a deacon in the Union Christian Church. Sometimes church services were held here when the church was too cold. A photograph of a Sunday school picnic is the only photograph of both Calvin and Abigail.

A first-floor bedroom contains the furniture from the upstairs bedroom where Grace and Calvin stayed while visiting. The quilt on the bed was made by Abigail Coolidge.

The kitchen has the original cast-iron wood stove and a table set for four. The shed bedroom has the bed in which the future president was born. A rare presidential artifact is the tumbling-block quilt made by ten-year-old Calvin, who also made the miniature chest of drawers. Displayed is Grandfather Coolidge's wool frock, which Calvin Coolidge frequently wore and in which he was photographed.

The Union Christian Church, a Congregational church that is owned by the Calvin Coolidge Memorial Foundation, was built in 1840 and is the church attended by the Coolidge family. The interior of the white frame Greek-revival structure was remodeled with golden oak in the carpenter gothic style in the 1890s.

The Wilder house was the childhood home of Calvin Coolidge's mother, Victoria Josephine Moor. She was married to John Coolidge in its front sitting room in 1868. Built as a tavern around 1830, it was remodeled in 1956 into a restaurant, which serves breakfast and lunch.

The Wilder barn, built in 1875 on the Moor-Wilder farm, is used for exhibits on Vermont rural life. Among these exhibits are a horse-drawn U.S. mail wagon and sleigh, newspapers relating to Harding's death and Coolidge's swearing in as president, maple-sugaring items, ice-cutting saws and tongs, and a one-horse open sleigh. The Wilder horse barn, a 2003 re-creation of the original 1875 barn, displays horse-drawn vehicles. The schoolhouse dates from 1890 and replaces the original schoolhouse that Calvin Coolidge attended, graduating from eighth grade in 1885.

John Coolidge was one of several farmers who in 1890 built the Plymouth Cheese Factory, where cheese was produced until 1934. The president's son John reopened the factory in 1960. In 1998 the Vermont Division for Historic Preservation purchased the factory. Since late 2004 Frog City Cheese has operated the cheese-making factory and a retail store.

President Calvin Coolidge is buried in Plymouth Cemetery along with six generations of the Coolidge family. Grace Coolidge and Calvin Coolidge Jr. are also buried there.

# Herbert Clark Hoover

THIRTY-FIRST PRESIDENT OF THE UNITED STATES
*March 4, 1929–March 3, 1933*

. . . . . . . . . . . . . . . . . . . . . . . . . . . . . . . . . . . . . . . . . . . . . . . . . . . . . . . . . . . . . . . . . . . . . .

Herbert Hoover was one of the most respected but also one of the most reviled of American political leaders. Honored as a great humanitarian and a great engineer, Hoover fed millions of starving people by organizing massive aid programs for a Europe devastated by World War I. During the Great Depression of the 1930s, however, he was viewed as an uncaring and remote president.

Herbert Clark Hoover was born on August 10, 1874, in West Branch, Iowa. He was the second of the three children of Huldah Randall Minthorn Hoover and Jesse Clark Hoover. Hoover spent his formative years in Quaker communities in Iowa, Oregon, and California. In 1738 Herbert's great-great-great-grandfather Andreas Huber, a Swiss, arrived in Philadelphia and Anglicized his name to Andrew Hoover. The Hoover family converted to the Society of Friends, the Quakers, and relocated to West Branch, Iowa, in 1854. Huldah Minthorn was born in 1848 in Burgersville, Ontario, Canada. Her family joined the Friends community of West Branch when Huldah was eleven years old.

Jesse Clark Hoover was a blacksmith and operated a farm-implement business. In 1880, at age thirty-four, he died. Herbert was six years old. Huldah Hoover turned to her relatives for help raising her children. From March to October 1881 young Bert, as Herbert was called, lived with his uncle Laban Miles, superintendent on the Osage Indian reservation in the Oklahoma Territory. Hulda died at age thirty-five on February 24, 1884, leaving her three children, ages twelve, nine, and seven, orphans.

In November 1885 eleven-year-old Bert Hoover, in the care of a Quaker family, traveled for seven days on a Union Pacific Railroad emigrant train to Newberg, Oregon, to live with his Aunt Laura and Uncle John Minthorn and their daughters. John Minthorn, Huldah's only brother, was a physician. He had practiced briefly in West Branch, where he had resuscitated two-year-old Herbert, whom his parents believed had died of the croup; they had even placed pennies on his eyes and covered his face with a sheet.

In Newberg, John Minthorn served as superintendent of a Quaker school, Friends Pacific Academy, which Bert attended. Later, Bert's brother, Theodore, his sister, Mary, and their grandmother joined the Minthorn family. In 1888 Dr. Minthorn moved his family to Salem, Oregon, where he established the

Oregon Land Company, which dealt in real estate and owned orchards, a hotel, and saw and flour mills. Herbert, now thirteen, left school and worked for three years as an assistant bookkeeper in the Oregon Land Company. He studied mathematics at night school.

Herbert was determined to become an engineer, though he did not have a high school education. Dr. Joseph Swain, a college recruiter and a Quaker, encouraged Hoover to apply to Stanford University in California, a new institution that specialized in engineering and technology. With the exception of mathematics, Hoover failed Stanford's entrance examination and spent the summer of 1891 in Palo Alto, California, receiving precollege tutoring. He was admitted to Stanford's first class as a major in geology. Although Stanford was tuition free, Herbert paid his living expenses from a two-thousand-dollar education fund that his mother had established. After graduating in May 1895, Hoover worked as a miner near Nevada City, California.

In 1897 the British firm Bewick, Moreing and Co. hired Hoover to assess the gold-producing potential of the desert of western Australia. Traveling by camel to remote mining sites there, Hoover prepared technical reports, surveys, and assessments of mines. In 1898 Hoover became Bewick's agent in China, a position that included a share of the profits. He was appointed as the Chinese government's resident chief engineer of the Bureau of Mines of Northern Chihli and Jehol Provinces.

While at Stanford, Herbert fell in love with Lou Henry, who also majored in geology and graduated from Stanford in 1898. Herbert and Lou were married on February 10, 1899, in her parents' Monterey, California, home. The couple would have two children: Herbert Jr., born on August 4, 1903; and Allan Henry, born on July 17, 1907.

The newlyweds arrived in Shanghai, China, in March 1899 and located in Tientsin's foreign compound. Suspicious of Western business motives, the imperial government imposed severe restrictions on foreign operators of Chinese mines.

A widespread reaction to foreign infringement occurred in 1900 when the Boxer Rebellion broke out. The Boxers, secret societies covertly supported by the imperial government, began a violent campaign to eradicate foreign influence in China and restore traditional values. They tried to destroy railroad and telegraph lines and attacked Christian schools and hospitals, killing missionaries and Chinese who worked with foreigners. Herbert and Lou were among hundreds of foreigners who sought refuge in the quarter-mile-wide and one-mile-long foreigners' settlement in Tientsin, which was besieged by shells and bullets for thirty days. Fifteen hundred lightly armed soldiers from several foreign countries aided by seven hundred Russian solders protected the foreign enclave from thousands of raging Boxer insurgents. Three hundred people were killed. Lou Hoover, armed with a .38 caliber pistol, served on guard duty.

Herbert helped barricade the town, fought fires, and delivered food and water to the six hundred anti-Boxer Chinese who had taken refuge in the quarter. The Boxers were crushed, and a combined force of European, American, and Japanese troops rescued the foreigners. Lou and Herbert Hoover left China on August 14, 1900.

With the failure of the Boxer Rebellion, European, American, and Japanese troops confiscated Chinese mines and mining equipment. Chang Yen-Mao, the imperial director of mines, reorganized China's mines under the control and protection of a British corporation that provided capital for development. Hoover, as trustee, accepted a deed to the properties. In England he assigned his power of attorney to Charles Moreing, who established the British-based Chinese Engineering and Mining Company. Hoover, a director of the new company, received a quarter of a million dollars of company stock.

In January 1901 the Hoovers returned to China, where Herbert was the acting general manager of the mining company. Caught in a power struggle between Belgian investors and the Chinese board, Hoover left China on October 1, 1901. He and Lou settled in London, where Hoover had become a partner in Bewick, Moreing and Co.

Hoover's business took him again to Australia, where he introduced a new separation process that he and his brother had invented to extract lead and silver from tailings. He became director and eventually chairman of the board of Burma Mines, which made large profits for Bewick and Moreing. In 1908 he resigned his partnership and worked as an independent mining engineer. Hoover's investments made him independently wealthy.

When World War I began in August 1914, the U.S. Embassy in London asked Hoover to help stranded American travelers in Europe get back home. Hoover organized the American Citizens' Relief Committee, a volunteer organization that aided 120,000 Americans.

When Emile Francqui, chairman of the Comite Nationale de Secours et d'Alimentation, asked Hoover to join relief efforts, he organized the Commission for Relief in Belgium, which provided millions of tons of food to feed seven million Belgians and two million French. Hoover became known as the "Great Humanitarian."

With America's entry into World War I in 1917, President Wilson appointed Hoover as the U.S. food administrator. Hoover successfully increased America's agricultural productivity and controlled prices so that the country could feed itself, provide for its troops, and aid war-devastated European countries. "To Hooverize" became a familiar slogan as Hoover encouraged Americans to observe designated meatless and wheatless days and to plant backyard "victory gardens." When the war ended, Hoover, as director general of the American Relief Administration, continued efforts to feed war-devastated Europe, especially Russia, which was in the grip of a communist revolution.

President Harding appointed Hoover as secretary of commerce. Calvin Coolidge, who took office upon Harding's death in 1923, retained Hoover. In 1927 the Mississippi River flooded an area one thousand miles long and forty miles wide, damaging seven hundred thousand homes and displacing six hundred thousand people. President Coolidge appointed a Mississippi Flood Committee with Hoover as chairman. Hoover, who established refugee camps for more than three hundred thousand people and organized myriad county health units, coordinated the efforts of Red Cross nurses, National Guardsmen, and thousands of volunteers. Hoover helped draft the Mississippi Flood Control Bill of 1928.

In 1928, at the Republican Party National Convention, Hoover received the presidential nomination. Sen. Charles Curtis of Kansas was his vice-presidential running mate. The Democratic candidate was Alfred E. Smith, New York's governor. Hoover won 21,391,993 popular and 444 electoral votes to Smith's 15,016,269 popular and 87 electoral votes.

The stock market plummeted on October 24, 1929, beginning the Great Depression of the 1930s. The country descended into an economic catastrophe with increasing unemployment. Hoover firmly believed that the American economy would recover, as it had in the past, through individual initiative, free enterprise, and the free market. He argued that federal aid would weaken local government. The economy went into a steep decline with mounting bank and business closings. A severe drought in the Great Plains caused a dust bowl, adding environmental disaster. Hoover was vilified in the press and condemned in Congress.

Hoover rejected Democrat efforts to provide federal relief for the unemployed. In February 1931 he vetoed a bill that would have enabled veterans of World War I to receive early payments of their bonuses, due in 1945. In the summer of 1932 twenty thousand veterans, loosely organized as the "bonus army," marched on Washington demanding early payment of their bonuses. They occupied abandoned buildings in Washington, D.C., and set up camp at Anacostia Flats in Maryland.

Hoover, working quietly through the District of Columbia Police Department, provided "clothing, beds, tents, medical supplies, kitchen equipment, and army food free or at cost" to the bonus marchers.[1] On July 15 Congress denied the bonus request, and while most veterans returned home, about two thousand remained. On July 28 Washington police evacuated several buildings near the White House, killing two bonus army veterans.

When local police said that they could no longer maintain order, the president ordered Patrick Hurley, the secretary of war, to use the army to clear Pennsylvania Avenue. Gen. Douglas MacArthur, in command of the operation, massed one thousand troops "including Third Cavalry troopers with sabers drawn," led by Maj. George S. Patton Jr., and "supported by six midget tanks, tear gas and a machine-gun unit."[2] Although Hoover had ordered Mac-Arthur to avoid attacking the bonus army camp at Anacostia, the general commenced an assault on the veterans, ignoring the advice of his aide, Col. Dwight Eisenhower. On July 21, 1932, MacArthur's troops routed the veterans from the camp. Twenty thousand spectators watched as troops burned down "bonus city," and the event was heavily covered in the press. Hoover's anger at Mac-Arthur's insubordination was unknown by the public, and the president took the brunt of the nation's disapproval. Franklin Roosevelt remarked that this fiasco assured his election in 1932.

That year the Republicans renominated Hoover and the Democrats nominated Franklin D. Roosevelt. Carrying forty-two of the forty-eight states and receiving more than 60 percent of the popular vote, Roosevelt won 22,809,638 popular and 472 electoral votes to Hoover's 15,758,901 popular and 59 electoral votes.

Herbert and Lou Hoover returned to their Palo Alto home. In 1934 they moved to the Waldorf Towers in the Waldorf-Astoria Hotel in New York City. On January 7, 1944, Lou Henry Hoover died of a heart attack. During Herbert Hoover's thirty years after serving as president in the White House, he wrote many books. Under President Harry Truman, Hoover served as chairman of the Famine Emergency Committee in 1946–47, helping to feed millions of people after World War II. He died on October 20, 1964, at the age of ninety and was buried in West Branch, Iowa.

........................................................................

## Herbert Hoover National Historic Site
## Hoover Presidential Library and Museum
## West Branch, Iowa

ADDRESS: 210 Parkside Drive, P.O. Box 488, West Branch, IA 52358

TELEPHONE: 319-643-5301 or 319-643-2541

WEB SITE: www.nps.gov/heho

LOCATION: In central Iowa, forty-five miles west of Davenport and ten miles east of Iowa City, one-half mile north of I-80, exit 254

OPEN: Daily, 9:00 A.M. to 5:00 P.M.; closed Thanksgiving, Christmas, and New Year's Day

ADMISSION: National Historic Site: free; library museum: adults, $6.00; seniors, $3.00

FACILITIES: The birthplace, childhood home, and presidential library of President Herbert Hoover; visitor center; gift shop and audiovisual program in museum; special events; President and Mrs. Hoover's grave sites; museum is handicapped accessible

Herbert Hoover National Historic Site,
West Branch, Iowa

*The Herbert Hoover National Historic Site,* located on 148 acres of rolling Iowa prairie at West Branch, portrays President Hoover's humble Quaker origins. Buildings open to the public are the Hoover birthplace cottage, the Hoover blacksmith shop, the West Branch School, and the Friends meetinghouse. Houses on adjoining properties with preserved exteriors contribute to the flavor of a nineteenth-century small town. One hundred acres of prairie grasses and wildflowers add to the atmosphere, as does Wapsinonoc Creek, which flows through the grounds where Hoover learned to fish using willow poles. Adjacent to the restored area is West Branch's downtown, which has buildings listed on the National Register of Historic Places.

West Branch was a predominately Quaker community when, in 1853, Herbert Hoover's great-grandfather Jesse Hoover moved there from Ohio. His namesake, Jesse Hoover, the president's father, bought two lots in West Branch, Iowa, for ninety dollars in 1871. Jesse and his father, Eli, built a two-room, board and batten cottage on one of those lots at the corner of Downey and Main streets. Its foundation was constructed of boulders from the open prairie to the west. Wisconsin timber was rafted down the Mississippi River, cut into lumber at the Muscatine sawmill, and then hauled thirty miles by oxcart to West Branch.

The 14 x 20–foot, whitewashed, two-room frame birthplace cottage was Herbert Hoover's home until he was five years old. The Hoovers used the larger room as a combination parlor, kitchen, and dining room, while the smaller room was the family's bedroom. The cottage has front and rear porches and an attached enclosed porch that was used as a summer kitchen. A wood shed at the rear of the cottage was used as sleeping quarters for a hired man. On August 10, 1874, the night of Herbert Hoover's birth, E. D. Smith, a hired hand who was sleeping there, was awakened and sent to get help for Mrs. Hoover, who was in labor. Most of the furniture is of the period, with the exception of Hoover's original cradle and high chair.

Jesse Hoover operated a blacksmith shop from 1871 to 1878. Reconstructed on the original site in 1957, the present blacksmith shop has a dirt floor, a forge, and smithy tools and equipment. Herbert Hoover wrote, "My recollection of my father is of necessity dim indeed. I retain one vivid memento from his time. Playing barefoot around the blacksmith shop, I stepped on a chip of hot iron and carry the brand of Iowa on my foot to this day."[3]

The white frame, one-room schoolhouse, built in 1853, was originally used by the Quakers as a school and a meetinghouse. Each of four desks seats two students, and also in the schoolhouse are a teacher's desk, an iron stove, and oil lamps. The children's lunch pails were stored in the entryway.

The meetinghouse, built by the Religious Society of Friends of West Branch in 1856, has two large rooms divided by partitions. The plain wooden structure, illuminated by lanterns, has pale green walls with wainscoting and an iron stove. Benches on the right were for the men, and those on the left were for the women. Elders sat facing the congregation. Hulda Hoover was a recorded minister, which meant that she had, because of her speaking ability, gained the respect of the meeting. Hoover wrote, "Since my mother had been educated above most women in those days—as a school-teacher—she was in demand as a speaker at Quaker meetings."[4]

In May 1878 Jesse Hoover sold the family cottage, the adjoining lot, and his nearby blacksmith shop for one thousand dollars and moved his family to a larger two-story house a block south. This house has been torn down. In 1890 the birthplace cottage was sold to R. P. Scellars. Mr. Scellars moved another house onto the property and joined the two houses together.

When Herbert Hoover became a well-known public figure, his birth home became a tourist attraction. Mrs. Scellars charged tourists ten cents admission. In 1927 Lou Hoover wanted to buy the cottage, but Mrs. Scellars refused to sell. After her death in 1934, Mrs. Scellars's heirs sold the property to Fred Albin, a friend of Herbert Hoover, who purchased it at Hoover's request. Albin immediately sold it to Allan Hoover, the president's son. Lou Hoover, the president's wife, supervised restoration of the cottage to its original condition. Additions to the house were removed.

On December 1, 1939, the property was transferred to the Herbert Hoover Birthplace Society, which purchased twenty-five additional acres of land surrounding the site. Jesse Hoover's blacksmith shop was reconstructed in 1957,

and in 1964 the Friends meetinghouse was moved to the site. In 1964 Herbert Hoover died at the age of ninety and was buried on a knoll overlooking the site. Lou Henry Hoover, who had died in 1944 and was buried in Palo Alto, California, was reinterred there shortly thereafter. The first West Branch schoolhouse was moved nearby in 1971.

When the Herbert Hoover Birthplace Society merged with the Herbert Hoover Birthplace Foundation in 1958, construction began on a museum of Hoover memorabilia. Two years later a library to house President Hoover's papers was added to the project. The Herbert Hoover Presidential Library and Museum was opened on August 10, 1962. In 1964 a fifteen-thousand-square-foot library addition was constructed. In 1965 the site was designated the Herbert Hoover National Historic Site under the administration of the National Park Service. Further additions to the library were built in 1971 and 1992, enlarging the building to forty-four thousand square feet.

The library, in a well-landscaped parklike setting, is a one-story building with six galleries depicting significant events in Herbert Hoover's life. The biographical exhibits in the museum galleries contain life-size figures, audiovisual stations, and interactive displays.

Gallery one begins with Hoover's birth in Iowa and covers his years at Stanford University, his mining experience in Australia, his wedding to Lou Henry, and his career in China. Gallery two focuses on the initial stages of Hoover's involvement in public life, 1901–14. Hoover's first assignment was to assist 120,000 Americans stranded on the Continent at the beginning of World War I. Hoover next headed the Belgium Relief Program and then directed the U.S. Food Administration. Gallery three centers on Hoover as secretary of commerce during the Harding and Coolidge administrations. Hoover was interested in conservation and wanted to reduce waste, conserve resources for the future, establish parks, and protect wildlife. Gallery four focuses on Hoover as the 1928 Republican presidential candidate against the Democrat Alfred E. Smith, the election, and the years in the White House.

Lou Henry Hoover is the subject of gallery five. She was one of the first American women to earn a geology degree. The exhibit features her extensive travels, her support of the Girl Scouts, and her contributions to the presidential retreat, Camp Rapidan, a Virginia fishing camp.

Herbert Hoover's post-presidential life is the centerpiece of gallery six. From late 1940 President Hoover lived in a suite at New York's Waldorf-Astoria Hotel, and its living room has been re-created. It features Hoover's desk and chair where the prolific author worked. Hoover died in the Waldorf Towers section of the hotel on October 20, 1964.

The National Park Service maintains a visitor center on the property. President and Mrs. Hoover are buried on a hill overlooking the Hoover birthplace, and their graves are marked by simple white Vermont marble gravestones.

..............................................................................

## Camp Rapidan
Shenandoah National Park
Luray, Virginia

ADDRESS: Shenandoah National Park, 3655 U.S. Highway 211 East, Luray, VA 22835

TELEPHONE: National Park: 540-999-3500; Camp Rapidan tours: 540-999-3283

WEB SITE: www.nps.gov/shen/historyculture/rapidancamp

LOCATION: Shenandoah National Park is in northern Virginia; Rapidan Camp is midway through the park, near Byrd Visitor Center and Big Meadows area; ranger-guided van tours leave from the Byrd Visitor Center at Big Meadows, milepost 51

OPEN: Shenandoah National Park is open year-round; most facilities are open mid-April through October; ranger-led programs to Camp Rapidan are from mid-June to early September and are by reservation only

ADMISSION: $15.00 per vehicle or $8.00 per individual entrance fee to Shenandoah National Park, March–November

FACILITIES: Summer White House of President Herbert Hoover; Shenandoah National Park has lodging, camping, restaurants, hiking trails, picnic areas, horseback riding, fishing, Skyline Drive; Big Meadows Lodge is the closest lodging to Rapidan Camp. National Historic Landmark

*Camp Rapidan, also known as Camp Hoover,* in Shenandoah National Park, was President Hoover's summer White House where he relaxed, fished, and entertained guests. Herbert Hoover wanted a getaway within one hundred miles of Washington, D.C., that was remote, scenic, and at an elevation of twenty-five hundred feet or higher to avoid mosquitoes.

Camp Rapidan, Luray, Virginia

The wooded site, selected by President and Mrs. Hoover in Virginia's Blue Ridge Mountains, was accessible only by horseback. Hoover purchased the land, located at the headwaters of the Rapidan River, with his own funds in July 1929, paying five dollars an acre. Two thousand acres of surrounding land were leased to insure privacy and security for the chief executive and his guests, and for hiking and riding trails. Hoover also paid for building materials while the Marine Corps cleared brush, erected structures, built furniture, erected bridges, and diverted water to create a new stream for running water, a waterfall, and a trout pond.

With an eye to impacting the natural terrain as little as possible, Lou Hoover and the architect James Rippin designed the campsite layout and its thirteen buildings, which included the president's lodge, two dining halls, staff and guest cabins, and a community center called Town Hall. The First Lady also oversaw work on the landscaping, pathways, and a fountain. Used from March through early November, the uninsulated buildings were heated only by fireplaces.

Because Hoover wanted the 164-acre property to serve as a weekend retreat for future presidents, he donated the land for incorporation into Shenandoah National Park, which was authorized in 1926 and established in 1935. President Franklin Roosevelt, Hoover's successor, used a wheelchair and found the terrain too rugged. The property was subsequently used for a variety of purposes and was designated as a National Historic Landmark in 1988.

Although it's a challenge to get to Camp Rapidan, the beautiful mountain scenery makes it worth the effort. The presidential retreat, a small area in a 280-square-mile national park, can be accessed either by hiking the four-mile-round-trip Mill Prong Trail, which begins at Milam Gap parking area (milepost 52.8 on Skyline Drive), or by ranger-guided van tours that leave from the Byrd Visitor Center at Big Meadows.

Ten of the thirteen wooden buildings on the site were torn down by the National Park Service in 1962. The Park Service has recently restored the remaining buildings to their appearance in 1931, midway through Hoover's presidential term. The cabins still standing are the President's Cabin or Brown House, the Prime Minister's Cabin, and the Creel Cabin. Other original features are an outdoor stone fireplace, a trout pool, a stone fountain, stone bridges, and trails. Although even Lou Hoover said that the camp was at the end of nowhere, it did have electricity and telephones, and the mail was flown in.

To return the rustic buildings to their original appearance, additions were removed, copper gutters were reinstalled, and newer roofs were replaced with asphalt shingle. The porch on the President's Cabin was restored, and the porch on the Prime Minister's Cabin was reconstructed. Stone masonry was rebuilt.

The rustic President's Cabin has a 60 x 20–foot living room, two bedrooms, two bathrooms, a screened sleeping porch, a large open porch with an opening for a tree, two fireplaces, and an open beam ceiling. Heart-of-pine wood was used for the walls, floors, and ceilings. Windows open inward, and there are copper-screened drop-down shutters. Deck chairs as well as silverware, china, and kitchen equipment came from the U.S. Navy's presidential yacht the *Mayflower*. Other furnishings were card tables, small mahogany tables, and locally purchased chairs and braided rugs.

An exhibit on Camp Rapidan, housed in the Prime Minister's Cabin, has photographs of the Hoovers and their guests, including Charles and Anne Lindbergh, British prime minister Ramsay MacDonald, Winston Churchill, and Thomas Edison. The Creel Cabin is used as housing for interpreters.

. . . . . . . . . . . . . . . . . . . . . . . . . . . . . . . . . . . . . . . . . . . . . . . . . . . . . . . . . . . . . . . . . . . . . . . . . . . . .

## Hoover-Minthorn House
## Newberg, Oregon

ADDRESS: 115 South River Street, Newberg, OR 97132
TELEPHONE: 503-538-6629
LOCATION: Newberg is twenty-three miles southwest of Portland, accessible from Routes 219 and 99W
OPEN: Wednesday–Sunday, 1:00 P.M. to 4:00 P.M., March–November; Saturday–Sunday, 1:00 P.M. to 4:00 P.M., December and February; closed January
ADMISSION: Adults, $3.00; seniors/students, $2.00; children 10 and under, $0.50
FACILITIES: Restored boyhood home of Herbert Hoover. National Register of Historic Places

*Herbert Hoover was born in 1874* in a Quaker community in West Branch, Iowa. After being orphaned at age nine, he went to live with his mother's brother Henry John Minthorn and his family, who resided in a Quaker community in Newberg, Oregon. In 1885 Herbert, in care of a Quaker family, traveled west for seven days on a Union Pacific train. The Minthorn family included Dr. John Minthorn, his wife Laura Ellen Miles, and their two daughters. Their only son had died.

Dr. Minthorn, a physician, had studied medicine at Iowa State Medical College. In 1883 the Minthorns settled in Oregon, where John was employed as superintendent of the Chemawa Indian School in Forest Grove. When Friends Pacific Academy was founded in Newberg, Dr. Minthorn became its superintendent in 1885 and Laura Minthorn became the principal of the grammar school. Friends Pacific Academy was the forerunner of Newberg's George Fox College, a Quaker institution. When eleven-year-old Herbert Hoover arrived in Newberg, he became a student at the academy.

Jesse Edwards, the founder of Newberg, was a scout for Indiana Quaker farmers. He bought a large amount of land and plotted out the town. In 1881 he built the house that would be purchased by the Minthorns in 1885. They lived there with their nephew until 1889, when the family relocated to Salem, Oregon.

Owned and operated by the National Society of Colonial Dames of America, the Hoover-Minthorn House was placed on the National Register of Historic Places in 2003. The oldest house still standing in Newberg, it has been well restored to its appearance in the late 1880s when President Hoover was a boy.

The Hoover-Minthorn House is a two-story, Italianate, cream-colored frame structure. On the first floor are a parlor, a dining room, a kitchen, and a pantry as well as an adjoining lean-to. Upstairs are three bedrooms: a master bedroom for John and Laura Minthorn; a bedroom for their daughters; and a small bedroom for Herbert. There are few original furnishings in the house, but similar furniture was obtained from homes in the region.

From the front porch visitors enter the dining room, which is furnished with a table and chairs, a large pie safe, and an original stove. There are photographs of the family as well as the house before restoration. Hoover artifacts include his fishing flies and his hat. Books by and about President Hoover are on the table.

In the parlor are Dr. Minthorn's sliding rocking chair and Laura Minthorn's rocking chair, a desk with bookcases, and family photographs. The kitchen has an iron stove. The lean-to off the kitchen was used for bathing and food preparation.

On the second floor, the master bedroom has its original stove. The girls' room has a trundle spindle bed, children's toys, and a small rocking chair. The bed and dresser in Herbert's small bedroom were used by the boy. Also on display are a bat, a ball, and a fishing rod.

Landscaping includes a perennial garden near the porch with blue asters and rudbeckias. A trellis supports grape vines. Behind the house is a raised herb garden.

# Franklin Delano Roosevelt

THIRTY-SECOND PRESIDENT OF THE UNITED STATES
*March 4, 1933–April 12, 1945*

Franklin Delano Roosevelt is the only president to be elected for third and fourth terms. He died just months into his fourth term after having served from March 4, 1933, until April 12, 1945, twelve years and thirty-nine days. He was president during the worst economic period in American history—the Great Depression—and a war-time president during World War II. A polio victim, he was confined to a wheelchair years before he became president.

Franklin Delano Roosevelt, born on January 30, 1882, in Hyde Park, New York, was the only child of Sara Delano Roosevelt and James Roosevelt. The Roosevelts were part of the Hudson River Valley's old patroon Dutch colonial aristocracy. Klaes Martenszen van Rosenvelt arrived from Holland in 1649. His son Nicholas had three sons, one of whom, Jacobus, was Franklin's direct ancestor, while another son, Johannes, was Theodore Roosevelt's direct ancestor, making Theodore and Franklin distant cousins. A wealthy family, the Roosevelts made money in real estate and merchandising.

James Roosevelt purchased 110 acres of land in Hyde Park with a seventeen-room house named Springwood, which had been built in 1826. His property grew to 1,000 acres of rolling farmland along the wooded bluffs of the Hudson River. Franklin Delano Roosevelt grew up at Springwood, spent summers at the family's summer home on Campobello Island in Canada, and traveled extensively with his parents. James, who was director of the Delaware and Hudson Railroad and the Louisville, Albany and Chicago Railroad, had a private railroad car.

Franklin's hobbies included stamp collecting and ornithology (birds). His father gave him a shotgun when he was eleven, and he shot hundreds of birds, which were stuffed by a taxidermist. When he was sixteen, Franklin's parents gave him a twenty-one-foot knockabout named *New Moon*. He became an able sailor and sailed all his life.

At age fourteen Franklin entered Groton School, a prestigious preparatory boarding school in Groton, Massachusetts. He then attended Harvard, where he majored in history and government. While Franklin was at Harvard, his cousin Theodore Roosevelt became vice president of the United States, and in September 1901 Theodore became president after President William McKinley's death.

Eleanor Roosevelt was a member of Franklin's social set, and she and Franklin became engaged in late 1904. Anna Eleanor, born on October 11, 1884, was the daughter of Anna Hall and Elliot Roosevelt, a younger brother of Theodore Roosevelt. Eleanor was orphaned when she was nine years old and was cared for by her Grandmother Hall. From the ages of fifteen to eighteen Eleanor attended Allenswood, a finishing school in London.

President Theodore Roosevelt gave the bride, his niece, away at the wedding of Franklin and Eleanor on March 17, 1905. On June 24, 1904, Franklin graduated from Harvard and entered Columbia Law School. He passed the bar exam in spring 1907 and worked for a Wall Street law firm. In 1908 Sara Roosevelt and the young couple moved into adjoining townhouses, built and designed by Sara, on New York City's East Sixty-fifth Street.

Franklin and Eleanor had six children. Their only daughter, Anna Eleanor, was born on May 3, 1906. James was born on December 23, 1907; Franklin Jr. was born on March 18, 1909, but died on November 8, 1909; Elliott was born on September 23, 1910; Franklin Delano Jr. was born on August 17, 1914; and John Aspinwall was born on March 13, 1916.

In 1910 Roosevelt, a Democrat, was elected to the New York Senate, and he was reelected two years later. President Wilson appointed Roosevelt as assistant secretary of the navy in March 1913. War broke out in Europe in the summer of 1914. When the nation entered the war on April 6, 1917, Congress authorized funds to build the navy to war strength.

Franklin took a European naval inspection trip in summer 1918. When he returned home, Eleanor discovered in his luggage love letters between her social secretary, Lucy Mercer, and Franklin. Devastated, Eleanor offered Franklin a divorce. Sara may have made threats to cut him off financially. His political assistant, Louis Howe, pointed out the consequences that divorce would have on Franklin's political future. Franklin ended the affair.

When World War I ended, Franklin ran unsuccessfully for the U.S. Senate. In 1920 James M. Cox, the Democratic candidate for president, selected Franklin as his running mate, but they lost to the Republican candidate, Warren Harding.

In August 1921 Franklin joined his family at their summer home on Campobello Island. He started to feel ill. Soon he could not walk and was paralyzed from the waist down. Dr. Robert Lovett diagnosed infantile paralysis—polio.

For the next seven years Franklin devoted himself to his recovery. He spent winters on a houseboat in Florida and then at a Georgia resort, Warm Springs, which had a spring-fed pool that was a constant eighty-eight degrees. As hard as he worked, Roosevelt would be confined to a wheelchair for the rest of his life.

In 1926 Franklin purchased Warm Springs. The nonprofit Georgia Warm Springs Foundation was established and purchased the hotel and grounds from Roosevelt for one dollar. Franklin built a small house on the foundation grounds. After he became president of the United States, this was known as the Little White House, and it was where Roosevelt would die in 1945.

In 1928 Roosevelt was elected as New York's governor, and he won reelection in 1930. At the Democratic presidential convention in 1932, Roosevelt was nominated on the fourth ballot with John Nance Gardner as vice president. President Herbert Hoover was renominated by the Republicans. Roosevelt won 472 electoral and 22,809,638 popular votes, or 57 percent, to Hoover's 59 electoral and 15,758,90l popular votes.

When Roosevelt was inaugurated on March 4, 1933, the nation's economy was on the brink of complete collapse, with unemployment at thirteen million and banks closed throughout the country. Announcing the New Deal agenda of relief, recovery, and reform, the president called Congress into a special emergency session. One day after his inauguration, Roosevelt by executive order closed the banks to prevent further runs on them. Congress on March 9 passed the Emergency Banking Relief Act, which provided for federal supervision and aid to the banks. The Reconstruction Finance Corporation provided federal loans to banks in financial difficulty. In June 1933 the Federal Deposit Insurance Corporation helped restore public trust.

During his first hundred days in office, Roosevelt launched a barrage of new legislation, which the Democratic-controlled Congress quickly passed. New Deal programs were directed at industrial and agricultural recovery, relief for the unemployed, and reform to correct weaknesses in the system.

The Tennessee Valley Authority was established to build dams that would provide hydroelectric power to bring electricity to the upper South. The Agricultural Adjustment Act set production limits to reduce the agricultural surplus, conserve soil to fight the dust bowl, and raise prices for agricultural crops. The Civilian Conservation Corps provided work for more than two million young men in the nation's parks and recreational areas. The Social Security Act, enacted in 1935, provided for a federally administered program of old-age pensions. The 1935 Wagner Act created a National Labor Relations Board to enable unions to engage in collective bargaining. The Fair Labor Standards Act established minimum wages and maximum hours of work per week. The National Youth Administration helped two million young people remain in high school and college by providing part-time employment in libraries and as research assistants. The Works Progress Administration provided eight million jobs in airports, post offices, hospitals, and schools.

In 1936 the Democrats renominated President Roosevelt and Vice President Garner, while the Republicans nominated Gov. Alfred Landon of Kansas. Roosevelt won by a landslide with 523 electoral and 27,752,869 popular votes to Landon's 8 electoral and 16,674,982 popular votes.

Roosevelt's Good Neighbor Policy renounced past American intervention in Latin America and, in 1934, its right to intervene in Cuba. By 1936 American troops no longer occupied any Latin American country.

When war began in Europe in 1939 with the German invasion of Poland, Roosevelt declared American neutrality and yet asked Congress to repeal the arms embargo to supply weapons to England and France. Congress allowed belligerent countries to purchase war supplies, provided they transported the goods in their own ships.

After Nazi Germany had conquered much of Europe and England was left standing alone, Roosevelt transferred fifty old American destroyers to England in exchange for rights to build air and naval bases on British possessions in the Western Hemisphere. Congress increased the defense budget to ten billion dollars and authorized the first peacetime draft, setting in motion the Selective Service in 1940.

In the election of 1940, the Democrats renominated Roosevelt for an unprecedented third term and nominated Henry A. Wallace as his vice-presidential running mate. The Republican presidential nominee was Wendell Willkie of Indiana. The results were another Roosevelt victory, with 27,263,448 popular and 449 electoral votes to Willkie's 22,336,260 popular and 82 electoral votes.

After his third inauguration, which for the first time was held in January, Roosevelt turned his attention to helping Britain fight the Nazis. Because Britain was financially exhausted, Roosevelt proposed the Lend-Lease Act, through which Britain and its allies received fifty billion dollars' worth of goods and services.

In September and October 1941 three American ships were sunk by German submarines, after which U.S. destroyers were ordered to attack U-boats on sight. Congress permitted American ships to deliver supplies to England and authorized the arming of U.S. merchant ships.

Japan signed the Tripartite Pact with Germany and Italy. On December 7, 1941, Japanese carrier-based planes bombed the American fleet at Pearl Harbor, sinking eight battleships, destroying 265 aircraft, and killing more than twenty-four hundred sailors. Congress declared war on Japan, and on December 11 Germany and Italy declared war on the United States. All four Roosevelt sons were in the military.

Roosevelt and Churchill forged a remarkable Anglo-American alliance, concentrating on first defeating Germany and then the Japanese. They endorsed a plan to create the United Nations. They also broadened the Allied alliance to include Joseph Stalin of the Soviet Union and Chiang Kai-shek of China. On June 6, 1944, the Allies invaded France at Normandy, and they liberated Paris on August 25. In the Pacific the turning point in the war was at Midway Island in June 1942.

On the home front, the War Production Board was created to mobilize American industry for full-scale war-time production. The Office of Price Administration sought to control prices and ration scarce goods. A blight on Roosevelt's civil rights record was the forced relocation of 120,000 Japanese Americans in 1942 to resettlement camps. This action was based on fears that they might commit acts of sabotage.

Roosevelt was renominated for a fourth term in 1944. Sen. Harry S. Truman of Missouri was the vice-presidential candidate. The Republicans nominated Thomas E. Dewey. Roosevelt received 25,611,936 popular and 432 electoral votes to Dewey's 22,023,372 popular and 99 electoral votes.

An Allied victory was in sight when Roosevelt met in February at Yalta in the Soviet Union with Churchill and Stalin. The president was clearly in ill health, suffering from congestive heart disease. In April 1945 Roosevelt went to Warm Springs, Georgia. In 1943 Franklin had resumed seeing Lucy Mercer Rutherfurd, and she was widowed in 1944. An artist, Elizabeth Shoumatoff, had been commissioned to do a portrait of the president. On April 12, 1945, while sitting for the artist in his cottage with Lucy Mercer in the room, Roosevelt suffered a massive cerebral hemorrhage; he died a few hours later.

On April 13 a funeral train carried the president's body to Washington, D.C. He was then taken to Hyde Park, New York, where on April 15 he was buried in his mother's rose garden at Springwood. Eleanor Roosevelt died on November 7, 1962.

. . . . . . . . . . . . . . . . . . . . . . . . . . . . . . . . . . . . . . . . . . . . . . . . . . . . . . . . . . . . . . . . . .

## Home of Franklin D. Roosevelt National Historic Site
## Franklin D. Roosevelt Presidential Library and Museum
## Hyde Park, New York

ADDRESS: 4097 Albany Post Road, Hyde Park, NY 12538

TELEPHONE: FDR home: 1-845-229-9115; library: 1-800-FDR-VISI (1-800-337-8474); Top Cottage: 845–229–5320

WEB SITE: www.nps.gov/hofr

LOCATION: In southeastern New York's Hudson Valley, on U.S. 9, six miles north of Poughkeepsie; ninety miles north of New York City; twelve miles from Rhinebeck

OPEN: FDR home and library: daily, 9:00 A.M. to 5:00 P.M.; closed Thanksgiving, Christmas, and New Year's Day; tours of Top Cottage are Thursday–Monday, May–October

ADMISSION: Adults 16 and older, $14.00; Top Cottage, $8.00; Val-Kill, $8.00; Vanderbilt estate, $8.00; combination tickets at reduced rates available

FACILITIES: Home, presidential library, museum, retreat cottage, and grave site of President Franklin Roosevelt; guided tours of the FDR home, which is

Home of Franklin D.
Roosevelt National
Historic Site, Hyde
Park, New York

handicapped accessible; rose garden; Henry A. Wallace Visitor and Education Center; Val-Kill; shuttle bus to Top Cottage

*The Home of Franklin D. Roosevelt National Historic Site* in Hyde Park, New York, is a three-hundred-acre site with the birthplace and boyhood home of President Franklin Delano Roosevelt, which is operated by the National Park Service, and the Franklin D. Roosevelt Presidential Library and Museum, which is operated by the National Archives. On adjoining property is Top Cottage, Franklin Roosevelt's retreat, and Val-Kill, Eleanor Roosevelt's retreat. In addition Franklin and Eleanor are buried on the grounds.

Franklin Delano Roosevelt was born and raised at Springwood, and he and his wife and children lived there for many years. During his years in the White House, President Roosevelt returned more than two hundred times to Hyde Park. The president donated Springwood and thirty-three acres of land to the government in 1943, with the provision that his family be allowed to live there after his death. The president's will specified that the house and grounds should remain as they were at the time of his death. After the president's death, the property was transferred to the U.S. Department of the Interior. The Roosevelt family relinquished their lifetime rights, and the home was opened to the public in 1946.

Franklin's father, James Roosevelt, purchased 110 acres of land in Hyde Park and a seventeen-room house named Springwood, which had been built in 1826. His property grew to 1,000 acres of rolling farmland along the wooded bluffs of the Hudson River. James Roosevelt married Sara Delano in 1880, and Franklin Delano was born on January 30, 1882, at Springwood.

Springwood was enlarged into a thirty-five-room house in 1915–16. Fieldstone wings were added at each end of the house along with a fieldstone terrace with a balustrade on the front of the house and a small columned portico at the front door.

Visitors begin at the Henry A. Wallace Visitor and Education Center, where a film about the Roosevelts can be viewed. Opened in 2003, the building has a café, an auditorium, and a museum store. Its design is based on early Dutch buildings in the Hudson River Valley.

Franklin designed Springwood's wings, one of which contained the large library and living room. The wood-paneled walls are lined with bookshelves. The high-backed leather chairs by the fireplace were used by FDR and his mother.

The music room is a formal parlor. Sara Roosevelt redecorated the room with chintz draperies and upholstery in 1939 when King George and Queen Mary of England visited Springwood. The oak dining room chairs have the Roosevelt crest carved on their backs. The spacious kitchen has built-in cabinets and drawers and a large stove. Six to ten servants, including a cook, staffed the house. Sara's Snuggery, with its red upholstered furnishings, was her office. Furnishings in Franklin's study include his desk, chairs, and bookshelves. His pince-nez and cigarette holder are on the desk.

On the second floor in the tower at the south end of the house is the master bedroom where Franklin was born. It has been restored to its 1882 appearance per a request that Sara made shortly before her death. Franklin's boyhood room is rather small with a brass bed, a dresser, a desk and chair, and bookshelves.

When the home was remodeled, Franklin designed a suite for himself and Eleanor with a bedroom, two dressing rooms, and a sitting room. After Franklin contracted polio, he and his Scotch terrier, Fala, shared the bedroom. Eleanor changed her dressing room into a bedroom, and Sara made their sitting room into her bedroom. Franklin's room had a White House telephone on the wall near the president's bed. His wheelchair, fashioned from a kitchen chair, is in the room.

Winston Churchill and King George VI occupied the pink room during their visits. Furniture includes a rosewood bed and chest. The servants' wing has eight bedrooms and two baths.

The laundry house was built about 1850 and was used by the Roosevelts until 1941; coal was stored in the other half of the building. James Roosevelt built the stables in 1886 for his saddle horses and carriage. The second floor has a hayloft and living quarters for the stablemen. An 1850 stable burned in 1971 and was reconstructed by the National Park Service in 1973. There were two icehouses, one of which dated from 1867 and a larger one that was built by James in 1898. Ice from the Hudson River was used by the Roosevelt household until 1941. The 1907 greenhouse has a rose house, a carnation wing, and a moist room for ferns. Other outbuildings on the site include the gardener's cottage, the garage, the coach house, and sheds.

In 1938 Franklin Roosevelt announced plans for a library at Hyde Park to house his public and private papers and donated sixteen acres of the

Springwood property for it. Franklin worked with the architect Henry Toombs to design the stone Dutch-colonial-style library building. The Franklin D. Roosevelt Presidential Library and Museum was dedicated by President Roosevelt on June 30, 1941. It is administered by the National Archives and Records Administration. Margaret "Daisy" Suckley, a relative and friend of the president, helped sort, classify, and annotate Franklin's personal and family papers.

Franklin Roosevelt designed his museum study, a spacious room with a fireplace, a desk and chair, and a wheelchair. Four fireside chats were broadcast from the study, which President Roosevelt also used for meetings with foreign leaders.

The library was enlarged in 1972 to house research facilities. Library holdings include more than forty thousand books and large collections of manuscripts, photographs, recordings, and films.

The museum chronicles Roosevelt's life through exhibits and photographs. FDR's White House desk is exhibited. Other exhibits focus on the 1932 election campaign, the Depression, World War II, and each of Roosevelt's four presidential terms. A gallery is devoted to Eleanor Roosevelt.

Franklin was a collector who had a personal library of fourteen thousand volumes; over two thousand naval paintings, prints, and lithographs; two hundred model ships; over one million stamps; more than three hundred mounted bird specimens; and thousands of coins, banknotes, and campaign buttons. Items from his collections are now housed in the museum.

Franklin Delano Roosevelt died in Warm Springs, Georgia, on April 12, 1945. On April 15 the president was buried in his mother's rose garden at Springwood. Franklin designed the simple white monument made of Imperial Danby marble quarried in Vermont. Fala, FDR's dog and constant companion, is buried near the sundial. Eleanor Roosevelt was buried beside her husband on November 10, 1962.

Springwood's grounds were personally overseen by Franklin Roosevelt, who planted thousands of trees of sixty-one varieties. He sometimes referred to himself as a tree farmer.

Top Cottage, Franklin Roosevelt's personal retreat on the Hyde Park estate, is located on Dutchess Hill overlooking the Hudson Valley with views of the Catskill and Shawangunk mountains. Roosevelt purchased the property adjacent to his Hyde Park estate in 1937, and the Dutch colonial fieldstone building was built in 1938. Top Cottage is distinctive in that it was designed to be handicapped accessible and was one of the first barrier-free buildings in the country. Like most paraplegics, Roosevelt found it almost impossible to be independent. He needed help to maneuver up and down stairs, through narrow doorways, and over doorway thresholds and to access high shelves.

Roosevelt had a strong interest in architecture and especially Dutch buildings in the Hudson Valley. Although Henry Toombs was the architect on most of his construction projects, FDR was very involved in the expansion of his Springwood home, the construction of the FDR Presidential Library and Museum, and the stone house built for Eleanor at Val-Kill. By the time Top Cottage was built, Roosevelt was a somewhat sophisticated amateur architect. He had designed the cottage and drawn the initial sketches himself. Toombs had supplied the revised drawings and was listed as associate architect. Top Cottage is not the only home designed by a president. Thomas Jefferson designed two Virginia homes: Monticello and his retreat Poplar Forest.

Located in a secluded wooded area, Top Cottage is a modest one-story, two-bedroom structure with a large living room, a kitchen and pantry, two bathrooms, and a wide porch. The cottage has a stone fireplace, low windows to enjoy the view while seated, barrier-free thresholds, entries without steps, and a ramp from the garage to the grounds. Exterior walls and fireplaces were built of fieldstone taken from the property's century-old fences. After the cottage was finished, bedrooms were added in the attic of the north wing for the resident caretaker and his family.

After Franklin's death in 1945, his son Elliott lived in the house. Elliott and Eleanor sold some Top Cottage furnishings through a New York gallery in late 1951. In 1952 or 1953 Elliot Roosevelt sold the house and 118 acres to Philip S. Potter Sr. The Potter family occupied the presidential retreat for over forty years. Top Cottage was acquired by Beaverkill Conservancy in 1996. It was leased to the Franklin and Eleanor Roosevelt Institute, and restoration took place between 1999 and 2000. Documents in the Roosevelt library were useful in restoring Top Cottage to its original appearance plus the changes overseen by President Roosevelt.

Top Cottage was added to the Roosevelt-Vanderbilt National Historic Sites at Hyde Park. In June 2001 the National Park Service assumed the management of Top Cottage and opened it for tours. Shuttle buses leave from the Henry A. Wallace Visitor Center for guided tours of the cottage.

Also at Hyde Park is the Eleanor Roosevelt National Historic Site. In 1925 a stone cottage, called Val-Kill, designed by Franklin Roosevelt and the architect Henry Toombs was built on the estate for Eleanor and her friends Nancy Cook and Marion Dickerman. Nancy and Marion lived there until 1947. The women also built a furniture factory to give employment to local people. After the furniture business closed in 1936, Eleanor remodeled the factory structure as a home for herself. After her husband's death in 1945, Val-Kill was Eleanor's Hyde Park home.

Eleanor Roosevelt died in 1962, and in 1970 the property was sold. In 1976 a preservation group acquired Val-Kill, and in May 1977 President Carter signed a bill creating the Eleanor Roosevelt National Historic Site. Val-Kill has been restored, and tours are given by the National Park Service. A visit to the simple, tranquil place evokes the spirit of the strong First Lady.

Nearby in Hyde Park is the Vanderbilt Mansion National Historic Site, which is managed by the National Park Service. Together, Franklin's home, Eleanor's Val-Kill, and the Vanderbilt house are called the Roosevelt-Vanderbilt National Historic Sites. In 1940 the Vanderbilt mansion was donated to the federal government. It had been carefully preserved with much of its original furnishings. The fifty-room house was built by Frederick and Louise Vanderbilt in the mid-1890s. Guided tours are available.

## Roosevelt's Little White House Historic Site
## Warm Springs, Georgia

ADDRESS: 401 Little White House Road, Warm Springs, GA 31830
TELEPHONE: 706-655-5870
WEB SITE: www.gastateparks.org
LOCATION: In west central Georgia, seventy miles south of Atlanta, forty miles north of Columbus, and fifteen miles east of Pine Mountain, on Ga. 85A and U.S. Highway 27A
OPEN: Daily, 9:00 A.M. to 4:45 P.M.; closed Thanksgiving, Christmas, and New Year's Day
ADMISSION: Adults, $8.00; seniors, $6.00; children 6–18, $4.00
FACILITIES: Vacation home of President Franklin D. Roosevelt; Museum with orientation film; handicapped accessible; picnic areas; living history programs; gift shop

*Roosevelt's Warm Springs home,* which he called the Little White House, is on a site that also includes a guesthouse and servants' quarters. The structures have been preserved as they appeared when President Roosevelt died on this site on April 12, 1945.

In 1924 Franklin Delano Roosevelt came to Warm Springs, Georgia, a resort community at the base of Pine Mountain, because of its warm springwater pool, which had a constant temperature of eighty-eight degrees. Desperate because of his unsuccessful search for a cure for his paralysis, Roosevelt had heard of a young man with polio who had improved dramatically after spending time in Warm Springs' pool.

Roosevelt was a forty-two-year-old Harvard-educated lawyer from a prominent New York family and had a promising political career when he became crippled by polio in 1921. He had served as assistant secretary of the navy and had been an unsuccessful Democratic nominee for vice president of the United States. Roosevelt's political career seemed at an end.

After spending hours swimming in the Warm Springs pool, Roosevelt's upper body grew stronger. The buoyancy of the water, due to the high concentration of mineral salts and its warmth, allowed polio patients to exercise

without becoming overtired. With his improved health, Roosevelt gained back some of his previous vitality, though he never was able to discard his leg braces.

He returned to Georgia to swim in the warm, mineral-rich, buoyant spring-fed pools more than forty times. Believing in the restorative powers of hydrotherapy, Roosevelt purchased the Warm Springs Resort in 1927. He then established the nonprofit Georgia Warm Springs Foundation, which purchased the property from Roosevelt for one dollar. It served as a treatment center for people with polio. Its fund-raising wing helped fund research, which led to effective vaccines against polio.

In 1928 Roosevelt was elected governor of New York, and he was reelected in 1930. After seven years of visits to Warm Springs during which the Roosevelts stayed in rented cottages, the governor built a house. Completed in 1932, the simple white frame, six-room dwelling was situated on a wooded site overlooking a deep ravine. Roosevelt also purchased twenty-two hundred acres of nearby farmland, on which cattle and chickens were raised and pine trees were planted.

Franklin Roosevelt was elected as president of the United States in 1932 and was reelected in 1936, 1940, and 1944. His Georgia home became known as the Little White House, and sentry houses for U.S. Marine guards were placed around the property. A guesthouse and servants' quarters were added.

After the Little White House was opened to the public in October 1948, visitors could tour not only the house but also the guesthouse and the servants' quarters. The surprisingly modest white frame buildings are located on the north slope of Pine Mountain. The Little White House has three bedrooms, two bathrooms, a combination living-dining room, a kitchen, and an entry. The three bedrooms were for the president, the president's secretary, and Mrs. Roosevelt.

All of the simply furnished rooms are paneled in native pine. Most of the maple furniture was produced at Val-Kill Industries, the Hyde Park, New York, furniture-making shop instituted by Eleanor Roosevelt to give work to the unemployed.

A floor-to-ceiling fieldstone fireplace in the living room is flanked by bookshelves. French doors from the living room open onto a large sun deck overlooking the ravine. President Roosevelt was handling mail at a revolving-top table in the living room while having his portrait painted by Elizabeth Shoumatoff on April 12, 1945, when about 1:15 P.M. he said, "I have a terrific headache" and then collapsed. Without regaining consciousness, the president died two hours later of a cerebral hemorrhage. The partially burned logs that were in the fireplace on that day remain. The unfinished portrait of the president was left just as it was when the president collapsed. Later the artist painted another canvas of the president, called *The Finished Portrait*. Both portraits are exhibited in the Franklin D. Roosevelt Memorial Museum located on the site.

The guesthouse consists of an entry, a living room, a bathroom, and a bedroom. It too is furnished with Val-Kill furniture. Visitors can also tour the garage and the servants' quarters.

Added to the Warm Springs property in 2004 is the twelve-thousand-square-foot Franklin D. Roosevelt Memorial Museum, which is located directly behind the historic entry building. It is a fully accessible one-story structure. Exhibits in the museum chronicle Roosevelt's life, including his struggle with polio. Artifacts on display include a table and a chair used on his sundeck, his wheelchair, his leg braces, and his saddle. Also on display are cars driven by the president, including a 1938 Ford V-8 convertible roadster equipped with hand controls so that the president could drive it and a 1940 Willys convertible. Visitors can listen to "Fireside Chats" playing on a 1930s radio in a replica of a kitchen from that era. A film on FDR's life narrated by Walter Cronkite features historic footage of Roosevelt swimming in the warm spring water.

Leading to the museum is the Walk of States, which features stones and flags from every state. A special "bump gate" could be opened by a driver with his bumper without exiting his car. Near the gate is the memorial fountain, which was dedicated in 1959.

Visitors can also see the historic campus of the Roosevelt Warm Springs Institute for Rehabilitation. The pools complex where Roosevelt and other polio patients swam for therapy is located one quarter of a mile north of downtown Warm Springs. The pools were used until 1942, when an indoor pool was built. Tours are provided by the Little White House staff.

In his will President Roosevelt gave the Little White House and its surrounding acreage to the Georgia Warm Springs Foundation, which in 1947 donated it to the state of Georgia. In 1980 the property was transferred to the Georgia Department of Natural Resources.

Roosevelt Cottage
Roosevelt Campobello International Park
Campobello Island, New Brunswick, Canada

ADDRESS: 459 Route 774, Welshpool, New Brunswick, Canada E5E 1A4; P.O. Box 129, Lubec, ME, United States 04652

TELEPHONE: 506-752-2922

WEB SITE: www.fdr.net

LOCATION: Campobello Island is on Fundy Bay in New Brunswick, Canada. The Roosevelt Memorial Bridge links Lubec, Maine, and Campobello Island. U.S. citizens will need a passport.

OPEN: Daily, 9:00 A.M. to 5:00 P.M., Memorial Day weekend to Columbus Day weekend

ADMISSION: Free

FACILITIES: Visitor center; guided tours of Roosevelt Cottage; twenty-eight hundred acres, hiking trails, golf course, campgrounds; much of the international park is handicapped accessible

*When Franklin Roosevelt was a child,* he and his parents often spent their summers on Campobello Island, located on Fundy Bay in New Brunswick, Canada, near the northeast coast of Maine. Franklin, Eleanor, and their children maintained the tradition of summering at Campobello, which Franklin referred to as his beloved island. There he and his family sailed, golfed, hiked, swam, played tennis, picnicked, and bird-watched. Sailing was their favorite activity. Despite the happy times at Campobello, sadly it was here in 1921 that Franklin suffered polio symptoms, which left him paralyzed.

Campobello Island is a place of natural beauty with bogs, beaches, forests, ponds, salt marshes, rocky headlands, and cliffs. The Native Americans who originally inhabited the island called it Abahquict, and Frenchmen who arrived at the end of the seventeenth century named it Port aux Coquilles. After Canada expelled the French Acadians in 1755, a Welshman, William Owen, was awarded this grant of land by Governor Campbell of Nova Scotia in 1767. The island was then named Outer Island of Passamaquoddy but was called Campobello after Governor Campbell.

The Owen family owned the island, now located in the province of New Brunswick, until 1881. It was sold to the Campobello Island Company, which developed the property as a summer resort. Between 1880 and 1910 the island was at the height of its popularity, but by 1910 the hotels had closed and land sales declined.

In 1883 James, Sara, and one-year-old Franklin Roosevelt visited the island. James purchased four acres of land and built a house, after which the family became regular summer visitors.

Roosevelt Cottage,
Roosevelt Campobello
International Park, New
Brunswick, Canada

The house referred to now as Roosevelt Cottage was built in 1897 next to James and Sara Roosevelt's summer home. It was designed by Willard T. Sears for Mrs. Hartman Kuhn, who in her will offered to sell her cottage to Sara Roosevelt for the reasonable price of five thousand dollars so that Eleanor and Franklin could have their own home. In 1909 Sara Roosevelt purchased the furnished cottage on five acres of land.

Sara, who died in 1941, left the Kuhn/Roosevelt house to Franklin. In 1952 Franklin's son Elliott sold it to the Hammer family. In 1963 it was deeded to the governments of Canada and the United State to be in a jointly administered international park. The twenty-eight-hundred-acre Roosevelt Campobello International Park was established on January 22, 1964, by President Lyndon Johnson and Prime Minister Lester Pearson of Canada.

The large red frame Roosevelt House is the centerpiece of the international park. Though the house built by James Roosevelt was demolished, there are four other beautifully restored summer homes that are used as lodgings for conference attendees. If it is unoccupied, the first floor of the Hubbard Cottage is open for touring July 1 through Labor Day.

The Roosevelt Cottage, in the Dutch colonial style, is an imposing two-and-one-half-story frame structure covered with cedar shingles painted red and with dark green shutters. In 1915 the younger Roosevelts expanded the cottage to accommodate their growing family. It has thirty-four rooms, eighteen of which are bedrooms and six of which are bathrooms. There are seven fireplaces. Without electricity, kerosene lamps were used for lighting, and there was no telephone. Water for washing and cooking was gravity fed from third-floor storage tanks supplied by well water pumped by windmill power to a holding tank on the tower. The first floor has both an open porch and a screened porch.

Eleanor decorated the house, and many furnishings in the charming, comfortable home are original Roosevelt items. Eleanor was particularly fond of hand-hooked rugs, which she purchased from local residents. Sheer white curtains hang on most windows, allowing in sunlight.

On the first floor are a living room, a dining room, a study, a kitchen, a laundry room, a food pantry, a butler's pantry, two bedrooms, and an office/playroom. The first room visitors enter was originally a school and play room; later, during the presidency, it was a reception room and office. Now used as exhibit space, it holds a fishing rod, FDR's sculling oars from Harvard, and model ship-building supplies. In addition the chair the president used when presiding over his first cabinet meeting and a desk made at the Val-Kill furniture factory are in this room.

The living room, with its stunning bay view, has wicker chairs, kerosene lamps, and Eleanor's Wedgwood tea set. A painting of the Confederate cruiser *Florida* that hangs above the fireplace was previously hung in FDR's White House office.

The dining room, which also has a view across the bay to Eastport, Maine, has a large dining room table and chairs. The two youngest Roosevelt sons often ate at a smaller table near the windows. The megaphones were used to call the children in and to talk to people on boats.

Eleanor and Franklin's son James and the children's tutor had bedrooms on the first floor. James's bedroom was later used by the Secret Service when the president was in residence, and the president stayed in the tutor's bedroom. On the first floor there is also a large kitchen with a white enamel coal-and wood-burning stove, a butler's pantry, a food pantry, and a laundry room.

On the second floor are four servants' rooms, three guest bedrooms, two baths, the master bedroom, Anna's bedroom, a school room, Elliott's bedroom, the boys' room, and a deck and covered porch. When Franklin first displayed polio symptoms in August 1921, he was nursed in the master bedroom by Eleanor and Louis Howe, Franklin's friend and political adviser. Roosevelt was in great pain, and doctors offered a variety of diagnoses. Here Franklin Roosevelt's life-long struggle with paralysis began. Eleanor slept in an adjacent guest bedroom after Franklin became ill. Howe, a frequent visitor, had his own room.

Anna's bedroom has a white brass and iron bed and wicker chairs. Franklin Jr. and John's bedroom, formerly a nursery, features a model sailboat built by President Roosevelt. A guest bedroom has Jenny Lind beds. On the third floor there are two servants' rooms, two guest rooms, and a bath.

Roosevelt Campobello International Park, an especially beautiful site, has flower gardens interspersed throughout the cottage area. The views from the shore are spectacular, with many birds, including eagles, visible. Tourists can drive on five kilometers of roads and hike on over five kilometers of walking trails on the twenty-eight-hundred-acre ruggedly natural island.

The Edmund S. Muskie Visitor Center has exhibits relating to Franklin Roosevelt and his family at Campobello Island. Overnight camping and a golf course can be enjoyed in the adjacent Herring Cove Provincial Park.

# Harry S. Truman

THIRTY-THIRD PRESIDENT OF THE UNITED STATES
*April 12, 1945–January 20, 1953*

. . . . . . . . . . . . . . . . . . . . . . . . . . . . . . . . . . . . . . . . . . . . . . . . . . . . . . . . . . . . . . . . . . . . . . . . . . . . .

Harry S. Truman led the United States to victory in the closing months of World War II, through its transition to a peace-time economy, and through the perils of what would be a long cold war with the Soviet Union. He was born on May 8, 1884, in Lamar, Missouri, to John Anderson Truman and Martha Ellen Young Truman. Harry was named after his uncle Harrison Young, and the middle initial "S" is not an abbreviation for a name but a compromise by the parents who couldn't decide which grandfather to name their child for—Solomon Young or Anderson Shipp Truman. Harry's siblings were John Vivian (known as Vivian) and Mary Jane.

Soon after their oldest son's birth, the Truman family moved to a farm near that of Solomon Young, Martha's father. In 1887 they moved to the Young farm, where John and Solomon became partners in the stock-trading business. Harry remembered his years on the Young farm as idyllic. In 1890 the Truman family moved to Independence, Missouri, where John was a livestock trader.

Martha Truman taught Harry to read by age five but realized that her son had a serious vision problem and needed glasses. Harry took piano lessons and dreamed of becoming a concert pianist. He graduated from Independence High School on May 30, 1901. College was out of the question because of John Truman's financial situation. After speculating on wheat futures in the summer of 1901, John eventually lost the home in Independence, his savings, and 160 acres of land that Martha had inherited. The family moved to Kansas City, where Harry worked in the mailroom of the *Kansas City Star* and was a construction timekeeper on the Santa Fe Railroad.

John and Martha Truman moved in October 1905 to Grandmother Young's farm in Grandview. When the six-hundred-acre farm proved too much work for John and his son Vivian, Harry became a farmer at age twenty-one. After John Truman died on November 2, 1914, Harry took on responsibility for the farm and the support of his mother and sister. He joined the National Guard of Missouri in June 1905.

When World War I started, thirty-three-year-old Harry Truman rejoined the National Guard and was commissioned as a first lieutenant in June 1917. Despite his poor eyesight, he passed his army physical. In March 1918 Truman was one of thousands of troops who sailed for France. In August the 129th Field Artillery joined the huge Meuse-Argonne offensive. Truman's Battery D was discharged in May 1919.

Harry had fallen in love with Elizabeth "Bess" Wallace, whom he had known since childhood. After Bess's father, David Willock Wallace, died, the Wallace family moved into her mother's (Madge) parents' home at 219 North Delaware. Wealthy and prominent, George Porterfield Gates, Madge's father and Bess's grandfather, was a partner in the Waggoner-Gates Milling Company. Bess and Harry, who had courted for nine years, were married on June 28, 1919, in Independence's Trinity Episcopal Church. Bess's mother insisted that the couple live in the Gates house with her as well as Bess's grandmother and brother Fred. Bess Truman gave birth to Mary Margaret on February 17, 1924.

Harry Truman and an army friend, Eddie Jacobson, opened a men's furnishings store called Truman & Jacobson in Kansas City. An economic depression affected the haberdashery, which failed in 1922.

In early 1921 Truman was asked to run for eastern judge of Jackson County by his friend Jim Pendergast and Jim's father, Mike Pendergast, of the politically powerful Pendergast Machine in Kansas City. Harry won a two-year term but was defeated in 1924. Two years later Harry won a four-year term as presiding judge of Jackson County, and he was reelected in 1930.

In May 1934 Tom Pendergast selected Truman as the Democratic candidate for the U.S. Senate with the backing of the Kansas City Machine; Harry won. Lloyd C. Stark was elected as governor of Missouri in November 1936. Truman had recommended Stark as the gubernatorial nominee to Tom Pendergast, and Stark was backed by the Kansas City Machine. During an investigation of vote fraud in Missouri's 1936 elections, Lloyd Stark cooperated fully, feeling no obligation to Tom Pendergast and his Kansas City Machine. Pendergast, a compulsive gambler heavily in debt to bookmakers, was indicted for tax evasion and sentenced to prison.

Stark received national accolades for being the righteous governor who turned against the corrupt Kansas City Machine. In September 1939 he declared his candidacy for the Senate seat occupied by Harry Truman. Stark had the support of President Roosevelt and the Missouri newspapers, while Truman was portrayed as a Pendergast lackey.

During Truman's senatorial campaign, the court-held mortgage on Martha Truman's Grandview farm was foreclosed by the Republican-controlled county court. Martha and Mary Jane Truman were evicted, and 195 acres of land were sold at public auction. Missouri newspapers printed photographs of the auction and identified the evictees as the mother and sister of Senator Truman. Truman won the primary by a slim margin and won the general election.

At the 1944 Democratic Convention, Franklin Delano Roosevelt was nominated for a fourth term and Harry Truman was chosen as the vice-presidential candidate. They were victorious. President Roosevelt died at 4:45 P.M. on April 12, 1945, at Warm Springs, Georgia. At 7:09 P.M. that evening, Harry S. Truman was sworn in as the thirty-third president in the Cabinet Room of the White House. On April 25, 1945, President Truman received a full briefing about the American-British scientific project called S-1 or the Manhattan Project. He learned that a test of the nuclear bomb was scheduled for July in New Mexico.

The German high command surrendered to the Allies on May 7, 1945, and the news became public the next day, V-E Day. The war in the Pacific continued as Japan refused to surrender. In July 1945 Truman met Churchill and Stalin at the Big Three meeting at Potsdam, Germany. While there Truman received word that the atomic bomb tests in New Mexico had been successful. Truman told Stalin privately that the United States had produced a new and powerful weapon. As it turned out, the Soviet Union was also engaged in nuclear research, and that country's espionage had provided it with detailed and reliable information about the S-1 project.

On July 24 Churchill and Truman agreed to use the atomic bomb against the Japanese. Although Truman had reservations, his military advisers and senior staff uniformly advocated using the new weapon and assured him that Roosevelt would have used it. On July 26 a joint statement to Japan by Truman, Clement Attlee, Britain's newly elected prime minister, and Chiang Kai-shek of Nationalist China was released. Called the Potsdam Declaration, it was both an ultimatum that threatened utter destruction unless the Japanese surrendered and a warning before the nuclear bomb was dropped. Prime Minister Kantar Suzuki of Japan ignored it.

On August 6 an American plane dropped the atomic bomb on Hiroshima. Approximately eighty thousand people were killed instantly, and in the next few months another fifty thousand died. After a second bomb hit Nagasaki on August 9 killing seventy thousand people, Emperor Hirohito and the Japanese government officially surrendered on August 14. On September 2, 1945, V-J Day, Japan accepted the surrender terms.

In 1948 President Truman issued an executive order that desegregated the armed forces. That year he was renominated at the Democratic National Convention, which chose Sen. Alban W. Barkley as the vice-presidential candidate. Liberal Democrats, led by Hubert Humphrey, included a strong civil rights plank in the party platform. Disgruntled southern delegates bolted the convention and nominated Strom Thurmond, South Carolina's governor, as the presidential nominee of the States' Rights Party, dubbed the "Dixiecrats." The Republicans nominated Thomas E. Dewey, the governor of New York, for president. Former vice president Henry A. Wallace was the presidential candidate of the Progressive Party. Truman scored an upset, winning the presidency and giving Democrats control of both houses of Congress.

During Truman's administration, the cold war with the Soviet Union intensified. Soviet armies had liberated Eastern Europe and much of Central Europe, giving them the opportunity to base Soviet troops in these countries and to set up communist governments. The Soviet Union consolidated its control of Eastern Europe in 1946 and 1947, establishing communist governments in Poland, Hungary, Romania, and Bulgaria. In March 1948 it staged a coup in Czechoslovakia, forcing the establishment of a communist government.

One of Truman's principal advisers was George Kennan, who proposed a containment policy designed to block the Soviets' attempts to expand their influence in Europe by meeting their incursions with a strong and sustained counterforce. Kennan correctly predicted that in time the Soviet system would collapse because of internal weaknesses.

The first phase of the containment policy, the Truman Doctrine, unfolded when Greece was torn by a bloody civil war, which pitted communist insurgents against the government. Truman requested $400 million for military and economic aid to Greece and Turkey.

The Marshall Plan was a major aspect of Truman's cold war policy. Secretary of State George C. Marshall in 1947 proposed an ambitious plan of American aid to finance Europe's economic recovery, which Truman and Marshall believed would create political stability. The Soviets and their Eastern European satellites refused to participate. Western European countries received more than $17 billion in aid over the next four years.

In 1945 Korea had been divided at the thirty-eighth parallel. The Russians, who liberated North Korea from the Japanese, installed a communist regime. In South Korea the Americans supported a nationalist government. On June 25, 1950, the North Korean army invaded South Korea. The U.N. Security Council condemned North Korea's aggression and called on member nations to force the North Koreans from South Korea. American troops entered the struggle, which at that time was called a "police action" rather than a war. The Korean War remained at a stalemate for the rest of Truman's term.

After Truman's presidency he and Bess returned to Independence, where establishing a Truman library was one of the former president's highest priorities. Since legislation to establish such a library had not yet been enacted, Truman collected private donations to establish a library and then turned over its maintenance and operation to the federal government. Harry Truman died on December 26, 1972, at the age of eighty-eight and was buried in the courtyard of the Harry S. Truman Presidential Museum and Library in Independence, Missouri. Bess Truman died on October 18, 1982, and was buried next to her husband.

## Harry S. Truman Birthplace State Historic Site
## Lamar, Missouri

ADDRESS: 1009 Truman, Lamar, MO 64759

TELEPHONE: 417-682-2279

WEB SITE: www.mostateparks.com/trumansite

LOCATION: Lamar is in southwestern Missouri, about twenty-six miles east of the Kansas state line, two miles east of U.S. 71

OPEN: Monday–Saturday, 10:00 A.M. to 4:00 P.M.; Sunday, noon to 4:00 P.M.; closed Easter, Thanksgiving, Christmas, and New Year's Day

ADMISSION: Free

FACILITIES: Gift shop. National Register of Historic Places

*The birthplace of Harry S. Truman* is a white frame house purchased in 1882 by his parents, John Anderson Truman and Martha "Mattie" Ellen Young Truman. On May 8, 1884, their first child, Harry, was born in the downstairs southwest bedroom. That day his proud father planted an Austrian pine tree near the house and nailed a mule shoe over the front door.

In the early 1880s Lamar was the county seat of Barton County. Located some 120 miles south of Kansas City, Lamar had a population of 2,780 in 1882. The town had several churches, two public schools, three newspapers, banks, hotels, factories, and an opera house and was surrounded by good farmland. Two railroads, the Fort Scott and Memphis and the Missouri Pacific, went through Lamar.

John Truman wanted to be a livestock trader like his father-in-law, Solomon Young. The house he purchased was one block from the Missouri Pacific tracks, and his mule barn, located diagonally across the street from his house, was adjacent to the railroad right-of-way and a block south of the depot. The house cost $685, while the mule barn and lot cost an additional $200.

In addition to John and Mattie, John's father, Anderson Truman, and his sister, Mary Martha Truman, lived in the Lamar house. When Harry was ten months old, the Truman family moved to Harrisonville, near the Solomon Young farm, and John Truman became the partner of Solomon Young.

The birthplace had many owners before Harry Truman became the thirty-third president of the United States in 1945. Interest in preserving the birthplace of a Missouri president surfaced. In April 1957 the United Auto Workers of America purchased the birthplace for six thousand dollars from Marie Earp, a descendant of Wyatt Earp, and offered the property to the state of Missouri. The Missouri State Park Board agreed to restore, operate, and maintain the birthplace. Work included restorations of the birthplace home and smokehouse; reconstructions of the well, privy, and landscape features; furnishing the home with period furniture; and the construction of a site office. President

Truman was consulted during the restoration period. On April 19, 1959, President Truman was present as his restored birthplace was dedicated and opened to the public. At that time the property was formally transferred to the state of Missouri.

The birthplace is a modest one-story frame dwelling just 20' x 28' and without electricity or indoor plumbing. There are four small rooms—two bedrooms, a kitchen, and a parlor—on the ground floor and two bedrooms in the finished attic space. Harry S. Truman was born on May 8, 1884, in the 6' 6" x 10' 9" southwest bedroom on the first floor. Simple furnishings are of the period.

Also on the property are the smokehouse, the outhouse, and a well. On May 6, 1984, a monument commemorating the 100th anniversary of Truman's birth was dedicated and placed on the site. Future plans include the reconstruction of a local school, which would be used as a visitor center and museum.

. . . . . . . . . . . . . . . . . . . . . . . . . . . . . . . . . . . . . . . . . . . . . . . . . . . . . . . . . . . . . . . . . . . .

## Harry S. Truman National Historic Site
## Independence, Missouri

ADDRESS: Visitor center: 223 North Main Street, Independence, MO 64050; Truman home: 219 N. Delaware, Independence, MO 64050; Farm Home: 12301 Blue Ridge Boulevard, Grandview, MO 64030

TELEPHONE: 816-254-9929

WEB SITE: www.nps.gov/hstr

LOCATION: Independence is in west central Missouri, near the Kansas border; the Truman house is in downtown Independence, twelve miles east of Kansas City; the Truman farm home is approximately twenty miles south of Independence in Grandview

OPEN: Truman home: daily, 8:30 A.M. to 5:00 P.M.; closed Thanksgiving, Christmas, and New Year's Day; tours are limited to eight people, and tickets sell out quickly during the summer and on weekends. Truman Farm Home in Grandview: Friday, Saturday, Sunday, 9:30 A.M. to 4:00 P.M., Memorial Day to Labor Day

ADMISSION: Truman Home and/or Truman Farm Home: adults 16 and older, $4.00

FACILITIES: Home of President Harry Truman, farm home of grandparents and parents; visitor center; guided tours; partially handicapped accessible; audiovisual orientation program. National Register of Historic Places, National Historic Landmark

*Harry S. Truman, the thirty-third president* of the United States, was born and raised, married, died, and was buried in Missouri. As a child and again as a young man, Harry lived with his family on his grandparents' farm in Grandview.

Truman Home, Harry S. Truman National Historic Site, Independence, Missouri

After his marriage he lived in the Independence family home of his wife, Elizabeth "Bess" Wallace Truman. The Harry S. Truman National Historic Site includes the Truman home in Independence; the adjoining homes of Bess Truman's brothers, George and Frank Wallace; the nearby home of Ethel Noland, Truman's aunt; and the Harry S. Truman farm home in Grandview.

On June 28, 1919, Harry S. Truman married Elizabeth Virginia Wallace in Independence, Missouri. The newlyweds moved into a second-floor bedroom of the Wallace family home at 219 Delaware in Independence with Bess's mother and grandmother. Two of Bess's brothers built houses on adjoining lots. Mary Margaret, the Trumans' only child, was born at this home in February 1924.

Truman regarded the Wallace mansion as his home for the rest of his life. The Delaware Street house served as the summer White House from 1945 to 1952. After he retired from the presidency, Truman and his wife returned there.

In 1867 George Porterfield Gates, Bess's grandfather, bought an Independence property with a small farmhouse. In 1885 Gates built an extensive addition to the house, resulting in an imposing fourteen-room Victorian mansion. George Gates's daughter, Madge, married David Willock Wallace, and they had four children, the oldest of whom was Elizabeth, called Bess. In 1904 David Wallace committed suicide. Subsequently Madge Gates Wallace and her children moved into her parents' house. Harry Truman's aunt, Ethel Noland, lived across the street from the Gates-Wallace house, which facilitated the courtship. Madge Gates Wallace acquired title to the house in 1925.

Harry Truman was elected to the U.S. Senate in 1934. When Congress was not in session, Bess and Margaret frequently returned to Independence, and Harry joined them when he was free. Truman was the vice-presidential running mate of President Franklin Delano Roosevelt, who was elected in 1944. Eighty-three days after the inauguration, President Roosevelt died and Harry S. Truman became the thirty-third president. Calling the White House the "Great White Jail," Truman regarded his Missouri house as a refuge.

In January 1953 the Trumans retired to Independence, where they lived for the rest of their lives. After Bess's mother died in December 1952, the Trumans purchased the house from Mrs. Wallace's estate. Harry Truman died in 1972, and Bess Truman died in 1982. In her will Bess left the Delaware Street house and its contents to the United States government. The National Park Service opened the house to the public on May 15, 1984.

The Truman House is a two-story, fourteen-room frame Victorian building on the corner of Truman Road and Delaware Street. Ninety-nine percent of the items in the house are original. There are family heirlooms owned by four generations of Gates and Wallaces and more than fifty thousand of the Trumans' possessions. Furnishings remain in their original places in the house; the house is just as the Trumans left it. Truman took daily brisk morning walks throughout his adult life. His coat and hat hang on a wooden hall rack seemingly ready to be donned.

Every night a formal dinner was served in the dining room, and the family wore formal wear. The dining room table is set with Bess's china and silver. Harry and Bess Truman ate breakfast and lunch in their cozy kitchen, which is in the oldest part of the house. Margaret Truman is responsible for the vivid apple green paint on the wainscoting, cupboards, table, and chairs.

In the music room the baby grand piano, a gift to Margaret, was played by both Harry and his daughter. It accompanied them to the White House and back. The study/library was a favorite room for both Harry and Bess for reading and listening to classical music. Over one thousand of their books are here. The upstairs rooms of the house are not open for touring.

The homes of Bess Truman's two brothers, Frank and George Wallace, are on adjoining properties. These brick bungalows were acquired by the National Historic Site in 1991 but are not open to the public. The home of Truman's Noland relatives is at 216 N. Delaware.

The Harry S. Truman Farm Home in Grandview, home to three generations of the Young/Truman family, was added to the Harry S. Truman National Historic Site in May 1994. In 1867 Harry Truman's maternal grandparents, Solomon and Harriet Young, purchased farmland in Grandview, where they built a house. Their daughter, Martha Ellen Young, married John A. Truman in 1881. From 1887 to 1890 the Truman family lived at the Young farm when John Truman was a business partner of Solomon Young. In 1893 the 1867 Young house burned down, and a new house was built in 1894.

In 1905 John and Martha Truman returned to Grandmother Young's Grandview farm. John Truman and his son Vivian operated the six-hundred-acre farm. Needing more help, they asked twenty-one-year-old Harry to work on the family farm, which he did. Grandmother Young and the five Trumans occupied the 1894 farmhouse. In 1911 John Truman made Harry his partner.

When Harriet Young died in late 1909, she left the farm to only two of her children, Harrison Young and Martha Truman, which resulted in protracted contesting of her will. After completing his military service in World War I, Harry Truman never returned to farming. The livestock and equipment from the Grandview farm were auctioned and the land was rented.

In July 1940, during Truman's Senate primary campaign, the court-held mortgage on Martha Truman's Grandview farm was foreclosed. Martha and Mary Jane Truman were evicted and 195 acres of land sold at public auction. Missouri newspapers printed photographs of the auction on their front pages and identified the evictees as the mother and sister of Senator Truman, much to his humiliation.

In May 1946 Harry Truman and his brother, Vivian, repurchased their mother's Grandview farm. Too elderly and infirm to move back, the president's mother, Martha Ellen Young Truman, died on July 26, 1947, in Grandview, Missouri, at the age of ninety-four.

After his presidency Truman selected the Grandview farm as the site of his presidential library. However, the Truman library was built in Independence because of its proximity to the Truman residence. The three Truman siblings sold 224 acres of the Grandview farm to a developer in early 1958.

The Harry S. Truman Farm Home Foundation, founded in 1978, acquired the Grandview farm. In 1978 the Truman farmhouse was listed on the National Register of Historic Places, and in 1984 it was designated as a National Historic Landmark. The farmhouse, which had fallen into disrepair, was renovated in 1983–84. A dedication ceremony for the restored building took place on May 5, 1984, and the house was opened to the public. The house was acquired by Jackson County in 1987, and. Jackson County transferred ownership to the National Park Service in the early 1990s. The Truman farm home was acquired by the Truman National Historic Site in May 1994.

The Truman farm home is a two-story, eight-room white frame house with dark green trim. No Truman artifacts remained. The house has been restored and a grove of sugar maple trees replanted. The home is open for tours on weekends.

. . . . . . . . . . . . . . . . . . . . . . . . . . . . . . . . . . . . . . . . . . . . . . . . . . . . . . . . . . . . . . . . . . . . . . . .

**Harry S. Truman Presidential Library and Museum**
**Independence, Missouri**

ADDRESS: 500 West U.S. Highway 24, Independence, MO 64050
TELEPHONE: 800-833-1225 or 816-268-8200
WEB SITE: www.trumanlibrary.org

LOCATION: In Independence, at U.S. Highway 24 and Delaware, less than a
mile from the Truman home; twenty minutes east of downtown Kansas
City, accessible from I-435

OPEN: Monday–Wednesday, Friday and Saturday, 9:00 A.M. to 5:00 P.M.; Sunday, noon to 5:00 P.M.; Thursday, 9:00 A.M. to 9:00 P.M., May–September;
closed Thanksgiving, Christmas, and New Year's Day

ADMISSION: Adults, $8.00; seniors, $7.00; children 6–15, $3.00

FACILITIES: Presidential museum of Harry Truman; research library; gift shop;
handicapped accessible; burial site of President Harry S. Truman and
Bess Truman

*The Harry S. Truman Presidential Museum and Library,* though not the first
presidential library, was the first one established under the 1955 Presidential
Libraries Act, which authorized the federal government to accept the papers
of any former president, as well as the building and equipment necessary to
preserve them, and make the presidential papers available to the public. Fund-
raising for presidential libraries is done by private foundations, and construction of the facilities is completed before they are transferred to government
ownership. Presidential libraries are administered by the National Archives
and Records Administration.

Harry Truman hoped to have his presidential library on the Grandview,
Missouri, farm that had been owned by his maternal grandparents and was in
his post-presidential years owned by the president and his brother and sister.
Instead a Truman Historic District was created in Independence, Missouri,
which includes the Truman home and the Truman library and museum,
which are less than a mile apart. The library, funded by the Harry S. Truman
Library, Inc., was built on land donated by the city of Independence. Ownership was transferred to the federal government at a dedication ceremony held
on July 6, 1957. Additions to the library were built in 1968 and 1980.

The one-story building has one hundred thousand square feet of floor
space, and its collection includes fifteen million manuscript pages, thirty thousand books, and an audiovisual collection of still pictures, motion pictures,
and tape recordings. The museum's twenty-eight thousand artifacts include
gifts from foreign heads of state and private citizens, personal possessions of
the Truman family, and political memorabilia. There is also a collection of
original artwork for more than twelve hundred political cartoons.

The Truman library/museum includes a replica of his Oval Office; a White
House gallery; President Truman's office; two major exhibits, "The Presiden-
tial Years" and "Harry S. Truman: His Life and Times"; and special exhibits.
In the lobby is a mural titled *Independence and the Opening of the West,* by
Thomas Hart Benton, depicting pioneers, traders, and Conestoga and freight
wagons leaving Independence for the Oregon, California, and Santa Fe trails.

The museum has interactive exhibits for children. An introductory film narrated by Jason Robards traces Truman's life.

Harry Truman maintained an office in the library and worked there five or six days each week. He walked to the library from his home on Delaware Street, often returning home for lunch. In his office Truman wrote his book of memoirs, *Mr. Citizen*. There he met with Presidents Hoover, Eisenhower, Kennedy, and Johnson and with other notable Americans. Truman participated actively in the day-to-day operation of the library, establishing themes for the first museum exhibits there.

Truman's office remains in the museum/library as it was on the day Harry S. Truman died. On his cluttered desk is the small photograph of Bess Wallace that she gave him in 1917 before he set off for his army service in France. A small stone and a block of wood are souvenirs of the White House renovation that took place during his presidency. The original mock-up of the presidential flag, redesigned in 1945 at the direction of President Truman, is displayed. The office desk is the one that President Truman used in his private study in the White House. A voracious reader, Truman kept in his office nearly five hundred books, many of which are inscribed with handwritten notes from the authors, including Winston Churchill, T. S. Eliot, Herbert Hoover, and Lyndon Johnson.

Truman's White House Oval Office has been re-created in the museum/library and has a Dumont television set; Truman was the first president to have a TV in his office. The White House gallery has four exhibits: "The Buck Stops Here"—displaying the famous "Buck Stops Here" sign indicating the president's acceptance of responsibility for his decisions; "The President's Day"—depicting activities during a typical workday of President Truman; "Dear Mr. President"—featuring correspondence written by citizens; and "The Changing President"—showing how technology and innovations have affected the role of the president.

The exhibit "Harry S. Truman: His Life and Times" features artifacts, photographs, and correspondence from Truman's life, including the early years, his family, his political career, life in the White House, and life as "Mr. Citizen" after his return to Independence following his presidency. "The Presidential Years" features two theaters, called Decision Theaters, that focus on major decisions faced by President Truman and interactive audio and video programs that portray the issues and events of Truman's presidency. Exhibits feature photos, videos, and documents from the library and excerpts from Truman's correspondence and diary. "The Decision to Drop the Atomic Bomb" describes Truman's agonizing choice of bombing Japan or authorizing an American invasion.

"Postwar America" illustrates Truman's efforts at meeting the challenges of the country's transition from a war-time economy to a peace-time economy. The economic boom that began in 1947 is illustrated by a period refrigerator filled with food, and a vintage television set displays a video loop of television shows, commercials, and weather forecasts from the early 1950s.

"The Origins of the Cold War" traces the history of the cold war between the United States and the Soviet Union. The gallery also features exhibits on the Truman Doctrine, the Marshall Plan, NATO, and the roles of George Marshall, Dean Acheson, Averell Harriman, and George Kennan in shaping the containment policy.

"Truman's Second Term" features Fair Deal programs such as proposals for national health insurance, public housing, civil rights legislation, and federal aid to education. Much of Truman's legislative agenda was blocked by a coalition of conservative Republicans and southern Democrats.

Harry Truman died on December 26, 1972, and was buried in the courtyard of the Truman library after a simple grave-side service. The ceremony was attended by President and Mrs. Nixon, President Lyndon Johnson, and seventy-five thousand mourners. Bess Truman, who died in 1982, is buried next to her husband.

..........................................................................

## Harry S. Truman Little White House Museum
## Key West, Florida

ADDRESS: 111 Front Street, Key West, FL 33040
TELEPHONE: 305-294-9911
WEB SITE: www.trumanlittlewhitehouse.com
LOCATION: Key West is the southernmost part of Florida and the United States, the last key in the string of keys south of Miami
OPEN: Daily, 9:00 A.M. to 5:00 P.M.
ADMISSION: Adults, $15.00; seniors, $13.00; children 5–12, $5.00
FACILITIES: Presidential retreat of Harry Truman, guided tours; audiovisual orientation film; gift shop

*A vacant commandant's residence* on a submarine base at Key West, Florida, became the winter vacation home of President Harry S. Truman. He and his staff spent working holidays at this southernmost point of the United States. The tropical-style home has been restored to its appearance in 1949.

President Franklin D. Roosevelt died on April 12, 1945, less than three months after the start of his fourth term, propelling Vice President Truman into the White House. In the winter of 1946 President Truman's personal physician ordered the overworked chief executive to take a vacation because of a persistent cold and cough. Fleet Admiral Chester W. Nimitz, chief of naval operations, suggested Key West, Florida, as the submarine base there was secure and the commandant's house was vacant.

President Truman's first trip to Key West occurred in November 1946. He returned many times, usually in November, December, February, or March, spending a total of 175 days at the "Little White House." Less than half the time Bess Truman joined her husband.

In 1890 Rowland A. Robbins was awarded a contract to construct a pair of two-story frame structures surrounded by both first- and second-story piazzas on a 2.27-acre waterfront tract that the U.S. Navy had purchased in January 1854. Quarters A and B, as they were called, were to house the base commandant and the paymaster. Early in the twentieth century Quarters A and B were converted to a single house for the base commandant. In 1903–4 the waterfront was filled in and bulkheaded so that the house was no longer on the water. After the commandant, Capt. Charles Edwin Reordan, retired in April 1946, the house was vacant.

Since trips to Key West were working vacations, the president usually was accompanied by about a dozen staff members. They would fly from Washington to the Boca Chica Naval Air Station. When the motorcade, with the president in an open car, reached the submarine base, it was greeted with full military honors, including 450 officers and enlisted men in white uniforms, a twenty-one-gun salute, and the presidential flag flying above the administration building.

Upon arrival Truman would phone his wife and change into a colorful Hawaiian shirt, his trademark. When he wasn't working, Truman liked to spend time on the beach, walking, swimming and fishing, or playing nightly games of poker with his all-male staff. A special poker table, built by the navy, was designed so that it would appear as an ordinary table when not in use. Since the poker games involved gambling, Truman did not want them to receive any publicity.

Because President Truman needed to keep in touch with Washington at all times, the Little White House switchboard had three direct circuits to the White House. The USS *Williamsburg*, the presidential yacht docked nearby, served as the communication center and received classified messages. Teletype equipment at the naval base was linked to the White House. Couriers brought the mail each day, and naval planes delivered official pouches from Washington several times a week. Each morning Truman held staff meetings, and cabinet members and political leaders were sometimes summoned to Key West.

After Truman's victory in the 1948 presidential election, Haygood Lassiter, a Miami interior designer, was hired to redecorate the Little White House. In addition to new carpeting, drapes, and furniture and repainting, the south porch was extended.

Presidents Eisenhower and Kennedy used the Key West house occasionally. In 1953 the Little White House became two houses again, and in 1957 it was returned to a single house, which was used by base commanders until the naval station closed in 1974. In 1986 the General Services Administration sold the naval station to a developer. The Little White House property and its furnishings were donated to the state of Florida and then leased to the Little White House Company for restoration of its appearance to the Truman era. The Little White House Museum opened in April 1991.

The Little White House has been restored to its appearance in early 1949 after the Lassiter redecorating. Entrance to the Truman Little White House property is through the presidential gates on Caroline Street. The white frame building, set among palm trees and native shrubs, has a tropical feel with wraparound screened porches furnished in rattan and wrought iron and louvered windows and doors. Lassiter's furnishings are off-the-floor items from Henredon and other manufacturers in traditional and early American styles. The color scheme includes avocado green, lime green, deep blue, and red. Tropical print fabrics are used for upholstery and drapes.

Tours of the house are guided and begin upstairs with an orientation video. On display in President Truman's bedroom are his desk, briefcase, Stetson hat, and white pith helmet. Margaret and Bess's bedroom holds blond wood twin beds and a dressing table. An adjoining porch, partitioned off and used as a sitting room, has its original iron and glass furniture.

On the first level the wooden floors in the north and south porches are original Dade County pine, which is termite and water resistant. The custom-made mahogany poker table, which could accommodate seven people, is on the south porch. Its built-in ashtrays were made from fifty-millimeter artillery shell casings. An extra top was designed to cover the table when it was not in use. There is a bar in the room.

Truman and his staff ate their meals in the dining room on a Sheraton table that extended to twelve feet. In this room there are two built-in corner cabinets and a fireplace. President Truman used the living room as his office, where he held staff meetings and handled correspondence at his desk. The tropical garden, replete with palm trees, native shrubs, and tropical fruit trees, has also been restored.

# Dwight David Eisenhower

THIRTY-FOURTH PRESIDENT OF THE UNITED STATES
*January 20, 1953–January 20, 1961*

Dwight Eisenhower was a West Point graduate, a career army officer, and during World War II the supreme commander of the Allied Expeditionary Force who led the D-Day invasion of Normandy. Descended from Pennsylvania Dutch Mennonites, the Eisenhauer family settled in Lancaster, Pennsylvania, in 1741.

David Dwight Eisenhower was born on October 14, 1890, in Denison, Texas, the third of seven sons of David Jacob Eisenhower and Ida Stover Eisenhower. Originally named David Dwight, when he entered West Point, the order of his given names was reversed.

The Eisenhower family located in Abilene, Kansas, in 1892. Dwight graduated from Abilene High School in 1909. He was accepted into the U.S. Military Academy at West Point in 1911 and graduated in the upper half of his class in 1915. Although he was from a pacifist family, his parents accepted Dwight's career decision.

Eisenhower was stationed with the Nineteenth Infantry at Fort Sam Houston, Texas; served with the Fifty-seventh Infantry at Leon Springs, Texas; and then was an instructor at the Officers' Training Camp at Fort Oglethorpe, Georgia. When America entered World War I, Eisenhower rose to the rank of lieutenant colonel and served at Camp Dix, New Jersey, and Fort Benning, Georgia.

In 1915 Dwight fell in love with Mamie Doud, who was born on November 14, 1896, in Boone, Iowa. Mamie completed her education at Miss Wolcott's, a private finishing school for young women. Dwight D. Eisenhower and Mamie Geneva Doud were married on July 1, 1916, in the Doud family home in Denver. Doud Dwight, who was born on September 24, 1917, contracted scarlet fever when he was three and died. John Sheldon Doud was born on August 3, 1922.

From 1916 until World War II, Mamie and Ike (his nickname from grade school) lived on army posts in the United States, Panama, France, and the Philippines. In 1933 Eisenhower was made chief military aide to Gen. Douglas MacArthur, the army chief of staff. During World War II, Eisenhower would command Allied forces in Europe while MacArthur commanded U.S. forces in the Pacific. In June 1941 Ike was appointed as chief of staff to Gen. Walter Krueger, commander of the Third Army, at Fort Sam Houston, Texas, and he was promoted to brigadier general in September 1941.

When the United States entered World War II, Eisenhower was appointed as assistant chief of staff in charge of the Operations Division under Gen. George S. Marshall. Recognizing his organizational and administrative abilities, Marshall secured Eisenhower's appointment as commanding general of the European theater, with headquarters in London, England.

Eisenhower commanded the American forces landing in North Africa in November 1942 and then was made commander in chief of Allied Forces in North Africa. In February 1943 his authority was extended as commander of forces in the Mediterranean basin, including the British Eighth Army, commanded by Gen. Bernard Law Montgomery. Eisenhower oversaw the Allied victory in North Africa over Erwin Rommel's Afrika Corps and the invasions of Italy in 1943.

Under Eisenhower's command the Allies staged a massive invasion of Europe on D-Day, June 6, 1944, when more than three hundred thousand troops crossed the English Channel and landed in Normandy. They pushed the Germans back through France and the Low Countries to Germany. On May 8, 1945, General Eisenhower accepted the unconditional surrender of all German forces, ending World War II in Europe. He was appointed as military governor of the United States Occupation Zone in Germany.

Eisenhower served as chief of staff of the U.S. Army from 1945 to 1948. In December 1950 he was named supreme commander of the North Atlantic Treaty Organization (NATO). He retired from active service on May 31, 1952. Eisenhower wrote his memoirs, *Crusade in Europe,* and was president of Columbia University.

In 1948 leaders in both major parties tried to persuade Eisenhower to seek their presidential nominations, but he declined. However, in 1952 he sought the Republican nomination for president and was in a close race with Sen. Robert A. Taft. Eisenhower won the nomination, and his vice-presidential running mate was Richard Nixon of California. The Democratic candidate for president was Adlai Stevenson, the governor of Illinois. Eisenhower won 33,936,000 popular and 442 electoral votes to Stevenson's 27,314,000 popular and 89 electoral votes.

During the Eisenhower years, from 1953 to 1961, America modernized its industrial and transportation infrastructure and generally enjoying economic prosperity, though it was engaged in a global cold war with the Soviet Union. Eisenhower rested his military and diplomatic policy on avoiding the catastrophe of nuclear war and maintaining national security through nuclear deterrence.

Although President Eisenhower suffered a heart attack in September 1955, he sought a second term. Again his Democratic opponent was Adlai Stevenson. Eisenhower won 35,585,000 popular and 457 electoral votes to Stevenson's 26,030,000 popular and 73 electoral votes.

Eisenhower signed the Highway Act of 1956, which provided federal funds to construct a forty-one-thousand-mile interstate highway system. The interstate system led to the growth of suburbs, to a thriving vacation industry, to the decline of railroads, and to a highly mobile population.

On May 17, 1954, the U.S. Supreme Court ruled in *Brown et al. v. Board of Education of Topeka et al.* that racial segregation was unconstitutional in public schools. During the Little Rock, Arkansas, school integration crisis in the fall of 1957, President Eisenhower was locked in conflict with Gov. Orval Faubus over school desegregation. The Little Rock School Board planned to integrate the senior high school, but Faubus claimed that order could not be maintained if desegregation were attempted. He ordered the Arkansas National Guard to prevent African American students from entering Little Rock Central High School. On September 14 Faubus met with Eisenhower, who recorded in his diary that he advised Faubus to "tell the Guard to continue to preserve order but to allow the Negro children to attend Central High School."[1]

On September 20 the Eighth Federal Circuit Court issued an injunction restraining Governor Faubus and the National Guard commanders from further interference in the court-ordered integration process. Faubus removed the National Guard on September 21. When school opened on September 23, even though a mob of approximately one thousand persons milled around outside, nine black students entered the school. After three hours of demonstrations outside, local officials, fearing for the black students' safety, had them removed from the school.

Mayor Woodrow Mann of Little Rock wired an urgent appeal for federal troops to President Eisenhower. On September 24 the president federalized the Arkansas National Guard and sent the 101st Airborne Division to Little Rock. For the rest of that year troops from the 101st Airborne Division escorted the African American students to classes.

During Eisenhower's two terms, the cold war between the United States and the Soviet Union escalated. Eisenhower, cautious but firm, was a reassuring father figure to a nation living with the threat of nuclear war. He maintained and strengthened the NATO alliance while he reduced spending on conventional weapons.

On July 2, 1953, American and North Korean emissaries signed an agreement that ended the fighting but kept the country divided at the prewar thirty-eighth parallel. As the French presence in Indo-China deteriorated, Eisenhower resisted requests to aid the French militarily. After the French were defeated and left Indo-China, Vietnam was divided into Communist North Vietnam and non-Communist South Vietnam. The United States then began to give aid to the South Vietnamese government.

On October 4, 1957, the Soviet Union successfully launched Sputnik, a space satellite, which orbited the earth. The Soviet success in space generated widespread criticism of American education. Congress enacted the National Defense Education Act (NDEA), which gave assistance to science, mathematics, and foreign language instruction. Alaska and Hawaii were admitted as the forty-ninth and fiftieth states in 1959.

President Eisenhower retired to his farm at Gettysburg, Pennsylvania, to write his memoirs and paint. He died on March 28, 1969, at Walter Reed Hospital and was buried in Abilene, Kansas. Mamie Eisenhower died on November 1, 1979.

. . . . . . . . . . . . . . . . . . . . . . . . . . . . . . . . . . . . . . . . . . . . . . . . . . . . . . . . . . . . . . . .

## Eisenhower Birthplace State Historic Site
## Denison, Texas

ADDRESS: 609 S. Lamar Avenue, Denison, TX 75021

TELEPHONE: 903-465-8908

WEB SITE: www.visiteisenhowerbirthplace.com

LOCATION: Denison is located seventy-five miles north of Dallas on U.S. Highway 75, in Grayson County, in downtown Denison

OPEN: Tuesday–Saturday, 9:00 A.M. to 5:00 P.M., and Sunday, 1:00 P.M. to 5:00 P.M.; closed Thanksgiving, Christmas Eve and Day, and New Year's Eve and Day

ADMISSION: Adults, $3.00; children 6–11, $2.00

FACILITIES: Birthplace home of President Dwight Eisenhower, handicapped accessible; visitor center with exhibits on Eisenhower; book and gift store; ten-acre park with hiking trails and picnic tables

*The Eisenhower Birthplace State Historic Site* is a ten-acre park in downtown Denison, Texas, in Grayson County. The citizens of Denison purchased the property in 1946. In 1958 the Eisenhower Birthplace Foundation donated the house to the state of Texas, and the following year it was opened to the public. It is now operated by the Texas Historical Commission.

Dwight's father, David, after suffering a total business failure in Kansas, found a job on the railroad in Denison at ten dollars per week in 1888. Ida Eisenhower, who was pregnant, stayed in Hope, Kansas. After the birth of their son Edgar in January 1889, Ida joined David in Denison with Edgar and their oldest son, Arthur. The Eisenhower family lived in a rented frame house. On October 14, 1890, Dwight, the only Eisenhower child to be born in Texas, was born in that house. When he was eighteen months old, the Eisenhower family returned to Kansas, and Dwight grew up in Abilene. Eisenhower was the first American president born in Texas.

Tours begin at the visitor center, which is located in a restored 1900s neighborhood residence. The center features exhibits on Eisenhower and World War II, including a bronze bust of Eisenhower and the "Ike Jacket," a brown short-waisted, tailored wool field jacket worn by the general. Two paintings by Eisenhower are displayed. Photographs document President Eisenhower's three visits to Denison between 1946 and 1965. The center also has a bookstore and videos about Eisenhower's life.

Eisenhower's birthplace is a modest two-story white frame home at the corner of Lamar Avenue and Day Street in east Denison. Here, Dwight David Eisenhower was born in 1890. Denison was a railroad town, and David Eisenhower was employed on the Missouri-Kansas and Texas Railroad, whose tracks ran near the home.

In 2003 the home was refurbished with period pieces from the 1890s era, some of which were donated by Denison residents. Eisenhower possessions include a quilt made by Ida Elizabeth Stover Eisenhower, the president's mother, and one of President Eisenhower's paintings.

A new education center is in the restored Red Store, which was built in 1890. On the grounds is an impressive statue of Eisenhower by the sculptor Robert Lee Dean Jr. The park encompasses several acres of scenic woods and creek bottomland intersected by an abandoned track that has been converted to a hiking path.

. . . . . . . . . . . . . . . . . . . . . . . . . . . . . . . . . . . . . . . . . . . . . . . . . . . . . . . . . . . . . . . . . . . . . . . .

## Dwight D. Eisenhower Presidential Library and Museum
## Abilene, Kansas

ADDRESS: 200 Southeast Fourth Street, Abilene, KS 67410

TELEPHONE: 785-263-6700

WEB SITE: www.eisenhower.archives.gov.

LOCATION: Abilene is located on I-70 approximately 150 miles west of Kansas City and 90 miles north of Wichita on K-15

OPEN: Daily, 9:00 A.M. to 4:45 P.M.; closed Thanksgiving, Christmas, and New Year's Day

ADMISSION: Adults, $8.00; seniors, $6.00; children 8–15, $1.00

FACILITIES: Family home, presidential library and museum, and burial site of President Dwight D. Eisenhower; visitor center; gift shop; handicapped accessible

*The Eisenhower Center is a five-building complex* on twenty-two acres of land located in Abilene, Kansas, the hometown of Dwight D. Eisenhower. The complex includes the visitor center, the family home, the museum, the library, and the Place of Meditation.

The Dwight D. Eisenhower Presidential Library and Museum is part of the presidential libraries system administered by the National Archives and Records Administration. In 1952 ground was broken for the museum, which was completed in 1954. The Eisenhower Presidential Library was completed in 1962,

Eisenhower Family
Home, Dwight D.
Eisenhower Presidential
Library and Museum,
Abilene, Kansas

269

DWIGHT DAVID EISENHOWER

opened to researchers in 1966, and enlarged with a new wing and rededicated in 1971. The Place of Meditation, where President Eisenhower, his wife, and his son are buried, was constructed in 1966, while the visitor center was completed in 1975. All of the buildings are constructed from native Kansas limestone. In 1985 a statue of Gen. Dwight D. Eisenhower, located between the museum and the library, was dedicated. The Eisenhower Center exhibits are self-guided. Tours begin at the visitor center, which has exhibits on Eisenhower and the center. An orientation film is shown there.

David and Ida Eisenhower and their sons Arthur, Edgar, and Dwight returned to Abilene from Denison, Texas, in 1891 when Dwight was just over one year old. David returned to his hometown to work at the Belle Springs Creamery. The family grew with the birth of Roy in 1892; in 1894 Paul, who died in infancy; Earl in 1898; and Milton in 1899.

The Eisenhower family home, a turn-of-the-century Kansas house, provides insights into the daily life of Ike and his family. Originally renting the house, which was owned by David's brother Abraham, David and Ida Eisenhower later purchased it. Crowded for a family of eight, it was located on several acres on which a vegetable garden was planted. There was a barn for the family's livestock. When Eisenhower laid the cornerstone for the museum on June 4, 1952, he said, "I found out in later years we were very poor but the glory of America is that we didn't know it then."[2]

The Eisenhower family home is an unpretentious two-story white frame structure. In the entry is a bookcase that contains the popular books of the time as well as religious books and the boys' textbooks.

The front parlor is dominated by Ida's piano, her most prized possession. The family Bible is displayed on a table. On the wall hangs David Eisenhower's framed diploma from a correspondence school in steam engineering. The kitchen, where Ida baked bread daily for her family, has cabinets, a sink, and a table.

On the second floor the parents' bedroom has a Singer sewing machine. Dwight's room, shared with Edgar, contains a chair, a dresser, and a marble-top washstand.

The house was Ida Eisenhower's home until her death in 1946, when her sons gave the house to the Eisenhower Foundation. The house, which was opened to the public in 1947, was given to the federal government in 1966.

The Eisenhower museum, with thirty-five thousand square feet of exhibit space, portrays the life and career of Dwight D. Eisenhower. The introductory gallery features exhibits on Eisenhower's ancestors and family. There are photographs of Dwight as a member of the high school football and baseball teams, and he is pictured in uniform as a cadet at West Point. Some exhibits relate to his service at Fort Sam Houston, Camp Gaillard, on the Battle Monuments Commission, and in the Philippines.

The First Lady's Gallery features Mamie Eisenhower as an army wife and as First Lady of the United States. It includes family photographs, clothing, jewelry, and other possessions.

The military gallery deals with Eisenhower's role in World War II and features military artifacts, uniforms, weapons, and equipment. There are exhibits about his role as commander in North Africa and in Europe during World War II. A large battle map details the Normandy invasion.

The presidential gallery focuses on political and international events during the Eisenhower presidency as well as social, cultural, and technological changes during the 1950s. Among the changes in American life was the rise of a new housing phenomenon—suburbia. In 1950, 3.9 million households had television sets; in the 1960s the number of households with TVs had skyrocketed to 46 million. The U.S. population grew from 152 million in 1950 to 181 million in 1960. The new highway transportation, linking cities across the country, reduced geographical isolation and created a highly mobile society.

Political exhibits feature Eisenhower's presidential campaigns of 1952 and 1956. Exhibits also cover the first fifteen years of the long cold war (1945–90) that pitted the United States and its allies against the Soviet Union and its satellites.

The massive glass entry to the library is highlighted with bronze work depicting a buffalo head and blue stem grass. There is an exhibit area on the second floor, while the remainder of the building contains archives, a photographic laboratory, and an auditorium.

The Place of Meditation is the final resting place of President Dwight D. Eisenhower, Mamie Doud Eisenhower, and their son, Doud Dwight Eisenhower. A meditation portion of the building is where Eisenhower hoped that visitors would reflect upon the ideals that made America a great nation.

Eisenhower National Historic Site
Gettysburg, Pennsylvania

ADDRESS: 250 Eisenhower Farm Drive, Gettysburg, PA 17325
TELEPHONE: 717-338-9114 or 877-874-2478
WEB SITE: www.nps.gov/eise
LOCATION: In south central Pennsylvania near the Maryland border, 143 miles
    west of Philadelphia, 39 miles southwest of Harrisburg, near Gettysburg
    National Military Park; due to a lack of on-site parking and space limita-
    tions in the Eisenhower home, visits can be made only by shuttle bus
    leaving from the Gettysburg National Military Park Visitor Center,
    approximately one mile south of Gettysburg on SR 134 (Taneytown
    Road) and U.S. 15 business route (Steinwehr Avenue)
OPEN: Daily, 9:00 A.M. to 4:00 P.M.; closed Thanksgiving, Christmas, and
    New Year's Day; Gettysburg National Military Park Visitor Center opens
    at 8:00 A.M.
ADMISSION: Adults, $7.50; children 6–12, $5.00
FACILITIES: The farm home and presidential retreat of President Dwight Eisen-
    hower, shuttle service from Gettysburg National Military Park Visitor
    Center to the Eisenhower farm

*Eisenhower National Historic Site, established in 1967,* preserves the home and
farm owned by President and Mrs. Eisenhower. The original 189-acre farm, with
its old farmhouse and dairy barn, was transformed into the 230-acre country
estate of the thirty-fourth president of the United States. When asked to recommend a place associated with his life as a National Historic Landmark,
Eisenhower chose his Gettysburg farm because, he said, that it was the only
home that was truly his and Mamie's. He added that they had lived in many
corners of the world during a half century of public service.

Located adjacent to the Gettysburg Battlefield, the farm served Eisenhower
as a weekend retreat and a meeting place for world leaders while he was president. With its peaceful setting and view of South Mountain, it provided a respite from Washington, D.C. Among the foreign visitors to Eisenhower's farm
were Prime Minister Jawaharlal Nehru of India, Chancellor Konrad Adenauer
of the Federal Republic of Germany, President Charles de Gaulle of France,
Winston Churchill, and Nikita Khrushchev.

The Eisenhowers purchased the Allen Redding farm, adjoining Gettysburg
National Military Park, in 1950. The Redding house was in such serious disrepair that it had to be dismantled and virtually replaced. The Eisenhowers instructed the builders to salvage as much of the original material as possible to
use in constructing the new home. Part of the brickwork, the kitchen fireplace,

Eisenhower Home, Eisenhower National Historic Site, Gettysburg, Pennsylvania. Photograph courtesy of the Eisenhower National Historic Site

and some wooden beams, floorboards, and shutters were salvaged. In March 1955 work on the two-story modified Georgian farmhouse was completed.

After Eisenhower left the presidency, he and Mamie spent their retirement, from 1961 to 1969, at Gettysburg, which is near the Pennsylvania Dutch country where Eisenhower's ancestors had first settled. Additional structures on the farm include a furnished guesthouse, a teahouse, greenhouses, an 1887 barn that housed the Secret Service office, garages, chauffeurs' quarters, a tack room, stables, and a carpentry shop. A skeet range and a putting green reflect some of Eisenhower's outdoor hobbies. Mamie's rose garden is still maintained. Lining the driveway to the house are fifty white pine trees, each the gift of a state Republican Party. Eisenhower's cattle operation was headquartered on the adjoining farm. The show barn serves as storage for hundreds of farm-related items. In 1967 the Eisenhowers deeded their property to the United States to be administered by the National Park Service.

Visits begin at the Eisenhower Tour Information Center in the lobby of the National Park Service visitor center. A farm visit includes a self-guided tour of the Eisenhower home and grounds, with a brief program in the home. The Eisenhower home, with five thousand original household furnishings, depicts the couple's public careers and private lives. On the first floor are the porch, the living room, the dining room, the kitchen, the office, and the den.

The living room contains many gifts that the couple received during their years of public life. The room was rarely used, but it provided a place to display Mamie's accumulations over the years—family photographs, figurines, and decorative items. For their thirty-eighth wedding anniversary, the White House staff presented the Eisenhowers with an 1870s marble fireplace from the White House.

The Eisenhowers' favorite room was the glassed-in porch on the east side of the house with a view of the rolling hills. Here they spent time reading, playing cards, watching television, or relaxing in the armchairs. Ike, a painter, took advantage of the room's natural light to paint his landscapes and portraits. He and Mamie often ate their meals on the spacious porch.

When family and friends visited, meals were served in the formal dining room. Mamie had purchased the dining room suite in 1927, and it traveled with the couple to various army posts. The tea service was a gift from Dwight to Mamie.

The 1950s kitchen and butler's pantry are in the old portion of the original house. The fireplace and oven were salvaged from a summer kitchen that once stood near the original farmhouse. Ike enjoyed making soups, stews, and especially a Pennsylvania Dutch–style breakfast.

Eisenhower used the den as a place to read or play cards. The office was used to conduct farm and presidential business. Both rooms were used as the temporary White House while President Eisenhower recuperated from a heart attack. The desk, a reproduction of one used by George Washington, is made of pine boards recovered from the White House when it was renovated in 1948–50.

On the second floor is the sitting room with paintings and books that reflect the Eisenhowers' interests in Westerns, biographies, and histories. The General's Room was used by Ike as his place to relax and take a nap. Eisenhower's portrait of his grandchildren, David and Anne, hangs on the wall. In the dressing room Cadet Eisenhower's West Point portrait is on Mamie's dressing table.

The master bedroom contains many photographs of family and friends. On display in the maid's room is some of the Eisenhowers' earliest furniture. Four paintings by President Eisenhower hang in the hallway.

# John Fitzgerald Kennedy

THIRTY-FIFTH PRESIDENT OF THE UNITED STATES

*January 20, 1961–November 22, 1963*

........................................................................

John Fitzgerald Kennedy, the first U.S. president born in the twentieth century, presided over an exciting and glamorous time in the White House. During his short term he led the country though the continuing cold war, averting nuclear war during the Cuban Missile Crisis. The nation was stunned and inconsolable when, on November 22, 1963, President Kennedy was assassinated in Dallas, Texas.

John F. Kennedy, born on May 29, 1917, in Brookline, Massachusetts, was the second of the nine children of Rose Elizabeth Fitzgerald Kennedy and Joseph Patrick Kennedy, both Roman Catholics and Irish Americans. Joe, a wealthy man, graduated from Harvard University and was involved in the automobile business and the Hollywood film industry. Kennedy's maternal grandfather and namesake, John Fitzgerald, was the mayor of Boston from 1906 to 1907 and again from 1910 to 1914.

Rose Fitzgerald and Joseph Kennedy married in 1914 and moved to Brookline, a Boston streetcar suburb. John Fitzgerald Kennedy, the future president, was born in the Brookline home. The growing Kennedy family moved to a larger house in Brookline in 1920 and then moved to Bronxville, New York, in 1927. They had a summer home in Hyannis Port, Cape Cod, Massachusetts, and an ocean-front house in Palm Beach, Florida.

John "Jack" Fitzgerald Kennedy began his education at the Devotion School, a Brookline public school, and at age seven attended Dexter, a prestigious boys' school. Jack then attended the Choate School, a highly selective private preparatory boarding school in Wallingsford, Connecticut, and graduated in 1935. He attended the London School of Economics followed by one year at Princeton University. In 1936 Jack Kennedy entered Harvard University.

Jack Kennedy spent part of 1938 in London, where his father, Joseph Kennedy, was ambassador at the Court of St. James. This experience heightened Jack's interest in world affairs and diplomacy. At Harvard he majored in government, reading extensively in history and politics. In the honors program Kennedy wrote a thesis on British prime minister Neville Chamberlain's appeasement of Hitler at Munich. He graduated from Harvard in 1940, receiving the bachelor of science degree with honors. Kennedy's thesis was later published as *Why England Slept*. He also wrote *A Nation of Immigrants*, in which he argues that immigrant groups could become American without losing their ethnic heritage.

During World War II, Kennedy joined the U.S. Navy. While he was serving in the Solomon Islands in August 1943, the Japanese destroyer *Amagiri* sliced Kennedy's PT-109 in half, and he and his crew were thrown into Ferguson Passage. Two men died, but the rest swam to safety. Kennedy towed an injured crew member by holding the strap of his life jacket in his teeth. The survivors were rescued from Olasana Island six days later. Kennedy was discharged in April 1945 and was awarded the Navy and Marine Corps Medal.

Kennedy worked briefly as a journalist for the *Chicago Herald-American* and the International News Service. He then entered Massachusetts Democratic politics, winning election to the U.S. House of Representatives in 1946.

Jack Kennedy met Jacqueline "Jackie" Lee Bouvier in 1951. Jackie, the daughter of Janet Lee Bouvier and John Vernon Bouvier III, was born on July 28, 1929, in South Hampton, Long Island, New York. The Bouviers divorced in 1940, and in 1942 Janet Bouvier married Hugh D. Auchincloss. Jackie attended Miss Porter's School in Farmington, Connecticut, followed by two years at Vassar. She spent her junior year at the Sorbonne in Paris and graduated from George Washington University in 1951. She worked as a columnist for the *Washington Times Herald*.

John Fitzgerald Kennedy and Jacqueline Lee Bouvier were married on September 12, 1953, in St. Mary's Roman Catholic Church in Newport, Rhode Island. In 1956 a stillborn daughter, unnamed, was born. Caroline Bouvier Kennedy was born to the couple on November 27, 1957, and John Fitzgerald Kennedy Jr. was born on November 25, 1960. Patrick Bouvier Kennedy was born in August 1963 and lived only a few days. Jackie, a young First Lady, was noted for her glamorous looks, her fashion style, her fine restoration of the White House, and her support of artistic and cultural endeavors.

John Kennedy, defeating the Republican incumbent Henry Cabot Lodge, was elected as senator from Massachusetts in 1952 and reelected in 1958. Kennedy wrote *Profiles in Courage*, published in 1956, about senators who took unpopular stands that endangered their political careers.

In the 1960 presidential election Kennedy, the Democratic nominee, and his running mate, Lyndon Johnson of Texas, were opposed by the Republican Richard M. Nixon, Eisenhower's vice president from 1953 to1961. The Republican vice-presidential candidate was Henry Cabot Lodge Jr., the Massachusetts senator whom Kennedy had defeated earlier.

An unprecedented high point in the 1960 campaign was the series of televised Kennedy-Nixon debates. Viewed by millions, the debates made clear that television would be a crucial dynamic in American politics. In an extremely close election Kennedy, with 49.7 percent of the vote, won 34,220,984 popular and 303 electoral votes. Nixon, with 49.5 percent, won 34,108,157 popular and 219 electoral votes.

Kennedy was the first Roman Catholic and the youngest man to be elected to the presidency. He was 43 years and 236 days old when he was inaugurated. However, Theodore Roosevelt was 42 years and 322 days when he became president after the assassination of President William McKinley.

Early in his administration Kennedy suffered a severe embarrassment in the Cuban Bay of Pigs debacle. Planned during the Eisenhower administration, the operation was a covert attempt to use Cuban exiles to depose the communist-backed Castro government. The Bay of Pigs invasion on April 17, 1961, was a complete failure. Twelve hundred invaders were taken prisoner, and four American pilots and more than one hundred Cubans were killed.

The cold war with the Soviet Union, which had preoccupied the Truman and Eisenhower administrations, continued to engage Kennedy. The Cuban Missile Crisis began on October 15, 1962, when U-2 reconnaissance intelligence discovered that the Soviets were constructing missile bases in Cuba. President Kennedy ordered the U.S. Navy to blockade Cuba. For fourteen days the two superpowers came close to nuclear war. On October 28 Nikita Khrushchev, the Soviet premier, yielded, agreeing to dismantle the missiles in Cuba in exchange for a noninvasion agreement and a secret removal of the U.S. missiles in Turkey.[1]

In a controversial move, President Kennedy appointed his brother Robert as attorney general. On March 1, 1961, President Kennedy created the Peace Corps by executive order and named R. Sargent Shriver, his brother-in-law, as its director. Volunteers worked overseas in education, community development, health care, and agriculture.

Civil rights for African Americans was a Kennedy priority. In September 1962 James Meredith, an African American, attempted to enroll at the University of Mississippi at Oxford. Mississippi's segregationist governor Ross Barnett intervened to block Meredith's admission to the university. The U.S. Court of Appeals had in 1961 found Barnett guilty of contempt and directed the Justice Department, headed by Robert Kennedy, to enforce its order that the university admit Meredith. When mob demonstrations erupted in Oxford, President Kennedy on September 30 ordered federal troops to the campus. A night of rioting followed, causing several deaths. The next morning, however, Meredith, protected by federal marshals, enrolled at the University of Mississippi.

President Kennedy supported space exploration. The Soviets had already successfully launched the first cosmonaut into space. In May 1961 the astronaut Alan Shepard traveled in space, and in February 1962 the astronaut John Glenn orbited Earth three times.

On November 22, 1963, President and Mrs. Kennedy arrived in Dallas, Texas. Accompanied by Vice President Lyndon Johnson, Lady Bird Johnson, Texas governor John Connally, and Nellie Connally, the Kennedys drove in a motorcade through downtown Dallas. The Kennedys and the Connallys were riding in an open-top 1961 Lincoln Continental. At 12:30 P.M., as the motorcade moved through Dealey Plaza, three shots were fired. A round entered President Kennedy's upper back, penetrated his neck, and exited his throat. A bullet that penetrated Governor Connally's back and chest is believed to be the same round that wounded Kennedy. The final shot hit Kennedy's head, inflicting a gaping wound.

At Parkland Memorial Hospital, President Kennedy was pronounced dead at 1:00 P.M. He was forty-six years old and had been president for less than one thousand days. At 2:38 P.M. Lyndon B. Johnson was sworn in as president by Judge Sarah Hughes aboard the presidential airplane, Air Force One. Jackie Kennedy, still in her blood-spattered pink suit, witnessed the ceremony.

The shots that killed the president were fired from the Texas School Book Depository at 411 Elm Street. Investigators found a rifle and other evidence of a sniper near a window on the sixth floor. A bullet found on Connally's hospital stretcher ballistically matched the rifle. Lee Harvey Oswald, who was employed at the Book Depository, was arrested on the evening of November 23 and charged with the murders of Dallas police officer J. D. Tippit and President Kennedy. Oswald, who denied involvement with either murder, was killed by Jack Ruby as he was being transferred to the county jail.

The president's body was returned to Washington, D.C., where it rested in the East Room of the White House. Millions of grief-stricken Americans watched on television as the president's coffin was taken to the Capitol Rotunda to lie in state and 250,000 mourners filed by over the next several days. A funeral was held at St. Matthew's Cathedral in Washington, D.C., and the president was buried in Arlington National Cemetery in Arlington, Virginia.

President Johnson on November 29, 1963, established a commission, chaired by Earl Warren, chief justice of the Supreme Court, to conduct an official investigation of the assassination. The Warren Commission concluded that it could not find any persuasive evidence of a domestic or foreign conspiracy. The commission determined that Lee Harvey Oswald was the lone assassin of Kennedy and that Jack Ruby acted alone in Oswald's murder.

In October 1968 Jackie Kennedy married Aristotle Onassis, a wealthy Greek businessman, who died in 1975. Jackie died on May 19, 1994, and was buried with John Kennedy at Arlington National Cemetery.

JOHN FITZGERALD KENNEDY

. . . . . . . . . . . . . . . . . . . . . . . . . . . . . . . . . . . . . . . . . . . . . . . . . . . . . . . . . . . . . . . . . . . . .

**John F. Kennedy National Historic Site**
**Brookline, Massachusetts**

ADDRESS: 83 Beals Street, Brookline, MA 02146
TELEPHONE: 617-566-7937

WEB SITE: www.nps.gov/jofi

LOCATION: Brookline is approximately seven miles from Boston's Logan Airport and can be reached from I-90 or from I-95/Rt. 128. From the MBTA/Subway Green Line (C-Cleveland Circle), exit at Coolidge Corner

OPEN: Wednesday–Sunday, 10:30 A.M. to 4:30 P.M., late May–September

ADMISSION: Adults 18 and older, $3.00

FEATURES: Birthplace of President John F. Kennedy, restoration by his mother, Rose Kennedy; visitor center in basement of house; orientation film; guided tours; bookstore; not handicapped accessible. National Register of Historic Places, National Historic Landmark

*John F. Kennedy National Historic Site* is unique in that the acquisition and restoration of the presidential birthplace were completed by the Kennedy family. Rose Kennedy, the mother of the assassinated president, wanted the house where she had given birth to her son to be a memorial to him.

President John F. Kennedy, the second child of Rose Fitzgerald and Joseph P. Kennedy, was born at 83 Beals Street, Brookline, Massachusetts, on May 29, 1917. The Kennedys had moved into the 1909 colonial-revival house shortly after their marriage in October 1914. Brookline was an attractive streetcar commuter suburb of Boston with tree-lined streets, good schools, and St. Aidan's Roman Catholic Church nearby. John F. Kennedy spent the first ten years of his life in

Brookline. The Kennedy family lived in the Beals Street house from 1914 until 1920, when they moved to a larger house two blocks away, where they resided until 1927.

In 1965 the Beals Street house was designated a National Historic Landmark; in 1966 the Kennedy family repurchased the home, and in 1967 it was placed on the National Register of Historic Places. Rose Kennedy supervised the restoration of the Beals Street house to its 1917 appearance based solely on her memory fifty years after John's birth, without interior photographs to guide her. Changes to the house that occurred after 1917 were removed. Mrs. Kennedy and a decorator assembled household furnishings and personal artifacts to decorate the house as she remembered it. In her memoirs Rose Kennedy said, "The house has been restored with most of the original furniture, some of which Joe and I had saved through the years and some we had lent or given away, but which could be traced and collected."[2]

The restoration was completed in 1967, and the house was donated to the National Park Service. In 1969 the John F. Kennedy National Historic Site was established, and the Beals Street house is administered by the National Park Service, U.S. Department of the Interior. National Park Service staff members were not involved in the restoration.

The John F. Kennedy National Historic Site, a small property, consists of a single house on a rather narrow lot with a tiny backyard on Beals Street in Brookline, a picturesque busy suburban Boston area. The visitor center is in the basement of the house, and parking is on the street. Neighboring houses are privately owned. Beals Street is lined with large frame houses situated on small lots.

The house is painted dark green with yellow trim, as it was in 1917. A bronze plaque indicates that John Fitzgerald Kennedy was born here on May 29, 1917. The tour begins on the porch, where a ranger, using family photos, introduces the Kennedy family and the house. There is a photograph of the large crowd that gathered spontaneously at the Kennedy birth house after Kennedy's assassination.

In some ways the Kennedy birth house is more about the mother than her famous son. Visitors hear Rose's story as the daughter of one of Boston's leading politicians, John "Honey Fitz" Fitzgerald, a mayor of Boston; as the wife of an ambitious and promising husband, Joseph Kennedy; and as the mother of John and the other Kennedy children and her experiences and attitudes related to family and children.

Before 3:00 P.M. the tour is led by a National Park Service ranger; after 3:00 P.M. visitors take a self-guided tour with an audio wand. The audio features Rose Kennedy describing the furnishings of each room and how the rooms were used by the family.

On the first floor are the front hall, the living room, the dining room, and the kitchen. In the living room, which runs from the front to the back of the house and has a gas-log fireplace, there is an Ivers and Pond grand piano. Also in this room is a large red chair where Joe Kennedy read his evening newspapers.

The dining room is furnished with an oval table formally set with crystal, silverware, and china dishes hand-painted by Rose's aunt. There is also a small children's table with places set for two. In a cabinet are Joe Jr. and John's monogrammed silver napkin rings, porringers, forks, and spoons. Meals were prepared in the kitchen, which has a large combination cast-iron Glenwood stove, a small table, and a sink.

On the second floor are the master bedroom, the bathroom, a guest room, a study, and a nursery. In the upstairs hallway there are framed newspaper clippings of Rose and Joseph Kennedy's wedding.

The large master bedroom contains twin beds. John Kennedy was born on May 29, 1917, on the bed nearest the window. Not only did the doctor have better light here during delivery, but also sunlight was believed to be healthy for a newborn. On display are photographs of the four oldest children when each was six months old.

Rose had a small upstairs office, adjoining the master bedroom, which she called her "Boudoir." It contains a mahogany desk where Rose did her correspondence and kept file boxes of index cards of her children's visits to the doctor and their vaccinations, illnesses, weights, and heights. The guest room became a children's bedroom after Rosemary was born. In addition to a bed with an Irish linen bedspread, there is a dresser with a monogrammed silver toilet set.

In the nursery is the bassinet that was used by all of the Kennedy newborn babies. The christening dress and bonnet are reproductions of the originals, handmade by Franciscan nuns and given to Rose and Joe by Joe's mother. The original dress, which all the Kennedy children wore at their baptisms and President Kennedy's son, John, wore at his baptism, is in the Kennedy Presidential Museum in Boston Massachusetts. Two rooms on the third floor were occupied by a maid and a nursemaid.

Tickets for a tour of the Kennedy home are provided on the lower level, which also houses a small gift shop, Kennedy photographs, and a time line of important events in their lives. A video, "A Life Remembered," features events in the lives of the Kennedys and the Fitzgeralds.

The Kennedy children who were born in Brookline were baptized at the 1911 medieval-revival Saint Aidan's Roman Catholic Church. John and his brother Joseph were altar boys there. St. Aidan's Roman Catholic Church, located at 207 Freeman Street, Brookline, has been converted to condominiums.

The larger house in which the Kennedy family lived from 1920 to 1927 is located at 51 Abbottsford Road. This house is privately owned and is not open to the public.

## Sixth Floor Museum at Dealey Plaza
Dallas, Texas

ADDRESS: 411 Elm Street, Dallas, TX 75202
TELEPHONE: 214-747-6660
WEB SITE: www.jfk.org
LOCATION: In West End Historic District in downtown Dallas; accessible from
I-35E, exit at Continental, take Continental to Houston Street, turn right
on Houston to Elm Street
OPEN: Monday, noon to 6:00 P.M., and Tuesday–Sunday, 9:00 A.M. to 6:00 P.M.;
closed Thanksgiving and Christmas
ADMISSION: Adults, $13.50; seniors and children 6–18, $12.50
FACILITIES: The site where the assassin Lee Harvey Oswald stood when he shot
President John F. Kennedy; audio tours available in English, French, German, Italian, Japanese, Portuguese, and Spanish; children's audio tours
available in English. National Register of Historic Places

*Not a presidential home, library, or burial site,* the Sixth Floor Museum at
Dealey Plaza is a unique site associated with the assassination of an American
president. Many people who come to Dallas visit the site of President John F.
Kennedy's death and the building from which the fatal bullets were fired. The
Sixth Floor Museum at Dealey Plaza is located in the former Texas School Book
Depository Building at 411 Elm Street. The assassin Lee Harvey Oswald shot
and killed President John F. Kennedy from a southeast corner window on the
sixth floor of that building at 12:30 P.M. on November 22, 1963. He also shot
and wounded Texas governor John Connolly.

Eyewitnesses reported that the shots came from the upper floors of the
depository. When the police searched its sixth floor immediately after the shooting, they found a barricade of boxes, a rifle, and three spent bullet cartridge
shells. Fingerprints and palm prints found on two of the boxes were later linked
to Oswald, who had been seen on the sixth floor thirty-five minutes before the
presidential motorcade passed the building. After Oswald shot and killed a
Dallas policeman, J. D. Tippit, police apprehended him in the Texas Theater an
hour and a half after the shooting of the president.

The seven-story masonry structure at 411 Elm Street was built in 1901 in
downtown Dallas by the Southern Rock Island Plow Company. In the mid-
1930s the Trinity River, which frequently flooded the downtown area, was
moved a mile west. A park in the reclaimed area was named for George Bannerman Dealey, publisher of the *Dallas Morning News*. The 411 Elm Street building is on Dealey Plaza. In 1937 the building was sold to the Carraway-Byrd
Corporation, and in 1939 it was purchased by Col. D. Harold Byrd, who owned
it until 1970.

In 1962 the Texas School Book Depository Company leased the building. The fifth through seventh floors were used as warehouse space, while the lower floors were used as publishers' offices. This private company distributed textbooks to Texas public schools. Lee Harvey Oswald became an order clerk for the Book Depository Company on October 15, 1963.

In 1970 the Texas School Book Depository Company vacated the 411 Elm Street Building, which was then purchased by Aubrey Mayhew, who hoped to open a Kennedy museum there. A fire in July 1972 damaged the building. The museum did not materialize, and purchase rights reverted to Dallas County in 1977. A bond issue raised money for Dallas County to acquire the building. The county used most of the building for office space and closed off the sixth floor.

The creation of the Sixth Floor Museum was a joint project of the Dallas County Historical Commission, the Texas Historical Commission, and the National Endowment for the Humanities. The Sixth Floor Museum at Dealey Plaza opened on President's Day, February 20, 1989, with historical exhibits on the life, times, death, and legacy of President Kennedy. Dallas county commissioners provided funds for a visitor center and exterior elevators behind the building. In 1997 the visitor center and museum store were completed. In 2002 the seventh floor was restored to its original 1901 appearance and is used as a gallery for temporary exhibits.

The museum's collection focuses on the Kennedy assassination and includes artifacts, newspapers, photographs, books, magazines, videos, and audiotapes. Its Oral History Collection includes hundreds of interviews with eyewitnesses, local law enforcement, local media people, politicians, White House officials, Kennedy family friends, and Parkland Hospital personnel.

The exhibit on the sixth floor includes an orientation film on the life and presidency of John F. Kennedy. Exhibits focus on the assassin of the president, the political reasons for Kennedy's trip to Texas, immediate post-assassination events, worldwide reactions to the news of the assassination, as well as the U.S. government's investigations into the assassination. Powerfully realistic installations include a re-creation of the sniper's area near the southeast corner window as it was found on November 22, 1963; the south windows that looked out on the presidential motorcade route through Dealey Plaza; and the corner staircase where the sniper allegedly exited and where the rifle and clipboard were found.

On display are acoustical evidence, photographs, and forensic and ballistics tests used in the investigations. Historic audio and video broadcasts feature President Lyndon Johnson being sworn in as the next president of the United States and talks about conspiracy theories that have continually surrounded the death of President Kennedy. The Dallas County Administration Building is a registered Texas Historical Landmark and is on the National Register of

Historic Places. The National Park Service designated the building as part of the Dealey Plaza Historic Landmark on November 22, 1993.

. . . . . . . . . . . . . . . . . . . . . . . . . . . . . . . . . . . . . . . . . . . . . . . . . . . . . . . . . . . . . . . . . . . . . . . . . . . . . . . .

## John F. Kennedy Burial Site
### Arlington National Cemetery, Arlington, Virginia

ADDRESS: Arlington, VA 22211

TELEPHONE: 703-607-8000

WEB SITE: www.arlingtoncemetery.org

LOCATION: In the Washington, D.C., area; across the Potomac River at the north end of Memorial Bridge, which is accessible from Constitution Avenue or Twenty-third Street NW; Arlington Cemetery is a blue line stop on the Metrorail

OPEN: Daily, 8:00 A.M. to 7:00 P.M., April–September; 8:00 A.M. to 5:00 P.M., October–May

ADMISSION: Free

FACILITIES: Paid parking lot; visitor center; Tourmobile (tour bus for a fee)

*On November 25, 1963, President John Fitzgerald Kennedy* was buried in Arlington National Cemetery, a five-thousand-acre military cemetery where U.S. veterans are interred. Kennedy qualified for burial here because he had served in the U.S. Navy during World War II and was commander in chief.

After lying in state in the Capitol Rotunda until the morning of the 25th, the president's coffin was placed on a caisson by nine military men while the U.S. Marine band played "Hail to the Chief." The funeral procession began to the sound of muffled drums. Seven horses slowly pulled the caisson, which was followed by a riderless horse. Black Watch pipers lent their mournful tunes. The solemn marchers proceeded to the White House and then to St. Matthew's Cathedral for a funeral mass conducted by Richard Cardinal Cushing, the archbishop of Boston.

At Arlington National Cemetery the state funeral of the president was held with full military honors. Irish Guardsmen stood at attention near the grave. Military personnel from the army, navy, air force, marines, and army special forces were present. The marine band and the air force bagpipe band provided music. Members of Congress stood near the grave. A Roman Catholic committal service was conducted by Richard Cardinal Cushing. The flag on the president's bronze coffin was folded and presented to his widow, Jacqueline Kennedy. She and Robert Kennedy lit the eternal flame. The Kennedy family, including Rose Kennedy, the president's mother, stood on one side of the grave. The ceremonies concluded with a twenty-one-gun salute, three musket volleys, and a bugler playing Taps. Fifty fighter planes, representing the fifty states, flew overhead, as did Air Force One, the presidential plane. Prominent mourners at the president's funeral included President Charles de Gaulle of France, Chancellor Ludwig Erhard of Germany, Emperor Haile Selassie of Ethiopia, Crown Princess Beatrix of the Netherlands, President Eamon de Valera of Ireland, and Prince Philip of the United Kingdom.

Two deceased Kennedy infants—an unnamed daughter who was stillborn in 1956 and a son, Patrick Bouvier Kennedy, who was born on August 7, 1963, and died on August 9, 1963—who had been buried elsewhere were reinterred with their father in the presidential plot in December 1963. Also buried with President Kennedy is his wife, Jacqueline Kennedy Onassis, who died in May 1994.

It was Jacqueline Kennedy's wish that her husband be buried in Arlington. In addition she wanted his funeral ceremonies to be similar to those of assassinated president Abraham Lincoln nearly one hundred years earlier. While lying in state in the Capitol Rotunda, Kennedy's coffin laid on the same black-draped catafalque on which Lincoln's coffin had rested. Jacqueline also wanted her husband's grave to be marked with an eternal flame similar to the one at the monument to the French Unknown Soldier in Paris. The flame burns from the center of a five-foot circular flat-granite stone at the head of the grave and is fueled by natural gas.

Kennedy's grave site is on a slope below the Custis-Lee Mansion. The original burial plot was twenty feet by thirty feet and was surrounded by a white picket fence. Large crowds visited the Kennedy grave site daily. Cemetery officials and Kennedy family members hired the architectural firm of John Warnecke and Associates to design a grave site that could accommodate the multitude of visitors. Construction began on the 3.2-acre site in 1965 and was completed in 1967.

President Kennedy and his two children were reinterred at the nearby site in a quiet ceremony attended by the president's widow, brothers, and President Johnson in March 1967. The grave area is covered with Cape Cod granite stones with clover and sedum planted in the spaces between the stones. The grave site inscription is taken from the inaugural address that President Kennedy delivered on January 20, 1961.

Arlington House and two hundred acres of land surrounding it were designated officially as a military cemetery on June 15, 1864, by Secretary of War Edwin M. Stanton. The cemetery is administered by the Department of the Army, while Arlington House, also known as the Custis-Lee Mansion, and its grounds are administered by the National Park Service. More than 260,000 veterans from all of the nation's wars have been interred at Arlington, including some from the Revolutionary War. William Howard Taft is the only president other than Kennedy who is buried there.

John F. Kennedy Presidential Library and Museum
Boston, Massachusetts

ADDRESS: Columbia Point, Boston, MA 02125
TELEPHONE: 617-514-1600 or 1-866-JFK-1960
WEB SITE: www.jfklibrary.org
LOCATION: Off Morrissey Boulevard, next to University of Massachusetts
   Boston campus; Red Line T to JFK/UMass
OPEN: Daily, 9:00 A.M. to 5:00 P.M.; closed Thanksgiving, Christmas, and New
   Year's Day. Research room: Monday–Friday, 8:30 A.M. to 4:30 P.M., by
   appointment; closed federal holidays
ADMISSION: Adults, $12.00; seniors and students, $10.00; children 13–17, $9.00
FACILITIES: Presidential library of President John F. Kennedy, museum,
   research library, café, museum store, museum is handicapped accessible,
   free parking

*The John F. Kennedy Library and Museum,* a presidential library administered
by the National Archives and Records Administration, was designed by the
famed Chinese American architect I. M. Pei, who was selected by Jacqueline
Kennedy. Originally the Kennedy Library was to be located in Cambridge,
adjacent to Harvard University, but in 1976 a decision was made to build the
library near the Harbor Campus of the University of Massachusetts Boston on
Columbia Point in Dorchester. Ground breaking occurred in mid-1977, and
the library was dedicated on October 20, 1979. President Carter accepted the
library, which was privately funded, on behalf of the American people.

The Kennedy Library and Museum is situated on ten acres of oceanfront
with a panoramic view of Boston Harbor and the city's skyline. Pei's building
is dramatic. It houses a glass pavilion soaring 115 feet high. A huge 26 x 45–foot
American flag hangs in the atrium. Landscaping includes pine tress, shrubs,
and wild roses.

On October 29, 1993, the new museum at the John F. Kennedy Library
opened, replacing the original 1979 museum as fewer museum patrons are old
enough to remember President Kennedy. Using video and sound recordings,
more than twenty chronologically arranged exhibits tell the story of John Kennedy's
life and presidency. A photo gallery at the theater's entrance portrays
John F. Kennedy and his family prior to his election as president. The exhibit
on the Democratic National Convention that nominated Kennedy for president
displays political posters, buttons, and delegates' credentials as well as
Kennedy's acceptance speech.

From the first exhibit onward television, the medium that Kennedy used so
well, re-creates the climate and mood of the Kennedy years. The campaign

286

trail and campaign office exhibits offer a study in contrasts—two storefronts, one of which is used as a campaign office, provide a nostalgic glimpse of Main Street, USA, in 1960. The campaign office, equipped with telephones and type-writers, displays photographs, itineraries, maps, signs, and documents from the Kennedy campaign, including anti-Catholic leaflets. Studio C, a re-created tele-vision studio similar to the site of the Kennedy-Nixon debate on September 16, 1960, shows the power of that medium. On display in the studio exhibit is the television camera used by the Chicago CBS affiliate WBBM-TV for the national telecast.

On election day, November 8, 1960, the nation watched the televised returns of what was then the closest presidential election in the United States. Walter Cronkite of CBS and Chet Huntley and David Brinkley of NBC covered the national drama. A large map of the states with their electoral votes shows the popular votes for each candidate. The election was not determined until No-vember 9, when Nixon conceded the close election. Kennedy had 49.7 percent of the popular vote and 303 electoral votes to Nixon's 49.5 percent of the popu-lar vote and 219 electoral votes.

On January 20, 1961, John F. Kennedy, age forty-three, the youngest person and the first Roman Catholic to be elected president of the United States, was inaugurated. Displayed is the Fitzgerald family Bible with which Kennedy took the oath of office that was administered by Chief Justice Earl Warren.

The re-created White House corridor that leads to the briefing room features photographs of the interior of the White House. Kennedy was the first president to hold live, televised press conferences. His repartee with the Washington press corps was quick, intelligent, and often humorous, as seen in the briefing room exhibit.

There is dramatic footage from Kennedy's speech on June 26, 1963, in Berlin, a city divided between the American, French, and British zones and the Russian zone. The East German government had built a fortresslike wall that separated the Communist-controlled part from the rest of the city. In West Berlin, President Kennedy said, "Let them come to Berlin" to see the repression of the Soviet system. Included in this speech are Kennedy's famous words "Ich bin ein Berliner," translated as "I am a Berliner."

President Kennedy created the Peace Corps by executive order and named R. Sargent Shriver, his brother-in-law, as its director. Peace Corps workers were young Americans who were trained and sent abroad to work on health, development, and educational projects in underdeveloped countries. The Peace Corps exhibit features photographs, documents, and artifacts from their projects.

The "From the Archives" exhibit provides linkage between the library and the museum. The library has nearly 48 million pages of documents from the collections of 340 individuals, organizations, and government agencies; oral history interviews with 1,084 people; and more than 35,000 books. Audiovisual materials in the archives include 400,000 still photographs; 7,550,000 feet of motion picture film; 2,300 hours of video recordings; 11,000 hours of audio recordings; and 500 original editorial cartoons.

The exhibit on the Cuban Missile Crisis dramatically portrays the events of October 1962 when America and the Soviet Union came precariously close to nuclear war. A film, highlighted by Kennedy's own commentary on the crisis, conveys the unfolding of the desperately dangerous events.

The Space Program exhibit features photographs of President and Mrs. Kennedy watching monitors showing Alan Shepherd's flight into space, the astronauts of Project Mercury, and Col. John Glenn's 1962 orbital space flight. The "Ceremonial and State Events" exhibit highlights White House ceremonies and diplomatic state visits by foreign heads of governments.

A re-creation of Robert F. Kennedy's Justice Department office depicts the attorney general's efforts against organized crime and his work to advance school integration and protect civil and voting rights. A photo of the Kennedy brothers Jack and Robert with their backs to the camera, casting long shadows, captures their special relationship.

In the reproduction of the Kennedy Oval Office, most of the furniture and artifacts are original, with the exception of the desk, which is a reproduction of the Resolute Desk. Kennedy was the first president to address the nation regularly through nationally televised broadcasts from the Oval Office.

Another exhibit features the multitalented Jacqueline Bouvier Kennedy as First Lady, especially her work in restoring and refurbishing the White House interior. The exhibit features her February 14, 1962, televised tour of the White House and displays the gowns she wore at state events. Jacqueline, who was an artist, painted several watercolors of the White House.

Featuring Jack Kennedy's love of the sea, another exhibit includes photos of him on his sailing boat, which is on display outside the museum, and as a lieutenant in the U.S. Navy. The exhibit also features President Kennedy's state visit to Ireland, his ancestral homeland, in 1963.

Rosemary Kennedy, the president's sister, was mentally handicapped, and the Kennedy family took a strong interest in the problems of mental retardation. The exhibit on this subject illustrates how family members worked through the Kennedy Foundation.

President Kennedy's assassination on November 22, 1963, his state funeral, and the days of public grief and mourning are indelibly etched in the American psyche. Using five screens, an exhibit shows Walter Cronkite, the CBS news anchor, announcing that the president was dead. The video continues with the funeral procession and the state funeral.

The "Legacy" exhibit portrays how foreign nations have honored President Kennedy's memory. On display is a piece of the Berlin Wall, which was given to the Kennedy Library by the city of Berlin.

In the large framed glass pavilion overlooking Boston Harbor, recipients of the John F. Kennedy Profile in Courage Award are honored. When he was a senator, Kennedy wrote *Profiles in Courage,* about senators who took unpopular stands that often cost them their political careers.

In addition to the main research room in the Kennedy Library, there is an Ernest Hemingway room, which houses an extensive collection of Ernest Hemingway's manuscripts, letters, and books as well as articles by and about the author. This room was dedicated in 1980 by Patrick Hemingway and Jacqueline Kennedy Onassis.

# Lyndon Baines Johnson

........................................................................

Lyndon Baines Johnson, who served as vice president from 1961 to 1963, became president on November 22, 1963. That was the day that President John F. Kennedy was assassinated in Texas, Johnson's home state.

Lyndon Johnson, the oldest of the five children of Sam Johnson and Rebekah Baines Johnson, was born on August 27, 1908, in a small farmhouse on the Pedernales River near Stonewall in Gillespie County, Texas. According to *A Family Album*, a family history book written by Rebekah Baines Johnson, three months passed before her first-born son was named. Sam finally suggested Linden, after his friend W. C. Linden, and Rebekah agreed on the condition that she could spell her son's name Lyndon.[1]

Rebekah Baines Johnson was the daughter of Joseph Wilson Baines, a lawyer, educator, state legislator, landowner, and lay preacher in the Baptist church in Blanco, Texas, and the granddaughter of Rev. George Washington Baines, who had been president of Baylor University. Sam Johnson, who did not finish high school, was a local politician, farmer, and trader in real estate and cattle.

Sam and Rebekah began married life in a dog-trot cabin in the barren Hill Country. They moved to Johnson City, population three hundred, in September 1913 when Lyndon was five years old. After Lyndon's grandparents' deaths, their 435-acre farm was not large enough to carve up among their eight children. In 1916 Sam Jr. mortgaged everything to buy it from his siblings. He failed as a farmer and was forced to sell the farm in 1922.

Sam was a steadfast progressive Democrat who served in the Texas state legislature from 1904 to 1908 and from 1918 to 1924. Lyndon often accompanied his father as he campaigned in the rural areas and also attended legislative sessions with him.

Lyndon Johnson graduated from Johnson City High School in 1924 and entered Southwest Texas State Teachers' College at San Marcos in February 1927. Twenty-year-old Johnson took a one-year assignment as principal and teacher at the Welhausen School in Cotulla, Texas, a largely Mexican American elementary school. In addition to teaching and administration, he also was coach of the boys' baseball team, debate coach, playground supervisor, and janitor when needed.[2] Johnson graduated from Texas State in August 1930 and taught public speaking at Sam Houston High School in Houston.

Johnson's entry into politics was unusual. In each election year a picnic was held in Henley at which candidates were invited to speak. In July 1930 Pat Neff, who was running for state railroad commissioner, did not appear when his name was called. Lyndon, who attended these picnics with his father, volunteered to give the speech for Neff. Willy Hopkins, a candidate for the state senate, heard Johnson speak and asked him to assist in managing his campaign.

Hopkins recommended Johnson to Texas congressman Richard Kleberg, who in 1931 hired Johnson as his legislative secretary. Richard Mifflin Kleberg was a grandson of Richard King, who developed the two-thousand-square-mile King Ranch, the largest ranch in the world; Kleberg owned 20 percent of it. Lyndon solved problems for Kleberg's constituents as he realized that was critical to reelection.

In 1934 Lyndon Johnson met Lady Bird Taylor, the daughter of Thomas Jefferson Taylor, a wealthy man who owned a store and extensive landholdings, and Minnie Patillo Taylor, the daughter of a wealthy Alabama plantation owner. Claudia Alta was born on December 22, 1912, in Karnack, Texas. When an African American cook employed by the family compared the pretty little girl to the ladybird beetles of East Texas, the nickname stuck. Lady Bird attended Marshall High School and St. Mary's School for Girls in Dallas. She received her B.A. degree in history in 1933 from the University of Texas in Austin. Lyndon and Lady Bird were married in San Antonio on November 17, 1934. On March 19, 1944, Lynda Bird was born, and Lucy Baines was born on July 2, 1947.

In 1943 the Johnsons purchased a Texas radio station, KTBC, with Lady Bird's inheritance from her mother. Lady Bird took an active role in running KTBC which became the basis for a multimillion-dollar media empire by the 1950s.

In August 1935 Lyndon was appointed as the Texas director of the National Youth Administration; he was the youngest NYA director in the country. The NYA, created by President Roosevelt during the Depression, was designed to put young people to work. By 1937 the Texas NYA employed eight thousand young people and assisted twenty thousand students.[3]

Lyndon ran for Congress when a seat became vacant due to the death of Congressman James P. Buchanan of the Tenth District in Central Texas. Lyndon won and served in the U.S. House of Representatives from 1937 until 1948. In 1941 Johnson ran for the Senate but lost.

In early 1940 Johnson was commissioned as a lieutenant commander in the U.S. Naval Reserve. After the United States entered World War II, Johnson, now on active duty, was sent to the South Pacific on an inspection tour. He was awarded a Silver Star after the military bomber he was flying in, the *Heckling Hare*, was attacked by Japanese planes. While he was in the military, Johnson retained his congressional seat. After President Franklin D. Roosevelt ordered congressmen in the military to resume their legislative duties, Johnson returned home in July 1942.

Johnson ran for the Senate again in 1948 and was opposed in the Democratic primary by former governor Coke Stevenson, whom he beat by a narrow margin of eighty-seven votes out of nine hundred thousand cast. Stevenson protested the election, and his challenge went to the Supreme Court. Johnson retained the Senate seat, but his victory was clouded by suspicion.

Johnson was elected as party whip three years later and in January 1953 as the leader of the Democrat caucus, serving as majority leader when his party held control. During his twelve years in the Senate, 1949 to 1961, Johnson successfully worked for legislation in the fields of farm subsidies, Social Security, aid to education, civil rights, NASA, conservation, flood control, rural electrification, public housing, and the minimum wage.

In 1949 Johnson purchased a family ranch on the Pedernales River between Fredericksburg and Johnson City. This grew into the LBJ Ranch. In July 1955 Johnson suffered a serious heart attack.

In the election of 1960, Johnson was John F. Kennedy's vice-presidential running mate. His ties to the South helped bolster the Democratic ticket, which proved victorious. Kennedy's assassination in Dallas on November 22, 1963, brought Johnson to the presidency. U.S. District Court judge Sarah T. Hughes administered the oath of office to Lyndon Johnson aboard Air Force One in Dallas' Love Field.

At the Democratic National Convention in August 1964, President Johnson was nominated by acclamation. Sen. Hubert Humphrey of Minnesota was the vice-presidential nominee. Johnson won a landslide victory over his conservative Republican opponent, Barry Goldwater.

Johnson launched his Great Society program in which the federal government would take a leading role in alleviating poverty in urban ghettoes and rural areas, especially Appalachia. The War on Poverty provided training and educational programs. Johnson proposed 200 major pieces of legislation on civil rights, poverty, education, health, housing, pollution, the arts, cities, occupational safety, consumer protection, and mass transit, and Congress passed 181 of these bills.

During Johnson's administration, sixty laws aiding education were passed. The Civil Rights Act of 1965 forbade racial discrimination in federally funded programs. Together with the ESEA, it stimulated school districts to desegregate and work toward racial integration.

Johnson's Great Society and War on Poverty initiatives included the Job Corps, VISTA, work training programs, Head Start, community action programs, education for migrant workers, and work-study programs for college students. In 1965 Congress passed the Medicare and Medicaid bills. Medicare provided hospital and medical insurance for those sixty-five and older, while Medicaid provided those same benefits for the poor of any age.

The presidency of Lyndon Johnson is largely associated in American minds with the Vietnam War and the protest movement. During the Kennedy administration, military advisers were sent to South Vietnam. Originally there were fewer than one thousand, but the number grew to sixteen thousand, though the Kennedy administration did not send combat forces.

In August 1964, in response to attacks by Vietnamese torpedo boats on U.S. destroyers in the Gulf of Tonkin, the United States attacked North Vietnamese naval installations from the air. Soon afterward Congress passed the Gulf of Tonkin Resolution, which gave the president power to take all necessary measures to repel armed attack against U.S. forces and to prevent further aggression. By 1968, 550,000 American troops were in Vietnam.

An undeclared war that lasted for eight years, the Vietnam War sparked violent protests and an antiwar movement, which was strongest among draft-age students on college campuses. President Johnson lost the support of the public, and his public appearances were marred by protestors. Because of that and a promise he had made to Lady Bird, Johnson stunned the nation when he announced in March 1968 that he would not seek reelection.

Lyndon Johnson oversaw the construction of the Johnson Presidential Library at the University of Texas in Austin, which was dedicated on May 22, 1971. After suffering his third heart attack at the LBJ Ranch, Johnson died on January 22, 1973. His body lay in state in the LBJ Library initially and then in the Capitol Rotunda. Funeral services were held in the National City Christian Church in Washington, D.C. The president was buried in the Johnson family plot near Johnson City, Texas. Lady Bird Johnson resided at the LBJ Ranch until her death on July 11, 2007.

..................................................................................

## Lyndon B. Johnson National Historical Park
## Johnson City, Texas

ADDRESS: P.O. Box 329, Johnson City, TX 78636
TELEPHONE: 830-868-7128
WEB SITE: www.nps.gov/lyjo
LOCATION: In south central Texas Hill Country; the park has two visitor areas separated by about fourteen miles
OPEN: Daily, 9:00 A.M. to 5:00 P.M.; closed Thanksgiving, Christmas, and New Year's Day; visitor center, 8:45 A.M. to 5:00 P.M.
ADMISSION: Adults, $1.00; to visit the Texas White House, it is necessary to obtain a free driving pass to the LBJ Ranch at the LBJ State Park and Historic Site visitor center
FACILITIES: The Johnson settlement / visitor center / boyhood home / park

Lyndon Johnson
Boyhood Home, Lyn-
don Baines Johnson
National Historical
Park, Johnson City,
Texas

293

headquarters in Johnson City and the LBJ Ranch near Stonewall; Texas
White House; reconstructed birthplace; presidential burial site

*Commemorating the Texas origins* of President Lyndon B. Johnson, the Lyndon B. Johnson National Historical Park consists of two units: one in Johnson
City and the other fifteen miles away at the LBJ Ranch. The National Historical Park cooperates with the Lyndon B. Johnson State Park, which has a visitor center where driving passes for the LBJ Ranch can be obtained.

Located in the Hill Country, a region in south central Texas with low, rolling
hills, extensive sites tell the story of Johnson's heritage, childhood, youth, and
retirement years. In the 1860s Samuel Ealy Johnson, Lyndon's grandfather, and
Sam's brother, Jesse Thomas Johnson, settled in Blanco County, where they
raised cattle for the eastern market. The cattle business was enormously profitable, and the Johnson brothers bought thousands of acres of ranch land in
Blanco, Hays, and Gillespie counties. When an overabundance of cattle hit the
market in 1871, prices dropped precipitously, and the Johnson brothers were
forced to sell land to pay their debts.

Sam Ealy Johnson Jr., the father of the president, was born on October 11,
1877. In 1889 the Johnson family moved to a 950-acre ranch in the Hill Country, where they were subsistence farmers.

Sam Johnson Jr. married Rebekah Baines on August 20, 1907. Their oldest
child, Lyndon Baines, was born in a dog-trot cabin on the Pedernales River
near Stonewall in Gillespie County on August 27, 1908. In 1964, at the direction
of President Johnson, his birthplace was reconstructed and opened for tours.

The Johnson family moved to Johnson City, named for James Polk Johnson, a nephew of Lyndon's grandfather, in 1913 when Lyndon was five years old.
In 1969 the Johnson family donated the boyhood home in Johnson City and
the reconstructed birthplace to the National Park Service.

When he was a teenager, Lyndon spent summers working on his aunt's cattle ranch. In 1951 Lyndon Johnson's aunt Frank Martin sold him her 250-acre ranch. After purchasing adjoining acreage, Lyndon's LBJ Ranch grew to 2,700 acres. The ranch house had been built in 1894, and in 1909, when Frank and Clarence Martin bought the property, they enlarged the house. When Lyndon Johnson acquired the house, he added the master bedrooms and an office wing. While he was president, the ranch house served as the Texas White House. In 1972 the Johnsons donated more than 200 acres of the LBJ Ranch, including the Texas White House and adjacent buildings, to the National Park Service. Junction School, attended by Lyndon Johnson, was acquired in 1972.

Lady Bird Johnson, the president's widow, resided at the LBJ Ranch until her death on July 11, 2007. During her life the Texas White House was closed to tourists, but it is now undergoing restoration. As of President Johnson's one hundredth birthday, August 27, 2008, the Texas White House may be visited on a guided tour. The president's office, the living room, and the dining room have been restored to their appearance in the 1963–68 period. As other rooms are completed, they will be added to the house tour.

In 1972 the Johnsons funded the purchase of the Johnson Settlement, a thirty-five-acre site in Johnson City originally settled by Johnson's grandfather and his brother in the 1860s. The Johnson family has since donated additional acreage.

Visitors start at the LBJ National Historical Park visitor center in Johnson City, where videos on the life of Lyndon Johnson are shown. The boyhood home of President Johnson, in Johnson City, has been restored to its appearance in the mid-1920s. Johnson lived in the house from the age of five until he was twenty-two years old, 1913–30. The folk Victorian house was built in 1901 by W. C. Russell, and it and a 1.75-acre lot were purchased by Sam Ealy Johnson Jr. in 1913. The house was donated to the National Park Service by the Johnson family in 1969, restored, and opened to the public in 1973.

The modest white frame one-story house with green trim and shutters has three bedrooms, a kitchen, a dining room, a parlor, a tub room, two front porches, a sleeping porch, and a back porch. In the hallway, used as an office by Sam Johnson Jr., are his rolltop desk, swivel chair, and bookcases.

The girls' bedroom was shared by Lyndon's sisters, Rebekah, Josefa, and Lucia Johnson. It was decorated with two double beds, wooden dressers, and a sewing machine. The dining room was the scene of family gatherings. Meals were eaten at the table, and the Johnson children studied, played games, and listened to the radio there. The parlor, a room reserved for formal occasions, contains period furniture.

The two youngest Johnson children were born in the master bedroom. Sam and his friends also met here for political discussions. The future president and his younger brother, Sam Houston, slept in the simply furnished boys' bedroom. The tub room was added in 1922 and had a bathtub and cold running water. The kitchen had a wood-burning stove and an oil range, a sink, and running water. There was an icebox on the sleeping porch.

The Johnson Settlement, located at the edge of Johnson City, includes the original log house, stone barns, and other outbuildings. Visitors start their tour at the Exhibit Center, which tells the story of the Johnson brothers as mid- to late-nineteenth-century cattle ranchers through photographs and artifacts.

Among the structures in the Johnson Settlement is the Johnson Headquarters, a log cabin that served as the headquarters of Tom and Sam Johnson's cattle-driving operations. Between 1867 and 1872 the cabin was a rendezvous point for ranch owners who would bring their cattle to the Johnson brothers for the long drive to the Kansas railroads.

The James Polk Johnson barn was purchased by James Polk Johnson, Sam Johnson's nephew, in 1872 as he made the transition from cattle drover to rancher. The James Polk Johnson house, a two-story frame home and smokehouse, was built in 1882. The large stone Bruckner barn was built in 1882 on land that was sold by James Polk Johnson to John Bruckner, a German immigrant.

At the LBJ Ranch visitors can feel the presence of the larger-than-life president from Texas. It is an operating ranch with wide open fields, pastures, a show barn, and cattle pens in addition to Junction School, the birthplace, the Johnson family cemetery, Sam Ealy Johnson's farmhouse, the Texas White House, the airplane hangar, ranch lands, and the Pedernales River. The small hangar was used for press conferences, parties, and as a movie theater. Johnson's Lincoln Continental and an amphibious car are exhibited, as are donkey carts and wagons.

Lyndon Johnson's birthplace, about a mile from the LBJ Ranch, was torn down in 1935 and was rebuilt in 1964 on the same site. It is a dog-trot-style cabin with a living room, a bedroom, and a kitchen. Sam Ealy Johnson's original farmhouse has been restored. Lyndon was a frequent visitor at his grandparents' house and loved to hear his grandfather's stories of his cowboy days.

Lyndon Baines Johnson died of a heart attack on January 22, 1973. Lady Bird Johnson, the president's widow, resided at the LBJ Ranch until her death on July 11, 2007. They are buried in the Johnson family cemetery at the LBJ Ranch.

..........................................................................................

**Lyndon Baines Johnson Presidential Library and Museum**
**Austin, Texas**

ADDRESS: 2313 Red River Street, Austin, TX 78705
TELEPHONE: 512-721-0200
WEB SITE: www.lbjlib.utexas.edu
ADMISSION: Free

LOCATION: In east central Texas, eighty-two miles north of San Antonio, on
the campus of the University of Texas at Austin, one block west of I-35,
between Martin Luther King Jr. Boulevard and Twenty-sixth Street
OPEN: Daily, 9:00 A.M. to 5:00 P.M.; closed Christmas
FACILITIES: Presidential library of Lyndon Johnson; museum; gift shop;
handicapped accessible

*The Lyndon Baines Johnson Presidential Library and Museum* is located on the
campus of the University of Texas at Austin. President Johnson oversaw the
construction of the library and museum. Housed in a ten-story building on a
thirty-acre site, the Johnson presidential library was dedicated in May 1971 and
is administered by the National Archives and Records Administration.

In the Lyndon Baines Johnson Library and Museum, an introductory film
on Johnson's life, using photographs and motion pictures, is narrated by a
variety of voices, including that of LBJ. The exhibit "A Walk through History"
places the life of President Lyndon Johnson in the context of the major periods
of American history through which he and his wife, Lady Bird, lived. "America, from 1908 to 1919" documents the year of Johnson's birth to World War I
and features family photographs.

"America from 1920–1929" features Johnson's biography through the post–
World War I period when Johnson was a student at Johnson City High School.
The Great Depression of the 1930s is the background for "America from 1929
to 1940," which covers the period when Lyndon was a student at Southwest
Texas State Teachers' College and then served as a principal and teacher at
Cotulla in south Texas. Johnson's public career began with his appointment as
Texas state director of the National Youth Administration and continued with
his campaigns for the U.S. House of Representatives and the U.S. Senate. When

World War II began, Johnson entered the U.S. Navy; he was the first member of Congress to go into the armed services.

From 1946 to 1953 Johnson was a U.S. senator. From 1954 to 1961, the Eisenhower years, Johnson was Senate majority leader. In the library/museum there is video and photograph coverage of the Kennedy-Johnson campaign in 1960. The exhibit "The Day the Nation Will Not Forget," referring to November 22, 1963, the day of President Kennedy's assassination in Dallas, Texas, begins with Mrs. Johnson using a tape recorder to record an entry in her diary. A photo depicts Johnson taking the oath of office as president on board Air Force One.

Campaign buttons, posters, and other memorabilia from the 1960s illustrate President Johnson's campaign against Barry Goldwater, the Republican nominee. During this period the Vietnam War escalated with the Gulf of Tonkin Resolution and the entry of more American troops in Operation Rolling Thunder.

Johnson wanted to be known as the "Education President," and exhibits highlight the Great Society and the War on Poverty. Among Johnson's achievements were the Civil Rights Act, the Elementary and Secondary Education Act, Medicare, the Job Corps, and Head Start. There are facsimiles from the first pages of the Great Society acts.

In "The Nightmare Year," 1968 is illustrated with newspaper headlines and photographs of Vietnam protests and urban disorders. On display are busts and photographs of Martin Luther King Jr. and Robert Kennedy, who were both assassinated in 1968.

In the Johnson library and museum there is a replica of the White House Oval Office as it was decorated during the Johnson administration. The East Room of the White House has also been re-created. Two automobiles on display are the Model T Ford that was a gift of Henry Ford II to Johnson and the 1968 stretch Lincoln that was the presidential limousine. "The Gifts of State" exhibit presents objects given by the leaders of ninety-four countries to Johnson during his presidency.

The First Lady's Gallery narrates Lady Bird Johnson's life, her role as the nation's First Lady, and her humanitarian and environmental interests. There are recorded excerpts from Mrs. Johnson's book *A White House Diary* and photographs of Mrs. Johnson's promotion of the use of wildflowers. Lady Bird Plaza is planted with vegetation typical of the Texas Hill Country.

# Richard Milhous Nixon

.........................................................................

Because of their deaths while in office, eight U.S. presidents did not complete their terms. Richard Nixon was the only president who did not complete his term because of resignation.

Richard Milhous Nixon, born on January 9, 1913, in Yorba Linda, California, was the second of the five sons of Francis (Frank) Anthony Nixon and Hannah Milhous Nixon. The Milhous family was Quaker.

Hannah Milhous and Frank Nixon met in East Whittier, California, and were married in 1908. In 1912 Frank bought a lemon ranch at Yorba Linda, ten miles from Whittier. He built a two-story frame house from a kit, and that is the house in which Richard Nixon was born. In 1922 the family moved to Whittier, where Frank Nixon operated a successful general store.

Richard Nixon entered Fullerton High School in 1926 and transferred to Whittier High School in 1928. He received the Harvard Club award as best all-around student and a scholarship to Harvard. He declined the scholarship because his father could not afford the living expenses at Harvard. Instead, Richard attended Whittier College.

At Whittier College, Richard Nixon won a scholarship to Duke University Law School. He entered Duke University in North Carolina in September 1934. After he passed the California Bar exam, Richard joined the firm of Bewley and Wingert, becoming a partner in 1939.

Nixon joined a local theater group, where he met his future wife, Pat Ryan, a teacher at Whittier High School. Pat Ryan was born on March 16, 1912, in Ely, Nevada, a mining town. Named Thelma Catherine, the baby girl was called "Pat" because she was born the day before St. Patrick's Day. When Pat was eighteen years old, she changed her name from Thelma to Patricia. Pat attended the University of Southern California, from which she graduated cum laude in 1937.

Richard and Pat married in a Quaker ceremony on June 21, 1940. On February 21, 1946, Patricia Nixon, called Tricia, was born. Julie Nixon was born on July 5, 1948.

In 1941 Nixon became an assistant attorney in the Rationing Coordination Section of the Office of Price Administration in Washington, D.C. As a birthright Quaker, Richard could have had conscientious-objector status with the draft board, but he enlisted in the navy. Nixon was ordered to the South Pacific

Combat Air Transport Command on the island of New Caledonia in the South Pacific and then transferred to Bougainville in the Solomon Islands.

In January 1946 Nixon successfully ran for California's twelfth congressional seat in the U.S. House of Representatives on the Republican ticket. During his decades-long political career, Nixon served from 1947 to 1950 in the U.S. House of Representatives, from 1951 to 1953 in the U.S. Senate, from 1953 to 1961 as vice president of the United States, and from 1969 to 1974 as president of the United States. In 1960 he was the Republican candidate for president but was defeated by John F. Kennedy. In 1962 he ran for governor of California and lost to Edmund G. Brown.

In 1948 the United States and the Soviet Union were locked in the cold war. The House Un-American Activities Committee (HUAC) launched an investigation of subversive activities among federal employees. Nixon's role in the HUAC investigation of Alger Hiss made him a nationally known figure. This was a complex case, and there still is no single factual account but rather many versions of the same story. Whittaker Chambers, senior editor of *Time* magazine, appearing before the HUAC committee, admitted to being a former member of the Communist Party and named others in his cell, including Alger Hiss, president of the Carnegie Endowment for International Peace and a former State Department aide at the Yalta Conference. Hiss denied the charges, including being acquainted with Chambers. Nixon arranged a face-to-face confrontation between Hiss and Chambers on August 17, during which Hiss admitted, based on overwhelming evidence, that he knew Chambers.

Because Chambers referred to Hiss as a communist on a "Meet the Press" show on August 27, 1948, Hiss filed a fifty-thousand-dollar libel suit against Chambers.[1] Under subpoena, Chambers turned over film taken of State Department documents. The film frames, which Chambers had sequestered in a pumpkin patch on his farm, indicated that Chambers and Hiss had engaged in espionage. Hiss was eventually convicted of two counts of perjury and sentenced to five years in prison.

On November 3, 1949, Nixon was a successful Republican candidate for the Senate. In 1952 he was the vice-presidential candidate on Dwight D. Eisenhower's successful ticket. At the Republican National Convention in July 1960, Richard Nixon was nominated for president on the first ballot with Henry Cabot Lodge as his vice-presidential running mate. John F. Kennedy was the choice of the Democratic Party, with Lyndon Johnson as the vice-presidential candidate.

The Nixon versus Kennedy campaign featured the first televised debates between presidential candidates. At the first debate on September 26, 1960, Nixon appeared weak, pale, and off his stride as a debater. Kennedy, in contrast, appeared well prepared and confident. Kennedy's victory was narrow in the popular vote with a margin of less than half a percentage point. Kennedy won 34,227,000 popular and 303 electoral votes to Nixon's 34,108,000 popular and 219 electoral votes.

At the Republican Convention held in August 1968, Richard Nixon was nominated for president, and he chose Gov. Spiro Agnew of Maryland as his vice-presidential running mate. The Democratic Convention, held in Chicago at the end of August, nominated Vice President Hubert Humphrey. Antiwar protestors and the Chicago police clashed violently outside the convention site. The scene was televised, and Americans were appalled. Nixon was the unintended beneficiary of the debacle. He won 31,770,000 popular and 301 electoral votes to Humphrey's 31,270,000 popular and 191 electoral votes.

Determined to end the Vietnam War, President Nixon and President Nguyen Van Thieu of South Vietnam met on June 8, 1969, and announced the immediate withdrawal of 25,000 American troops. By December 1969 the number of American troops in Vietnam had been reduced by 115,000.

President Nixon authorized an invasion of Cambodia in late April 1970 to destroy stockpiles of supplies. College students began marching, picketing, and striking in protest. At a demonstration at Kent State University in Ohio on May 2, a Reserve Officers' Training Corps building was burned. Gov. James Rhodes declared martial law and dispatched National Guard units. On May 4 the National Guard opened fire on a group of protestors, killing four students and wounding eleven. Protests erupted at eleven hundred campuses. A week later over four hundred colleges and universities had closed.

Nixon's Vietnamization policy reduced U.S. involvement while expanding the fighting into Cambodia and Laos. To protest the invasions into Cambodian and Laos, Vietnam Veterans Against the War, led by John Kerry, a future senator from Massachusetts and Democratic presidential candidate, camped on the Washington, D.C., mall in April 1971. Hundreds of thousands of protestors marched throughout the country. American combat troops withdrew from Vietnam in August 1972, and a peace agreement was signed in Paris in January 1973.

A groundbreaking meeting between President Nixon and Chairman Mao Tse-tung and Premier Chou En-Lai of the People's Republic of China took place in February 1972. The two countries agreed to broaden scientific, cultural, and trade contacts. The United States and the Soviet Union signed a Chemical Weapons Treaty in 1971, and in May 1972 Nixon and Soviet leader Leonid Brezhnev signed the Strategic Arms Limitation Talks, known as SALT.

Although he removed President Johnson's recording systems when he became president, Nixon had recording devices installed in the Oval Office, the cabinet room, his private office in the Executive Office Building, the Lincoln sitting room, and the Aspen Lodge at Camp David. He had taps placed on three of his phones.

On June 15, 1971, the *New York Times* began publication of a classified study, commissioned by Secretary of Defense Robert McNamara in June 1967, of the presidential role in the Vietnam War. Daniel Ellsberg, one of its authors, leaked a copy of the report, dubbed the Pentagon Papers, to the *New York Times*. A U.S. district judge enjoined the newspaper to stop publishing the Pentagon Papers. In *New York Times v. U.S.* the Supreme Court ruled six to three in favor of the newspaper. A unit called the "plumbers" (with the task of plugging media leaks from administration officials and others to the media), under the direction of Bud Krogh, broke into the office of Daniel Ellsberg's psychiatrist, Dr. Lewis Fielding, on September 3, 1971.

A team from Nixon's election committee bugged the offices of the Democratic National Committee in the Watergate office complex on May 28, 1972. On June 17 there was a second incursion into the DNC's office to replace a malfunctioning bug. A building guard called the police, who arrested James McCord, Frank Sturgis, Virgilio Gonzalez, Eugenio Martinez, and Bernard Barker. E. Howard Hunt and G. Gordon Liddy, who were monitoring the operation from the Watergate Hotel across the street, fled and inadvertently left an address book with Hunt's name and White House telephone numbers as well as thirty-two consecutively numbered one-hundred-dollar bills, which were discovered by the police. Recording devices in the president's office eventually revealed his knowledge of and participation in the cover-up of the burglary scheme.

On August 22 the Republican National Convention renominated Nixon. George McGovern, senator from South Dakota, became the presidential nominee of the Democratic Party. On November 7, 1972, President Nixon was reelected with 46,740,000 popular and 520 electoral votes. McGovern took 28,900,000 popular and 17 electoral votes.

On September 15 a federal grand jury indicted McCord, Gonzalez, Hunt, Liddy, Barker, Felipe De Diego, and Martinez for wiretapping and stealing documents. Bob Woodward and Carl Bernstein, *Washington Post* reporters, wrote a front-page story about Donald Segretti and his team of fifty people whose assignment was to disrupt the campaigns of Democratic presidential candidates. In February the Senate formed a committee to investigate presidential campaign activities.

E. Howard Hunt's wife Dorothy distributed more than two hundred thousand dollars of presidential campaign funds to Howard Hunt and the other burglars. On January 16, 1973, four of the Watergate burglars pleaded guilty to charges of second-degree burglary and wiretapping. On January 30 Liddy and McCord were found guilty. Judge John Sirica issued forty-year sentences for Frank Sturgis, Virgilio Gonzalez, Eugenio Martinez, and Bernard Barker, from six to twenty years for Liddy, and thirty-five years for Hunt. James McCord admitted that perjury had occurred in the trial and that the break-in was not a CIA operation.

On March 21 seventy-five thousand dollars in cash, taken from a White House safe and authorized by the president, was paid to Hunt, who was threatening to expose presidential aide John Ehrlichman's involvement. On April 30, 1973, President Nixon announced the resignations of his aides Ehrlichman and Bob Haldeman and that of Attorney General Richard Kleindienst as well as the firing of White House counsel John Dean. On May 10 John Mitchell, former attorney general under President Nixon, and Maurice Stans, President Nixon's finance committee chairman, were indicted

The Watergate Committee hearings, held from May until early August, were televised. A Democrat, Archibald Cox, served as the Watergate special prosecutor. When the Watergate Committee subpoenaed the tapes from the White House recording system, Nixon, claiming executive privilege, supplied edited transcripts. The Supreme Court ruled that the president had to release the tapes.

Vice President Agnew resigned on October 10, 1973, due to charges stemming from his days as governor of Maryland. On October 22 the House Democratic leadership ordered the Judiciary Committee to begin considering impeachment charges against the president. House minority leader Gerald Ford was sworn in as vice president on December 6.

On March 1, 1974, the former presidential aides John Mitchell, Bob Haldeman, John Ehrlichman, Charles Colson, Robert Mardian, Kenneth Parkinson, and Gordon Strachan were indicted in the Watergate cover-up conspiracy. Secretly the president had been named an unindicted coconspirator. The Judiciary Committee voted to submit articles of impeachment to the House of Representatives charging Nixon with obstruction of justice, abuse of power, and failure to comply with congressional subpoenas. Tapes confirming that the president was aware of the crimes and tried to hinder the investigations were delivered to Judge John Sirica on August 2.

Richard Nixon resigned as president on August 9, 1974, and Vice President Gerald Ford was inaugurated the same day. On September 8, 1974, President Ford granted a full and absolute pardon to Richard Nixon for all federal offenses he committed.

Patricia Nixon died on June 22, 1993, at the age of eighty-one, and Richard Nixon, eighty-one, died on April 22, 1994. They are buried on the grounds of the Richard Nixon library and birthplace in Yorba Linda, California.

. . . . . . . . . . . . . . . . . . . . . . . . . . . . . . . . . . . . . . . . . . . . . . . . . . . . . . . . . . . . . . . . . . . . . . . . . . . .

### Richard M. Nixon Presidential Library and Museum
### Yorba Linda, California

ADDRESS: 18001 Yorba Linda Boulevard, Yorba Linda, CA 92886-3949
TELEPHONE: 714-983-9120
WEB SITE: www.nixonlibrary.gov
LOCATION: In southern California, thirty miles south of Los Angeles
OPEN: Monday–Saturday, 10:00 A.M. to 5:00 P.M.; Sunday, 11:00 A.M. to 5:00
    P.M.; closed Thanksgiving, Christmas, and New Year's Day

ADMISSION: Adults 12–61, $9.95; seniors and military, $6.95; students, $5.95; children 7–11, $3.75

FACILITIES: Restored birthplace; presidential museum, library, and archives; burial sites of Patricia and Richard Nixon

*The Richard M. Nixon Presidential Library and Museum* is located on a nine-acre site in Yorba Linda, California, with a museum, library, archives, restored 1912 birthplace of Richard Nixon, gardens and the burial sites of Patricia and Richard Nixon. More than eight acres of museum property were owned by Francis Nixon, the president's father, from 1912 to 1922. The Richard Nixon Library & Birthplace, a privately supported, nonprofit institution under the direction of the Richard Nixon Library & Birthplace Foundation, opened on July 19, 1990. In January 2004 the U.S. Congress passed legislation to establish a federally operated Nixon Presidential Library in Yorba Linda, California, under the auspices of the National Archives and Records Administration system. Transfer of the Nixon Library to the NARA system occurred on July 11, 2007. An addition to the library was completed in spring 2010 to accommodate the Nixon materials that have since been moved from Maryland. In addition museum exhibits, which were designed without any input from the National Archives system, are being redesigned over time.

In 1974, after Nixon's resignation, Congress enacted the Presidential Recordings and Materials Preservation Act, which authorized the seizure of Nixon's presidential materials. To prevent Nixon from destroying these materials, they were transferred to the National Archives in College Park, Maryland. The Nixon Presidential Materials Project was under the jurisdiction of the National Archives and Records Administration.

President Nixon protested the seizure of the presidential materials, which he believed belonged to him. In 1978 Congress passed a law making the records of future presidents, beginning with Ronald Reagan, public property, but Nixon's

case predated that law. President Ford also objected to the government seizure of Nixon's presidential papers and wanted them moved to the Nixon Library archives, as did Julie Nixon Eisenhower and Tricia Nixon Cox, Nixon's daughters. Nixon pursued litigation over custody of and compensation for his presidential materials until his death in 1994, and his estate continued the fight, winning an $18 million settlement in 2000.

After the settlement, negotiations between the Nixon Library and the National Archives and Records Administration resulted in a 2004 agreement to move the Nixon Presidential Materials to the Yorba Linda Library, which is the twelfth and newest member of the NARA Presidential Library System. The Yorba Linda facility has been enlarged to accommodate this massive amount of data.

The 1990 opening of the privately funded Richard Nixon Library & Birthplace was attended by Presidents Nixon, Bush, Reagan, and Ford and their wives. Its archives housed Nixon's private pre-presidential papers from 1913 to 1968, his post-presidential papers from 1974 to 1994, and Pat Nixon's papers.

Visitors begin their tour of the museum with a film about Nixon's life and career. In the museum's main gallery is a re-creation of the Lincoln Sitting Room from the White House private quarters. There is also a re-creation of the study used by Nixon in his post-presidential New Jersey home.

Opened in 2004, the forty-seven-thousand-square-foot Katherine B. Loker Center, a $13.4 million expansion that has nearly doubled the size of the building, has a full-size replica of the White House East Room and gallery space for traveling museum exhibitions. The gallery "Richard Nixon and the History of America in Space" focuses on the space program and its inception under Eisenhower when Nixon was vice president.

Nixon's legacy is overshadowed by the Watergate scandal. The president was instrumental in the design of the Watergate exhibit when the library was privately owned. Presented from a pro-Nixon perspective, it portrayed the animosity that existed between the president and a Democratic Congress. The federal acquisition of the library means that the Watergate exhibit will be redone from an objective historical perspective. The older exhibit has been digitally photographed and will be shown on a screen in the revamped Watergate exhibit so that visitors can access Nixon's version of events.

The small house on the library grounds is the birthplace of Richard Nixon, who was born on January 9, 1913. Richard's father, Frank, constructed the family home from a kit in 1912, the year he bought a lemon ranch at Yorba Linda. The restored two-story frame house is on its original site, and many of the furnishings are original. An audio tour is narrated by Richard Nixon. In his parents' bedroom on the first floor of the house is the bed where Richard Nixon was born. The living room has a brick fireplace built by Frank Nixon and the piano on which Richard took piano lessons. Richard and his three brothers slept in a small bedroom on the second floor.

Patricia and Richard Nixon are buried on the library grounds in an English garden setting. Richard Nixon, eighty-one, died on April 22, 1994, in New York City. Nixon's funeral service, conducted by Billy Graham, was held on April 27 at the library and was attended by Presidents Ford, Carter, Bush, Reagan, and Clinton and their wives. Patricia Ryan Nixon died on June 22, 1993, at age eighty-one.

# Gerald Rudolph Ford Jr.

THIRTY-EIGHTH PRESIDENT OF THE UNITED STATES
*August 9, 1974–January 20, 1977*

Gerald Ford is the only vice president who became president because of the resignation of his predecessor, and he is the only person to become president without having been elected to national executive office. In addition he is the longest-lived U.S. president, having died at the age of ninety-three on December 26, 2006.

Gerald Rudolph Ford, who was born on July 14, 1913, in Omaha, Nebraska, was named Leslie Lynch King Jr. at birth. His parents were Leslie Lynch King, a wool trader, and Dorothy Ayer Gardner King of Harvard, Illinois.

Charles Henry King, the president's grandfather, was a multimillionaire who owned general stores, lumberyards, banks, wool-trading companies, a freight-hauling business, and real estate in Nebraska and Wyoming and was involved in the western expansion of the Burlington Railroad line. His son, Leslie, was manager of the family's Omaha Wool and Storage Company.

Leslie King began physically abusing his wife on their honeymoon. Dorothy gave birth to the future president in her in-laws' Omaha home on July 14, 1913. After the birth King threatened to shoot her and their son. Dorothy sent a telegram to her father, who rushed to Omaha, but Leslie King obtained a court order to bar the Gardners from visiting their daughter. When the future president was sixteen days old, Dorothy Gardner King escaped with him across the Missouri River to Council Bluffs, Iowa, where her parents were waiting.

A divorce was granted to the Kings on December 19, 1913, and Dorothy was awarded sole custody of their son. Because King was ordered to pay alimony and child support, he moved to Wyoming, where the Nebraska court had no jurisdiction. Charles King, the baby's grandfather, made the monthly payments during his lifetime.

Embarrassed by the scandalous divorce, Dorothy and her parents moved from Illinois to Grand Rapids, Michigan. When Junie, a derivative of Junior, was two years old, Dorothy married Gerald Rudolph Ford, a paint salesman for the Grand Rapids Wood Finishing Company. The child became known as Junie Ford and eventually as Gerald "Jerry" Ford Junior. Three other sons were born to Dorothy and Gerald Ford.

Young Jerry Ford did not learn that Gerald Ford was not his biological father until about age thirteen. During high school Jerry worked at Bill Skougis's restaurant. One day in 1930 Leslie King came into the restaurant and told Jerry that he was his father. King, who had not contacted his son before, asked Jerry if he would like to live with him in Wyoming. Ford replied that he liked where he was.

Ford was captain of the football team his senior year when South High School won the state championship. He was in the National Honor Society. When he was a senior, Ford won a trip to Washington, D.C. Impressed by his visit to Congress, Ford decided to become a lawyer.

When Ford graduated from South High School in 1931, his family was financially unable to send him to college. Dorothy Ford won a judgment against her former husband to pay one hundred dollars a month for their son's education, but the Nebraska judgment could not be enforced in Wyoming. The principal of South High School arranged for Ford to get a part-time job at the University of Michigan at Ann Arbor, and the high school bookstore sponsored a one-hundred-dollar scholarship for him.

Although in his senior year the Michigan football team did poorly, Ford played every game and was named to the All Big Ten. He was recruited to play professional football by the Green Bay Packers and the Detroit Lions, but he declined because he wanted to attend law school. He graduated with a bachelor of arts in economics.

To earn money for law school, he accepted a coaching job at Yale University. At this time he decided to change his name legally, and on December 3, 1935, he became Gerald Rudolph Ford Jr. Although many accounts of Ford's life indicate that he was adopted by his stepfather either shortly after Ford married his mother or in 1935, Ford was never adopted.

After a year coaching football, Jerry worked in Yellowstone National Park for the summer. On his way there he visited his father and his family in Wyoming. That fall his mother hired a lawyer to recover the money owed by Leslie King and was awarded over six thousand dollars. When King didn't comply with the court order, he was arrested. Eventually, Dorothy Ford received two thousand dollars, which she sent to Jerry. He returned it to her, saying that he had paid off his college debt and saved money for law school.

In 1937 Jerry Ford was admitted to Yale Law School, and he graduated in the top third of his class of 1941. After passing the Michigan Bar exam, Ford practiced law in Grand Rapids. Pearl Harbor was bombed on December 7, 1941, and the following April, Ford joined the navy. He was assigned to the USS *Monterey*, which joined Adm. William Halsey's Third Fleet in the Western Pacific. Ford was discharged in January 1946 after serving nearly four years and being awarded ten battle stars. In 1948 Ford successfully ran for the U.S. House of Representatives in the Republican primary against the incumbent, Bartel J. Jonkman, from the Fifth District of Michigan.

In Grand Rapids, Ford met Betty Bloomer Warren. She was born in Chicago on April 8, 1918, and had lived in Grand Rapids since she was two. She studied dancing at the Martha Graham Studio in New York City and modeled for the Powers modeling agency. She married William Warren in 1942 and was in the process of divorcing him when she and Ford met.

Gerald Ford and Betty Warren were married on October 15, 1948, in East Grand Rapids, Michigan. They had four children. Michael Gerald was born on March 14, 1950; John Gardner, called Jack, was born on March 16, 1952; Steven Meigs was born on May 19, 1956; and Susan was born on July 6, 1957.

Winning his congressional election every two years, Ford grew to be a senior and powerful member of the House during the administrations of Presidents Truman, Eisenhower, Kennedy, Johnson, and Nixon. After President Kennedy's assassination, President Johnson appointed Ford, well-known for his integrity, as the only Republican on the Warren Commission investigating Kennedy's death. In 1964 Ford became the House minority leader. He was elected minority leader five times.

In 1973 Vice President Spiro T. Agnew was investigated by federal prosecutors for taking bribes from contractors on public works projects while he was a Baltimore County executive, governor, and vice president. Agnew resigned on October 10, 1973. President Nixon offered the vice presidency to Ford. Confirmed by the Senate Committee on Rules and Administration and the House of Representatives, Ford was sworn in as vice president on December 6, 1973.

During this period President Nixon was embroiled in the Watergate scandal and his potential impeachment. On October 20, 1973, the White House announced that Special Prosecutor Archibald Cox had been fired, and the Office of the Special Prosecutor, which had been conducting the Watergate investigation, was abolished. The "Saturday Night Massacre," as the actions were dubbed, stunned the country, including Jerry Ford, who had believed Nixon's protestations of innocence. On October 23 Speaker of the House Carl Albert ordered the House Judiciary Committee to begin a formal inquiry into grounds for the impeachment of President Nixon.

On July 27, 1974, the House Judiciary Committee voted 27–11 for Article I of the Articles of Impeachment, charging Nixon with obstruction of justice. Several days later they voted for Article II, charging him with abusing presidential power. Alexander Haig informed Ford of the president's possible resignation and handed Ford documents written by Nixon's lawyer Joseph F. Buzhardt, including a ''half-page summary of the President's power to pardon a person before indictment or trial. The second, also in Buzhardt's handwriting, was the draft of a Ford pardon for Nixon."[1] Ford told Haig that he refused to be a party to a deal in which the president resigned only if Ford would pardon him. Nixon informed Ford on Thursday, August 8, around noon that he was going to resign, which he did that evening on national television.

On August 9, 1974, at 12:03 P.M., Gerald R. Ford Jr. was sworn in as the thirty-eighth president of the United States by Chief Justice Warren Burger in the East Room of the White House. Ford chose Nelson Rockefeller as his vice president.

Ford agonized about pardoning Nixon but determined that it was in the national interest. On September 8, 1974, President Ford publicly announced his decision to pardon President Nixon. The country reacted with horrified shock and anger, and Ford never overcame the distrust generated by his decision.

Ford ran for the presidency in 1976, and so did Ronald Reagan. Ford won the hotly contested nomination at the Republican National Convention and selected Sen. Robert Dole as his running mate. The Democratic candidate was Jimmy Carter, a Georgia governor. Ford lost to Carter, who received 49.9 percent of the votes to Ford's 47.9 percent. Carter won 40,830,763 popular and 297 electoral votes to Ford's 39,147,793 popular and 240 electoral votes. Eugene McCarthy, running as an Independent, took 756,000 popular votes.

The Fords moved to Rancho Mirage, California. Ford helped establish the Gerald R. Ford Library in Ann Arbor, Michigan, and the Gerald R. Ford Museum in Grand Rapids, both of which were dedicated in 1981.

Gerald Ford died at his California home on December 26, 2006, at the age of ninety-three. The longest-living U.S. president, he outlived the previous record holder, Ronald Reagan, by one month. After a funeral in California, Ford's casket lay in state in the Capitol. Funeral services, held at Washington National Cathedral on January 2, 2007, were attended by President George W. Bush and former presidents George H. W. Bush, Bill Clinton, and Jimmy Carter. On January 3 President Ford was interred on a hillside north of the Gerald R. Ford Museum in Grand Rapids, Michigan.

. . . . . . . . . . . . . . . . . . . . . . . . . . . . . . . . . . . . . . . . . . . . . . . . . . . . . . . . . . . . . . . . . . .

## Gerald R. Ford Presidential Library and Museum
### Ann Arbor, Michigan, and Grand Rapids, Michigan

ADDRESS: Library: 1000 Beal Avenue, Ann Arbor, MI 48109; museum: 303 Pearl Street NW, Grand Rapids, MI 49504-5353

TELEPHONE: Library: 734-205-0555; museum: 616-254-0400

WEB SITE: www.fordlibrarymuseum.gov

LOCATION: The Gerald R. Ford Library is on the campus of the University of Michigan in Ann Arbor, 130 miles east of Grand Rapids; the Gerald R. Ford Museum is in downtown Grand Rapids, in west central Michigan, about 25 miles east of Lake Michigan and 77 miles north of the Michigan-Indiana border

OPEN: Library: Monday–Friday, 8:45 A.M. to 4:45 P.M., closed federal holidays;

Gerald R. Ford Museum, Grand Rapids, Michigan. Photograph courtesy of Gerald R. Ford Presidential Library and Museum, Grand Rapids, Michigan

museum: daily, 9:00 A.M. to 5:00 P.M., closed Thanksgiving, Christmas, and New Year's Day

ADMISSION: Museum—Adults, $7.00; seniors and military, $6.00; college students, $5.00; children 6–18, $3.00

FACILITIES: Museum with audiovisual presentation, accessible to handicapped; gift and book shop; burial site of President Ford. The library contains archives that are open to researchers.

*The Gerald R. Ford Presidential Library and Museum* is under the auspices of the Presidential Libraries System of the National Archives and Records Administration. However, the library and the museum are in separate Michigan locations: the Ford Library is in Ann Arbor; while the Ford Museum is in Grand Rapids.

The Ford Library and Archives is on the campus of the University of Michigan, Ford's alma mater, in Ann Arbor, Michigan, 130 miles east of Grand Rapids. Geared primarily to scholars and researchers, it contains Ford's presidential papers along with many other documents and audiovisual materials related to the Ford era.

The museum in Grand Rapids originated with local people, the Gerald R. Ford Commemorative Committee, who did the planning and raised funds. They wanted the museum to be a testament to the esteem the people of Grand Rapids felt for Ford. The museum opened in 1981, and ownership of the museum was transferred to the National Archives and Records Administration.

President Gerald R. Ford, the thirty-eighth president of the United States, was appointed as vice president on December 6, 1973. The successful candidates in the presidential election of 1972 were Richard Nixon for president and Spiro Agnew for vice president. Spiro Agnew resigned in disgrace in October 1973. When the Watergate scandal resulted in the resignation of President Nixon on August 9, 1974, the appointed, not elected, vice president, Gerald Ford, was sworn in as president the same day.

The Gerald R. Ford Museum, modern and impressive architecturally, is a triangular, two-story building with a mirrored east wall situated on a six-acre site on the west bank of the Grand River. Ah-Nab-Awen Bicentennial Park, which is a memorial to the Indian tribes who used this site as a trading place, separates the museum from the Grand River. On the other side of the Grand River are the imposing Amway Plaza Hotel and the Grand Center, a convention facility.

Interactive exhibits in the museum use multimedia to involve visitors. The 1970s gallery sets the stage for the Ford era with fashions, music, and other aspects of pop culture. The "Constitution in Crisis" exhibit explores the Watergate scandal, which led to the resignation of President Richard Nixon and the unexpected presidency of Gerald Ford.

The exhibit "Young Jerry Ford" features a re-creation of Gerald R. Ford Sr.'s Ford Paint and Varnish Company store and focuses on the future president's boyhood through his congressional years. "At Work in the Oval Office" is a full-scale replica of the White House Oval Office as it looked during the Ford years. "Leader in Diplomacy" focuses on the international situations dealt with by President Ford and Secretary of State Henry Kissinger and includes a Vietnam-era helicopter.

The Cabinet Room has been re-created as it appeared during the Ford era. The exhibit "Life in the White House" features a holographic tour of the White House as well as gifts from dignitaries and heads of state. Ford's unsuccessful 1976 campaign includes campaign artifacts and videos of the presidential debates with Jimmy Carter.

"America at 200" refers to the 1976 Bicentennial and displays gifts marking the occasion that were made by Americans from every state. "Gerald R. Ford Becomes President" is an exhibit on the series of events culminating in the inauguration of President Ford.

President Ford died on December 26, 2006. On January 3 he was interred on a hillside north of the Gerald R. Ford Museum. His grave site can be visited.

# James Earl Carter Jr.

THIRTY-NINTH PRESIDENT OF THE UNITED STATES
*January 20, 1977–January 20, 1981*

............................................................................

Jimmy Carter came to the presidency as a little-known southern governor but left the office known worldwide for the Camp David Accords. Carter's achievements after leaving office—receiving the Nobel Prize for Peace, founding the Carter Center, and writing highly acclaimed books—mark a distinguished career as a humanitarian.

James Earl Carter Jr., known as Jimmy Carter, was born on October 1, 1924, at Wise Hospital in Plains, Georgia. He is the oldest of the four children of James Earl Carter Sr. and Besse Lillian Gordy Carter. James Earl was a successful businessman and civic leader who owned farms in Webster County and Archery. Lillian Gordy, who came to Plains to study nursing at Wise Hospital, was born and raised in Richland, twenty miles from Plains.

James Earl Carter Sr. and Lillian Gordy were married on September 26, 1923, in the Plains Baptist Church. When the Carters' first child, the future president, was born, their next-door neighbors were the Smiths, parents of Jimmy's future wife, Rosalynn. Jimmy's siblings were Gloria who was born on October 22, 1926, Ruth who was born on August 7, 1929, and William Alton (Billy) who was born on March 29, 1937.

In 1928, when Jimmy was four years old, the family moved to the Archery farm. James Earl continued to operate businesses in Plains while sharecroppers and laborers worked on his farms, which increased to several thousand acres. James Earl Carter, a conservative Democrat who served in the Georgia House of Representatives, opposed Roosevelt's New Deal.

Jimmy grew up on the farm in Archery until he left for college. Most people in Archery were poor African American farm laborers and sharecroppers, and their children were Jimmy's playmates. Although the community was racially segregated, rural children played with each other regardless of race. That changed as the children grew older and attended segregated schools. All white children in and near Plains, including Archery, attended Plains High School from the first grade through the eleventh grade. Black children went to school in a variety of churches and private homes.

Jimmy Carter recalled that during his youth he did not question racial segregation, which was part of life in rural Georgia. Lillian Carter continued her nursing career while raising her family and provided medical care for her black neighbors. An African American woman named Annie Mae Hollis took care of the Carter children.[1]

Jimmy graduated from Plains High School in 1941. He aspired to go to sea as his uncle Tom Watson Gordy had done. To prepare for the U.S. Naval Academy, he enrolled in Georgia Southwestern College in Americus and followed that up with a year of engineering studies and ROTC at the Georgia Institute of Technology in Atlanta. Carter entered the U.S. Naval Academy at Annapolis in June 1943 and graduated in June 1946.

In July 1945 Jimmy fell in love with Rosalynn Smith. The daughter of Frances Allethea Murray and Wilburn Edgar Smith, Eleanor Rosalynn Smith was born on August 18, 1927, in Plains, Georgia. Her younger sister, Lillian, was named for Lillian Carter, who nursed Wilburn Smith before he died of leukemia.

Jimmy and Rosalynn were married on July 7, 1946, in the Methodist church in Plains. They had three sons and one daughter. John William Carter was born on July 3, 1947; James Earl Carter III, called Chip, was born on April 12, 1950; and Donnel Jeffrey was born on August 18, 1952. In October 19, 1967, Rosalynn gave birth to a long-awaited daughter, Amy.

In June 1948 Jimmy began a six-month period at a submarine officer training school. He then was assigned as an electronics officer to the USS *Pomfret,* whose home port was Pearl Harbor. In February 1951 Jimmy became the senior officer of the precommissioning detail overseeing the building of the K-1 submarine in the shipyards of the Electric Boat Company in New London, Connecticut. The vessel was commissioned on November 10 with Carter as the engineering officer. On June 1, 1952, Jimmy, promoted to full lieutenant, qualified as a submarine commander. He wrote a thesis dealing with a method of underwater range finding using passive listening devices. Later the navy used this method extensively.

Jimmy entered the navy's nuclear submarine program and was assigned to duty with the U.S. Atomic Energy Commission, Division of Reactor Development, Schenectady Operations Office. He became the senior officer of the precommissioning detail for the *Sea Wolf.*

In 1953, when Carter's father was diagnosed with terminal pancreatic cancer, Jimmy resigned his navy commission and returned to Georgia. James Earl Carter died on July 23, 1953, leaving an estate estimated at a quarter of a million dollars.[2] Jimmy took over his father's farm and business interests.

There was a housing shortage in Plains, and because Carter had no income initially, the family qualified for public housing. They moved into an apartment in a red brick housing project built during the Roosevelt era. Jimmy Carter is the only U.S. president to have lived in government-subsidized public housing.[3] A year later the Carters rented a house. In 1961 they built a ranch house on over two acres of land near downtown Plains.

As an adult, Jimmy Carter no longer accepted Georgia's traditional attitudes toward race. During the 1960s civil rights movement in the South, Jimmy declined to join the local White Citizens' Council. As chairman of the Sumter County School Board, he recommended a referendum for school consolidation that would have resulted in black and white children attending the same schools. Carter was branded as an integrationist, and there was a short-lived boycott of his business.

Jimmy Carter, a Democrat, ran for the office of state senator in 1962 but lost to Homer Moore. Because of voting irregularities in Quitman County, Carter challenged the election. As a result, he won the general election by fifteen hundred votes and served in the Georgia Senate from 1963 to 1967.

Carter announced his candidacy for the U.S. House of Representatives in March 1966 but withdrew three months later when he became a candidate for governor. He was defeated in the Georgia Democratic gubernatorial primary by Lester Maddox, a rigid segregationist who opposed civil rights laws. Jimmy had great difficulty in accepting his defeat by Maddox. After engaging in deep, soul-searching discussions with his sister Ruth, he became a born-again Christian. Ruth Carter Stapleton was an international evangelist and author.

On April 3, 1970, Carter again announced his candidacy for governor. He and former governor Carl Sanders faced a run-off election, which Carter won. He served as Georgia's governor from 1971 to 1975.

Carter formally announced his presidential candidacy on December 12, 1974. Most Americans had never heard of Jimmy Carter. In the two years of his campaign, he traveled over five hundred thousand miles and visited every state.

Because of the Watergate scandal, which had culminated in the resignation of President Nixon, Democrats were hopeful about winning the presidency. The 1976 Democratic primary field was crowded with candidates, including Henry Jackson, Morris Udall, Lloyd Bentsen, Frank Church, Birch Bayh, Milton Shapp, Sargent Shriver, Fred Harris, Edmund Brown Jr., and George Wallace. At the Democratic National Convention, Carter was nominated on the first ballot. Sen. Walter Mondale of Minnesota was the vice-presidential nominee.

Jimmy Carter defeated the incumbent, President Gerald Ford. Carter won 40,830,763 popular and 297 electoral votes to Ford's 39,147,793 popular and 240 electoral votes. Eugene McCarthy, running as an Independent, took 756,000 popular votes.

Carter was inaugurated on January 20, 1977. Rather than being sworn in as James Earl Carter Jr., he took the presidential oath as Jimmy Carter. President Carter pardoned an estimated ten thousand Vietnam War draft evaders.

Carter's years in office were plagued by escalating inflation rates and rising energy costs. Nevertheless he tried to balance the budget and maintain social and educational programs. He established the Department of Energy and the Department of Education. The Alaska Lands Act increased the size of the national park system.

In 1977 Carter signed treaties that restored Panama's sovereignty over the five-hundred-square-mile Canal Zone and operation of the Panama Canal. The canal would be returned to Panama in 2000. In 1979 the United States established diplomatic relations with the People's Republic of China, formally recognizing it as the legitimate government of China.

At the presidential retreat at Camp David, Maryland, President Carter spent thirteen days, September 5–17, 1978, brokering negotiations between Egyptian president Anwar Sadat and Israeli prime minister Menachem Begin. Two documents, "Framework for Peace in the Middle East" and "Framework for the Conclusion of a Peace Treaty," led to a formal peace treaty in March 1979 that ended a thirty-one-year state of war between Egypt and Israel.

The shah of Iran was ousted in January 1979 by Islamic fundamentalists led by Ayatollah Khomeini. When the shah, in exile in Mexico, developed lymphoma, Carter allowed him to receive medical treatment at Sloan-Kettering Institute in New York in October. Despite assurances from Iran that there would be no reprisals, on November 4, 1979, a mob attacked the U.S. Embassy in Tehran and kidnapped sixty-six Americans. Televised pictures of mobs burning the American flag and blindfolded hostages on public display enraged the public. In April a commando raid to free the hostages failed and eight American soldiers were killed. American negotiators enlisted the help of Crown Prince Fahd of Saudi Arabia, and on November 17 thirteen African American and female hostages were freed.

Although Sen. Edward Kennedy strongly opposed Carter in the primaries, the Democratic National Convention renominated President Carter in 1980. The Republicans nominated Ronald Reagan for president and George H. W. Bush for vice president. John Anderson ran as an Independent.

Reagan carried forty-four states with 489 electoral votes and won 43,899,000 popular votes, 51 percent of the total cast. Carter won six states with 49 electoral votes and 35,481,000, or 41 percent, of the popular vote. John Anderson garnered 5,719,000, 8 percent of the popular vote. The hostages were freed on the day Carter left office and Reagan was inaugurated.

When the Carters returned to Plains, they found that their peanut business was $1 million in debt. Fortunately they were able to sell it to Archer-Daniel-Midland Company. President Carter, a prolific author, has written books that range from autobiography, to poetry, to public-policy commentaries. His well-written *An Hour before Daylight: Memories of a Rural Boyhood* is an illuminating and candid autobiography. In 1982 he was appointed as University Distinguished Professor at Emory University in Atlanta, Georgia.

The former president founded the Carter Center, which addresses national and international issues of public policy and endeavors to resolve conflict, promote democracy, protect human rights, and prevent disease and other world afflictions. Carter has been a frequent volunteer with Habitat for Humanity, an organization that builds and rehabs houses for the poor.

On December 10, 2002, the Norwegian Nobel Committee awarded the Nobel Peace Prize for 2002 to Jimmy Carter "for his decades of untiring effort to find peaceful solutions to international conflicts, to advance democracy and human rights, and to promote economic and social development."[4]

................................................................................

## Jimmy Carter National Historic Site
## Plains, Georgia

ADDRESS: 300 North Bond Street, Plains, GA 31780
TELEPHONE: 229-824-4104
WEB SITE: www.nps.gov/jica
LOCATION: Plains is in southwestern Georgia, 120 miles southwest of Atlanta, 10 miles west of Americus on U.S. 280; the Carter boyhood home is 2.5 miles west of Plains on Old Plains Highway
OPEN: Plains High School: daily, 9:00 A.M. to 5:00 P.M.; train depot: daily, 9:00 A.M. to 4:30 P.M.; Carter boyhood farm: daily, 10:00 A.M. to 5:00 P.M.; all are closed Thanksgiving, Christmas, and New Year's Day
ADMISSION: Free
FACILITIES: Plains High School museum and visitor center; Plains depot museum; restored boyhood home of Jimmy Carter

*President Jimmy Carter's Georgia roots* are commemorated in the Jimmy Carter National Historic Site and Preservation District established by Congress in 1987. Carter was born, raised, educated, and married and operated a peanut business in or near Plains, Georgia. He served in the Georgia Senate and as governor of Georgia.

The site, operated by the National Park Service, includes Plains High School, the old Plains railroad depot, Jimmy Carter's boyhood home and farm, and the Carter residence. Because the Carter residential complex is the current home of Jimmy and Rosalynn Carter, it is not open to the public.

The preservation district consists of a historic district and 650 acres of agricultural land in and around Plains. Founded in 1885, Plains incorporated earlier communities, including the Plains of Dura, established in the 1830s on Creek Indian land. Plains, a rural southern town of 634 people, retains a late nineteenth- or early twentieth-century character.

Plains High School, which both Jimmy and his wife, Rosalynn Smith Carter, attended from first grade through high school graduation, was built in 1921,

Jimmy Carter National
Historic Site, Plains,
Georgia. Boyhood Home.
Photograph courtesy of
Jimmy Carter National
Historic Site

317

JAMES EARL CARTER, JR.

integrated in 1966, and closed in 1979. In 1996 Plains High School was opened as a museum and visitor center. A classroom, the principal's office, and the auditorium have been restored to their appearance in the 1930s when the school was segregated. Exhibits focus on Carter's family, boyhood, navy career, peanut business, and pre-presidential political career in Georgia.

The old Plains railroad depot, on Main Street and South Hudson Street, served as Jimmy Carter's 1976 Presidential Campaign Headquarters. The depot dates to 1888 and was used until 1951, when passenger train service to Plains was discontinued. The depot, restored to its appearance in 1976, tells the story of Carter's presidential campaign through videos, photographs, posters, buttons, and written materials. Carter, a peanut farmer, used peanuts in his campaign materials. His campaign workers were called the Peanut Brigade.

Carter's boyhood home, the family farm in Archery, opened as a unit of the Carter National Historic Site in November 2000. Jimmy and Rosalynn Carter attended the dedication ceremony. The National Park Service spent four years restoring the property. On 15 acres of the original 360-acre farm are the house, a reconstructed barn, a farm store, a windmill, and a tenant farmer's house.

Jimmy Carter and his family moved to this farm in 1928 when he was four years old, and he lived here until he started college. Cotton, peanuts, and corn were grown on the farm. The family raised vegetables for their own use and kept some animals. The Carter family left the farm in 1949.

The Carter farmhouse, built circa 1922, is a one-story frame bungalow. Designed in the shotgun style with one room behind another, it includes a living room, a dining room, three bedrooms, a kitchen, and a screened porch across the back of the house. The privy was outdoors. In 1935 James Earl Carter, Jimmy's father, purchased a windmill with a tank and pipes so that there would be an indoor toilet and running water in the kitchen. The farm was electrified in the 1930s. On the property were a dirt tennis court, a pond, and a pond house with Ping-Pong tables, a jukebox, and a patio. Other structures on the farm were a frame commissary, blacksmith and carpentry shops, a large barn, a pump house with a well, a harness shed, and five small clapboard tenant farmers' houses.

The farmhouse has been restored to its appearance in the 1930s before electrification, when fireplaces and wood stoves were used for heating. Visitors see the future president's simply furnished bedroom, a battery-operated radio in the living room, the indoor bathroom, and the wood stove in the kitchen.

The frame commissary store, run by James Earl Carter, was stocked with food, household goods, and clothing. Visitors can also see the reconstructed barn and the simple home of the African American tenant farmer Jack Clark and his wife Rachel.

The pecan grove was planted by James Earl and Jimmy Carter. Not far from the boyhood home is Lebanon Cemetery, where James Earl, Lillian, and Billy Carter, Jimmy's brother, are buried.

........................................................................

## Jimmy Carter Presidential Library and Museum
## Atlanta, Georgia

ADDRESS: 441 Freedom Parkway, Atlanta, GA 30307-1498
TELEPHONE: 404-865-7100
WEB SITE: www.jimmycarterlibrary.gov
LOCATION: Northeast of downtown Atlanta, at Cleburne and North Highland Avenue, accessible from I-75/85
OPEN: Library: Monday–Friday, 8:30 A.M. to 4:30 P.M.; museum: Monday–Saturday, 9:00 A.M. to 4:45 P.M., and Sunday, noon to 4:45 P.M.
ADMISSION: Adults 17 and over, $8.00; seniors, military, and students, $6.00
FACILITIES: Museum, library, and archives; Japanese garden; shop; restaurant; handicapped accessible

*The Jimmy Carter Presidential Library and Museum* in Atlanta is in a series of connecting modern concrete and glass circular structures with an adjacent Japanese garden. The Carter Presidential Library houses the papers and artifacts related to the Carter presidency in its archives, while the museum focuses not only on Jimmy Carter as president but also on Carter the man.

Built at a cost of $26 million in private donations, the seventy-thousand-square-foot Jimmy Carter Library was completed in October 1986. The architecturally impressive modern concrete and glass presidential library was designed by Jova, Daniels, Busby of Atlanta and Lawton, Umemura & Yamamoto of Honolulu. The Japanese garden was designed by the Japanese master gardener Kinsaku Nakane.

When it was dedicated and opened to the public, the Carter Library was turned over to the National Archives and Records Administration, which

administers more than twenty-seven million pages of material and more than a million photographs, motion picture film, videotapes, and audiotapes. The state-of-the-art museum exhibits include an interactive town meeting in which visitors can question Carter about his daily activities in the White House or peace negotiations with Sadat and Begin.

The full-scale replica of Jimmy Carter's White House Oval Office is furnished as it was during the Carter administration. Carter's presidential desk was made of wood from a nineteenth-century English ship that was lost after being stuck in ice near the North Pole. Captain Buddington of the U.S. whaler *George Henry* found the HMS *Resolute* and returned it to England. In gratitude, Queen Victoria had a desk made from timbers from the *Resolute* and presented it to President Hayes. A reproduction of that desk is in the replica Oval Office, as is President Carter's Bible. Carter kept a bust of Harry Truman, one of his favorite presidents, along with a sign reading "The Buck Stops Here," which was a gift from Margaret Truman Daniel.

Campaign materials from the gubernatorial and presidential races are displayed. The exhibit "The Race to the White House" portrays Carter's presidential campaign in 1976. The exhibit outlines his campaign strategy and is illustrated with campaign buttons, bumper stickers, and posters. He debated President Gerald Ford in three televised debates. On Inauguration Day when he was sworn in as the thirty-ninth president of the United States, Jimmy Carter used the Bible that his mother had given him.

Carter's international policies, including the Camp David Accords and the Middle East peace process, are the subjects of the exhibit "Peace in the Middle East," which illustrates one of Carter's major diplomatic achievements. In July 1978 President Carter invited Egyptian president Anwar Sadat and Israeli prime minister Menachem Begin to Camp David for face-to-face talks.

Gifts given to the president by leaders of foreign countries are presented. Artifacts from Carter's personal life include family photographs along with his baby book, his report cards, and the clothes worn by Jimmy and Rosalynn on their wedding day.

The Carter Center contains offices for Jimmy and Rosalynn Carter, the Carter Center of Emory University, and the Task Force for Child Survival and Global 2000. The Japanese garden, designed by the Japanese master gardener Kinsaku Nakane, is a simulation of a landscape of deep mountains, secluded valleys, and two symbolic waterfalls.

# Ronald Wilson Reagan

FORTIETH PRESIDENT OF THE UNITED STATES
*January 20, 1981–January 20, 1989*

. . . . . . . . . . . . . . . . . . . . . . . . . . . . . . . . . . . . . . . . . . . . . . . . . . . . . . . . . . . . . . . . . . . . . .

Beginning his career as a radio sports announcer and then a Hollywood movie actor, Ronald Reagan, known as the "great communicator," effectively carried his message of patriotism and conservatism to the nation. Ronald Wilson Reagan was born in Tampico, Illinois, on February 6, 1911, to Nelle Clyde Wilson Reagan and John Edward Reagan. His paternal ancestors originated in the town of Doolis in County Tipperary, Ireland, where the family name was O'Regan. In 1856 Ronald's great-grandparents Michael and Catherine Reagan immigrated to Canada, and from there they traveled to Carroll County, Illinois.

In November 1904 Jack Reagan and Nelle Wilson were married in the rectory of the Immaculate Conception Catholic Church in Fulton. They moved to Tampico, whose population was less than thirteen hundred people. Jack worked at the H. C. Pitney General Store, and he and Nelle lived in a five-room flat over a bakery on Main Street. There John Neil Reagan was born on September 16, 1908, followed by Ronald Wilson Reagan on February 6, 1911. When Jack saw his newborn son Ronald, Jack called him "Dutch," a nickname that stayed with him into adulthood. Dutch people lived in Fulton, and Jack believed that his baby son resembled them.

Jack had an almost lifelong problem with alcohol, which caused frequent job losses and evictions. In 1914 the Reagan family moved to Chicago. After less than a year they moved to Galesburg and then to Monmouth in late 1917. In August 1919 the Reagan family moved back to Tampico and then to Dixon in December 1920. Though only nine years old, Ronald had already lived in nine, possibly ten, different residences in four different towns.

Until Ronald was twenty-one years old, Dixon, with a population of ten thousand, was the future president's home. Even in Dixon the Reagan family lived in five rented houses. Their residence on Hennepin Avenue is now designated as the Reagan boyhood home.

At North Dixon High School, Dutch was student body president and a member of the drama club and the football team. He took swimming lessons at Lowell Park, a three-hundred-acre nature preserve on the swift and dangerous Rock River. Every summer several swimmers at Lowell Park drowned. Dutch, the first lifeguard at Lowell Park, worked seven days a week, twelve hours a day for eighteen dollars a week.[1] During the six summers Dutch was a lifeguard, he is credited with saving seventy-seven lives. Although that figure sounds inflated, the Rock River was wide and deep at that point, and inexperienced swimmers quickly got into trouble.

In 1928 Ronald Reagan entered Eureka College, a small Christian Church liberal arts school founded in 1855 in Eureka, Illinois. He financed his college education with funds from his jobs as a lifeguard and a caddy and with an athletic scholarship. During his senior year he was the president of the student body. A member of the Dramatics Club, he starred in several student productions.

Ronald Reagan graduated from Eureka in June 1932 with a B.A. in economics. Radio Station WOC in Davenport, Iowa, hired him as a sports announcer.[2] When WOC merged with WHO in Des Moines, Iowa, Dutch became WHO's chief sports announcer. Because he loved to ride horses, he enlisted as a reserve officer in the Fourteenth Cavalry Regiment stationed at nearby Camp Dodge and was commissioned as a second lieutenant.

Reagan became a well-known radio announcer who broadcast the Chicago Cubs' home games. In February 1937 he went to California to cover the Chicago Cubs' spring training camp on Catalina Island. After a screen test at the Warner Brothers studio, Reagan won a seven-year contract with six-month options. After initially playing leads in B films and small roles in A films, Reagan appeared in fifty-three feature films. He purchased a ranch and bought his parents a house in California.

Reagan met the movie star Jane Wyman in 1939 when they worked together on *Brother Rat and a Baby*. Jane was born Sarah Jane Mayfield on January 5, 1917, in St. Joseph, Missouri. Jane married Myron Futterman in 1936, but when Jane and Ronald met, she was in the final stages of a divorce. Ronald Reagan and Jane Wyman were married on January 26, 1940, at the Wee Kirk O'Heather Church in Glendale. A daughter, Maureen, was born on January 4, 1941. Ronald and Jane adopted an infant son, Michael, in March 1945. In June 1947 Jane gave birth to a premature baby, who died the next day. Jane filed for divorce in June 1948, and the divorce was final in July 1949.

Reagan's role in *Knute Rockne—All American* was a turning point in his career. The movie opened in South Bend, Indiana, the home of Notre Dame University, and thousands of people attended the movie premiere events and a Notre Dame football game. Because of the movie's good reviews, Warner Brothers cast Reagan in the studio's A movies.

During World War II, Reagan was called to active duty in April 1942. He served in Culver City, California, in the First Motion Picture Unit at the Hal Roach Studio. He and thirteen hundred other actors, directors, and writers produced war propaganda films.[3] Reagan was discharged in July 1945.

Reagan served as president of the Screen Actors Guild from 1947 to 1952 and again from 1959 to 1960. He was the host of a television series, *General Electric Theater*, and as a spokesperson for General Electric he traveled the country giving speeches that included his conservative vision for America.

In 1952 Reagan married Nancy Davis. Born in New York City on July 6, 1921, Nancy was named Anne Frances Robbins. Her parents were Edith Luckett, a stage actress, and Kenneth Seymour Robbins. Her mother called her baby girl "Nancy." Edith and Kenneth separated in 1923, and Edith resumed her acting career, leaving Nancy with Edith's sister Virginia and her husband, C. Audley Galbraith, for the next five years. In 1929 Edith married Loyal Davis, a wealthy Chicago neurosurgeon, who adopted Nancy when she was fourteen. Nancy was a drama major at Smith College, graduating in 1943.

In 1949 Nancy received a seven-year contract from Metro-Goldwyn-Mayer, and she was in nine films. Nancy and Ronald Reagan were married on March 4, 1952. Patricia Anne (Patty) was born on October 22, 1952, and Ronald Prescott Jr. was born in May 1958.

Reagan became an articulate spokesman for the conservative wing of the Republican Party. His political ideology was strongly anticommunist, antitax, patriotic, and opposed to the Roosevelt-era welfare programs, although the first time Reagan voted in a presidential election, he voted for Roosevelt. Reagan was the Republican candidate for governor of California in 1966, running against Pat Brown, the Democratic incumbent. Reagan won and was reelected in 1970.

Reagan unsuccessfully challenged Richard Nixon for the Republican presidential nomination in 1968 and the incumbent Gerald Ford in 1976. In November 1979 Reagan won twenty-nine primaries and the Republican nomination. George Bush was his vice-presidential running mate. The incumbent president, Jimmy Carter, was the Democratic candidate.

In the election of 1980 Reagan carried forty-four states with 489 electoral votes and won 43,899,000 popular votes, or 51 percent of the total votes cast. President Carter won six states with 49 electoral votes and 35,481,000, or 41 percent, of the popular votes. John Anderson, running as an Independent, garnered 5,719,000, or 8 percent, of the popular vote.

After Reagan was inaugurated on January 20, 1981, Iran freed fifty-two American hostages whose release President Carter had been unable to secure. Determined to end the liberal economics and social policies associated with the welfare state, Reagan launched an attack on "big government" and federal bureaucracy. The term "Reaganomics" was coined for his free-enterprise, free-market, and nongovernment interventionist economics. Under Reagan military spending increased from under $144 billion to almost $295 billion. He reduced funding of welfare programs, lowered taxes, and through appointments created a more conservative federal court and Supreme Court. In 1981 the country slipped into a recession, which lasted almost two years. In 1983 an economic recovery began, and Reagan credited the rebounding economy to his economic policy.

On March 20, 1981, John W. Hinckley, a mentally ill young man, shot President Reagan in the chest with a 22-caliber handgun, inflicting a life-threatening injury. In 1985 Ronald Reagan had major cancer surgery.

President Reagan was concerned about the leftist, procommunist orientation of the Sandinistas in Nicaragua and directed William Casey, the CIA director, to fund the training of Contras, anti-Sandinista guerrillas. In a covert operation money and arms were channeled through Gen. Manuel Noriega, Panama's president. Reagan and the CIA ignored the Boland Amendment of 1982, which reduced financial aid to the Contras, as well as Boland II, which forbade further assistance to the Contras. Oliver North was charged with secretly raising funds to continue the aid program.

The Republicans renominated President Reagan and Vice President Bush in 1984. The Democrats nominated Walter Mondale for president and Geraldine Ferraro for vice president. Reagan won 54,455,472 popular votes, or 58.7 percent of the total, and 525 electoral votes. Mondale won 37,577,352 popular votes, or 40.6 percent, and 13 electoral votes.

While seven Americans were held hostage in Lebanon, National Security Adviser Robert McFarlane was approached in July 1985 by David Kimche, an Israeli citizen. He introduced McFarlane to an Iranian businessman, Manucher Ghorbanifar, who proposed a hostage-for-arms deal. President Reagan approved the arms sales in January 1987. Initially weapons were sold with Israel acting as the middle man, but no hostages were released. On September 15 a single hostage was released.

In December, McFarlane resigned and was replaced by Adm. John Poindexter. Oliver North directed the continuing arms sales to Iran. In what was called the Iran-Contra affair, North used profits from the arms sales to Iran to support the Contras in Nicaragua. In the summer of 1986 a second hostage was freed, and a third followed in November. In fall 1986 the scandal broke. The White House denied involvement. North, Poindexter, and others were indicted and convicted, but their convictions were later overturned.

From 1985 to 1988 President Reagan met several times with the Soviet leader Mikhail Gorbachev. Speaking at the Berlin Wall, Reagan said, "Mr. Gorbachev, tear down that wall." In December 1987 Reagan and Gorbachev signed the Intermediate-Range Nuclear Forces (INF) treaty, in which the two superpowers agreed to remove all intermediate-range nuclear tipped missiles from Europe. By 1988 the cold war had ended. The Berlin Wall, a symbol of communism, fell in 1989.

After the presidency the Reagans returned to their home in Bel Air, California. Reagan was active in creating the Ronald Reagan Presidential Library and Museum, north of Los Angeles. In November 1994 Ronald Reagan revealed publicly that he suffered from Alzheimer's disease. Ten years later, on June 5, 2004, he died in his Bel Air home.

Reagan's body first lay in state at the Reagan Presidential Library in Simi Valley, California, and then was moved to the Capitol Rotunda in Washington, D.C. The funeral, held in Washington's National Cathedral, was attended by former presidents Ford, Carter, Bush, and Clinton, and President George W. Bush was one of the eulogists. Reagan was buried at his presidential library in Simi Valley, California, on June 11.

..................................................................................

## Birthplace of President Ronald Reagan
## Tampico, Illinois

ADDRESS: 111 S. Main Street, P.O. Box 344, Tampico, IL 61283
TELEPHONE: 815-438-2130
WEB SITE: www.tampicohistoricalsociety.citymax.com
LOCATION: Tampico is in northwestern Illinois, 127 miles west of Chicago, accessible from I-88, 28 miles southwest of Dixon, about 50 miles east of the Quad Cities at the Illinois-Iowa border
OPEN: Monday–Saturday, 10:00 A.M. to 4:00 P.M., and Sunday 1:00 P.M. to 4:00 P.M., April–October; Saturday, 10:00 A.M. to 4:00 P.M., and Sunday, 1:00 P.M. to 4:00 P.M., March
ADMISSION: Free; donations appreciated
FACILITIES: Restored birthplace apartment; visitor center; guided tours

*Ronald Wilson Reagan, the fortieth president* of the United States, was born in Tampico, Illinois, on February 6, 1911. He is the only president born in Illinois. His parents, Nelle and Jack, and his older brother, Neil, lived in a spacious apartment above a bakery at 111 Main Street. On that cold February day, Ronald was born in a bedroom that fronted the street.

Tampico was incorporated as a village in February 1875. It was a small town then, and it is a small town today. Three months after Ronald's birth, the family moved to a two-story house nearby on Glassburn Street, so Ronald had no memory of the apartment. When he toured the restored apartment, he commented that it was so nice he wondered why his parents moved. The Glassburn Street house is privately owned and occupied.

The Reagan family lived in Tampico until December 1914, after which they lived in Chicago, Galesburg, and Monmouth. They returned to Tampico in August 1919 and lived on Main Street again in an apartment above the shoe store in which Jack Reagan worked. They moved to Dixon, Illinois, in December 1920.

The restoration of the Reagan birthplace was a labor of love for two local couples, the Nicelys and the McElhineys. Helen Woods Nicely, daughter of the

Ronald Reagan Birthplace, Tampico, Illinois

town banker, and her husband, Paul Nicely, acquired the Main Street property from her family. In 1976 they began restoring the apartment to its 1911 appearance, and they opened the apartment and a first-floor museum to tourists in 1981 after Ronald Reagan's election as president.

In the late 1990s the McElhineys became involved with the Reagan birthplace through the Tampico Area Historical Society, also located on Main Street. When the Nicelys were no longer able to act as tour guides, the McElhineys filled that void. Since Lloyd McElhiney's death in 2006, members of the Tampico Area Historical Society lead the tours.

After Mrs. Nicely's death in 2003, Wayne Whalen, a Chicago attorney, purchased from her estate the two adjoining Main Street buildings, which house the birthplace and the museum. Whalen is interested in restoring the First National Bank, which was on the first floor of the Reagan birthplace. There is some debate whether the first floor housed a bakery or a bank at the time the Reagan family lived upstairs.

Tampico is proud of President Reagan, and a visit to the site projects a positive, admiration-filled picture of the fortieth president. On the first floor is a visitor center and a museum filled with Reagan artifacts.

On Main Street owners of first-floor businesses built large apartments for their families above their stores. The spacious three-bedroom apartment has a parlor, a dining room, a kitchen, and a back porch. The decor of the apartment reflects the early 1900s era when the Reagans occupied it. The furniture was not owned by the Reagans but is of the period. The outhouse was in the yard.

Across the street from the Reagan birthplace is the building that housed the shoe store where Jack Reagan was employed. Nearby is the house the Reagans moved to, which is privately owned and occupied, and the park where the children played.

## Ronald Reagan Boyhood Home
## Dixon, Illinois

ADDRESS: 816 S. Hennepin Avenue, Dixon, IL 61021
TELEPHONE: 815-288-5176
WEB SITE: www.ronaldreaganhome.com
LOCATION: One hundred miles west of Chicago, accessible from East-West
Tollway, I-88
OPEN: Monday–Saturday, 10:00 A.M. to 4:00 P.M., and Sunday, 1:00 P.M. to
4:00 P.M., April–October; Saturday, 10:00 A.M. to 4:00 P.M., and Sunday
1:00 P.M. to 4:00 P.M., March; closed Easter
ADMISSION: Adults and children 13 years and older, $5.00
FACILITIES: Restored boyhood home; visitor center; orientation film; gift shop;
guided tours. National Register of Historic Places

RONALD WILSON REAGAN

*Praising the fine restoration of his boyhood home* on a 1984 visit to Dixon,
Ronald Reagan said that if the house on Hennepin had looked that good when
he lived there, he might never have left. He did leave, however, and became a
famous movie actor, governor of California from 1967 to 1975, and president
of the United States from 1981 to 1989.

Although born in Tampico, Illinois, Ronald Reagan considered Dixon his
hometown. "Everyone has a place to come back to, and for me that place is
Dixon, a place on the Rock River," Reagan said in the 1950 movie *The Hasty
Heart*. The original line referred to Boston, but Reagan got permission to change
the line.

Ronald Reagan's parents, John Edward and Nelle Wilson Reagan, and their
sons, Neil, twelve, and Ronald, nine, moved to Dixon (population ten thousand) in 1920 after having lived in Tampico, Chicago, Galesburg, and Monmouth. The future president resided in Dixon until he was twenty-one years
old, and his parents lived there until 1937, when they moved to California.

Known as Jack, Ronald Reagan's father, an Irish Catholic, worked in the retail shoe business. His wife, a Scottish Protestant, taught Sunday school at the
First Christian Church, as did Ronald. Neil and Ronald attended South Side
School and different campuses of Dixon High School. After learning to swim
at the YMCA, Ronald worked as a lifeguard at Lowell Park for six summers
and is credited with saving seventy-seven lives.

The Reagans rented a house on Hennepin Avenue that was built in 1891 by
William C. Thompson. It was then sold to Edward Donovan, who rented it to
the Reagans from 1920 until 1923. This house was the first of five residences
rented by the Reagan family in Dixon; one house has been torn down, and the
other three are privately owned. The Reagan Boyhood Home is listed on the
National Register of Historic Places.

In 1980 the house on Hennepin Avenue was purchased for $31,500 by local citizens. In poor condition, the house had undergone substantial changes. It has been beautifully restored to its appearance in the early 1920s when it was occupied by the Reagans. It is now owned by the Ronald Reagan Home Preservation Foundation, with most of its funding provided by the Norman Wymbs Family Foundation. The U.S. Department of the Interior has shown interest in acquiring the house from the foundation. The house was formally dedicated on February 6, 1984, President Reagan's seventy-third birthday. Ronald, Nancy, and Neil Reagan toured the house and ate lunch in the dining room.

Tours of the Reagan home begin in the Victorian house next door, which serves as a visitor center. An orientation film that focuses on President Reagan's 1984 visit to Dixon is shown there.

On a tree-lined street of similar residences, the two-story, white-frame, Queen Anne–style Reagan house has a front porch and a wood shingle roof. On the first floor are a parlor, a family sitting room, a dining room, and a kitchen. Three bedrooms and a bathroom are upstairs. A modern house, it was complete with indoor plumbing and central heat.

The woodwork, light fixtures, and light switches are original, though none of the furnishings is original. Rooms are simply furnished. President Reagan and his brother were given pre-1920 Sears catalogs and asked to indicate the type of furniture that they remembered from their childhood.

The formal parlor has a tile fireplace with an oak mantel and a mirror above. During his 1984 visit Reagan reminisced about keeping pennies under a loose tile. He found the loose tile and left a few pennies under it. The flowered wallpaper in the parlor is a reproduction of the 1920s wallpaper unearthed during restoration. The children did their homework and played board games on the oak table in the sitting room.

Oak dining room furniture includes an exact replica of Nelle Reagan's buffet. The dining room table is set with dishes that were bonuses from Jewel Tea food stores and are identical to Nelle Reagan's. A china cabinet contains Nelle's collection of china cups and saucers. Mrs. Reagan took in sewing, and some of her customers paid her with cups.

The 1920s modern kitchen has a Detroit Jewel gas stove, a wooden icebox with a metal top, a metal sink, and a free-standing Hoosier cabinet with a built-in flour bin.

On the second floor the parents' bedroom has a brass bed, and a second brass bed is in the guest bedroom / sewing room. The Reagan brothers shared a bedroom and an iron bed. Banners from Dixon High School and Eureka College decorate the wall. The bathroom has a footed bathtub.

The barn behind the house has been reconstructed on its original site. Jack Reagan used the barn as a garage, and now it houses a Model T Ford similar to the one he owned. There is a vegetable garden in the backyard like the one Nelle had. Next to the Reagan home is a small park with a bronze statue of Ronald Reagan.

Approximately three blocks from the boyhood home is South Side School, later called South Central School, where Ronald attended sixth and seventh grades. The sixth-grade classroom has been restored to its 1920s look. Known as the Dixon Historical Center, it is owned by the Ronald Reagan Home Foundation Inc. A four-story brick and steel structure built in 1908, it is located at Hennepin Avenue and Fifth Street.

Located at 123 S. Hennepin Avenue is the First Christian Church attended by Nelle Reagan and her sons. Also in Dixon is the Loveland Community Center and Historical Museum, 513 West Second Street. Its second-floor museum displays Reagan artifacts.

. . . . . . . . . . . . . . . . . . . . . . . . . . . . . . . . . . . . . . . . . . . . . . . . . . . . . . . . . . . . . . . . . . .

## Ronald Reagan Presidential Library and Museum
## Simi Valley, California

ADDRESS: 40 Presidential Drive, Simi Valley, CA 93065
TELEPHONE: 800-410-8354 or 805-577-4000
WEB SITE: www.reaganlibrary.com
LOCATION: In southern California, north of Los Angeles, in Simi Valley
OPEN: Museum: daily, 10:00 A.M. to 5:00 P.M., closed Thanksgiving, Christmas, and New Year's Day; library research room: Monday–Friday, 9:00 A.M. to 5:00 P.M., closed federal holidays

Ronald Reagan Presidential Library and Museum, Simi Valley, California

ADMISSION: Museum: adults, $12.00; seniors, $9.00; children 11–17, $6.00
FACILITIES: Museum and shops; café; research library; presidential burial site

*Located in picturesque Simi Valley, California,* the Ronald Reagan Presidential Library is on a one-hundred-acre hilltop site overlooking the Pacific Ocean, the Simi Valley, and nearby mountains. The stunning location, about midway between the Reagan home in Bel Air and their Rancho del Cielo ranch in Santa Ynez, is on property donated by the land developers Don Swartz and Gerald Blakeley.

The Ronald Reagan Presidential Library and Museum, dedicated on November 4, 1991, is a four-level Spanish-mission-style structure with a central courtyard. The museum is housed in two above-ground stories, and the library is in two stories below ground. The well-visited site has 153,000 square feet, 22,000 of which are devoted to museum exhibits. Privately funded by the Ronald Reagan Presidential Foundation, it was built at a cost of $57 million. At its 1991 dedication ceremony, the presidential library was turned over to the National Archives and Records Administration.

In 2010 the Ronald Reagan Presidential Library and Museum began redesigning the majority of its museum exhibits in preparation for the Reagan Centennial. Ronald Reagan was born February 6, 1911, and, by the centennial celebration in February 2011, new exhibits were installed. Previous exhibits focused on Reagan's early years and his acting, military, and political careers as well as his presidency.

Exhibits that are unchanged include the Reagan Oval Office and Air Force One. The White House Oval Office has been replicated with reproduction furniture as it appeared on Reagan's last day of office. There are couches and chairs upholstered in cream-colored fabric, a beige oval rug, and a replica of the Resolute Desk sent from Queen Victoria to President Hayes. Air Force One, a fabulous exhibit, displays the Boeing 707 plane used by Presidents Reagan,

Nixon, Ford, Carter, and Bush until 1990, after which it was used as a backup plane. Called the *Spirit of '76*, it sits in a three-level pavilion with a glass wall overlooking the mountains. Museum visitors tour the interior of the presidential plane and see the communications center, the president's office, a conference room, a galley for the president and crew, a staff room with four seats and two desks, the staff and guest compartment, the security staff compartment, and the passenger and media compartment. A flying White House, it could handle fifty passengers and eighteen crew members.

The same pavilion houses a Secret Service van, a presidential limousine, a police car, and two motorcycles. A helicopter is on the lower level. On the balcony is an exhibit on Check Point Charlie with soldiers on either side of the Berlin Wall. A video and photographs document the end of the cold war.

Outside the museum is a section of the Berlin Wall that was given to President Reagan on April 12, 1990. The wall, a physical barrier between East and West Berlin, Germany, was the symbol of the separation of communism from Western democracies. In June 1987 Reagan called on Mikhail Gorbachev to tear down the wall. Two years later Germans tore down the barrier.

Landscaping includes a rose garden and a re-creation of the White House South Lawn. The Reagan Library contains 55 million pages of government records, more than 1.5 million photographs, and almost 770,000 feet of motion picture film.

On June 5, 2004, at age ninety-three, Ronald Reagan died in his Bel Air, California, home. On June 11 the Reagan family and seven hundred invited guests attended the sunset service for the former president at his presidential library. Reagan's coffin was sealed inside an underground tomb. The memorial site has an ivy-covered curved granite wall.

# George Herbert Walker Bush

........................................................................

Only two U.S. presidents, John Adams and George H. W. Bush, were the fathers of presidents. Skilled in foreign policy, George H. W. Bush was president during the turbulent era of the collapse of the Soviet Union and the liberation of Kuwait from Iraq.

George Herbert Walker Bush, the son of Prescott Bush and Dorothy Walker, was born in Milton, Massachusetts, on June 12, 1924. Prescott Bush, a Yale graduate, served in the U.S. Senate from 1953 to 1963. In 1936 George H. W. Bush entered Phillips Academy, a prestigious preparatory school in Andover, Massachusetts.

In 1942 George enlisted in the U.S. Navy on his eighteenth birthday, determined to become a navy pilot. He was assigned to Torpedo Squadron (VT-51). Bush's squadron was based on the USS *San Jacinto,* which was part of a navy task force engaged in operations against the Japanese in the Pacific. On June 19, 1944, Bush's plane was forced to make a water landing. A destroyer rescued the young pilot and his crew, although the plane was lost. Bush and another aviator were credited with sinking a Japanese cargo ship off the island of Palau.

The *San Jacinto* was in action against the Japanese in the Bonin Islands. On September 2 Bush was piloting a Grumman TBM Avenger plane that attacked Japanese installations on Chichi Jima. Bush's flying group met strong Japanese anti-aircraft fire; his plane was hit, and its engine caught fire. Bush and another crew member were forced to bail out. Bush waited four hours in his inflated raft until the submarine USS *Finback* rescued him. He was awarded the Distinguished Flying Cross. Bush was honorably discharged in September 1945.

In late 1941 George met Barbara Pierce in Greenwich, Connecticut. A student at Ashley Hall in Charleston, South Carolina, Barbara was born in New York City in 1925. Her father, Marvin Pierce, was president of the McCall Corporation.[1]

George Bush and Barbara Pierce were married on January 6, 1945, in Rye, New York. Their first child, George W. Bush, a future president, was born on July 6, 1946. Pauline Robinson "Robin," who was born in 1949, died of leukemia in 1953. John Ellis "Jeb" Bush, a future Florida governor, was born in 1953, followed by Neil Mallon in 1955, Marvin Pierce in 1956, and Dorothy Walker in 1959.

Using benefits from the GI Bill, George entered Yale University. Graduating in 1948, he earned a bachelor of arts in economics with Phi Beta Kappa honors. Bush went into the oil business in Texas, working for Dresser Industries, a subsidiary of Brown Brothers Harriman. In 1951 Bush and John Overbey founded the Bush-Overbey Oil Development Company, and two years later Bush and others established the Zapata Petroleum Corporation. In 1954 the Zapata Off-Shore Company, a subsidiary, was founded which specialized in offshore drilling operations.

In 1964 Bush received the Republican Party's nomination as a U.S. senator from Texas, running against the liberal incumbent Democrat, Sen. Ralph Yarborough. Bush lost by three hundred thousand votes. In 1966 Bush was the Republican candidate for the U.S. House of Representatives in the Seventh Texas District against Frank Briscoe, the Democrat. Bush won and was reelected to a second term.

In 1970 Bush ran again for the Senate but was defeated by the Democrat Lloyd Bentsen. President Nixon appointed Bush as U.S. ambassador to the United Nations, a post he held from 1971 to 1973. He was named chairman of the Republican National Committee in 1972. As the Watergate scandal investigation led to President Nixon, Bush wrote to Nixon that his resignation would be best for the country.

Under President Ford, Bush was appointed as chief of the U.S. Liaison Office in the People's Republic of China. He then served as director of the Central Intelligence Agency, a post he held from January 30, 1976, to January 20, 1977.

In 1980 George H. W. Bush and Gov. Ronald Reagan of California were the leading candidates for the Republican nomination for president. Reagan received the nomination at the Republican National Convention and selected Bush as his vice-presidential running mate. The Reagan-Bush ticket swept the 1980 election, winning 43,899,000 popular votes, or 51 percent, and carrying forty-four states with 489 electoral votes. President Carter won six states with 49 electoral votes and 35,481,000 popular votes, or 41 percent. John Anderson, a Republican congressman from Illinois running as an Independent, garnered 5,719,000, or 8 percent of the popular vote.

In 1984 the Republicans again nominated Reagan and Bush, while the Democrats nominated Walter Mondale for president and Geraldine Ferraro for vice president. The Reagan-Bush ticket won again by a huge margin.

In 1988 Vice President Bush received the Republican nomination for president and chose Dan Quayle, a senator from Indiana, as his vice-presidential running mate. The Democratic nominee was Gov. Michael Dukakis of Massachusetts. Bush and Quayle won 426 electoral votes to 111 for Dukakis and his running mate, Lloyd Bentsen. Bush took 53.4 percent of the popular votes to Dukakis's 45.6 percent.

Bush conducted an assertive foreign policy that he called "a New World Order." In December 1989 Bush ordered "Operation Just Cause," a U.S. military invasion to depose Gen. Manuel Noriega of Panama. Noriega, using Panama to facilitate drug traffic from South America to the United States, had grown increasingly unpopular among Panamanians. A force of twenty-five thousand U.S. troops quickly toppled Noriega and took control of Panama.

In 1990 and 1991 Iraq, led by Saddam Hussein, the Iraqi dictator, invaded and occupied Kuwait, Iraq's small, oil-rich neighbor. An overwhelming majority of the world's nations, acting through the United Nations, condemned Iraqi aggression and imposed economic sanctions to force its withdrawal from Kuwait. President Bush and Secretary of State James Baker built a UN coalition to liberate Kuwait. Operation "Desert Shield" commenced on January 17, 1991, and successfully liberated Kuwait. Bush then ordered the end of combat operations, which allowed Saddam Hussein to stay in power in Iraq.

In 1989 and 1990 an avalanche of events occurred in the Soviet satellites in Central and Eastern Europe. Beginning with the solidarity movement in Poland led by Lech Walesa, the people in the Soviet satellite countries showed a restlessness that galvanized into a momentous surge for their political self-determination. The Soviet Union had ruthlessly suppressed earlier attempts at independence in Hungary in 1956 and in Czechoslovakia in 1968. Facing a stagnating Soviet economy, the new leader of the Soviet Union, Mikhail Gorbachev, chose not to intervene as the people of Eastern Europe challenged their communist governments in 1989–90. First in Poland and then in Hungary, Czechoslovakia, and East Germany, noncommunist governments were elected. Long-standing and unresolved nationalist and ethnic feelings for autonomy and independence surfaced in the Baltic republics of Latvia, Lithuania, and Estonia and in Georgia, Ukraine, and Uzbekistan.

In the Soviet Union the monolithic structure created by Lenin and Stalin showed signs of crumbling. As the Soviet Union was disintegrating, President Bush and President Gorbachev declared a U.S.-U.S.S.R. strategic partnership at their summit in July 1991, which decisively marked the end of the cold war.

Bush appeared unbeatable in the 1992 presidential election. However, the Democratic nominee, Gov. Bill Clinton of Arkansas, charged that Bush was unaware of the country's economic recession. Another factor was the strong third party bid of Ross Perot, who continually referenced the country's precarious economic situation. Clinton was victorious with 44,909,806 popular and 370 electoral votes; Bush won 39,304,550 popular and 168 electoral votes. Perot, with 19,743,821 popular votes, claimed 19 percent of the popular vote.

George and Barbara Bush retired to their home in Houston, Texas. President Bush was actively involved in the establishment of the George Bush

Presidential Library and Museum on the campus of Texas A&M University at College Station, Texas. George Bush's son and almost-namesake, George W. Bush, became president of the United States in 2001 and was reelected in 2005.

......................................................................

## George Bush Presidential Library and Museum
### College Station, Texas

ADDRESS: 1000 George Bush Drive West, College Station, TX 77845
TELEPHONE: 979-691-4000
WEB SITE: http://bushlibrary.tamu.edu
LOCATION: One hundred miles northwest of Houston, on the campus of Texas A&M University at College Station
OPEN: Library research room: Monday–Friday, 9:00 A.M. to 4:30 P.M., closed federal holidays; museum: Monday–Saturday, 9:30 A.M. to 5:00 P.M., and Sunday, noon to 5:00 P.M., closed Thanksgiving, Christmas, and New Year's Day
ADMISSION: Adults, $7.00; seniors and military, $6.00; children 6–17 and college students, $3.00
FACILITIES: Presidential library of George H. W. Bush; museum

*The George Bush Presidential Library and Museum* is part of the academic environment of Texas A&M University. The museum depicts the career of George Herbert Walker Bush, the forty-first president of the United States, who served from 1989 to 1993. Before his presidency Bush was vice president of the United States, serving in the administration of Ronald Reagan. He also served as a member of the U.S. House of Representatives from the Seventh District of Texas from 1967 to 1971, as U.S. ambassador to the United Nations from 1971 to 1973, as chairman of the Republican National Committee from 1973 to 1974, as chief of the U.S. Liaison Office in the People's Republic of China from 1974 to 1976, and as director of the Central Intelligence Agency from 1976 to 1977.

Presidents Ford, Carter, Bush, and Clinton, accompanied by their wives and by First Ladies Lady Bird Johnson and Nancy Reagan, attended the dedication of the George Bush Presidential Library and Museum on November 6, 1997. The library/museum cost $83 million and is part of the Presidential Library System administered by the National Archives and Records Administration. The library's collections include 43 million pages of documents and letters, 1 million photographs, and 2,500 hours of videotape. The museum holds a collection of 100,000 objects. In 2007 the main exhibit on the life of George Bush was updated using substantial amounts of video as well as touch screens and interactive technology.

The Bush Library is constructed of beige Texas granite and limestone marble. At the entrance is a large sculpture of five bronze mustangs jumping over

a 4 x 12–foot section of the Berlin Wall. Visitors enter the rotunda, which is 50 feet tall and 100 feet across, surrounded by five pillars forming a circle. It houses the admissions desk, a museum store, a donors' wall, and an orientation theater, which features an introductory film.

"The Life and Presidency of George Bush" narrates the personal story of George Bush and his family. Photographs of the Bush and Pierce families feature George and Barbara's childhood and youth. The exhibit on World War II highlights the service of George Bush as a U.S. Navy pilot. A large map of the Pacific theater of war enables visitors to locate major battles related to Lieutenant Bush. Displayed is the restored 1944 TBM Avenger, similar to the aircraft Bush flew as a navy pilot. A flight simulator allows visitors to attempt landing the TBM on the deck of the *San Jacinto*. Bush being shot down while on a mission on Chichi Jima in 1944 and being rescued by the USS *Finback* are the subjects of another exhibit. The *Finback* is on display.

An exhibit on George Bush's years at Yale and his marriage to Barbara focuses on the period after George was discharged from the navy. It then follows George and Barbara to Texas, a state with which the Bush name would be henceforth associated. A 1947 Studebaker, like the one George drove to Texas in 1948, is displayed. This exhibit focuses on Bush's entry into the oil business, the formation of the Bush-Overbey Oil Development Company in 1951 and in 1954 the Zapata Off Shore Oil Company.

The next exhibits focus on Bush's political career in Texas as the Harris County Republican chairman, his years as a U.S. congressman, and his failed runs for the U.S. Senate. Included are campaign photographs, posters, and memorabilia. Also on display are a thirty-foot replica of the capitol dome in Washington, D.C., and a window with view of the White House. Another exhibit features Bush as U.S. ambassador to the United Nations. Headlines, photographs, and text highlight the major issues: the continuance of cold war tensions with the Soviet Union and the admittance of the People's Republic of

China and the expulsion of Taiwan from the United Nations. Another exhibit concentrates on Bush's role as the chairman of the Republican National Committee during the Nixon administration. During the Watergate scandal Bush tried to keep the controversy from negatively impacting the Republican Party. Another exhibit topic is Bush's role from 1973 to 1974 as the chief of the U.S. Liaison Office in the People's Republic of China. At the time the United States did not have an embassy there, but Bush's job was equivalent to that of an ambassador.

From 1976 through 1977 Bush served as director of the Central Intelligence Agency. He sought to reform the agency and restore the confidence of its operatives. In the exhibit a reconnaissance satellite hangs overhead depicting intelligence gathering and the part it plays in national security.

The exhibits on the vice presidency and the campaign of 1988 deal with Bush's service as vice president under President Reagan and his campaign and election as president in 1988. Vice President Bush headed the Crisis Management Team and chaired task forces on the wars on illegal drugs, air pollution, and illegal immigration.

In the White House exhibit a video wall portrays a day in the life of Bush as president. A re-creation of the north portico celebrates the two hundredth anniversary of the White House. There are replicas of Bush's Oval Office and Press Room in the White House and his Air Force One Office.

Other exhibits on Bush's presidency deal with the major domestic legislation enacted during his term, such as the Clean Air Act and the Americans with Disabilities Act. An exhibit on Camp David includes a replica of Bush's office there.

The exhibit on the Berlin Wall features a sixty-five-hundred-pound piece of the Berlin Wall presented by the German people to President Bush. The wall was erected by the East German communist government in 1961 to prevent East Germans from fleeing to the democratic Federal Republic of Germany. Photographs tell the story of the wall and the oppression of people living behind the Iron Curtain.

The Gulf War exhibit portrays the role of the United States and the UN coalition in liberating Kuwait from its occupation by Saddam Hussein's Iraqi army. The exhibit details the strategy and military operations of Desert Shield and Desert Storm. A fiber-optic light show illustrates the stages of the war in January and February 1991. Suspended from the ceiling are replicas of Patriot, Scud, and Tomahawk missiles.

A special exhibit is devoted to First Lady Barbara Bush and her efforts for literacy, AIDS prevention, and volunteering. Another exhibit features gifts that President Bush received from heads of state, including a tea service from Vaclav Havel, president of Czechoslovakia, and a carriage clock from Princess Diana of England. There are also exhibits on the 1992 presidential election, which Bush lost to Bill Clinton.

# William Jefferson Clinton

FORTY-SECOND PRESIDENT OF THE UNITED STATES
*January 20, 1993–January 20, 2001*

...............................................................................

Bill Clinton, a relatively unknown Arkansas governor, won a surprising victory over incumbent president George H. W. Bush in 1992. Clinton presided over a period of economic growth and prosperity but also was the second president to be impeached but not removed from office.

The forty-second president of the United States was born on August 19, 1946, in Hope, Arkansas, to Virginia Dell Cassidy Blythe and William Jefferson Blythe III, to whom he was born posthumously. The baby was named William Jefferson Blythe IV. Years later, as a teenager, he changed his last name to Clinton, his stepfather's name, and thus became William Jefferson Clinton.

Virginia Cassidy, born on June 6, 1923, was the only child of Edith Valeria Grisham Cassidy and James Eldridge Cassidy of Arkansas. William Jefferson Blythe III was born on February 27, 1918, in Sherman, Texas. Virginia and Bill met in July 1943 at Shreveport, Louisiana's Tri-State Hospital, where Virginia was a student nurse. They married in Texarkana, Arkansas, on September 3, 1943. Bill Blythe, who had been drafted, was awaiting his military orders.

In October, Bill Blythe shipped out to Egypt initially and then to Caserta, Italy. He was a technician third grade with the 3030th Company, 125th Ordnance Base Auto Maintenance Battalion.[1] After he was honorably discharged in December 1945, Blythe got a job with the Manbee Equipment Company in Chicago. He and Virginia purchased a house in Forest Park, a Chicago suburb, but were unable to take immediate possession, so Virginia, who was pregnant with the future president, remained in Hope, Arkansas. When the Forest Park house became available, Bill drove to pick up his wife. On his way William Jefferson Blythe III died on May 17, 1946, when his car went off the road near Sikeston, Missouri. Three months later Virginia gave birth to William Jefferson Blythe IV, whom she called "Billy."

Virginia studied for two years at Charity Hospital in New Orleans to become a nurse anesthetist. One-year-old Billy stayed with the Cassidys, who were devoted grandparents. In June 1950 Virginia married Roger Clinton. Billy then lived with his mother and Roger, whom he called Daddy, although Roger never adopted him.

After his junior year at Hot Springs High School, Bill attended the American Legion Boys Nation program held at the University of Maryland in

College Park. The young men toured Washington, D.C., and also met President Kennedy.

Roger Clinton was an alcoholic and a gambler who verbally and physically abused Virginia. In 1962 she filed for divorce on grounds of mental cruelty and abuse.[2] The divorce was granted on May 15, 1962, but the couple remarried that August.[3] At this time Billy legally changed his last name from Blythe to Clinton. Roger Clinton died in 1967. In 1969 Virginia married Jeff Dwire, who died in 1974. She married Richard Kelley in 1982.

Bill Clinton attended the School of Foreign Service at Georgetown University and worked in Sen. J. William Fulbright's Washington office. During his college years Clinton had a student draft deferment. He opposed the war in Vietnam, though he did not actively protest it. In early 1968 draft deferments for graduate students were abolished and Clinton was reclassified 1-A, eligible for the draft upon graduation.

Clinton won a Rhodes Scholarship for graduate study at Oxford University in England. He took his preinduction armed forces physical examination at a U.S. airbase near London on January 13, 1969. On April 30 he received an induction notice, which had been sent to England by surface mail. Since the induction date had already passed, Clinton's draft board allowed him to finish his current term at Oxford.

In June 1969 Bill returned home facing a July 28 induction date. Looking for alternatives to active military service, Clinton was admitted to the Reserve Officers' Training Corps at the University of Arkansas in conjunction with admission to law school. After Clinton signed a letter of intent regarding the ROTC program, his draft board reclassified him 1-D Reservist and waived his induction date.[4]

Clinton returned to Oxford. In his autobiography Clinton says that he "wanted to be put back in the draft. . . . On October 30, the draft board reclassified me 1-A."[5] Now classified 1-A, he was no longer committed to the University of Arkansas ROTC program. Due to the deescalation of the Vietnam conflict and the fact that his birthday was number 311 in the draft lottery that had been instituted on December 1, 1969, Clinton was never drafted. While at Oxford, Bill became involved with antiwar activities and attended small peace demonstrations in London.

Because he did not complete the requirements, Clinton did not receive an Oxford degree.[6] He was accepted at Yale Law School, where he met his future wife, Hillary Rodham. Hillary Diane Rodham was born on October 26, 1947, in Chicago's Edgewater Hospital. She attended Wellesley College and Yale Law School. Hillary and Bill were married on October 11, 1975, in Fayetteville, Arkansas. On February 27, 1980, Hillary gave birth to a daughter, Chelsea Victoria.

After graduating from Yale in 1974, Bill was an assistant professor at the University of Arkansas Law School at Fayetteville. Hillary was a staff lawyer for the House impeachment inquiry that was building a case against President Nixon. After Nixon resigned, she too joined the faculty of the University of Arkansas Law School.

In 1975 Bill was an unsuccessful candidate for Congress. He then ran for the office of attorney general of Arkansas, won the May 1976 primary, and had no Republican opponent. In 1978 he won the race for governor of Arkansas. Governor Clinton ran for reelection in 1980 against the Republican Frank White and lost, but he successfully opposed Governor White two years later. Clinton remained governor for the next ten years. In Little Rock, Hillary joined the Rose Law Firm.

On October 3, 1991, Governor Clinton announced his candidacy for the presidency of the United States. Early in the campaign rumors about Bill's marital infidelities surfaced. In 1992 a story in the tabloid newspaper the *Star* asserted that Gennifer Flowers, an Arkansas state employee, had had a twelve-year affair with Clinton. Hillary and Bill asserted on the CBS television show *60 Minutes* that Flowers's story was untrue.

The *Wall Street Journal* published a story about Clinton's involvement with the University of Arkansas ROTC in 1969 in which Col. Eugene Holmes stated that Clinton had misled him. Clinton had written a letter to Colonel Holmes explaining his opposition to the Vietnam War after he had chosen to have his draft status returned to 1-A. Clinton believed that the letter to Holmes had been removed from his file at his request. When it surfaced, Clinton's campaign staff published the letter in the *New Hampshire Manchester Union Leader* to defuse the issue. Although Clinton had a draft deferment while at Oxford, he had publicly denied it. This, plus his lack of military service during the Vietnam War, was the basis of his being labeled a draft dodger and war resister by political opponents.

In July 1992 the Democratic Party nominated Clinton for president and Sen. Al Gore of Tennessee as his running mate. President George Bush had been renominated by the Republicans. H. Ross Perot, a Texas billionaire, entered the presidential race as an Independent. Clinton won 44,909,806 popular, or 43 percent, and 370 electoral votes. Bush won 39,104,550 popular, or 37.4 percent, and 168 electoral votes. Ross Perot won 19,743,821 popular votes, or 18.9 percent.

President Clinton named Hillary Rodham Clinton as head of the President's Task Force on National Health Care Reform. Lacking sufficient support in Congress, health care reform failed. One of the first issues that faced Clinton was allowing gay people to serve openly in the military. Current policy was to bring discharge procedures against military personnel who were found to be gay. Clinton sought to buy time by directing military personnel not to ask recruits their sexual orientation. This was referred to as "Don't Ask. Don't Tell."

In February 1993 Clinton signed the Family and Medical Leave Act, which protected jobs of parents who cared for seriously ill children. Clinton supported affirmative action and also welfare reform, which cut in half the number of people on welfare. In 1996 a bill increasing the minimum wage was passed as was a bill enabling employees to carry their health plans from one job to another.

NAFTA, or the North American Free Trade Agreement, which removed tariffs and other trade barriers between the United States and Mexico and Canada, had been negotiated by President Bush and was passed under the Clinton administration.

Clinton was a proponent of the expanded NATO, a move opposed by the Russian president at the time, Boris Yeltsin. After the two leaders met at Helsinki, Finland, in early 1997, Yeltsin reluctantly agreed to the expansion. At a summit held in Madrid in June 1997, the sixteen NATO nations approved the expansion with the first new members to be Poland, Hungary, and the Czech Republic.

The Clintons were investigated for a prepresidential, unprofitable investment in property on the Arkansas White River called "Whitewater." James McDougal of Arkansas was the managing partner and also the proprietor of Madison Guaranty Savings and Loan, which failed, costing taxpayers $50 million.[7] President Clinton asked for a special prosecutor to look into the Whitewater matter. Attorney General Janet Reno appointed a Republican, Robert Fiske, who was later replaced by Kenneth Starr.

The Democratic Party renominated Clinton and Gore in 1996. Sen. Robert Dole was the Republican nominee. Clinton won 47,402,357 popular, or 49.24 percent, and 379 electoral votes. Dole received 39,198,755 popular, or 40.71 percent, and 159 electoral votes. Perot got 8 percent of the popular votes.

When Paula Jones filed a lawsuit alleging sexual harassment by Governor Clinton, the president argued that sitting presidents should be immune from civil lawsuits. The U.S. Supreme Court, in a unanimous decision, ruled in favor of Jones. She refused a settlement offer, and her lawyers used the discovery process to delve into Clinton's sexual history.

On January 21, 1998, a *Washington Post* story alleged that the president had had a sexual affair with Monica Lewinsky, a young White House intern. Lewinsky had confided in Linda Tripp, who had taped their telephone conversations. Kenneth Starr, the special prosecutor in the Whitewater matter, learned of the relationship and, with the permission of the Justice Department, looked into possible obstruction-of-justice issues in the Jones case. The Jones suit, the Whitewater investigation, and the Lewinsky story became entangled. Clinton was subpoenaed in January 1998. By that time Jones's lawyers, Kenneth Starr, and a *Newsweek* reporter knew the Lewinsky story. The president issued a strong denial of ever having sexual relations with Monica Lewinsky.

In April, Judge Susan Webber Wright dismissed Paula Jones's lawsuit. However, Kenneth Starr pursued his investigation. In July, Monica Lewinsky agreed to testify before a federal grand jury in exchange for immunity. President

Clinton testified before the grand jury in mid-August. Starr issued a report to Congress detailing the sexual encounters between the president and Ms. Lewinsky and accused Clinton of lying under oath and obstruction of justice.

Articles of impeachment charging that Clinton had lied under oath to the grand jury and had obstructed justice and tampered with witnesses in the Jones case were passed by the House of Representatives in December 1998. A Senate trial ensued, and the Senate voted 50–50 to reject the obstruction-of-justice article of impeachment and 45–55 to reject the perjury article. A two-thirds vote was required to remove the president from office. President Clinton was impeached but not removed from office.

In his postpresidential years Bill Clinton has been occupied with establishing the Clinton Presidential Library in Little Rock, Arkansas. The Clintons purchased a house in Chappaqua, in suburban New York. First Lady Hillary Clinton was a successful senatorial candidate in November 2000, and she made a strong but unsuccessful bid to win the Democratic presidential nomination in 2008. President Barack Obama appointed Senator Hillary Clinton as his secretary of state.

. . . . . . . . . . . . . . . . . . . . . . . . . . . . . . . . . . . . . . . . . . . . . . . . . . . . . . . . . . . . . . . . . . . .

### President William Clinton's Birthplace Home
### Hope, Arkansas

ADDRESS: 117 South Hervey Street, P.O. Box 1925, Hope, AR 7180l

TELEPHONE: 870-777-4455

WEB SITE: www.clintonbirthplace.org

LOCATION: In southwest Arkansas, about thirty miles northeast of the Texas border, about one hundred miles southwest of Little Rock on I-30

OPEN: Monday–Saturday, 10:00 A.M. to 5:00 P.M.

ADMISSION: Adults, $5.00; seniors, $4.00; children 6–18, $3.00

FACILITIES: Restored birthplace and childhood home of President William Clinton; visitor center and gift shop; Virginia Clinton Kelley Garden; guided tours. NHS

*As president, Bill Clinton often referred fondly* to his hometown in Arkansas as "a place called Hope." Bill Clinton was born in Hope on August 19, 1946, and lived there until he was about seven years old. He and his widowed mother lived in his grandparents' house until his mother married Roger Clinton in June 1950 and the Clinton family moved to another house in Hope.

Bill Clinton depicted Hope as "a town of about six thousand in southwest Arkansas, thirty-three miles east of the Texas border at Texarkana."[8] Hope was a small town with hardworking people. Today, Hope has a population of fewer than eleven thousand people. It was not prosperous when Clinton was born and does not look prosperous today.

The Cassidys, Clinton's maternal grandparents, were people of modest means who had lived on a farm in nearby Bodcaw and moved to Hope when their only child, Virginia, started high school. The home owned by Eldridge and Edith Cassidy from 1939 to 1956 is known now as the Clinton Birthplace Home. In his autobiography Clinton says, "The people of Hope raised the funds to restore it and fill it with old pictures, memorabilia, and period furniture. They call it the Clinton Birthplace. It certainly is the place I associate with awakening to life—to the smells of country food; to buttermilk churns, ice-cream makers, washboards and clotheslines; to my 'Dick and Jane' readers, my first toys, including a simple length of chain I prized above them all; to strange voices talking over our 'party line' telephone; to my first friends and the work my grandparents did."[9]

In the visitor center, located in a neighboring house, the biography of Clinton from his childhood as Bill Blythe in Hope to his inauguration as the forty-second president of the United States is traced through photographs. The time-line room documents key events in Clinton's life. A docent takes tourists on a guided tour of the Clinton Birthplace.

The birthplace house was originally built by Dr. H. S. Garrett, a Hope physician, in 1912. Built in the four-square style, it is a two-story white frame house with green trim. Today the house is owned by the Clinton Birthplace Foundation. Located next door is the home of Vince Foster, Clinton's childhood friend.

After 1956 Clinton's family did not own the house where Clinton was born, and it deteriorated. In the early 1990s the structure was condemned and slated to be torn down. A group of interested citizens purchased it in 1992 and restored it, and it was dedicated in March 1999. At the dedication President Clinton said, "In this house I learned to walk and talk; I learned to pray; I learned to read: I learned to count from the playing cards my grandparents tacked up on the kitchen windows."

Hervey Street was residential when the Cassidys occupied the house, but the road has been widened and is now a busy thoroughfare. Furniture in Clinton's Birthplace Home includes period pieces from the 1940s and 1950s as well as the Cassidys' coffee table and couch. Wood floors and light fixtures are original. On the front porch is a swing.

On the first floor are the living room, the dining room, the laundry room, and the kitchen. The living room has a fireplace with a mirror hanging above it. There is a telephone on a telephone table. A card table and chairs are set up as they were when the Cassidys frequently played cards. Doors open from the living room to the dining room, which was used only on holidays. At other times the dining room table was used for folding laundry, and a ironing board is set up. The kitchen has a Formica table, chairs, a high chair, and a period Blackstone gas stove.

The second floor includes a bathroom, the grandparents' bedroom, and Virginia's bedroom. The sun porch was converted into Billy's room. In the wood-paneled room on display are a crib, a dresser, and a children's book that Billy liked, *The Kitten's Surprise*. The bathroom has its original tub. In the grandparents' bedroom there are two iron beds. Virginia's bedroom has blond wooden furniture and striped wallpaper. Next to the house is the Virginia Clinton Kelley Garden, which was dedicated by President Clinton in 1999.

Also in Hope is Rosehill Cemetery, the site of the Clinton-Kelley-Blythe grave site, which is surrounded by a black wrought-iron fence. Many of President Clinton's family members are buried here. Stone markers identify the graves of Clinton's grandparents, Eldridge Cassidy, August 19, 1900–March 11, 1957, and Edith V. Cassidy, November 2, 1901–January 17, 1968; and his parents, William Jefferson Blythe, February 27, 1918–May 17, 1946, and Virginia Clinton Kelley, June 6, 1923–January 6, 1994.

. . . . . . . . . . . . . . . . . . . . . . . . . . . . . . . . . . . . . . . . . . . . . . . . . . . . . . . . . . . . . . .

## Hope Visitor Center and Museum
## Hope, Arkansas

ADDRESS: South Main and Division Streets, P.O. Box 596, Hope, AR 71802

TELEPHONE: 870-722-2580

WEB SITE: www.hopearkansas.net/

LOCATION: Hope is in the southwestern part of Arkansas and is accessible from I-30; the Hope Visitor Center and Museum is located in downtown Hope, in the old train depot

OPEN: Monday–Friday, 8:30 A.M. to 5:00 P.M.; Saturday, 9:00 A.M. to 5:00 P.M.; Sunday, 1:00 P.M. to 4:00 P.M.

ADMISSION: Free

FACILITIES: Museum about President Bill Clinton in the restored railroad station in his hometown; video

*The Hope Visitor Center and Museum* is located in the restored Iron Mountain / Missouri Pacific Railroad depot. This small, exceptionally well-done museum situates President Bill Clinton in the context of Hope, the small town in which he was born and spent part of his childhood.

The original station was built in 1912 at a cost of twenty-nine thousand dollars. As in other small towns, the railroad for much of the twentieth century was an important link to the outside world. Passenger service was discontinued in 1971. Bill Clinton returned in the summer of 1992 to have campaign photos taken at the train depot. When he was elected president, local residents began an effort to restore the depot for use as a museum about President Clinton, the city of Hope, and the station.

The Union Pacific Railroad donated the station to the city of Hope in 1994, and the museum was dedicated in August 1996. On March 12, 1999, two Hope natives visited the Hope Visitor Center and Museum: Bill Clinton and his former chief of staff Thomas Franklin McLarty Jr., known as "Mack."

An excellent video on Clinton's childhood in Hope and his parents, grandparents, stepfather, and marriage can be viewed. The film is narrated by Bill Clinton; his mother, Virginia; his half brother, Roger; his daughter, Chelsea; and his wife, Hillary. In addition to the exhibits on the station's operations as a railway depot and on the city of Hope, there is a photo exhibit on Bill Clinton and his family and friends in Hope. Some of the Clinton family photos include Clinton's mother, Virginia Cassidy, at age four and in high school; Bill's great uncle H. O. Grisham, whom Bill called Uncle Buddy; Bill's father, Bill Blythe, in army uniform, which shows the remarkable resemblance between father and son; and his grandfather in his grocery store and in a family photo when Eldridge Cassidy was five years old.

The former baggage room of the depot has been restored and converted into the McLarty Conference Room, named for Mack McLarty, Clinton's boyhood friend and first chief of staff. It is furnished with an antique conference table and chairs.

The William J. Clinton Presidential Library and Museum
Little Rock, Arkansas

ADDRESS: 1200 President Clinton Avenue, Little Rock, AR 72201
TELEPHONE: 501-374-4242
WEB SITE: www.clintonlibrary.gov
LOCATION: On the northeastern edge of downtown Little Rock, along the
   Arkansas River; accessible from I-30
OPEN: Monday–Saturday, 9:00 A.M. to 5:00 P.M., and Sunday, 1:00 P.M. to 5:00
   P.M.; closed Thanksgiving, Christmas, and New Year's Day

ADMISSION: Adults, $7.00; senior citizens, college students, and retired military, $5.00; children 6–17, $3.00

FACILITIES: Presidential museum and library of President Bill Clinton; handicapped accessible; free parking; Café 42. The Clinton Museum Store is off-site at 610 President Clinton Avenue, Little Rock, AR 72201; telephone: 501–748–0400; fax: 501–748–0417; Web site: www.clintonmuseumstore .com. The store is open Monday–Saturday, 10:00 A.M. to 5:30 P.M., and Sunday, 2:00 P.M. to 5:30 P.M.

*The Clinton Presidential Museum,* which is located within the Clinton Presidential Center and Park, a thirty-acre landscaped site, reflects the personality of its subject. In this way it is like the museums of other modern presidents, such as Jimmy Carter, Richard Nixon, Ronald Reagan, and George H. W. Bush, who were active participants in erecting impressive monuments to their presidencies. They oversaw the site locations, chose the architects, approved the designs, selected and approved the exhibits, and generally put their own personal stamps on their museums. As in an autobiography, they get to tell their stories their own ways.

As the site of the twelfth and largest national presidential library and museum, the Clinton Presidential Center is massive, impressive, loaded with technology, and interactive. The man from Hope's presence permeates the museum; Clinton's face can be seen and his voice can be heard on videos throughout the site.

The Clinton Foundation raised $165 million from private donors for the museum and oversaw its construction. When the Clinton Presidential Library and Museum officially opened on November 18, 2004, the foundation turned it over to the National Archives and Records Administration.

Designed by the noted architect James Polshek, the stunning elongated, rectangular-shaped glass and steel building is cantilevered out over the banks of the Arkansas River like a bridge. Bridge building inspired the museum's design as "Building a Bridge to the Twenty-first Century" was a major theme in Clinton's presidential campaign. In addition to the museum building, the Clinton Presidential Center and Park site includes the presidential library and archives as well as the Clinton Foundation and the Clinton School of Public Service of the University of Arkansas (which offers a master's degree), the latter two of which are housed in the restored 1899 red brick Choctaw railroad station.

The museum is an environmentally sound 150,000-square-foot structure employing solar energy. On display in the great hall of the museum is a presidential limousine, a 1993 Cadillac Fleetwood made by General Motors in Warren, Michigan. A soaring space with glass walls allowing natural light, the museum has a long exhibit area running down the middle of the rectangular

William J. Clinton
Presidential Library and
Museum, Little Rock,
Arkansas

347

WILLIAM JEFFERSON CLINTON

main gallery. Wooden piers are filled with blue archive boxes with the presidential seal that contain White House documents.

Major museum exhibits are on the second floor. Key events and highlights of the Clinton administration are illustrated by a time line, with videos introducing each year from the inauguration in 1993 to the completion of the second term in 2000. Photographs depict the major world events that took place during a particular year and the Clinton administration's initiatives. On the other side of the time line exhibit is an interactive station where visitors can access photos, documents, and excerpts from the president's speeches and letters for specific years.

Arranged on either side of the main gallery are fourteen multimedia alcoves, each of which focuses on a significant area of policy. "Confronting Conflicts" highlights the Clinton administration's efforts for human rights, the Middle East Camp David talks, and peace in Africa, the Balkans, and Northern Ireland. "Building a Global Community" features presidential travel, trade cooperation, NAFTA, and the Asia-Pacific Rim. "The Work of the First Lady" details Hillary Clinton's work on the health care initiative, education, and child care. "Protecting the Earth" deals with the environment, the creation of national monuments, the Kyoto protocol, global warming, and clear air and water. "Putting People First" highlights the Family and Medical Leave Act and the Moving Families from Welfare to Work policy.

The "Fight for Power" exhibit focuses on Clinton's impeachment, sexual scandals, and right-wing opposition during his presidency. The "Politics of Persecution" exhibit connects Republican Newt Gingrich's "Contract with America" and independent counsel Kenneth Starr's Whitewater investigation. Republicans are blamed for the incessant investigation of Clinton's finances and personal behavior. There is an admission that Clinton was not forthcoming regarding his relationship with White House intern Monica Lewinsky.

The Orientation Theater presents a film on the president's life and political career. In a replica of the White House Cabinet Room, visitors can sit at the large table and use the interactive program to take part in decision-making on important policies of the Clinton administration. The "Work of the Vice-President" exhibit describes Al Gore's role in the Clinton administration, especially Gore's interest in the environment and the electronic highway.

The mezzanine level, which has the best views of Little Rock and the Arkansas River, contains personal as well as administrative exhibits. In "Life in the White House" visitors see the grandeur of state events, holiday festivities, and celebrations with family and friends. Gifts to the president on display include a stunning Chihuly glass tree.

One of the most outstanding exhibits is the only full-scale replica of the Oval Office outside the White House. Appearing as it was during the Clinton administration, the office features a reproduction of the desk used by President Clinton and previously used by President Kennedy; the desk was a gift from Queen Victoria. Near the entrance of the office is an interactive room-by-room tour of the Clinton White House narrated by President and Mrs. Clinton.

The exhibit "The Work Continues" describes the ongoing projects of President Clinton and the William J. Clinton Foundation's philanthropic works, including those on HIV/AIDs and disaster relief. Traditional exhibit cases on the mezzanine contain biographical materials, mementos, and photographs of Clinton's prepresidential years.

The Clinton library archives are open to the public. Materials are stored in two subterranean levels. One of the largest archival collections in the history of the country, it includes approximately 76.8 million pages of paper documents, 1.85 million photographs, and over 75,000 artifacts. Over 620 tons of materials were sent from Washington to Little Rock, including 30,000 cubic feet of restricted materials. Each document has to be reviewed by an archivist, placed in order, and be included in a finding aid. The Clinton archives present new problems for archivists and researchers in that they reflect the first genuinely electronic presidency.

# George Walker Bush

FORTY-THIRD PRESIDENT OF THE UNITED STATES
*January 20, 2001–January 20, 2009*

President George Walker Bush is the son of President George Herbert Walker Bush. The younger Bush shares the unique distinction of being a former president's son with President John Quincy Adams, son of President John Adams.

George W. Bush was born in New Haven, Connecticut, on July 6, 1946, the oldest of the six children of George Herbert Walker and Barbara Pierce Bush. When George W. was two years old, his family moved to Midland, Texas, and they later moved to Houston. He enrolled at Phillips Academy in Andover, Massachusetts, in 1961 and in 1964 entered Yale University, where he majored in history. George graduated in 1968 with a bachelor of arts degree and next attended Harvard Business School, where he earned his master's in business administration in 1975.

Bush joined the Texas Air National Guard in May 1968, taking basic training at Lackland Air Base in San Antonio and flight training at Moody Air Force Base in Valdosta, Georgia. He was assigned to his home unit in Houston and was discharged in 1973.

In 1977 Bush met Laura Lane Welch, who was born on November 4, 1946, in Midland, Texas, the only child of Harold Welch and Jenna Louise Hawkins Welch. Laura earned a bachelor of science degree in education from Southern Methodist University in 1968 and a master's degree in library science from the University of Texas at Austin in 1973.

George and Laura were married on November 5, 1977, at the First United Methodist Church in Midland. In 1978 Bush ran unsuccessfully for the U.S. House of Representatives. Laura gave birth to twin daughters, Jenna Welch and Barbara Pierce, on November 25, 1981.

George W. Bush entered the oil industry and formed his first company, Arbusto Energy (*arbusto* is the Spanish word for "bush"), which invested more than $3 million in low-risk wells. In 1982 he expanded his oil interests to Bush Exploration, an operating company. He then merged his interests with Spectrum 7 in 1983, becoming its CEO. The company did well until 1985, when oil prices crashed.[1] Spectrum 7 was then purchased by Harken Energy.

During this time Bush had several incidents of substance abuse. He was arrested in 1976 for driving under the influence of alcohol in Kennebunkport,

Maine. Bush gave up alcohol in 1986, a decision he attributes to his religious faith and to his wife's positive influence.

After working on his father's presidential campaign in 1988, Bush invested in the Texas Rangers baseball team and served as managing general partner for five years. In 1994 he was the Republican candidate for governor of Texas and won, serving from 1995 to 2000.

In 2000 Bush was a candidate for the Republican nomination for president of the United States. Running as a "compassionate conservative," Bush won the Republican nomination and selected Dick Cheney, CEO of Halliburton and a former White House chief of staff, as his vice-presidential running mate. Vice President Al Gore was the Democratic presidential nominee, and Sen. Joseph Lieberman of Connecticut was the vice-presidential candidate.

The election of 2000 was extremely close and ended in controversy. Both candidates claimed victory in Florida. After several recounts and lower-court decisions, the U.S. Supreme Court, on December 9 in *Bush v. Gore*, reversed a Florida Supreme Court ruling ordering a third recount. As a result Bush won the 25 Florida electoral votes and in all received 271 electoral votes to Gore's 266.

Nine months into Bush's first term, Al-Qaeda terrorists on September 11, 2001, crashed hijacked passenger planes into the World Trade Center's twin towers in New York City and the Pentagon in Washington, D.C. The terrorist suicide attacks caused the deaths of nearly three thousand people. President Bush announced that the nation was fighting a global war on terrorism. To capture Osama bin Laden, who had ordered the attacks, and to destroy Al-Qaeda, Bush ordered an invasion of Afghanistan. U.S. troops supporting the Northern Alliance toppled the Taliban regime. However, bin Laden eluded capture.

In his State of the Union Address on January 29, 2002, Bush condemned Saddam Hussein's Iraq as part of an "axis of evil" supporting terrorists and possessing weapons of mass destruction. Bush urged the United Nations Security Council to enforce its mandates requiring Iraq's disarmament.

In November 2002 Hans Blix, heading a team of UN inspectors, began searching for weapons of mass destruction in Iraq. Though they found no weapons and asked for more time, the inspectors left Iraq when U.S. military action appeared imminent. Joined by twenty other countries, especially the United Kingdom, the United States mobilized a military force that Bush called the "coalition of the willing" to invade Iraq. The invasion began on March 20, 2003. Although the Iraqi army was quickly defeated, coalition forces faced a growing insurgency of various sectarian groups.

In the 2004 election President Bush and Vice President Cheney were renominated by the Republicans, running against John Kerry, the Democratic presidential candidate, and John Edwards, the vice-presidential candidate. Bush won 50.7 percent of the vote and carried 31 of 50 states with 286 electoral votes.

From 2004 on the situation in Iraq was unsettled. Critics charged that Bush's allegations that Iraq had weapons of mass destruction were either based on faulty intelligence or deliberately manipulated. They called for a timetable to withdraw troops from Iraq. On January 10, 2007, Bush announced a "surge," in which 21,500 additional troops would be sent to Iraq.

President Bush used his 1,583-acre Prairie Chapel Ranch, seven miles northwest of Crawford, Texas, as his unofficial western White House. In 1999 Bush had purchased the property for an estimated $1.3 million. After the presidency the Bushes moved to Dallas. The former president planned to oversee the establishment of his presidential library on the campus of Southern Methodist University in Dallas.

......................................................................................

## George W. Bush Presidential Library and Museum (proposed)
## Dallas, Texas

ADDRESS: Bush Library Foundation, P.O. Box 600610, Dallas, TX 75206
TELEPHONE: 214-890-9943
WEB SITE: www.georgewbushlibrary.com
E-MAIL: info@georgewbushlibrary.com

*On February 22, 2008, the George W. Bush* Presidential Library Foundation announced that Southern Methodist University in Dallas, Texas, had been chosen as the site of the George W. Bush Presidential Library. SMU, a private institution, was founded in 1911 by the United Methodist Church and opened in 1915. The location was controversial as some members of the university's Perkins School of Theology objected to locating the Bush Center at SMU. On July 20, 2008, the South Central Jurisdiction of the United Methodist Church gave final approval to its location at SMU.

Groundbreaking for the facility occurred on November 16, 2010, with the opening and dedication in spring 2013. Construction is expected to cost from $200 million to $500 million. Robert A. M. Stern, dean of the architecture school at Yale University, will design the library.[2] Located five miles north of downtown Dallas on approximately twenty-five acres of the SMU campus, the center will overlook the downtown. The three-part presidential center will consist of the presidential library, containing documents and artifacts of the Bush administration; a museum with permanent and traveling exhibits; and an independent public-policy institute along with the offices of the George W. Bush Foundation.

## Thomas Jefferson

1. S. Allen Chambers Jr., "Revelations from the Records: The Documentary Research at Poplar Forest," in *Notes on the State of Poplar Forest,* vol. 1, reprinted from *Lynch's Ferry: A Journal of Local History* 4, no. 1 (1991): 4.

## Andrew Jackson

1. Robert V. Remini, *The Life of Andrew Jackson* (New York: Harper & Row, 1988), 23.
2. Ibid., 25.

## Martin Van Buren

1. The early nineteenth-century Republican Party, derived from Jefferson's Democratic-Republicans, was different from the contemporary Republican Party that was established in 1856.

## Franklin Pierce

1. Larry Gara, *The Presidency of Franklin Pierce* (Lawrence: University Press of Kansas, 1991), 161.

## James Buchanan

1. Philip Shriver Klein, *President James Buchanan* (University Park: Pennsylvania State University Press, 1962), 402.
2. Ibid., 410.
3. James Buchanan, *Mr. Buchanan's Administration on the Eve of the Rebellion* (New York: John Appleton, 1866).

## Abraham Lincoln

1. David H. Donald, *Lincoln* (New York: Simon & Schuster, 1995), 27.
2. Ibid., 151–52.
3. Ibid., 222–23.
4. Ibid., 471–72.
5. Ibid., 599.

## Ulysses Simpson Grant

1. Ulysses S. Grant, *Personal Memoirs of U. S. Grant,* vol. 1 (New York: Charles L. Webster & Company, 1885), 229–31.

## Rutherford Birchard Hayes

1. http://MillerCenter.org/academic/ Americanpresident/hayes/essays /biography 4.
2. Ibid.

## James Abram Garfield

1. Speech by James A. Garfield in Ravenna, Ohio, July 4, 1865, in John M. Taylor, *Garfield of Ohio: The Available Man* (New York: W.W. Norton & Company, 1970), 103.

## Chester Alan Arthur

1. Thomas Reeves, *Gentleman Boss: The Life of Chester Alan Arthur* (New York: Knopf, 1975), 62–63.
2. Ibid., 121.
3. Sean D. Cashman, *America in the Gilded Age: From the Death of Lincoln to the Rise of Theodore Roosevelt* (New York: New York University Press, 1988), 208–9.

## Grover Cleveland

1. Allan Nevins. *Grover Cleveland: A Study in Courage* (New York: Dodd, Mead, 1933), 163–66.
2. Ibid., 169.
3. Cashman, *America in the Gilded Age,* 216–17.

## William McKinley

1. H. Wayne Morgan, *William McKinley and His America* (Syracuse, N.Y.: Syracuse University Press, 1963), 12.
2. Ibid., 30.

## Theodore Roosevelt

1. Nathan Miller, *Theodore Roosevelt: A Life* (New York: Morrow, 1992), 180.
2. G. Wallace Chessman, *Theodore Roosevelt and the Politics of Power* (Boston: Little, Brown, 1969), 88–89.

## Woodrow Wilson

1. Erick Montgomery, *Thomas Woodrow Wilson: Family Ties and Southern Perspectives* (Augusta, Ga.: Historic Augusta, 2006), 21.

2. Ibid., 29.

3. Ibid., 142–47.

### Warren Gamaliel Harding

1. Carl Sferrazza Anthony, *Florence Harding: The First Lady, the Jazz Age, and the Death of America's Most Scandalous President* (New York: William Morrow, 1998), 24.

### Calvin Coolidge

1. Robert Sobel. *Coolidge: An American Enigma* (Washington, D.C.: Regnery Publishing, 1998), 144.

### Herbert Clark Hoover

1. David Burner, *Herbert Hoover: A Public Life* (Norwalk, Conn.: Easton Press, 1996), 309.

2. Richard Norton Smith, *An Uncommon Man: The Triumph of Herbert Hoover* (New York: Simon and Schuster, 1984), 138–39.

3. Herbert C. Hoover, *Memoirs of Herbert Hoover: Years of Adventure, 1874–1920* (New York: Macmillan, 1951), 3–4.

4. Ibid.

### Dwight David Eisenhower

1. Notes dictated by the president on October 8, 1957, concerning the visit of Gov. Orval September 14, 1957, in Eisenhower diary, Archives, Dwight D. Eisenhower Presidential Library and Museum, Abilene, Kansas.

2. Stephen E. Ambrose, *Eisenhower,* vol. 1: *Solder, General of the Army, President-Elect, 1890–1952* (New York: Simon & Schuster, 1983), 19.

### John Fitzgerald Kennedy

1. Graham Allison and P. Zelikow, *Essence of Decision: Explaining the Cuban Missile Crisis* (New York: Longman, 1999).

2. Rose Fitzgerald Kennedy, *Times to Remember* (New York: Doubleday, 1974), 72.

### Lyndon Baines Johnson

1. Rebekah Baines Johnson, *A Family Album* (New York: McGraw-Hill, 1965), 18.

2. Robert A. Caro, *The Years of Lyndon Johnson: The Path to Power* (New York: Knopf, 1982), 165.

3. Robert Dallek, *Lone Star Rising: Lyndon Johnson and His Times, 1908-1960* (New York: Oxford University Press, 1991), 141–42.

### Richard Milhous Nixon

1. Fawn M. Brodie, *Richard Nixon: The Shaping of His Character* (New York: W. W. Norton, 1981), 225.

### Gerald Rudolph Ford

1. James Cannon, *Time and Chance: Gerald Ford's Appointment with History* (New York: HarperCollins, 1994), 287

### James Earl Carter Jr.

1. Jimmy Carter, *An Hour before Daylight: Memories of a Rural Boyhood* (New York: Simon & Schuster, 2001), 75.

2. Kenneth E. Morris, *Jimmy Carter: American Moralist* (Athens: University of Georgia Press, 1997), 25.

3. Ibid., 115.

4. Norwegian Nobel Committee announcement, December 10, 2002.

### Ronald Wilson Reagan

1. Anne Edwards, *Early Reagan: The Rise to Power* (New York: William Morrow, 1987), 64.

2. William E. Pemberton, *Exit with Honor: The Life and Presidency of Ronald Reagan* (Armonk, N.Y.: M. E. Sharpe, 1997), 14.

3. Ibid., 26.

### George Herbert Walker Bush

1. Barbara Bush, *A Memoir: Barbara Bush* (New York: St. Martin's Press, 1994), 6–7.

## William Jefferson Clinton

1. David Maraniss, *First in His Class: A Biography of Bill Clinton* (New York: Simon & Schuster, 1995), 26.

2. Ibid., 39.

3. Ibid., 41.

4. Bill Clinton, *My Life* (New York: Alfred A. Knopf, 2004), 154–55.

5. Ibid., 159.

6. Maraniss, *First in His Class,* 223.

7. John F. Harris, *The Survivor: Bill Clinton in the White House* (New York: Random House, 2005), 103.

8. Clinton, *My Life,* 4.

9. Ibid., 8.

## George Walker Bush

1. George W. Bush, *A Charge to Keep: My Journey to the White House* (New York: Perennial; imprint of Harper-Collins publisher, 1999), 63–64.

2. See http://en.wikipedia.org/wiki/George_W._Bush.

375